D1608031

CONTENTS

HONG KONG

•RESTAURANTS

•HOTELS

MACAU

•RESTAURANTS

•HOTELS

MAPS

目錄

DEAR READER

It's our great pleasure to present the 8th edition of the MICHELIN Guide Hong Kong Macau.

The dining scenes of these two regions are now recognised throughout the world for their variety and vitality. Our recommendations within these pages bring you the best of the best across all styles and price bands, with every establishment chosen first and foremost for the quality of its cooking.

In this year's guide, for the first time, we are delighted to include a selection of our favourite spots for street food – such an intrinsic part of local life.

Every entry has been selected by our team of local, full-time Michelin inspectors who are the eyes and ears of our readers. They always pay their own bills and their anonymity is key to ensuring that they receive the same treatment as any other guest. Entry into the guide is free of charge.

Our famous Michelin Stars ✿ are awarded to restaurants with exceptional cooking, but look out too for the Bib Gourmands ⊛; these are places offering a carefully prepared but simpler style of cooking for under $300. We've kept this price limit the same for yet another year and have found even more 'Bibs' for you to try.

Our independent inspectors have also chosen a selection of the best hotels, ranging from intimate townhouses to grand palaces. The standard of accommodation has always been high in the region and now, with many new openings planned to meet the rapidly increasing demand, we are finding even greater levels of comfort and service.

We are always very interested to hear what you, our readers, think. Your opinions and suggestions matter enormously to us and help shape the guide, so please do get in touch.

You can email us at michelinguide.hongkong-macau@cn.michelin.com

We hope you enjoy all your dining and hotel experiences.

Bon appétit!

親愛的讀者

很開心香港澳門米芝蓮指南已踏入第八個年頭。

香港和澳門是美食匯聚之都,含蘊豐富的飲食文化,獲得本指南推薦的餐廳,其食材質素與食物水準全屬優質之列;餐廳種類涵蓋各種類型、價格。

每個地方均有其土產特色小食,今年開始我們在指南內增加了街頭小吃店推介。透過此推介,讀者能進一步以味覺去體驗港澳兩地的地道風味與飲食文化。

本指南內推薦的餐廳全部由本地全職米芝蓮評審員團隊嚴格挑選,只有最佳食店才獲推介。為確保經驗到與一般顧客同等的服務待遇,讓評審結果更客觀公正,我們的評審員會以匿名身份到訪各大食肆。

除了聞名遐邇的米芝蓮星級 ✿ 食肆推介那些食物質素特佳的食店外,還有車胎人 ⊕ 美食推介。車胎人美食推介推薦的是裝潢簡單、烹調和選料用心卻價格實惠,個人消費額不到HK$300的食店。

與餐廳食肆一樣,米芝蓮評審員團隊在芸芸酒店中挑選了一系列優質酒店,推薦給廣大讀者。從時尚型格到優雅舒適,以致豪華典雅,各個級別和風格的酒店,那怕是新開幕者,只要服務水準高、房間舒適及設備完善也會獲本指南推薦。

我們向來重視讀者的回饋,渴望聆聽閣下的意見。如閣下對本指南有任何意見或提議,歡迎電郵至下列電子郵箱:

michelinguide.hongkong-macau@cn.michelin.com

祝閣下在香港和澳門擁有愉快的美食和住宿體驗!

Bon appétit!

THE MICHELIN GUIDE'S COMMITMENTS

"This volume was created at the turn of the century and will last at least as long".

This foreword to the very first edition of the MICHELIN Guide, written in 1900, has become famous over the years and the guide has lived up to the prediction. It is read across the world and the key to its popularity is the consistency of its commitment to its readers, which is based on the following promises:

Anonymous inspections:
Our inspectors make regular and anonymous visits to restaurants and hotels to gauge the quality of the products and services offered to an ordinary customer. They settle their own bill and may then introduce themselves and ask for more information about the establishment. Our readers' comments are also a valuable source of information, which we can then follow up with another visit of our own.

Independence:
Our choice of establishments is a completely independent one, made for the benefit of our readers alone. The decisions to be taken are discussed around the table by the inspectors and the editor. Inclusion in the guide is completely free of charge.

Selection and choice:
Our guide offers a selection of the best restaurants and hotels. This is only possible because all the inspectors rigorously apply the same methods.

Annual Updates:
All the practical information, the classifications and awards are revised and updated every single year to give the most reliable information possible.

Consistency:
The criteria for the classifications are the same in every country covered by the MICHELIN Guide.

...And our aim:
To do everything possible to make travel, holidays and eating out a pleasure, as part of Michelin's ongoing commitment to improving travel and mobility.

承諾

「這冊書於世紀交替時創辦,亦將繼續傳承下去。」

這是1900年首冊米芝蓮指南的前言,多年來享負盛名,並一直傳承下去。指南在世界各地均大受歡迎,關鍵在其秉承一貫宗旨,履行對讀者的承諾。

匿名評審

我們的評審員以匿名方式定期到訪餐廳和酒店,以一般顧客的身份對餐廳和酒店的食品和服務質素作出評估。評審員自行結賬後,在需要時會介紹自己,並會詳細詢問有關餐廳或酒店的資料。讀者的評語和推薦也是寶貴的資訊來源,我們會根據讀者的推薦到訪該餐廳。

獨立性

餐廳的評選完全是我們獨立的決定,純以讀者利益為依歸。經評審員和編輯一同討論後才作出決定,亦不會向收錄在指南內的餐廳和酒店收取任何費用。

選擇

全賴一眾評審員使用一致且嚴謹的評選方法,本指南才能向讀者推介一系列優質餐廳和酒店。

每年更新

每年都會修訂和更新所有實用資訊、分類及評級,務求為讀者提供最可靠的資料。

一致性

每個國家地區的米芝蓮指南均採用相同的評審和分類準則。

我們的目標

盡全力令旅遊、度假及在外用膳成為一大樂事,實踐米芝蓮一貫優化旅遊和生活的承諾。

ONCE UPON A TIME,
IN THE HEART OF FRANCE...

It all started way back in 1889, in Clermont-Ferrand, when the Michelin brothers founded the Manufacture Française des Pneumatiques Michelin tyre company — this was at a time when driving was considered quite an adventure!

In 1900, fewer than 3,000 cars existed in France. The Michelin brothers hit upon the idea of creating a small guide packed with useful information for the new pioneers of the road, such as where to fill up with petrol or change a tyre, as well as where to eat and sleep. The MICHELIN Guide was born!

The purpose of the guide was obvious: to track down the best hotels and restaurants across the country. To do this, Michelin employed a veritable armada of anonymous professional inspectors to scour every region — something that had never before been attempted!

Over the years, bumpy roads were replaced by smoother highways and the company continued to develop, as indeed did the country's cuisine: cooks became chefs, artisans developed into artists, and traditional dishes were transformed into works of art. All the while, the MICHELIN Guide, by now a faithful travel companion, kept pace with — and encouraged — these changes. The most famous distinction awarded by the guide was created in 1926: the "étoile de bonne table" — the famous star which quickly established itself as the reference in the world of gastronomy!

Bibendum — the famous tyre-clad Michelin Man — continued to widen his reach and by 1911, the guide covered the whole of Europe.

In 2006, the collection crossed the Atlantic, awarding stars to 39 restaurants in New York. In 2007 and 2008, the guide moved on

to San Francisco, Los Angeles and Las Vegas, and in 2011 it was the turn of Chicago to have its own Michelin guide — The Michelin Man had become truly American!

In November 2007, The Michelin Man took his first steps in Asia: in recognition of the excellence of Japanese cuisine, stars rained down on Tokyo, which was gripped by culinary fever! A guide to Kyoto, Kobe, Osaka and Nara followed, with Yokohama and Shonan then joining Tokyo.

Hong Kong and Macau arrived in 2009, putting the Red Guide firmly on the map in the Far East. Today the collection covers 24 titles in 24 countries, with over 30 million copies sold in a century. Quite a record!

Meanwhile, the search continues... Looking for a delicious pot-au-feu in a typical Parisian bistro, or a soothing bowl of congee in Hong Kong? The Michelin Man continues to span the globe making new discoveries and selecting the very best the culinary world has to offer!

從前，在法國中部……

這一切始於1889年，米芝蓮兄弟在法國克萊蒙費朗 (Clermont-Ferrand) 創辦 Manufacture Française des Pneumatiques Michelin 輪胎公司 – 當年駕駛汽車仍被視為一大冒險。

在1900年，法國的汽車總數量少於3,000輛。米芝蓮兄弟靈機一觸，想到為道路駕駛的先驅提供含實用資訊的小指南，如補充汽油或更換輪胎，以至用餐和睡覺的好去處。米芝蓮指南就這樣誕生了!

指南的宗旨非常清晰：搜羅全國各地最好的酒店和餐廳。為達目的，米芝蓮招攬了一整隊神秘專業評審員，走遍全國每一個角落尋找值得推介的酒店和餐廳，這在當時是前所未有的創舉。

多年來，崎嶇不平的道路早已被平順的高速公路取代，米芝蓮公司持續茁壯成長。同時間，全國各地餐飲業的發展亦一日千里：廚子成為大廚、傳統手藝成為藝術，傳統菜餚亦轉化成為藝術傑作。現今米芝蓮指南已成為廣受信賴的旅遊夥伴，不僅與時並進，更致力推動這些轉變。指南中最著名的是早在1926年面世，並迅即成為美食界權威指標的「星級推介」。

由米芝蓮車胎人必比登為代言人的米芝蓮指南，不斷拓展其版圖，到1911年已覆蓋全歐洲。

2006年，米芝蓮指南系列成功跨越大西洋，授予紐約39家餐廳星級推介。在 2007 及 2008 年，米芝蓮指南在三藩市、洛杉磯和拉斯維加斯出版，2011已拓展至芝加哥，米芝蓮車胎人必比登也正式落戶美國。

2007年11月，米芝蓮車胎人首次踏足亞洲，在東京廣發星級推介，以表揚日本料理的卓越成就，同時亦掀起美食熱潮。其後，旋即推出京都、神戶、大阪及奈良指南，並繼東京之後推出橫濱和湘南指南。

香港和澳門指南亦於2009年推出，令這本以紅色為標誌的指南，在遠東地區的覆蓋範圍更見廣泛。

時至今日，米芝蓮指南系列共計24本，涵蓋24個國家，一個世紀以來，總銷量超過三千萬。這是個令人鼓舞的紀錄！

此時此刻，我們仍然繼續對美食的追尋……是巴黎餐廳的美味雜菜鍋，還是香港令人窩心的粥品？米芝蓮車胎人將會努力不懈，發掘全球美食，為你們挑選最出色的佳餚美饌！

HOW TO USE
THIS RESTAURANT GUIDE
如何使用餐廳指南

Map number / coordinates
地圖號碼 / 座標

New entry in the guide
新增推介

Cuisine type
菜式種類

Name of restaurant
餐廳名稱

Stars for good food
美食星級
❀ to ❀❀❀

Bib Gourmand
(Inspectors' favourite
for good value)
(評審員推介榜)
☺

Restaurant classification
according to comfort
餐廳 — 以舒適程度分類

Particularly pleasant if in red
紅色代表上佳

	Simple shop
	簡單的食店
X	Quite comfortable
	顏舒適
XX	Comfortable
	舒適
XXX	Very comfortable
	十分舒適
XXXX	Top class comfort
	高級舒適
XXXXX	Luxury
	豪華

Thai 泰國菜   MAP 地圖 19/D-2

Namo NEW

X   🏠 ≼ ⇔10 🕐

A great harbour-facing terrace isn't the only attraction of this contemporary Thai restaurant in Empire Centre. The food, prepared by Thai chefs, brings together Thai and international ingredients as well as different cooking techniques. Try Iberico pork rib in northern Thai curry sauce, bouchot mussels in chili-galangal coconut broth, or Japanese tofu with crispy coconut coating. They also do interesting cocktails – sticky rice martini anyone?

海風、陽光和泰國菜往往是最佳配搭！坐在Namo的露天用餐區，邊欣賞對岸的港島景色，邊享用別具特色的泰式美食，的確十分寫意。這裡的菜式全由泰籍廚師按傳統方法烹調，配上國際化食材；試試西班牙豬肋骨伴清邁咖喱或椰香焗脆炸日本軟豆腐，必定令你感到驚喜。

TEL. 2739 1133
Shop G18, Empire Centre, 68 Mody Road,
Tsim Sha Tsui
尖沙咀麼地道 68號帝國中心 G18號鋪

■ PRICE 價錢
Lunch 午膳
set 套餐 $ 88-238
à la carte 點菜 $ 200-300
Dinner 晚膳
à la carte 點菜 $ 200-300

■ OPENING HOURS 營業時間
12:00-01:00 (L.O.)

194

A new section - Street Food - is listed separately from Recommended restaurants. Please refer to P.306 - P. 311 for Hong Kong Street Food; and P. 440 - 442 for Macau Street Food.

French contemporary 時尚法國菜

MAP 地圖 41/C-2

The Tasting Room
御膳房

XXXX　　　　　　　　　　　 ⬅ ♨ ⇔14 ▥ ⌘　✿✿

Finding respite on the Cotai Strip away from the lively casino vibe can be hard but this relaxing restaurant could help. It's an elegant circular room and offers discreet service. The food is largely French and the Bresse pigeon is the favoured dish of the locals. The chef adds his own unique touches, like onion ice cream to the onion soup. Be sure to have the Chef's Menu.

欲在金光大道賭場內找個地方歡歇，可以到這家氣氛輕鬆的餐廳。圓形的主餐室華麗優雅，侍應服務細心周到。以供應法國菜為主，最著名的是法國乳鴿。大廚喜歡將自己的創意融入菜式中，如洋蔥湯加上洋蔥雪糕。八道菜的總廚精選套餐絕對非試不可。

TEL. 8868 6681
3F, Crown Towers, City of Dreams,
Estrada do Istmo, Cotai
路氹連貫公路新濠天地皇冠度假酒店 3樓
www.cityofdreamsmacau.com/restaurant

■ PRICE 價錢
Lunch 午膳
set 套餐 MOP 388-528
à la carte 點菜 MOP 650-2,150
Dinner 晚膳
set 套餐 MOP 828-2,088
à la carte 點菜 MOP 650-2,150

■ OPENING HOURS 營業時間
Lunch 午膳　12:00-14:30 (L.O.)
Dinner 晚膳　18:00-22:30 (L.O.)

440

Restaurant symbols
餐廳標誌

⑤ Cash only
只收現金

♿ Wheelchair access
輪椅適用

⛱ Terrace dining
陽台用餐

⬅ Interesting view
上佳景觀

🅿 Valet parking
代客泊車

🅿 Car park
停車場

⇔ Private room with maximum capacity
私人房間及容納人數

⬛ Counter
櫃枱式

☎🍴 Reservations required
需訂座

🚫🍴 Reservations not accepted
不設訂座

🍷 Interesting wine list
供應優良的酒類

想知道香港及澳門有甚麼馳名小吃，請翻看第 306-311 頁香港街頭小吃及第 440-442 頁的澳門街頭小吃部分。

HOW TO USE
THIS HOTEL GUIDE
如何使用酒店指南

Map number / coordinates
地圖號碼 / 座標

New entry in the guide
新增推介

MAP 地圖

Name of hotel
酒店名稱

The Ritz-Carlton NEW
麗思卡爾頓

Hotel classification according to comfort
酒店 — 根據舒適程度分類

Particularly pleasant if in red
紅色代表上佳

All bedrooms are suites at the exclusive Ritz-Carlton hotel, which is located on the upper floors at Galaxy Macau. They are impeccably dressed and come with particularly luxurious marble bathrooms. They also provide great views of Cotai, as does the outdoor pool. Along with a state-of-the-art spa is an elegant bar and stylish, very comfortable lounges.

講究的裝潢、精緻的藝術擺設、舒適的座椅，甫踏進設在51樓的接待處，心已給溶化！風格典雅的套房除了設有舒適奢華的大理石浴室外，還能俯瞰欣賞銀河渡假村景觀或遠眺市內風光。與接待處同層的麗思酒廊設計優雅，且能飽覽氹仔景致，是與摯愛親朋把酒談心的歇息處。

Quite comfortable
頗舒適

Comfortable
舒適

Very comfortable
十分舒適

Top class comfort
高級舒適

Luxury
豪華

Restaurants recommended in MICHELIN Guide
米芝蓮指南內的推薦餐廳

TEL. 8886 6868
FAX. 8886 6600
Galaxy, Estrada da Baia da Nossa
Senhora da Esperança, Cotai
路氹望德聖母灣大馬路澳門銀河渡假城
www.ritzcarlton.com/macau

Suites 套房 = MOP 3,588-6,888
Suites 套房 254

RECOMMENDED RESTAURANTS 餐廳推薦
Lai Heen 麗軒 ✕✕✕✕
The Ritz-Carlton Café 麗思咖啡廳 ✕✕

Grand Hyatt
君悅

With its striking 22m ceiling and fabulous artwork, the lobby sets the tone – the droplets appear to be falling from a cloud. The contemporary bedrooms are split between two towers. Along with contemporary and luxurious suites, the Grand Club on the top floor provides a dining service where customers can order any kind of cuisine they choose.

君悅酒店的大堂設計獨特，從22米天花上空墜下的吊飾，配合藝術設計營造出水珠從雲層落下再匯聚一起的壯觀景象。設計時尚的房間分佈在兩棟大樓內。位於頂層的嘉賓軒裝潢高雅，有多間貴賓廂房，按客人喜好提供不同餐飲服務，是舉辦私人商務聚會的理想場地。

TEL. 8868 1234
FAX. 8867 1234
City of Dreams, Estrada do Istmo, Cotai
路氹連貫公路新濠天地
www.macau.grand.hyatt.com

♦	MOP 5,588-6,588
♦♦	MOP 5,588-6,588
Suites 套房	MOP 6,088-33,788
☷	MOP 228

Rooms 客房 503
Suites 套房 288

RECOMMENDED RESTAURANTS 餐廳推薦
Beijing Kitchen 滿堂彩 ※※
Mezza9 ※※

4

○─ Hotel symbols
酒店標誌

    Wheelchair access
輪椅適用

    Interesting view
上佳景觀

    Valet parking
代客泊車

P   Car park
室外停車場

    Garage
室內停車場

    Non smoking rooms
非吸煙房室

    Conference rooms
會議室

    Outdoor/Indoor
swimming pool
室外 / 室內游泳池

Spa   Spa
水療

    Exercise room
健身室

    Casino
娛樂場

Michelin is committed to improving the mobility of travellers

ON EVERY ROAD AND BY EVERY MEANS

Since the company came into being – over a century ago – Michelin has had a single objective: to offer people a better way forward. A technological challenge first, to create increasingly efficient tyres, but also an ongoing commitment to travellers, to help them travel in the best way. This is why Michelin is developing a whole collection of products and services: from maps, atlases, travel guides and auto accessories, to mobile apps, route planners and on-line assistance: Michelin is doing everything it can to make travelling more pleasurable!

A tyre...
⇨ what is it?

Round, black, supple yet solid, the tyre is to the wheel what the shoe is to the foot. But what is it made of? First and foremost, rubber, but also various textile and/or metallic materials... and then it's filled with air! It is the skilful assembly of all these components that ensures tyres have the qualities they should: grip to the road, shock absorption, in two words: 'comfort' and 'safety'.

1 TREAD
The tread ensures the tyre performs correctly, by dispersing water, providing grip and increasing longevity.

2 CROWN PLIES
This reinforced double or triple belt combines vertical suppleness with transversal rigidity, enabling the tyre to remain flat to the road.

3 SIDEWALLS
These link all the component parts and provide symmetry. They enable the tyre to absorb shock, thus giving a smooth ride.

4 BEADS
The bead wires ensure that the tyre is fixed securely to the wheel to ensure safety.

5 INNER LINER
The inner liner creates an airtight seal between the wheel rim and the tyre.

Michelin
⇒ *innovation in movement*

Created and patented by Michelin in 1946, the belted radial-ply tyre revolutionised the world of tyres. But Michelin did not stop there: over the years other new and original solutions came out, confirming Michelin's position as a leader in research and innovation.

⇒ *the right pressure!*

One of Michelin's priorities is safer mobility. In short, innovating for a better way forward. This is the challenge for researchers, who are working to perfect tyres capable of shorter braking distances and offering the best possible traction to the road. And so, to support motorists, Michelin organises road safety awareness campaigns all over the world: «Fill up with air» initiatives remind everyone that the right tyre pressure is a crucial factor in safety and fuel economy.

The Michelin strategy:
→ *multi-performance tyres*

Michelin is synonymous with safety, fuel saving and the capacity to cover thousands of miles. A MICHELIN tyre is the embodiment of all these things – thanks to our engineers, who work with the very latest technology.

Their challenge: to equip every tyre – whatever the vehicle (car, truck, tractor, bulldozer, plane, motorbike, bicycle or train!) – with the best possible combination of qualities, for optimal overall performance.

Slowing down wear, reducing energy expenditure (and therefore CO_2 emissions), improving safety through enhanced road handling and braking: there are so many qualities in just one tyre – that's Michelin Total Performance.

MICHELIN
Total Performance

Every day, **Michelin** is
working towards
sustainable
mobility

OVER TIME,
WHILE
RESPECTING
THE PLANET

Sustainable mobility
→ is clean mobility... and mobility for everyone

Sustainable mobility means enabling people to get around in a way that is cleaner, safer, more economical and more accessible to everyone, wherever they might live. Every day, Michelin's 113 000 employees worldwide are innovating:

• by creating tyres and services that meet society's new needs,

• by raising young people's awareness of road safety,

• by inventing new transport solutions that consume less energy and emit less CO_2.

→ *Michelin Challenge Bibendum*

Sustainable mobility means allowing the transport of goods and people to continue, while promoting responsible economic, social and societal development. Faced with the increasing scarcity of raw materials and global warming, Michelin is standing up for the environment and public health. Michelin regularly organises 'Michelin Challenge Bibendum', the only event in the world which focuses on sustainable road travel.

HONG KONG
香港

RESTAURANTS
餐廳

STARRED RESTAURANTS
星級餐廳

Within this selection, we have highlighted a number of restaurants for their particularly good cooking. When awarding one, two or three Michelin Stars there are a number of factors we consider: the quality and compatibility of the ingredients, the technical skill and flair that goes into their preparation, the clarity and combination of flavours, the value for money and above all, the taste. Equally important is the ability to produce excellent cooking not once but time and time again. Our inspectors make as many visits as necessary, so that you can be sure of the quality and consistency.

A two or three star restaurant has to offer something very special that separates it from the rest. Three stars – our highest award – are given to the very best.

Cuisines in any style of restaurant and of any nationality are eligible for a star. The decoration, service and comfort levels have no bearing on the award.

在這系列的選擇裡，推薦的是食物質素特別出色的餐廳。給予一、二或三粒米芝蓮星時，我們考慮到以下因素：材料的質素和配搭、烹調技巧和特色、氣味濃度和組合、價錢是否相宜及味道層次。同樣重要的是該餐館的食物恆常保持在高水平。閣下對我們的推薦絕對可以放心！我們的評審員會因應需要多次到訪同一家餐館，以確認其食物品質能恆常保持高水準。

二或三星餐廳必有獨特之處，比同類型其他餐廳更出眾。最高評級－三星－只會給予最好的餐廳。

星級評定不會受到餐廳風格、菜式、裝潢陳設、服務及舒適程度影響。只要烹調技巧出色，食物品質特別優秀，都有機會獲得米芝蓮星星。

Exceptional cuisine, worth a special journey.
卓越的烹調，值得專程造訪。

Our highest award is given for the superlative cooking of chefs at the peak of their profession. The ingredients are exemplary, the cooking is elevated to an art form and their dishes are often destined to become classics.

獲得最高級別的餐館，其廚師的烹調技巧卓絕，選材用料堪稱典範，並將烹飪提升至藝術層次，菜式大多會成為經典。

Bo Innovation	ᐵᐵᐵ	Innovative 創新菜	79
L'Atelier de Joël Robuchon	ᐵᐵ	French contemporary 時尚法國菜	162
Lung King Heen 龍景軒	ᐵᐵᐵ	Cantonese 粵菜	182
8 1/2 Otto e Mezzo - Bombana	ᐵᐵᐵ	Italian 意大利菜	205
Sushi Shikon 志魂	ᐵ	Sushi 壽司	253
T'ang Court 唐閣	🛏 ᐵᐵᐵ	Cantonese 粵菜	259

Excellent cooking, worth a detour.
烹調出色，值得刻意造訪。

The personality and talent of the chef and their team is evident in the refined, expertly crafted dishes.

主廚的個人風格與烹飪天賦及其團隊的優秀手藝完全反映在精巧味美的菜式上。

Amber	ᐵᐵᐵ	French contemporary 時尚法國菜	69
Caprice	ᐵᐵᐵᐵ	French 法國菜	84
Celebrity Cuisine 名人坊	ᐵᐵ	Cantonese 粵菜	87
Duddell's 都爹利會館	ᐵᐵ	Cantonese 粵菜	113
Forum 富臨飯店	🛏 ᐵᐵ	Cantonese 粵菜	120
Ming Court 明閣	🛏 ᐵᐵᐵ	Cantonese 粵菜	190
Pierre	ᐵᐵᐵ	French contemporary 時尚法國菜	212
Ryu Gin 天空龍吟	ᐵᐵ	Japanese 日本菜	221
Shang Palace 香宮	ᐵᐵᐵ	Cantonese 粵菜	230

High quality cooking, worth a stop!
優質烹調，不妨一試！

Within their category, these establishments use quality ingredients and serve carefully prepared dishes with distinct flavours.
此名單上的餐館，在同類型餐館中，其食材較具質素，烹調細緻用心、味道出色。

NEW : New entry in the guide 新增推介
🍃 : Restaurant promoted to a Bib Gourmand or Star 評級有所晉升的餐廳

美 食 會 萃

Gourmet ParadisE
@ Harbour City

位處香港的中心，毗鄰維多利亞港，海港城是香港領先的商場，匯集超過四百五十間不同類型的商店、五十多間中外餐廳、三間星級酒店、兩大電影院以及美術館。除了於廣東道的十多個國際頂尖時裝品牌旗艦店和場內多個世界著名品牌外，我們亦有超過二十間飽覽維港美景餐廳，為大家提供與別不同的一站式時尚購物、美食享受及精彩體驗。

海港城現誠邀所有「知味」之友於商場內餐廳用餐時拍攝美食，將相片以 #hcfood 為主題標籤及於該餐廳簽到，並於 Instagram 分享。追尋城中「知味」，齊齊品「相」海港城 #hcfood Instagram Menu。

Located in the heart of Hong Kong and next to Victoria Harbour, Harbour City is a leading shopping mall in Hong Kong houring over 450 shops of all kinds, more than 50 food & beverage outlets, 3 hotels, 2 cinemas and an art galler. With more than 10 international fashion flagship stores on Canton Road and many other leading luxury brands, we also have over 20 harbour view restaurants, ensuring visitors from all over the world enjoy an incredible one-stop shopping, dining and enterainment experience.

Share photos taken at any F&B outlets of Harbour City on Instagram, hashtag #hcfood and check-in. Search #hcfood to check out our menu on Instagram, kick-start your Taste-FULL Journey @ Harbour City!

電話 Tel : (852) 2118 8666

地址 Address：九龍尖沙咀廣東道3-27號 3-27, Canton Road, Tsim Sha Tsui, Kowloon

前往方法 Access：

港鐵尖沙咀站A1出口或港鐵尖東站L5出口步行約10分鐘 ｜ 中環或灣仔乘坐天星小輪至尖沙咀約7分鐘
10-minute walk from MTR Tsim Sha Tsui station (Exit A1) or East Tsim Sha Tsui station (Exit L5) to Harbour City
7-minute ride from Central or Wan Chai Star Ferry Pier to Tsim Sha Tsui Pier

一個海港，只有一個
www.harbourcity.com.hk

BIB GOURMAND RESTAURANTS
車胎人美食推介餐廳

This symbol indicates our inspectors' favourites for good value. These restaurants offer quality cooking for $300 or less (price of a 3 course meal excluding drinks).

這標誌表示評審員認為最超值的餐廳：費用在 300 元或以下（三道菜式但不包括飲料）。

NEW : New entry in the guide 新增推介

ᵗᵉ : Restaurant promoted to a Bib Gourmand or Star 評級有所晉升的餐廳

RESTAURANTS BY AREA
餐廳 — 以地區分類

Hong Kong Island 香港島

Admiralty 金鐘

Ammo	XX	Mediterranean 地中海菜	70
Café Gray Deluxe	XX	European contemporary 時尚歐陸菜	81
Golden Leaf 金葉庭	XxX	Cantonese 粵菜	131
Lobster Bar and Grill 龍蝦吧	XX	Seafood 海鮮	179
Nicholini's 意寧谷	XxX	Italian 意大利菜	197
Petrus 珀翠	XxXxX	French 法國菜	211
Shanghai Garden 紫玉蘭	XX	Shanghainese 滬菜	231
Summer Palace 夏宮	✿✿ XxX	Cantonese 粵菜	245
The Continental NEW	XX	European contemporary 時尚歐陸菜	266

Causeway Bay 銅鑼灣

An Nam 安南	XX	Vietnamese 越南菜	71
Din Tai Fung (Causeway Bay) 鼎泰豐 (銅鑼灣)	⊛ X	Shanghainese 滬菜	107
Farm House 農圃	XX	Cantonese 粵菜	115
Forum 富臨飯店	✿✿ XX	Cantonese 粵菜	120
Fu Sing (Causeway Bay) 富聲 (銅鑼灣)	⊛ XxX	Cantonese 粵菜	122
Gonpachi 權八	X	Japanese 日本菜	133
Ho Hung Kee 何洪記	✿ X	Noodles and Congee 粥麵	140
Iwanami 岩浪 NEW	X	Japanese 日本菜	149
Kung Tak Lam (Causeway Bay) 功德林 (銅鑼灣)	⊛ XX	Vegetarian 素食	159

NEW : New entry in the guide 新增推介
↗ : Restaurant promoted to a Bib Gourmand or Star 評級有所晉升的餐廳

Central 中環

Wan Chai 灣仔

Western District 西環

Kowloon 九龍

Cheung Sha Wan 長沙灣

Hung Hom 紅磡

Jordan 佐敦

| Yau Yuen Siu Tsui 有緣小敘 | 🍴 | Shaanxi 陝西菜 | 299 |

Kowloon Bay 九龍灣

| Lei Garden (Kowloon Bay)
利苑酒家 (九龍灣) | ❄ | XX | Cantonese 粵菜 | 169 |
| Siu Shun Village Cuisine (Kowloon Bay)
肇順名匯河鮮專門店 (九龍灣) | 🍴 | X | Shun Tak 順德菜 | 240 |

Kowloon City 九龍城

| Gainmore Cuisine
桂寶雞窩米線 | 🍴 | Hotpot 火鍋 | 128 |

Kwun Tong 觀塘

Dragon King (Kwun Tong) 龍皇 (觀塘)	XX	Cantonese 粵菜	112
Lei Garden (Kwun Tong) 利苑酒家 (觀塘)	🍃	❄	XX	Cantonese 粵菜	170
Lucky Indonesia 好運印尼餐廳	🍴	Indonesian 印尼菜	180
MIC Kitchen	❄	X	Innovative 創新菜	189
Wonton Master 灃家	🍴	Noodles and Congee 粥麵	294

Mong Kok 旺角

Chuen Cheung Kui (Mong Kok) 泉章居 (旺角)	🍴	X	Hakkanese 客家菜	98
Fung Shing (Mong Kok) 鳳城 (旺角)	🍴	X	Cantonese 粵菜	126
Good Hope Noodle (Fa Yuen Street) 好旺角麵家 (花園街)	🍴	Noodles and Congee 粥麵	134
Lei Garden (Mong Kok) 利苑酒家 (旺角)	❄	XX	Cantonese 粵菜	171
Ming Court 明閣	🍃	❄❄	XXX	Cantonese 粵菜	190

Prince Edward 太子

| Ah Chun Shandong Dumpling
阿純山東餃子 | 🍴 | Dumplings 餃子 | 66 |

New Territories 新界

Sai Kung 西貢

Loaf On 六福菜館	❀	X	Cantonese 粵菜	178
May's Sawaddee Thailand 旺泰特食	⊛	🍜	Thai 泰國菜	186
Sai Kung Sing Kee 勝記	❀	X	Seafood 海鮮	223

Sha Tin 沙田

Fung Lum 楓林小館	⊛	XX	Cantonese 粵菜	125
Lei Garden (Sha Tin) 利苑酒家 (沙田)		XX	Cantonese 粵菜	173
Sha Tin 18 沙田18		XX	Chinese 中國菜	229

Sham Tseng 深井

| Yue Kee 裕記 | ⊛ | X | Cantonese 粵菜 | 308 |

Tseung Kwan O 將軍澳

| Jin Cuisine 晉薈 | | XX | Cantonese 粵菜 | 151 |
| Tze Yuet Heen 紫粵軒 | | XX | Cantonese 粵菜 | 285 |

Tsuen Wan 荃灣

| Yin Yue 殷悅 | | XX | Cantonese 粵菜 | 302 |

Tuen Mun 屯門

| Dragon Inn 容龍 | ⊛ | XX | Seafood 海鮮 | 111 |
| Yuè (Gold Coast) 粵 (黃金海岸) | | XX | Cantonese 粵菜 | 306 |

Yuen Long 元朗

Chiu Chow Rice Roll 潮式腸粉		🍜	Chiu Chow 潮州菜	97
Ho To Tai 好到底	⊛	🍜	Noodles 麵食	141
Tai Wing Wah 大榮華	⊛	X	Cantonese 粵菜	256

RESTAURANTS BY CUISINE TYPE
餐廳 — 以菜式分類

American 美國菜

Beef & Liberty		X	Wan Chai 灣仔	77

British contemporary 時尚英國菜

Aberdeen Street Social		X	Central 中環	64
The Pawn	NEW	X	Wan Chai 灣仔	267

Cantonese 粵菜

Above & Beyond 天外天		XXX	Tsim Sha Tsui 尖沙咀	65
Ah Yat Harbour View 阿一海景飯店	✿	XXX	Tsim Sha Tsui 尖沙咀	67
Celebrity Cuisine 名人坊	✿✿	XX	Central 中環	87
Celestial Court 天寶閣		XXX	Tsim Sha Tsui 尖沙咀	88
Che's 車氏粵菜軒		XX	Wan Chai 灣仔	91
Cuisine Cuisine at The Mira 國金軒 (The Mira)		XXX	Tsim Sha Tsui 尖沙咀	104
Dragon King (Kwun Tong) 龍皇 (觀塘)		XX	Kwun Tong 觀塘	112
Duddell's 都爹利會館	✿✿	XX	Central 中環	113
Farm House 農圃		XX	Causeway Bay 銅鑼灣	115
Fook Lam Moon (Tsim Sha Tsui) 福臨門 (尖沙咀)		XXX	Tsim Sha Tsui 尖沙咀	118
Fook Lam Moon (Wan Chai) 福臨門 (灣仔)	✿	XXX	Wan Chai 灣仔	119
Forum 富臨飯店	⤴ ✿✿	XX	Causeway Bay 銅鑼灣	120
Fu Ho (Tsim Sha Tsui) 富豪 (尖沙咀)	✿	XXX	Tsim Sha Tsui 尖沙咀	121
Fu Sing (Causeway Bay) 富聲 (銅鑼灣)	㉿	XXX	Causeway Bay 銅鑼灣	122

NEW : New entry in the guide 新增推介

⤴ : Restaurant promoted to a Bib Gourmand or Star 評級有所晉升的餐廳

Cantonese Roast Meats 燒味

Dumplings 餃子

Ah Chun Shandong Dumpling 阿純山東餃子	🏠	🍴	Prince Edward 太子	66
Wang Fu (Central) 王府(中環)	🏠	🍴	Central 中環	290

European 歐陸菜

Hugo's 希戈	XxX	Tsim Sha Tsui 尖沙咀	143

European contemporary 時尚歐陸菜

Arcane	NEW	XX	Central 中環	73
Café Gray Deluxe		XX	Admiralty 金鐘	81
Felix		XX	Tsim Sha Tsui 尖沙咀	116
Mandarin Grill + Bar 文華扒房+酒吧	✿	XxxX	Central 中環	184
Penthouse		XX	Causeway Bay 銅鑼灣	210
The Continental	NEW	XX	Admiralty 金鐘	266
Whisk		XX	Tsim Sha Tsui 尖沙咀	291

French 法國菜

Bibo		XX	Central 中環	78
Caprice	✿✿	XxXxX	Central 中環	84
Cocotte		X	Central 中環	101
Épure		XxX	Tsim Sha Tsui 尖沙咀	114
Gaddi's 吉地士		XxxX	Tsim Sha Tsui 尖沙咀	127
ON	NEW ✿	XX	Central 中環	203
Petrus 珀翠		XxXxX	Admiralty 金鐘	211
Seasons	✿	XxX	Causeway Bay 銅鑼灣	225
Spoon by Alain Ducasse	✿	XxxX	Tsim Sha Tsui 尖沙咀	243
Upper Modern Bistro		XX	Sheung Wan 上環	286

French contemporary 時尚法國菜

Akrame	✿	XX	Wan Chai 灣仔	68
Amber	✿✿	XxX	Central 中環	69
L'Atelier de Joël Robuchon	✿✿✿	XX	Central 中環	162

Le Dôme de Cristal	NEW	XxX	Central 中環	164
Pierre	✿✿	XxxX	Central 中環	212
Serge et le Phoque	🍃 ✿	X	Wan Chai 灣仔	227

Fujian 福建菜

Putien (Causeway Bay) 莆田(銅鑼灣)	NEW	🔞	XX	Causeway Bay 銅鑼灣	214

Hakkanese 客家菜

Chuen Cheung Kui (Mong Kok) 泉章居 (旺角)	🔞	X	Mong Kok 旺角	98

Hang Zhou 杭州菜

Hong Zhou 杭州酒家	XX	Wan Chai 灣仔	142

Hotpot 火鍋

Gainmore Cuisine 桂寶雞窩米線	🔞	🍴	Kowloon City 九龍城	128
King's Garden 東來居	🔞	X	Wan Chai 灣仔	158

Hunanese 湖南菜

Café Hunan (Western District) 書湘門第 (西環)	🔞	X	Western District 西環	82

Indian 印度菜

Bombay Dreams	🔞	XX	Central 中環	80
Tulsi (North Point) 羅勒 (北角)	🔞	X	North Point 北角	283
Tulsi (Quarry Bay) 羅勒 (鰂魚涌)		X	Quarry Bay 鰂魚涌	284

Indonesian 印尼菜

Lucky Indonesia 好運印尼餐廳	🔞	🍴	Kwun Tong 觀塘	180
Restoran Indonesia 1968 印尼餐廳1968	✿✿	X	Central 中環	219

Innovative 創新菜

Bo Innovation		✿✿✿	XxX	Wan Chai 灣仔	79
MIC Kitchen		✿	X	Kwun Tong 觀塘	189
Ta Vie 旅	NEW	✿	XX	Central 中環	255
Tate		✿	XX	Central 中環	261
Town	NEW		XX	Causeway Bay 銅鑼灣	278
Wagyu Takumi		✿✿	XX	Wan Chai 灣仔	289

Italian 意大利菜

CIAK - In The Kitchen		✿	X	Central 中環	100
Grissini			XxX	Wan Chai 灣仔	137
Nicholini's 意寧谷			XxX	Admiralty 金鐘	197
No.5 Italian (Tai Hang)			X	Tai Hang 大坑	199
8½ Otto e Mezzo - Bombana		✿✿✿	XxxX	Central 中環	205
Tosca		✿	XxxX	Tsim Sha Tsui 尖沙咀	277

Italian-American 美國意大利菜

Carbone	NEW		XX	Central 中環	85

Japanese 日本菜

Gin Sai 吟彩			X	Wan Chai 灣仔	129
Go Ya 五谷			🍜	Tai Hang 大坑	130
Gonpachi 權八			X	Causeway Bay 銅鑼灣	133
Inakaya 田舍家			XX	Tsim Sha Tsui 尖沙咀	145
Iwanami 岩浪	NEW		X	Causeway Bay 銅鑼灣	149
Kazuo Okada 岡田和生		✿	XxX	Hung Hom 紅磡	157
Nishiki 錦		🏮	X	Tsim Sha Tsui 尖沙咀	198
Robatayaki 爐端燒	NEW		X	Hung Hom 紅磡	220
Ryu Gin 天空龍吟		✿✿	XX	Tsim Sha Tsui 尖沙咀	221
Shiba	NEW	🏮	🍜	Kennedy Town 堅尼地城	234
Takeya 竹家		🏮	🍜	Hung Hom 紅磡	258
Wa-En 和宴	NEW		XX	Tsim Sha Tsui 尖沙咀	287

Wagyu Kaiseki Den	✿	ХХХ	Sheung Wan 上環	288
Youka 八日		Х	Wan Chai 灣仔	304
Zenpachi 禪八	NEW	ХХ	Tsim Sha Tsui 尖沙咀	310

Japanese contemporary 時尚日本菜
Nobu		ХХ	Tsim Sha Tsui 尖沙咀	200

Korean 韓國菜
Arisu (Tsim Sha Tsui) 阿利水 (尖沙咀)		ХХ	Tsim Sha Tsui 尖沙咀	74
Chang Won 莊園		Х	Tsim Sha Tsui 尖沙咀	90
Sorabol (Causeway Bay) 新羅寶（銅鑼灣）		ХХ	Causeway Bay 銅鑼灣	242

Malaysian 馬拉菜
Sabah (Wan Chai) 莎巴(灣仔)	⊛	Х	Wan Chai 灣仔	222

Meat and Grills 烤肉小餐館
Atelier Vivanda	NEW	Х	Wan Chai 灣仔	75

Mediterranean 地中海菜
Ammo		ХХ	Admiralty 金鐘	70
Isono	NEW	Х	Central 中環	148

Middle Eastern 中東菜
Le Souk		Х	Central 中環	166

Noodles 麵食
Dandan 四川擔擔麵	NEW	🍜	Sheung Wan 上環	106
Ho To Tai 好到底	⊛	🍜	Yuen Long 元朗	141
Kau Kee 九記	⊛	🍜	Central 中環	155
Kwan Kee Bamboo Noodle(Cheung Sha Wan) 坤記竹昇麵(長沙灣)	⊛	🍜	Cheung Sha Wan 長沙灣	160
Sister Wah (Tin Hau) 華姐清湯腩 (天后)	⊛	🍜	Tin Hau 天后	239

Shaanxi 陝西菜

Yau Yuen Siu Tsui 有緣小敍	⊕	ᴮ⃒	Jordan 佐敦	299

Shanghainese 滬菜

Din Tai Fung (Causeway Bay) 鼎泰豐（銅鑼灣）	⊕	X	Causeway Bay 銅鑼灣	107
Din Tai Fung (Silvercord) 鼎泰豐（新港中心）	⊕	X	Tsim Sha Tsui 尖沙咀	108
Grand Cuisine Shanghai Kitchen 君頤上海小廚		X	Tai Koo Shing 太古城	135
Jardin de Jade 蘇浙滙	❀	XXX	Wan Chai 灣仔	150
Liu Yuan Pavilion 留園雅敍		XX	Wan Chai 灣仔	176
Nanxiang Steamed Bun (Causeway Bay) 南翔饅頭店（銅鑼灣）	⊕	X	Causeway Bay 銅鑼灣	195
New Shanghai 新滬坊	⊕	XXX	Wan Chai 灣仔	196
Shanghai Garden 紫玉蘭		XX	Admiralty 金鐘	231
Snow Garden 雪園	⊕	XX	Causeway Bay 銅鑼灣	241
Wu Kong (Causeway Bay) 滬江（銅鑼灣）		XX	Causeway Bay 銅鑼灣	295
Yè Shanghai (Tsim Sha Tsui) 夜上海（尖沙咀）	❀	XXX	Tsim Sha Tsui 尖沙咀	300
Zhejiang Heen 浙江軒	❀	XX	Wan Chai 灣仔	311

Shun Tak 順德菜

Siu Shun Village Cuisine (Kowloon Bay) 肇順名滙河鮮專門店（九龍灣）	⊕	X	Kowloon Bay 九龍灣	240

Sichuan 川菜

Chilli Fagara 麻辣燙			X	Central 中環	95
Da Ping Huo 大平伙			X	Central 中環	105
Mask of Sichuen & Beijing 面譜京川料理		⊕	X	Tsim Sha Tsui 尖沙咀	185
Qi 丼	♫	❀	XX	Wan Chai 灣仔	215
Yun Yan 雲陽		⊕	X	Causeway Bay 銅鑼灣	309

Singaporean and Malaysian 星馬菜

Ancient Moon 古月	NEW	🏮	🍴	North Point 北角	72

Spanish 西班牙菜

Catalunya		XX	Wan Chai 灣仔	86
FoFo by el Willy		X	Central 中環	117
Olé		XX	Central 中環	202

Steakhouse 扒房

Grand Hyatt Steakhouse		XX	Wan Chai 灣仔	136
Morton's of Chicago	NEW	XX	Tsim Sha Tsui 尖沙咀	192
The Bostonian 美岸海鮮廳		XX	Tsim Sha Tsui 尖沙咀	264
The Steak House Wine bar + grill		XXX	Tsim Sha Tsui 尖沙咀	269

Sushi 壽司

Sushi Ginza Iwa		✿	X	Central 中環	249
Sushi Mori Tomoaki	NEW		X	Tin Hau 天后	251
Sushi Rozan 鮨魯山			X	Wan Chai 灣仔	252
Sushi Shikon 志魂		✿✿✿	X	Sheung Wan 上環	253
Sushi Ta-ke 竹 寿司			X	Causeway Bay 銅鑼灣	254
Xuan Sushi 玄鮨			X	Central 中環	296

Swiss 瑞士菜

Chesa 瑞樵閣	XX	Tsim Sha Tsui 尖沙咀	92
The Swiss Chalet 瑞士餐廳	X	Tsim Sha Tsui 尖沙咀	270

Tempura 天婦羅

Ippoh 一宝	NEW	X	Central 中環	146

Teppanyaki 鐵板燒

IM Teppanyaki & Wine	XX	Tai Hang 大坑	144

Thai 泰國菜

Vegetarian 素食

Vietnamese 越南菜

Xinjiang 新疆菜

RESTAURANTS WITH INTERESTING WINE LISTS
供應優質餐酒的餐廳

NEW : New entry in the guide 新增推介

❞ : Restaurant promoted to a Bib Gourmand or Star 評級有所晉升的餐廳

RESTAURANTS WITH VIEWS
有景觀的餐廳

NEW : New entry in the guide 新增推介
❀ : Restaurant promoted to a Bib Gourmand or Star 評級有所晉升的餐廳

STREET FOOD
街頭小吃
Popular places for snack food
馳名小食店

Looking for a taste of local life? Check out our top street food picks.
到哪兒尋找本土特色小食？請翻閱本年度新增的街頭小吃推介。

Read 'How to use this guide' for an explanation of our symbols, classifications and abbreviations.
請細閱「如何使用餐廳／酒店指南」，當中的標誌、分類等簡介助你掌握使用本指南的訣竅，作出智慧選擇。

Aberdeen Street Social

🍴

🏠 🍽18 🕐🍴

It's now home to Hong Kong's creative industries but PMQ was originally built back in the '50s as Police married quarters. British chef Jason Atherton occupies two units inside, with a bar on the ground floor and a comfortable restaurant on the second which serves good looking modern dishes. From the private room you can look into the kitchen and admire the skills on show.

原是已婚警察宿舍，獲列為三級歷史建築，保留下來後活化為現在的元創坊。餐廳在靠近荷里活道那邊佔了兩層樓，地下是氣氛輕鬆的酒吧和露天座位，一樓是感覺舒適的餐室及一間能觀看廚房工作的私人房。精心炮製的時尚英國菜外型吸引。

TEL. 2866 0300
PMQ, 35 Aberdeen Street, Central
中環鴨巴甸街35號
www.aberdeenstreetsocial.hk

■ PRICE 價錢
Lunch 午膳
set 套餐 $ 238-288
à la carte 點菜 $ 550-850
Dinner 晚膳
set 套餐 $ 950
à la carte 點菜 $ 550-850

■ OPENING HOURS 營業時間
Lunch 午膳　12:00-14:30 (L.O.)
Dinner 晚膳　18:00-22:30 (L.O.)
Weekends & Public Holidays
週末及公眾假期　11:30-15:30 (L.O.)

Above & Beyond
天外天

XXX ⟨ 🖐 🍽30 🕐🍴 ⅋

Designed by Sir Terence Conran, the restaurant of the Hotel Icon (partly run by the education sector and staffed by keen students) is unsurprisingly contemporary and boasts a chic lounge and bar and stunning harbour views. What is unexpected is that this Western-style restaurant serves authentic Cantonese cuisine – dishes like smoked pigeon with Oolong tea leaves, and braised tofu with morels and Chinese mushrooms stand out.

由泰倫斯‧康藍爵士（Sir Terence Conran）設計的唯港薈中菜廳，時尚典雅的酒吧大廳，是其一貫的設計風格，加上醉人的維港景致，叫人讚歎不已。令人驚喜的是，裝潢如此西化的餐廳，卻以提供傳統粵菜為主，如凍頂烏龍茶燻鴿、野生羊肚菌炆腐皮等，都做得十分出色。

TEL. 3400 1318
28F, Hotel Icon, 17 Science Museum Road,
East Tsim Sha Tsui
尖東科學館道 17 號唯港薈 28 樓
www.hotel-icon.com

■ PRICE 價錢
Lunch 午膳
à la carte 點菜 $ 300-1,200
Dinner 晚膳
à la carte 點菜 $ 300-1,200

■ OPENING HOURS 營業時間
Lunch 午膳　11:00-14:30 (L.O.)
Dinner 晚膳　18:00-22:30 (L.O.)

HONG KONG 香港

Ah Chun Shandong Dumpling
阿純山東餃子

Shandong people are famed for their hospitality and when entertaining at home that means serving handmade dumplings. Using fresh ingredients, the owner's wife makes an abundance of authentic dumplings each day – and the daily speciality could be traditional or something more innovative such as mackerel dumpling. Other recommended dishes are Shandong roast lamb and minced meat pie. A menu in English is available.

山東人以好客聞名，喜歡在家中以自製餃子招待客人。東主的太太採用新鮮食材，每天親自包製多款不同味道的傳統餃子，其中以京葱羊肉餃最受歡迎，此外，每日特色推介如馬鮫魚餃，常給顧客帶來驚喜!其他推介菜式還有山東紅燒羊肉和餡餅。

TEL. 2789 9611
60 Lai Chi Kok Road, Prince Edward
太子荔枝角道 60號

■ PRICE 價錢
à la carte 點菜 $ 30-100

■ OPENING HOURS 營業時間
11:00-22:30 (L.O.)

■ ANNUAL AND WEEKLY CLOSING 休息日期
Closed 6 days Lunar New Year and Wednesday
農曆新年休息 6 天及週三休息

Ah Yat Harbour View
阿一海景飯店

❄️

XXX   👤 ✈ 🚪60 🍽

The first thing you notice as you leave the lift is the photo of owner chef Yeung Koon Yat enjoying his most famous dish – Ah Yat abalone. Ah Yat signature fried rice and stewed oxtail with homemade sauce and red wine casserole are also worth a try. The good value set lunch menu is a great way of experiencing many more of their Cantonese specialities. The contemporary dining room takes full advantage of the wonderful views, as do the smart private rooms.

身處位於iSquare29樓的阿一海景，不光可以欣賞宜人的維港兩岸美景，更能品嘗名廚老闆楊貫一的名菜：阿一鮑魚。此外，不妨試試其他馳名菜如一哥招牌砂窩炒飯及紅酒醬炆牛尾。飯店為客人供應來自波爾多、加洲、新西蘭和澳洲的高級紅酒。店內設有四間私人廂房。

TEL. 2328 0983
29F, iSquare, 63 Nathan Road, Tsim Sha Tsui
尖沙咀彌敦道 63 號 iSquare 29 樓

SPECIALITIES TO PRE-ORDER 預訂食物
Poached sliced fresh sea whelk 白灼響螺盞 / Baked chicken filled with abalone matsutake mushroom and morchella mushroom 松茸羊肚菌吉濱鮮鮑魚焗雞 / Baked salty chicken 一哥白灼響螺盞鹽焗雞

■ PRICE 價錢
Lunch 午膳
set 套餐 $ 268
à la carte 點菜 $ 270-1,100
Dinner 晚膳
set 套餐 $ 788-2,088
à la carte 點菜 $ 320-1,100

■ OPENING HOURS 營業時間
Lunch 午膳　12:00-15:30 (L.O.)
Dinner 晚膳　18:00-22:30 (L.O.)

French contemporary 時尚法國菜　　　　　　　MAP 地圖　28/B-3

Akrame

🍴🍴　　　　　　　　　　　　　　　　　🛋10　◐🍴

Having conquered Paris, Chef Akrame Benallal then turned his attention to Hong Kong. His eponymous, contemporary French restaurant comes in monochrome and is an understated yet comfortable space. Only set menus are offered – they change monthly and you decide on the number of courses (3-6 at lunch, 4-8 at dinner). The emphasis is on seafood and the ingredients are sourced largely from France. Sommeliers are on hand to recommend the best wine pairings.

總店設在巴黎的時尚法國菜餐廳，廚師Akrame Benallal選址船街開設香港分店，室內空間以黑白色作主調，線條簡潔且具時尚魅力。午餐和晚餐均提供以海鮮為主的套餐，大部分食材由法國購入，配合本地時令食材烹調，餐單平均每兩月更新一次。你可讓侍酒師為你配搭餐酒用餐，饒有興味。

TEL. 2528 5068
9 Ship Street, Wan Chai
灣仔船街 9號
www.akrame.com.hk

■ PRICE 價錢
Lunch 午膳
set 套餐 $ 280-580
Dinner 晚膳
set 套餐 $ 888-1,398

■ OPENING HOURS 營業時間
Lunch 午膳　12:00-14:30 (L.O.)
Dinner 晚膳　18:30-22:00 (L.O.)

French contemporary 時尚法國菜

MAP 地圖　25/C-3

Amber

❁ ❁

XXXX　　　　　🚻 🖐 🍽 20 🕐🍴 🎀

The hanging ceiling sculpture, which features over 3,500 copper tubes, is the most striking element of Adam Tihany's bold restaurant design. Service is detailed and courteous yet never overbearing, but it is the adventurous and creative French cuisine, made with superb ingredients, which attracts diners to these plush surroundings. Try Hokkaido sea urchin in a lobster Jell-O or charcoal-grilled Bresse pigeon, and don't miss the chocolate soufflé.

天花懸着由超過3,500條銅管造成的雕塑令人神搖目眩，細心有禮且恰到好處的服務，令食客感到放心舒適，然而，最吸引食客光顧的是選用優質材料製作、大膽與創意兼備的法國菜。

TEL. 2132 0066
7F, The Landmark Mandarin Oriental Hotel,
15 Queen's Road, Central
中環皇后大道中 15號置地文華東方酒店 7樓
www.amberhongkong.com

■ PRICE 價錢
Lunch 午膳
set 套餐 $ 580-1,200
à la carte 點菜 $ 1,400-2,200
Dinner 晚膳
set 套餐 $ 1,988
à la carte 點菜 $ 1,400-2,200

■ OPENING HOURS 營業時間
Lunch 午膳　12:00-14:30 (L.O.)
Dinner 晚膳　18:30-22:30 (L.O.)

HONG KONG 香港

Mediterranean 地中海菜

MAP 地圖　27/B-2

Ammo

🍴🍴   🚇

Copper tubes and pipes have been used to great effect to create a striking and quite futuristic looking restaurant, here at the Asia Society Center. The name refers to the building's former life as an explosives depot. The cooking is largely Mediterranean based, with a strong Italian element, but the kitchen also adds some subtle Asian twists. Homemade pasta is something of a speciality – try the squid ink tagliolini with mussels.

Ammo因所處建築物前身是炸藥倉庫而命名。一如其名，吧枱後用銅管堆砌的牆身猶如火球炸開的形態，配上三面落地玻璃牆，風格前衛且予人強烈的空間感。餐館供應的地中海菜混入了意大利與亞洲風味，自製意大利粉是最有特色的食物，可試試墨魚汁麵配青口。

TEL. 2537 9888
Asia Society, 9 Justice Drive, Admiralty
金鐘正義道 9 號亞洲協會香港中心
www.ammo.com.hk

■ PRICE 價錢
Lunch 午膳
set 套餐 $248
à la carte 點菜 $250-500
Dinner 晚膳
à la carte 點菜 $250-500

■ OPENING HOURS 營業時間
Lunch 午膳　12:00-14:30 (L.O.)
Dinner 晚膳　18:00-22:00 (L.O.)

70

An Nam
安南

🅿 🍽 14 ☎🍴

There is a subtle colonial element to the decoration at this elegant Vietnamese restaurant, thanks to the antique panels, painted walls and tiled flooring. The restaurant offers delicacies from all parts of Vietnam but the dishes that really stand out are those from Huế, the former capital in the middle of the country, such as steamed rice flan and lotus root salad with banana flower. The food is as attractive as it is flavoursome.

到安南用膳是一件賞心樂事：甫踏進餐廳便會為其氣氛和環境吸引。古董越南傢俱、牆飾、懷舊地磚及吊燈，帶着濃濃的殖民地情懷，東西方色彩融合得自然優雅。提供菜式包括越南各地美食及中部城市順化菜式，賣相吸引且味道清新。順化浮萍餅和安南藕藤沙律尤為出色。

TEL. 2787 3922
4F, Lee Gardens One, 33 Hysan Avenue, Causeway Bay
銅鑼灣希慎道 33號利園一期 4樓
www.annam.com.hk

■ PRICE 價錢
Lunch 午膳
à la carte 點菜 $ 250-700
Dinner 晚膳
à la carte 點菜 $250-700

■ OPENING HOURS 營業時間
11:30-24:00 L.O. 23:00

■ ANNUAL AND WEEKLY CLOSING 休息日期
Closed Lunar New Year
農曆新年休息

HONG KONG 香港

Ancient Moon NEW
古月

It was Singaporean and Malaysian street food enjoyed whilst travelling that inspired owners Funni and Lico to open their fun little place. The small menu lists about 12 items and avoids serving the more standard dishes. Instead, it's one of the few places to offer Malaysian chilli pan mee (a flavoursome white noodle dish with dried fish and homemade chilli sauce) and Singaporean bak kut the, made with pork ribs and garlic.

藏身於鬧市中，古月的位置確是有點隱閉，你須從書局街進入方能找到。看着牆上帶有地方特色的卡通繪畫，不難猜中這裡提供的是星、馬兩地美食。餐單貴精不貴多，當中多是在香港較少見，甚或是首家供應的菜式，包括以胡椒和生蒜作湯底的星加坡肉骨茶及配自製辣椒乾進食非常惹味的馬來西亞板麵等。

TEL. 3568 4530
29A, Kam Ping Street, North Point
北角錦屏街 29號 A舖

■ PRICE 價錢
Lunch 午膳
à la carte 點菜 $ 50-100
Dinner 晚膳
à la carte 點菜 $ 50-100

■ OPENING HOURS 營業時間
Lunch 午膳 12:00-15:00 (L.O.)
Dinner 晚膳 18:00-22:00 (L.O.)

■ ANNUAL AND WEEKLY CLOSING 休息日期
Closed Sunday 週日休息

Arcane NEW

🍴 ╳╳　　　　　　　　　　　　　　　　　　　🕐🍴 ᙚ

Aussie Shane Osborn, who made his name and reputation at Pied à Terre in London, has returned to basics with this contemporary little 35-seater restaurant. From an open kitchen he shares with his customers his passion for cooking and shows his respect for the exemplary ingredients by using simple recipes but a refined edge. His menu changes frequently and could include Wagyu 6+ sirloin with roast garlic mash, or steamed kinmedai with broccolini.

店內僅有三十五個座位，然而小小的開放式廚房卻拉近了主廚Shane Osborn與顧客的距離，讓顧客感受他對烹飪的熱情及對食材的尊重。主廚致力為顧客提供製作簡單但講究的食物。這兒以日本海鮮、澳洲牛肉、意大利小牛肉及法國有機雞肉作主要食材，每日新鮮運到；菜單經常更新，還提供素食餐單。

TEL. 2728 0178
3F, 18 On Lan Street, Central
中環安蘭街 18號 3樓
www.arcane.hk

■ PRICE 價錢
Lunch 午膳
set 套餐 $ 350
à la carte 點菜 $ 700-1,000
Dinner 晚膳
à la carte 點菜 $ 700-1,000

■ OPENING HOURS 營業時間
Lunch 午膳　12:00-14:30 (L.O.)
Dinner 晚膳　18:30-22:30 (L.O.)

■ ANNUAL AND WEEKLY CLOSING 休息日期
Closed 4 days Christmas; 4 days Lunar New Year; Saturday lunch and Sunday 聖誕節及農曆新年休息 4 天，週六午膳及週日休息

Arisu (Tsim Sha Tsui)
阿利水 (尖沙咀)

✗✗   🍽10 ☎️🍸

Steam rather than smoke is more likely to fill the air at this bright, contemporary Korean restaurant because hotpot is the popular dish here, with the seafood hotpot being a particular highlight. Other attractively presented dishes include grilled yellow corvine, kimchee and pork pancake; and the noodles are good too. The restaurant is housed within a new building, standing in juxtaposition to its more traditional surroundings.

這家韓國餐廳位於一座新落成大廈內，窗外所見全是舊式樓宇，店內環境卻明亮時尚，以火鍋馳名，在室內常看到火鍋產生的蒸氣，而非燒烤的煙燻。此店以海鮮火鍋最受歡迎，其他招牌菜式包括烤黃花魚和泡菜豬肉煎餅，麵食亦非常美味。

TEL. 2369 8008
3F, H8, 8 Hau Fook Street, Tsim Sha Tsui
尖沙咀厚福街 8號 H8 3樓
www.arisuhk.com

■ PRICE 價錢
Lunch 午膳
set 套餐 $ 55-130
à la carte 點菜 $ 180-550
Dinner 晚膳
à la carte 點菜 $ 180-550

■ OPENING HOURS 營業時間
Lunch 午膳   11:00-15:00 (L.O.)
Dinner 晚膳   17:30-22:30 (L.O.)

■ ANNUAL AND WEEKLY CLOSING 休息日期
Closed 2 days Lunar New Year
農曆新年休息 2 天

Atelier Vivanda　NEW

🍴　　　　　　　　　　　　　　　　　　口12　�. ◔🍴

Akrame Benallal's third Atelier Vivanda is his first outside France and is in the same street as his eponymous restaurant. It specialises in meat – with an unlimited supply of potato – and, with chopping boards as tables, somewhat resembles a butcher's. Start with slices of 50-day matured beef and then try Black Angus flank or sirloin, chicken or duck breast, veal or pork rib –seasoned with a little salt and their own brand of peppered olive oil.

法籍廚師Akrame Benallal旗下法式概念小餐館，以肉店作主題的砧板桌面、舊式切肉機及彷古羅馬層刀款餐刀，進餐時趣味頓添。其焦點有機草飼肉如黑安格斯牛、法國雞和鴨、伊比利亞豬肋骨，全以少許鹽及自家橄欖油調味後用紅外線爐烹煮。主菜前來點五十天熟成的煙燻牛肉，後以經典法式甜品終結。

TEL. 2109 1768
9 Ship Street, Wan Chai
灣仔船街 9號

■ PRICE 價錢
Lunch 午膳
set 套餐 $ 298
Dinner 晚膳
set 套餐 $ 448

■ OPENING HOURS 營業時間
Lunch 午膳　12:00-14:00 (L.O.)
Dinner 晚膳　18:30-22:30 (L.O.)

HONG KONG 香港

Ba Yi 😊
巴依

Lamb lovers will be glad they made the effort to find this somewhat out of the way Xinjiang restaurant. The special lamb dishes include traditional stewed lamb, roast leg and mutton skewers, with most of the meat being imported from Xinjiang. The handmade Xinjiang noodles are only available at lunchtime. The interior, dominated by a map of the Silk Route, has been refurbished and is now a little more up-to-date.

食店位置有點偏僻，但嗜羊的食客絕對不會後悔遠道而來。重新裝修後餐廳更富時代氣息，帶有標誌性的巨型絲路圖仍放置在店中央。大部分肉類均由新疆入口，羊肉特式菜包括手抓肉、烤羊腿和羊肉串燒等。三款新疆特色手打麵只於午餐時段供應。

TEL. 2484 9981
43 Water Street, Sai Ying Pun
西營盤水街 43號

■ PRICE 價錢
Lunch 午膳
set 套餐 $ 40-80
à la carte 點菜 $ 150-250
Dinner 晚膳
à la carte 點菜 $ 150-250

■ OPENING HOURS 營業時間
Lunch 午膳　12:00-15:00 L.O.14:30
Dinner 晚膳　18:00-23:00 L.O.22:30

■ ANNUAL AND WEEKLY CLOSING 休息日期
Closed 2 weeks Lunar New Year and Monday
農曆新年休息兩星期及週一休息

Beef & Liberty

This burger specialist uses grass-fed beef from Hereford cattle raised in Cape Grim on Tasmania's west coast. Different cuts are used and the meat is ground twice a day to ensure the burgers are fresh, juicy, and full of flavour – and the homemade sourdough bun proves an ideal companion. The choice also includes a Welsh lamb burger and there's a falafel burger for Veggies. Don't even think about resisting the warm skillet cookie and cream.

鍾情優質漢堡的你，定能在Beef & Liberty得到滿足。選用塔斯曼尼亞格津角，自然生長無激素草飼牛三個不同部位混合而成的牛肉餅，於每天午、晚餐前人手製作，保持了牛肉的鮮味與肉汁，配合特製麵包，滋味無窮。以威爾斯羊肩肉和法垃費素漢堡也十分美味；暖曲奇配奶油更是令人難以抗拒。

TEL. 2811 3009
2F, 23 Wing Fung Street, Wan Chai
灣仔永豐街 23號 2樓
www.beef-liberty.com

■ PRICE 價錢
set 套餐 $ 128-152
à la carte 點菜 $ 160-250

■ OPENING HOURS 營業時間
Monday - Thursday 週一至週四
11:30-22:30 (L.O.)
Friday - Weekends 週五及週末
11:00-23:00 (L.O.)

Bibo

🍴🍴   ⊕10 ☎🍽 ⚬

It's all about creativity here at Bibo. Descend into the restaurant and you find yourself in a space that's more gallery than restaurant, with works that include street art, paintings and sculpture. This unique and arresting space plays host to French cooking that is not afraid to mix the classical with the more modern. The inexorable link between art and food is also celebrated in the striking way these dishes are presented.

金色滑門後的樓梯通往這間感覺神秘、像藝廊般的餐廳。藝術品、街頭壁畫及雕塑遍佈整間餐廳。菜式結合傳統法國烹調藝術與世界不同地區食材，展現細膩且充滿時代感的法國風味。或許你的注意力也會隨着其他食客的目光一起遊走於藝術物件之上。

TEL. 2956 3188
163 Hollywood Road, Sheung Wan
上環荷李活道 163號
www.bibo.hk

■ PRICE 價錢
Dinner 晚膳
set 套餐 $ 650-1,300
à la carte 點菜 $ 700-1,600
Weekends & Public Holidays
週末及公眾假期
brunch 早午併餐 $ 580

■ OPENING HOURS 營業時間
Dinner 晚膳   18:30-22:15 (L.O.)
Weekend & Public Holiday brunch
週末及公眾假期早午併餐   11:15-14:30 (L.O.)

Bo Innovation

❀❀❀

✗✗✗   ⌂ ⎺ ☏❙ ⽊

Having the open kitchen in a raised position in front of the dining room seems entirely fitting as there's a strong theatrical element to owner-chef Alvin Leung's highly imaginative and innovative cooking. It's clear that this is not creativity for its own sake but a modern interpretation of traditional Chinese flavours. Examples include 'molecular cha siu bao', suckling pig with Sichuan pineapple and pork jus, and saga-gyu beef with black truffle.

於食客用膳區前方較高位置設有開放式廚房，正好配合餐廳老闆兼廚師梁經倫的強烈表演欲及創新煮意。侍應會給客人介紹每道菜的材料和做法。梁經倫熱衷為傳統食譜作全新演繹，務求為食客帶來嶄新的味覺感受，其分子料理如分子叉燒包、烤乳豬配四川風味鳳梨及和牛黑松露甜豉油腸粉便是絕佳例子。

TEL. 2850 8371
2F, J Residence, 18 Ship Street,
Wan Chai
灣仔船街 18 號嘉薈軒 2 樓
www.boinnovation.com

■ PRICE 價錢
Lunch 午膳
set 套餐 $ 430-730
Dinner 晚膳
set 套餐 $ 1,680-2,380

■ OPENING HOURS 營業時間
Lunch 午膳 12:00-14:00
Dinner 晚膳 19:00-22:00

■ ANNUAL AND WEEKLY CLOSING 休息日期
Closed 3 days Lunar New Year, Saturday lunch and Sunday 農曆新年 3 天，週六午市及週日休息

Bombay Dreams

🍴🍴

Although most regions of India are represented, the kitchen's strengths lie with dishes from more northerly parts of the country. Lunch sees a well-stocked buffet; at dinner you can experience dishes like spicy prawns with garlic and mustard or spring lamb marinated in yoghurt and spices. The authentic cooking and appealing prices mean that booking is recommended. The pleasantly contemporary room allows for interesting views into the kitchen.

這裡提供印度大部份地區的菜式，當中最出色為印度北部地區之佳餚。午市供應豐富的自助餐，晚市則可一嘗蒜香芥末辣味大蝦，或乳酪香草滷羔羊等美食。食物以正宗方法烹調，而且價錢相宜，建議預先訂座；環境舒適且富現代氣息，用餐時可一窺廚房的工作情況，饒富趣味。

TEL. 2971 0001
4F, 75-77 Wyndham Street, Central
中環雲咸街 75-77號 4樓
www.diningconcepts.com.hk

■ PRICE 價錢
Lunch 午膳
set 套餐 $ 148
à la carte 點菜 $ 200-400
Dinner 晚膳
à la carte 點菜 $ 200-400

■ OPENING HOURS 營業時間
Lunch 午膳　12:00-15:00 (L.O.)
Dinner 晚膳　18:00-23:00 (L.O.)

Café Gray Deluxe

    P ⌂12 ☺️

Café Gray Deluxe is a suitably cool restaurant to have on the 49th floor of the fashionable Upper House hotel. It comes with a terrific bar – homage, perhaps, to consulting chef Gary Kunz's New York background – spectacular views and fluent, confident service. The kitchen adds its own twists to mostly European dishes with the likes of pasta fiore; braised short rib of beef with soft grits and Meaux mustard sauce; and Alaskan halibut.

型格餐廳Café Gray Deluxe，位處奕居酒店49樓。充滿活力的酒吧大概與顧問主廚Gray Kunz的紐約背景有莫大關係。用餐的同時能欣賞維港的超凡美景，服務亦極為周到。廚師在歐陸佳餚中混入獨特的材料變化，如香草汁鮮茄車輪意粉、芥茉汁牛小排及阿拉斯加比目魚等均別具風味。

TEL. 3968 1106
49F, The Upper House Hotel,
Pacific Place, 88 Queensway,
Admiralty
金鐘道 88號太古廣場奕居 49樓
www.cafegrayhk.com

■ PRICE 價錢
Lunch 午膳
set 套餐 $355-395
à la carte 點菜 $600-1,300
Dinner 晚膳
set 套餐 $725
à la carte 點菜 $600-1,300

■ OPENING HOURS 營業時間
Lunch 午膳　12:00-14:30 (L.O.)
Dinner 晚膳　18:00-22:30 (L.O.)

HONG KONG 香港

Café Hunan (Western District)
書湘門第 (西環)

The young Hunanese chef developed his skills while working in his mother's restaurant and has a passion for the dishes of his home town. To ensure authenticity he insists on using ingredients from Hunan, like the different types of chilli and the smoked pickled pork which is supplied directly by the farmer. Try the rich tasting braised pork elbow – it involves 4 complicated stages and around 2 hours of cooking to get the texture just right.

年輕廚師自小在母親的菜館幫忙，入廚經驗豐富。來自湖南的他對家鄉菜充滿熱誠，最怕菜式不辣。此店大部分材料採購自湖南，如向農戶購買的煙燻臘肉及各種辣椒，確保風味正宗。經四個工序以五個小時製作的霸王肘子，味道層次豐富，紅黃二色辣椒蒸煮的鴛鴦魚頭王亦不遑多讓。

TEL. 2803 7177
420-424 Queen's Road West,
Western District
西環皇后大道西 420-424號

SPECIALITIES TO PRE-ORDER 預訂食物
Steamed fish head with diced red and yellow pepper 鴛鴦魚頭王／Braised pork elbow Hunan style 霸王肘子

■ PRICE 價錢
Lunch 午膳
set 套餐 $ 48　　à la carte 點菜 $ 100-200
Dinner 晚膳
à la carte 點菜 $ 100-200

■ OPENING HOURS 營業時間
Lunch 午膳　11:00-15:00 (L.O.)
Dinner 晚膳　18:00-22:30 (L.O.)

■ ANNUAL AND WEEKLY CLOSING 休息日期
Closed 4 days Lunar New Year
農曆新年休息 4 天

Café Siam

For lovers of Thai food, Café Siam has been a reassuring presence in Central for over 15 years, albeit at two different addresses. It now occupies two floors of a building in LKF and keeps its regulars happy with satisfying and aromatic curries, mouth-wateringly fresh salads like Som Tam, hotpots and dishes like spicy stir-fried prawns. Local office workers crowd in at lunchtime for the Pad Thai and Khao Pad.

Café Siam開業十五年，向以正宗風味泰國菜吸引食客。充滿椰香的泰式青咖喱、各式清新可口的沙律，以至香辣刺激的炒蜆都不乏追隨者。各款河粉和泰飯是上班族在午餐時段的最愛。位於蘭桂坊的這家店子佔了兩層樓，室內環境雅致舒適，透出一種閒逸情調，與街道上的繁囂有極大對比。

TEL. 2851 4803
2-3F, 21 D'Aguilar Street, Central
中環德己立街 21 號 2-3 樓
www.cafesiam.com.hk

■ PRICE 價錢
Lunch 午膳
set 套餐 $ 98-128
à la carte 點菜 $ 150-200
Dinner 晚膳
à la carte 點菜 $ 200-300

■ OPENING HOURS 營業時間
Lunch 午膳 12:00-14:30 (L.O.)
Dinner 晚膳 18:30-23:00 (L.O.)

■ ANNUAL AND WEEKLY CLOSING 休息日期
Closed Sunday lunch 週日午膳休息

Caprice

A raised open kitchen, framed by a jewelled canopy, dominates this glamorous room. From here, the large brigade of chefs produce highly accomplished French dishes such as foie gras terrine, and roasted Bresse chicken with a herb and black truffle butter – be sure to also sample the impressive selection of cheeses. Along with highly skilled cooking, you can expect great harbour views and charming service – this is a true destination restaurant.

水晶珠簾圍着的開放式廚房華麗且具氣派；陣容鼎盛的廚師團隊精心炮製各款法國佳餚，如鴨肝凍批及香草黑松露牛油烤法國雞等；超水準的特選芝士系列令人一試難忘。精湛的廚藝、迷人的維港景色與一絲不苟的服務，令顧客萬分愜意。

TEL. 3196 8860
6F, Four Seasons Hotel,
8 Finance Street, Central
中環金融街 8號四季酒店平台 6樓
www.fourseasons.com/hongkong

■ PRICE 價錢
Lunch 午膳
à la carte 點菜 $ 1,200-2,000
Dinner 晚膳
set 套餐 $ 1,990
à la carte 點菜 $ 1,200-2,000

■ OPENING HOURS 營業時間
Lunch 午膳   12:00-14:30 (L.O.)
Dinner 晚膳   18:30-22:30 (L.O.)

Carbone NEW

✕✕ ⛁30 ☺︎❢

Following the lead of the original Carbone in Greenwich Village, this colourful restaurant in LFK Tower pays homage to the Italian-American eateries of the 1950s. Tiles, wood panelling, red armchairs and a counter bar all help create that typical NYC feel. The menu features classic dishes such as minestrone, meatballs, prawns Fra Diavola, and linguine vongole; you choose dessert, such as cheesecake or tiramisu, from the five on the trolley.

色彩明艷式樣懷舊的地磚、牆上的木窗框裝飾、懷舊天花、紅色扶手靠背椅和入口處的小吧枱，將你帶進五十年代的紐約。餐單以美國意大利菜如皮埃蒙特生牛肉片、辣醋香草大蝦意粉等為主。侍應會於餐後推着載有紐約芝士蛋糕、意大利芝士蛋糕等甜品的餐車服務顧客。餐酒單上羅列的均是意國佳釀。

TEL. 2593 2593
9F, LKF Tower, 33 Wyndham Street, Central
中環雲咸街 33號 LKF Tower9樓
www.carbone.com.hk

■ PRICE 價錢
Lunch 午膳
à la carte 點菜 $ 430-1,160
Dinner 晚膳
à la carte 點菜 $ 430-1,160

■ OPENING HOURS 營業時間
Lunch 午膳　12:00-14:30 (L.O.)
Dinner 晚膳　18:00-23:30 (L.O.)

■ ANNUAL AND WEEKLY CLOSING 休息日期
Closed Sunday lunch 週日午膳休息

Catalunya

🍴🍴   🪑16 ☎️🍴 🍇

The clue is there: yes, Catalan cuisine is celebrated here at this comfortable and well run restaurant, found in one of Wan Chai's quieter spots. The chef's inspiration comes from his mother's cooking but to these traditional recipes are added some innovative touches and techniques. The resulting dishes are striking in looks yet still authentic in flavour. Tapas is popular but also try Segovian-style suckling pig, which is cooked for 14 hours.

餐廳在灣仔區較寧靜的一隅,與店內懶洋洋的氣氛很一致。顧名思義這裡主要提供加泰隆尼亞美食。來自當地的廚師,秉承世代相傳的飲食文化,配合優質食材和創新烹飪技術,製作出賣相有創意、味道正宗的小菜。焦店食物是Tapas系列。經十四個小時烹調的烤乳豬皮脆肉嫩,值得一試。

TEL. 2866 7900
GF, Guardian House, 32 Oi Kwan Road,
Wan Chai
灣仔愛群道 32號愛群商業大廈地下
www.catalunya.hk

■ PRICE 價錢
Lunch 午膳
set 套餐 $ 188-268
à la carte 點菜 $ 400-900
Dinner 晚膳
à la carte 點菜 $ 400-900

■ OPENING HOURS 營業時間
Lunch 午膳   12:00-14:30 (L.O.)
Weekend lunch 週末午膳
12:00-15:00 (L.O.)
Dinner 晚膳   18:00-22:30 (L.O.)

Celebrity Cuisine
名人坊

🍴🍴   ⛩20 ◎🍴

Having just six tables and a host of regulars makes booking ahead vital at this very discreet and colourful restaurant concealed within the Lan Kwai Fong hotel. The Cantonese menu may be quite short but there are usually plenty of specials; highlights of the delicate, sophisticated cuisine include whole superior abalone in oyster sauce; baked chicken with Shaoxing wine and, one of the chef's own creations, 'bird's nest in chicken wing'.

這家隱藏於蘭桂坊酒店內的餐廳，看似不甚出眾但別具魅力，地方雖小卻常客眾多，故此必須提早預約。這裡的廣東菜餐牌頗為精簡，但全是大廚富哥的特選菜式，精美菜餚推介包括富哥頂級鮑魚、花雕焗飛天雞及自創菜式燕窩釀鳳翼。

TEL. 3650 0066
1F, Lan Kwai Fong Hotel, 3 Kau U Fong, Central
中環九如坊 3號蘭桂坊酒店 1樓

■ PRICE 價錢
Lunch 午膳
à la carte 點菜 $ 200-400
Dinner 晚膳
à la carte 點菜 $ 350-1,000

■ OPENING HOURS 營業時間
Lunch 午膳   12:00-14:30 (L.O.)
Dinner 晚膳   18:00-22:30 (L.O.)

■ ANNUAL AND WEEKLY CLOSING 休息日期
Closed 3 days Lunar New Year
農曆新年休息 3 天

HONG KONG 香港

Celestial Court
天寶閣

✗✗✗   ♿ 🍴 🍽100 ◑🍴

Silks and woods adorn this large dining room within the Sheraton Hotel, where service comes courtesy of an experienced team. Despite its size, scores of regulars mean that queuing for a table is sometimes required. A large selection of Cantonese and Chinese specialities includes roasted whole suckling pig, pearl barley, black truffles, glutinous rice with Yunnan ham and deep-fried prawns, spicy termite mushrooms and crispy rice toast.

位於喜來登酒店內的天寶閣，以灰白作主色調、配以絲綢與木材作裝飾。眾多常客令這間面積寬敞的中菜廳偶然也需要排隊輪候入座。餐牌選擇甚多，包括廣東和其他中國地方的佳餚，黑松露薏米燒釀乳豬和飯焦雞琮菌鳳尾蝦。

TEL. 2732 6991
2F, Sheraton Hotel, 20 Nathan Road,
Tsim Sha Tsui
尖沙咀彌敦道 20號喜來登酒店 2樓
www.sheraton.com/hongkong

SPECIALITIES TO PRE-ORDER 預訂食物
Roasted whole suckling pig, pearl barley,
black truffles, glutinous rice, Yunnan ham
黑松露薏米燒釀乳豬

■ PRICE 價錢
Lunch 午膳
à la carte 點菜 $ 300-800
Dinner 晚膳
à la carte 點菜 $ 300-800

■ OPENING HOURS 營業時間
Lunch 午膳   11:30-14:30 (L.O.)
Dinner 晚膳   18:00-23:00 (L.O.)

Chan Kan Kee Chiu Chow (Sheung Wan)
陳勤記鹵鵝飯店 (上環)

Ms Chan's grandfather set up this family business in 1948 in Sheung Wan; it moved to its current location in 1994 and was completely refurbished in 2010, when the kitchen was also expanded. Chiu Chow goose, cooked in a secret family recipe, remains the main event here, but there are other Chiu Chow specialities on offer such as fried noodle with vinegar and sugar, steamed goby fish with salted lemon, and double-boiled pig's lung and almond soup.

陳小姐的祖父於1948年在上環開創此家族生意，1994年遷至現址，及後於2010年大規模翻新，廚房規模亦加以擴充。家傳秘方炮製的潮州鹵鵝仍然是招牌菜，另外還提供其他潮州特色美食，如潮州糖醋麵、檸檬蒸烏魚和杏汁燉白肺湯等。

TEL. 2858 0033
11 Queen's Road West, Sheung Wan
上環皇后大道西 11號

■ PRICE 價錢
Lunch 午膳
set 套餐 $ 50-70
à la carte 點菜 $ 100-400
Dinner 晚膳
à la carte 點菜 $ 100-400

■ OPENING HOURS 營業時間
11:00-21:45 (L.O.)

■ ANNUAL AND WEEKLY CLOSING 休息日期
Closed 3 days Lunar New Year
農曆新年休息 3 天

Chang Won
莊園

Where better to come for tasty and authentic Korean food than so-called Korean Street? Chang Won's appearance was previously more about practicality than prettiness but a makeover has made it more attractive. Their wide choice of barbecued meats includes venison, pork, lamb, chicken and ox heart, liver and tripe; try the rich and intense beef short ribs or the various noodles, such as the seafood noodle stew or the noodles with black bean sauce.

座位或有點擠逼，你亦可能要跟其他食客拼桌共坐，但這裡的韓國美食確有其吸引之處。店內提供多種燒烤肉食：豬肉、羊肉、雞肉、牛心、牛肝及牛肚等。此外，味道濃郁的炆牛肋骨及多款麵食，如海鮮火鍋麵條或韓式炸醬麵均值得一試。

TEL. 2368 4606
1 Kimberley Street, Tsim Sha Tsui
尖沙咀金巴利街 1 號

■ PRICE 價錢
à la carte 點菜 $ 150-350

■ OPENING HOURS 營業時間
12:00-05:00 (L.O.)

Che's
車氏粤菜軒

🍴 ✕   🍽35   ☎🍴

This unremarkable-looking little restaurant is popular with the local businessmen who come here in their droves for speedy service of the house speciality - crispy pork buns. But there are other reasons to visit: the dim sum at lunch; the extensive menu of classic dishes like crispy chicken or crab and dry scallop soup with bitter melon; simpler offerings such as congee or braised claypot dishes; and the blueberry pudding with which to end.

這家小餐館看似不起眼，但在本地商界人士間卻享負盛名，選擇豐富的經典粤菜如脆皮炸子雞，簡單卻美味的粥品和煲仔菜，還有午市點心，都使一眾食客趨之若鶩。服務快速且有效率，午餐時分往往座無虛席。

TEL. 2528 1123
4F, The Broadway,
54-62 Lockhart Road, Wan Chai
灣仔駱克道 54-62 號博匯大廈 4 樓

■ PRICE 價錢
Lunch 午膳
à la carte 點菜 $ 120-350
Dinner 晚膳
à la carte 點菜 $ 200-750

■ OPENING HOURS 營業時間
Lunch 午膳   11:30-14:15 (L.O.)
Dinner 晚膳   18:00-22:15 (L.O.)

Chesa
瑞樵閣

An imposing wood door leads into an intimate Swiss-style chalet with wooden objects left, right and centre – for over forty years this charming spot has played host to the cuisine of Switzerland. Traditional dishes sit alongside the cheese specialities: fondue moitié-moitié (gruyère and vacherin cheese fondue) or raclette du Valais (hot melted cheese with potatoes, pickled onions and gherkins). For dessert: chocolate fondue or Swiss chocolate mousse.

瑞士美食在香港佔一席位超過四十年。氣派莊嚴的木門後是親切的瑞士農舍，四處都有木製的裝飾。傳統瑞士菜式與特選芝士系列互相輝映：瑞士芝士火鍋或瓦萊州烤芝士(熱熔的芝士配馬鈴薯、醃洋葱及青瓜)。至於甜品，巧克力火鍋或瑞士巧克力慕絲是兩大必吃之選！

TEL. 2696 6769
1F, The Peninsula Hotel,
Salisbury Road, Tsim Sha Tsui
尖沙咀梳士巴利道半島酒店 1 樓
www.peninsula.com

■ PRICE 價錢
Lunch 午膳
à la carte 點菜 $ 550-950
Dinner 晚膳
à la carte 點菜 $ 550-950

■ OPENING HOURS 營業時間
Lunch 午膳　12:00-14:30 (L.O.)
Dinner 晚膳　18:30-22:30 (L.O.)

Chili Club
辣椒會

It's fair to say that customers aren't attracted to Chili Club by its looks. However, if you're strolling along Lockhart Road in search of sustenance you'll find yourself drawn inexorably into this Thai restaurant by the enticing aromas emanating from it. Proving further than one shouldn't judge by appearance, the kitchen is less preoccupied with presentation and instead focuses on delivering authentic and very satisfying flavours.

每次經過駱克道這幢大廈門前，都會嗅到陣陣香味，有時是混着椰香的泰式咖喱、有時是烤豬沙嗲的肉香。推門進去經過曲折的樓梯，是這家開業逾二十年的辣椒會。菜式雖無佳美的外型，卻有正宗而味道層次豐富的泰國風味。室內裝潢亦很簡樸，透過大型玻璃窗能一覽駱克道的繁華景象。

TEL. 2527 2872
1F, 88 Lockhart Road, Wan Chai
灣仔洛克道 88號 1樓

■ PRICE 價錢
Lunch 午膳
à la carte 點菜 $ 100-350
Dinner 晚膳
à la carte 點菜 $ 100-350

■ OPENING HOURS 營業時間
Lunch 午膳   12:00-14:30 (L.O.)
Dinner 晚膳   18:00-22:30 (L.O.)

Enjoy good food without spending a fortune!
Look out for the Bib Gourmand symbol ☺ to find
restaurants offering good food at great prices!

既想省錢又想品嘗美食，便要留心注有這個 ☺ 車胎人標
誌的餐廳，她們提供的是價錢實惠且高質素的美食。

Looking for a taste of local life? Check
out our top street food picks.

到哪兒尋找本土特色小食？請翻閱本年度新
增的街頭小吃推介。

Chilli Fagara
麻辣燙

Those orange flames in the window represent a warning – chillies are a passion here! The walls come in a suitably rich red colour and a sweet ambience prevails, courtesy of the small team who ensure that all runs smoothly. The heat is turned up as you progress from mild 'natural' dishes through to the likes of red hot chilli prawn – which is only for the very brave. You can even round things off with a chilli chocolate ice cream.

窗上掛滿辣椒，橙色的火焰是預警。濃艷的紅牆意外地帶給顧客一份親切感！當你從溫和的普通菜式吃到味道濃郁的辣椒蝦之類菜餚時，便會渾身發熱。不少食客更喜歡以辣椒朱古力雪糕作為完美終結。服務小團隊運作順暢，氣氛融洽和諧。

TEL. 2893 3330
Shop E, GF, 51A Graham Street, Soho, Central
中環蘇豪嘉咸街 51A 地下 E 舖
www.chillifagara.com

■ PRICE 價錢
Lunch 午膳
set 套餐 $ 98
Dinner 晚膳
à la carte 點菜 $ 220-400

■ OPENING HOURS 營業時間
Lunch 午膳　11:30-14:30 (L.O.)
Dinner 晚膳　17:00-23:30 L.O.23:00

■ ANNUAL AND WEEKLY CLOSING 休息日期
Closed 4 days Lunar New Year and Monday
農曆新年 4 天及週一休息

China Tang
唐人館

XXX   P   24

Conceived and designed by Sir David Tang, this is the sister to the original branch in London's Dorchester hotel. It's a handsome room, decorated with a mix of traditional Chinese art and contemporary Western design, with hand-embroidered wallpaper, mirrors, antique lamps and books. Dishes from Beijing, Sichuan and Canton feature, along with dim sum; try the signature barbecue pork, the wok-fried crystal king prawn, or the stewed Wagyu beef.

由鄧永鏘爵士構思及設計,是其繼倫敦唐人館後又一傑作。人手刺繡的牆紙、獨特的鏡飾、古董燈飾及線裝中式排版菜譜,中式傳統藝術與西方美學結合得天衣無縫,流露出典雅貴氣。菜單涵蓋粵、京、川等地美食及精製南北點心:老北京傳統掛爐烤鴨、唐人館叉燒、琉璃蝦球及三蔥炆和牛肩肉等,滋味無窮。

TEL. 2522 2148
Shop 411-413, 4F, Landmark Atrium,
15 Queen's Road, Central
中環皇后大道中 15 號
置地廣場 4 樓 411-413 號舖
www.chinatang.hk

SPECIALITIES TO PRE-ORDER 預訂食物
Traditional Beijing roasted duck 老北京傳統掛爐烤鴨 / Hangzhou Vagabond chicken 火焰杭州富貴雞

■ PRICE 價錢
Lunch 午膳
set 套餐 $638 　à la carte 點菜 $300-1,000
Dinner 晚膳
à la carte 點菜 $300-1,000

■ OPENING HOURS 營業時間
Lunch 午膳 12:00-14:30 (L.O.)
Dinner 晚膳 18:00-22:30 (L.O.)

■ ANNUAL AND WEEKLY CLOSING 休息日期
Closed 3 days Lunar New Year
農曆新年休息 3 天

HONG KONG 香港

Chiu Chow Rice Roll
潮式腸粉

 🍜 🍴 ⑤ ⊘🍴

One way of attracting passing customers into your little restaurant is to name it after your speciality. The owner-chef here sells an assortment of Chiu Chow dishes and snacks but it is his rice roll that is the undoubted star of the show. It comes with a variety of toppings that include shrimp, squid or baby oyster with vegetables. You can also ask the owner for Chiu Chow specialities not listed on the menu, such as peach glutinous rice cake.

吸引顧客的最佳方法莫過於以店內著名菜式為餐廳命名。身兼店東的主廚精於製作各式各樣潮式小菜和小吃，當中潮式腸粉為其招牌菜，可以配搭不同餡料，如蝦、魷魚或蠔仔及蔬菜。食客可預訂多款潮州食品如紅桃粿及小米粿等。

TEL. 2418 9638
Shop 5, GF, Kin Fai Building,
69 Fung Cheung Road, Yuen Long
元朗鳳翔路 69號建輝大廈地下 5號舖

■ PRICE 價錢
à la carte 點菜 $30-90

■ OPENING HOURS 營業時間
11:00-22:30 (L.O.)

Chuen Cheung Kui (Mong Kok)
泉章居 (旺角)

Highlights of the menu of this first floor restaurant, which overlooks the street below, are those dishes based largely on traditional Hakkanese recipes, such as chicken baked in salt or stewed pork with preserved vegetables. In the afternoon, the smaller ground floor room is used for the serving of simpler, rice-based dishes. The restaurant has been owned by the same family since the 1960s and relocated to its current location in 2004.

在餐館一樓可看到街景。精選菜式以傳統客家菜為主,為人津津樂道的有鹽焗雞和梅菜扣肉。下層地舖面積較小,在下午時分主要供應烹調工序較簡單的碟頭飯。菜館自1960年代起一直由同一家族經營,直至2004年才遷至現址。

TEL. 2396 0672
Lisa House, 33 Nelson Street,
Mong Kok
旺角奶路臣街 33號依利大廈

■ PRICE 價錢
à la carte 點菜 $ 100-330

■ OPENING HOURS 營業時間
11:00-23:15 (L.O.)

■ ANNUAL AND WEEKLY CLOSING 休息日期
Closed 4 days Lunar New Year
農曆新年休息 4 天

Chuen Kee Seafood
全記海鮮菜館

Two family-run restaurants overlook a pleasant harbour to distant islands; choose the one with the rooftop terrace and the quayside plastic seats. An extraordinary range of seafood is available from adjacent fishmongers: cuttlefish, bivalve, crab and lobster, mollusc, shrimps, prawns…Go to the tank, select your meal, and minutes later it appears in front of you: steamed, poached, or wok-fried. Then settle back and watch the boats go by.

這兩家餐廳是家族生意，位置優越，可選擇有陽台的那一家，坐在碼頭邊的膠座椅上觀賞怡人海灣及離島景致。魚缸內的海鮮種類繁多，包括墨魚、貝類、蟹、龍蝦、瀨尿蝦、大蝦小蝦等等，任你隨意挑選。蒸、灼、炒也好，不一會就奉到餐桌上，然後你便可輕鬆地邊品嘗海鮮邊細覽海上景色。

TEL. 2791 1195
53 Hoi Pong Street, Sai Kung
西貢海傍街53號

■ PRICE 價錢
à la carte 點菜 $180-500

■ OPENING HOURS 營業時間
11:00-23:00 L.O. 22:30

HONG KONG 香港

CIAK - In The Kitchen

✕　　　　　　　　　　　　　　　　　　　　♿ ⛶6 🍴 ❁

There are four sections to this casual eatery in the Landmark Atrium which comes courtesy of celebrity chef Umberto Bombana: the kitchen, bakery, charcoal grill, and pasta bar. The decoration is simple yet contemporary and the atmosphere is bustling and busy. The food focuses on the tastes of an Italian home and the produce is available to take away. Afternoon tea is popular, as is brunch which is offered on weekends and public holidays.

此間以地道意大利市集風味作主打的餐廳，設計簡約時尚，置身其中猶如在家中般舒適自在，適合與三五知己共膳閒談。店內分為廚房、麵包店、炭燒食品及意粉吧四個區域，食客可以享受不同烹調風格的意大利家常美食。下午茶套餐格外受歡迎。此外，週末及公眾假期還會供應早午合餐。

TEL. 2522 8869
3F, Landmark Atrium, Shop 327-333,
15 Queen's Road Central
皇后大道中 15號置地廣場 3樓
327-333號舖
www.ciakconcept.com

■ PRICE 價錢
Lunch 午膳
set 套餐 $ 298-358
à la carte 點菜 $ 350-700
Dinner 晚膳
set 套餐 $ 680
à la carte 點菜 $ 350-700

■ OPENING HOURS 營業時間
Lunch 午膳　11:30-15:00 (L.O.)
Dinner 晚膳　18:00-23:00 (L.O.)

French 法國菜

Cocotte

The French food at this charming little restaurant is presented in a very contemporary style but the dishes are underpinned by traditional combinations of flavours. The cooking skills are accomplished and the seasonal ingredients excellent; dishes are also large enough to satisfy those who like to share. The room has a lively atmosphere and a bright, attractive look, with striking wallpaper, marble-topped tables and green velvet seating.

黑色鐵框玻璃門後是一個空間狹長的餐室。花俏的牆紙、雲石餐桌、橡木地板和綠色絲絨長沙發，創造出亮麗的環境與輕鬆的氣氛。喜歡法國菜的食客定會享受這裡的美食。廚師選用時令食材並以精細的烹調方式製作傳統菜，展現出時尚法國口味。份量較大的分享菜式，適合多人聚會，感覺更親密。

TEL. 2568 8857
9 Shin Hing Street, Central
中環善慶街 9號
www.cocotte.hk

■ PRICE 價錢
Dinner 晚膳
set 套餐 $ 628
à la carte 點菜 $ 450-800

■ OPENING HOURS 營業時間
Dinner 晚膳　18:00-23:00 (L.O.)
Weekend & Public Holiday brunch
週末及公眾假期早午併餐　11:00-16:00 (L.O.)

Come-Into Chiu Chow
金燕島

🍴🍴   🍴16   📞🍴

The restaurant may have moved in 2014 but that hasn't stopped all the regulars coming along for their regular fix of Chiu Chow dishes. The team spirit of the staff, many of whom have been working together for over three decades, is clear to see and the restaurant itself has quite a grand feel and comes complete with assorted calligraphy and paintings. The standout Chiu Chow dishes include bird's nest and soyed meat such as goose web and wings.

餐廳在2014年遷至現址，共佔兩層，二樓有多間設備齊全的廂房，一樓的主餐室飾以書畫作品，裝潢甚具中式大宅氣派。由早年在星光行開業起，此店一直以高級朝州菜馳名，共事已久的員工默契十足，熟客也追隨至今。馳名潮州美食有燕窩菜式和鹵味如鹵水鵝掌翼。

TEL. 2322 0020
1F & 2F, Guang Dong Hotel,
18 Prat Avenue, Tsim Sha Tsui
尖沙咀寶勒巷 18號粵海酒店 1-2樓
www.come-into.com.hk

■ PRICE 價錢
Lunch 午膳
à la carte 點菜 $ 150-200
Dinner 晚膳
à la carte 點菜 $ 300-500

■ OPENING HOURS 營業時間
Lunch 午膳   11:00-15:00 (L.O.)
Dinner 晚膳   17:30-22:30 (L.O.)

■ ANNUAL AND WEEKLY CLOSING 休息日期
Closed 3 days Lunar New Year
農曆新年休息 3 天

Congee and Noodle Shop
粥麵館

Just pull up a plastic chair, be willing to share your table with a stranger and simply enjoy traditional congee prepared by a chef with over 30 years' experience. Fresh crab congee and bitter melon and salty spare rib congee are bestsellers, but many of the customers also order congee to accompany a combination of their favourite ingredients, like fish belly and beef. The surroundings may be modest but everyone's here for the congee.

店內裝潢並不講究，然而食客全是為了美味粥品而來。為了品嘗逾三十年經驗老師傅精心炮製的傳統靚粥，客人都不介意坐塑膠椅及跟陌生人拼桌。暢銷粥品有原味蟹皇粥及涼瓜鹹排骨粥，但食客通常會選自己喜愛的配粥材料，如魚腩及牛肉等。

TEL. 2750 0208
2F, Kerry Centre, 683 King's Road, Quarry Bay
鰂魚涌英皇道 683號嘉里中心 2樓

■ PRICE 價錢
à la carte 點菜 $ 25-100

■ OPENING HOURS 營業時間
10:30-20:15 (L.O.)

■ ANNUAL AND WEEKLY CLOSING 休息日期
Closed 3 days Lunar New Year
農曆新年休息 3 天

Cuisine Cuisine at The Mira
國金軒 (The Mira)

XXX   ♿ 🖐 ⛶24 🎎

When you come across a stylish and contemporary dining room such as this one, with its eye-catching chandeliers, intimate spaces and modern furniture, you can be fairly certain that its Cantonese food will also come with a few modern twists. Along with the dim sum at lunch, try signature dishes like honey-glazed barbecue pork and marinated abalone in Hua Diao. The restaurant is on the 3rd floor of the equally fashionable Mira hotel.

當你踏入這家別具型格又充滿現代感的餐廳：引人注目的吊燈、私人空間和摩登家具，你幾乎可以肯定這裡的廣東美食，也會融入精巧的現代變化。除了午市供應的精美點心以外，招牌菜如蜜餞叉燒皇及酒香鮑魚等值得一試。餐廳座落於同樣時尚的The Mira酒店三樓。

TEL. 2315 5222
3F, The Mira Hotel, 118 Nathan Road, Tsim Sha Tsui
尖沙咀彌敦道118號 The Mira 3樓
www.themirahotel.com

■ PRICE 價錢
Lunch 午膳
set 套餐 $ 398
à la carte 點菜 $ 200-1,350
Dinner 晚膳
set 套餐 $ 948-1,128
à la carte 點菜 $ 350-1,350

■ OPENING HOURS 營業時間
Lunch 午膳   11:30-14:30 (L.O.)
Dinner 晚膳   18:00-22:30 (L.O.)

Da Ping Huo
大平伙

The Sichuan couple who founded this somewhat hidden restaurant have a more consultative role these days but their restaurant remains as charming and as popular as ever. An 11 course menu is offered at dinner; at lunch there is a 6 course menu plus an à la carte. The signature dishes include Da Ping Huo braised beef brisket and the special chilled rice noodles.

這家獨具魅力的餐廳由來自四川的王先生夫婦創辦。時尚典雅的餐室由本身是藝術家的王先生親自設計，曾為歌手的太太負責統籌廚房團隊的運作，為客人烹調正宗四川家常小菜。中午除了套餐外，還提供自選餐單，晚上則只供應十多道菜的套餐。

TEL. 2559 1317
LG, Hilltop Plaza, 49 Hollywood Road, Central
中環荷李活道 49號鴻豐商業中心地下低層
https://dapinghuo.com.hk

■ PRICE 價錢
Lunch 午膳
set 套餐 $ 120
à la carte 點菜 $ 150-200
Dinner 晚膳
set 套餐 $ 430

■ OPENING HOURS 營業時間
Lunch 午膳　12:00-14:30 (L.O.)
Dinner 晚膳　18:30-23:00 (L.O.)

HONG KONG 香港

Dandan NEW
四川擔擔麵

$

'Soul food from Sichuan' is how the young couple behind this very busy operation describe their food – she is from Sichuan and is in charge of the kitchen, while her French husband takes care of the service. The focus of the small menu is on authentic dandan noodles following a traditional recipe, along with some cold dishes and dumplings. You have to pay for your food at the cashier counter by the entrance before it's served at your table.

來自重慶的女東主和其法籍丈夫在上環鬧市中開設小館子，推廣家鄉美食，焦點是擔擔麵。經典重慶式湯麵及成都式拌麵，均以從當地入口的芽菜與其他配料按傳統方法烹調，每一碗都讓你品嘗到香、濃、麻、辣的滋味。小店環境明亮整潔，配上漫畫商標，成功建立了獨特的形象。

TEL. 6920 8125
Grand Millennium Plaza,
181 Queen's Road Central,
Sheung Wan
上環皇后大道中 181號新紀元廣場
www.dandanhk.com

■ PRICE 價錢
set 套餐 $ 65-85
à la carte 點菜 $ 50-100

■ OPENING HOURS 營業時間
10:30-21:30 (L.O.)

Shanghainese 滬菜

Din Tai Fung (Causeway Bay)
鼎泰豐 (銅鑼灣)

🍴   ⊡14 🚫🍴

Queuing can be a tiresome bind but occasionally the reward for waiting in line makes it worthwhile. Din Tai Fung's Xiao Long Bao are so terrific you'll find it hard not to re-order a second basket – and you can even watch them being made while waiting for a table. Other standouts are double-boiled chicken soup and braised beef brisket noodle soup. The place is bigger than the Tsim Sha Tsui branch and is run with impressive efficiency.

這間位於銅鑼灣的分店不但更摩登，而且佔地更廣，也同樣備受追捧，很多時都需要輪候入座。菜牌包括上海小菜與點心，小籠包是其重點所在。熱賣菜式有原盅雞湯與紅燒牛肉湯麵。飯店還為初次光顧的客人提供進食名小籠包的說明，非常周到。

TEL. 3160 8998
Shop G3-G11, GF, 68 Yee Woo Street,
Causeway Bay
銅鑼灣怡和街 68號地下 G3-G11號舖
www.dintaifung.com.hk

■ PRICE 價錢
à la carte 點菜 $ 110-280

■ OPENING HOURS 營業時間
11:30-22:00 (L.O.)

■ ANNUAL AND WEEKLY CLOSING 休息日期
Closed 3 days Lunar New Year
農曆新年休息 3 天

HONG KONG 香港

Din Tai Fung (Silvercord)
鼎泰豐 (新港中心)

✗ 　　　　　　　　　　　　　🍴12 ⓧ🍴

Mr Yang opened up his dumpling shop in Taiwan back in 1958 and focused on delivering service, price and quality; there are now branches in all major Asian cities. Fresh, handmade Shanghai dumplings are their speciality and they are extremely good; the steamed pork ones being especially tasty. Queues are the norm here, but don't worry: a team of 130 smart and efficient staff serve at least 1000 people a day and take it all in their stride.

楊先生在1958年於台灣開辦首家小籠包店，特別注重服務、價格及品質；如今，在所有主要亞洲城市均有分店。新鮮、以人手炮製的上海小籠包是主打，餡料充足，令人食指大動。店前常擠滿排隊輪候的食客，由一百三十名員工組成的服務團隊非常有效率。

TEL. 2730 6928
Shop 130 & Restaurant C,
3F Silvercord, 30 Canton Road,
Tsim Sha Tsui
尖沙咀廣東道 30號新港中心 3樓 C130號舖
www.dintaifung.com.hk

■ PRICE 價錢
à la carte 點菜 $ 100-250

■ OPENING HOURS 營業時間
11:30-22:30 (L.O.)

■ ANNUAL AND WEEKLY CLOSING 休息日期
Closed 3 days Lunar New Year
農曆新年休息 3 天

Dong Lai Shun (Tsim Sha Tsui)
東來順 (尖沙咀)

♿ 🤘 🍽 24 🍽

The first Dong Lai Shun was founded in 1903 in Peking, and has been successfully transplanted to the basement of the Royal Garden hotel. Its décor is contemporary with distinct Asian nuances, panels and paintings; there's also a water feature which creates a relaxing atmosphere. The mix of Beijing and Huaiyang recipes includes hotpot, Peking duck and 'shuan yang rou': paper thin slices of Mongolian black-headed mutton.

餐廳的裝修揉合了現代和傳統格調；鮮明細緻的亞洲特色，從牆板和壁畫便可略窺一二。這裡的人工噴泉營造了閒適的氣氛。食物方面，餐廳的北京和淮陽菜共冶一爐，包括火鍋、北京填鴨及涮羊肉：採用蒙古黑頭白羊的上乘部分，肉質薄如紙，軟如棉。

TEL. 2733 2020
B2F, The Royal Garden Hotel,
69 Mody Road, East Tsim Sha Tsui
尖東麼地道 69 號帝苑酒店地庫 2 樓
www.rghk.com.hk

■ PRICE 價錢
Lunch 午膳
à la carte 點菜 $ 250-800
Dinner 晚膳
à la carte 點菜 $ 250-800

■ OPENING HOURS 營業時間
Lunch 午膳　11:30-14:30 (L.O.)
Dinner 晚膳　18:00-22:30 (L.O.)

Dot Cod

✕✕ 20 ☎️

It's back to basics at this seafood restaurant owned by the Hong Kong Cricket Club: the menu now concentrates on simpler dishes and more classic recipes which ensures the focus is on the freshness of the fish. Your waiter will present the catch of the day on a tray at your table – Wednesday night is 'Oyster night'. The bar gets busy, especially when a match is being shown, but the dining room is a slightly more relaxing spot.

由香港木球會主理、位於地庫，是中環一族經常流連之處。內裡的酒吧在球賽進行期間特別繁忙，用餐區則相對悠閒。海鮮是這裡一大賣點，侍應會把一大盤當日精選海鮮放在餐桌旁供你點選；逢星期三是生蠔之夜。

TEL. 2810 6988

B4, Prince's Building, 10 Charter Road, Central
中環遮打道 10 號太子大廈地庫 B4
www.dotcod.com

■ PRICE 價錢
Lunch 午膳
set 套餐 $ 328
à la carte 點菜 $ 480-800
Dinner 晚膳
à la carte 點菜 $ 480-800

■ OPENING HOURS 營業時間
Lunch 午膳　11:00-14:30 (L.O.)
Dinner 晚膳　18:00-22:30 (L.O.)

■ ANNUAL AND WEEKLY CLOSING 休息日期
Closed Sunday and Public Holidays
週日及公眾假期休息

Dragon Inn
容龍

　&　⫷　**P**　⫸72　◐¶

There aren't many locals who haven't heard of Dragon Inn as it's been here in one form or another since 1939. It may have great views to the sea across tropical gardens but it's the seafood most come for – some regulars don't even look at the main menu but just pick from the seafood speciality list. Baked baby lobster with cheese or baked oysters with port are favourites and dim sum is now offered during the day. Ask for a window table.

容龍海鮮酒家在本區可謂無人不曉，不少人都喜愛到這裡欣賞海景，受歡迎是意料中事。但最吸引客人的是這裡的海鮮。個別食客完全不看主菜牌，而直接從海鮮單上挑選食物。芝士焗龍蝦與砵酒焗生蠔是必然之選。日間有點心供應。預訂時可選擇靠窗座位。

TEL. 2450 6366
Castle Peak Road, Miles 19, Tuen Mun
屯門青山公路 19咪

■ PRICE 價錢
à la carte 點菜 $ 150-500

■ OPENING HOURS 營業時間
10:00-22:30 (L.O.)

■ ANNUAL AND WEEKLY CLOSING 休息日期
Closed 2 days Lunar New Year
農曆新年休息 2 天

HONG KONG 香港

Dragon King (Kwun Tong)
龍皇 (觀塘)

🍴🍴　　　　　　　　　　　　　　♿ 🅿 ⛶60 ☎️🍴

Creative Cantonese dishes with a seafood slant are the draw at this contemporary dining room owned by famous local chef Wong Wing Chee. Standout dishes include Australian Tiger Jade abalone double-boiled with herbs, and Mantis prawns steamed in a bamboo basket. From time to time the chefs enter group culinary competitions to aid their cooking skills and creative thinking – the results can be seen in some of the more innovative dishes on the menu.

這家富現代感的中菜館，提供以海鮮為主的創新廣東菜式，東主為香港著名廚師黃永幟。在芸芸美食中，最出眾的有石決明燉老虎鮑和清蒸斑馬富貴蝦。所屬集團會定期舉行廚藝比賽，讓各分店主廚施展實力與創意，同時亦會將配搭新穎的得獎菜式上市供食客品嘗。

TEL. 2955 0668
2F, Yen Sheng Centre,
64 Hoi Yuen Road, Kwun Tong
觀塘開源道 64 號源成中心 2 樓
www.dragonking.com.hk

■ PRICE 價錢
Lunch 午膳
à la carte 點菜　$ 80-100
Dinner 晚膳
à la carte 點菜　$ 150-200

■ OPENING HOURS 營業時間
Lunch 午膳　11:00-16:30 (L.O.)
Sunday & Public Holiday lunch
週日及公眾假期午膳　10:00-16:30 (L.O.)
Dinner 晚膳　18:00 23:00 (L.O.)

Duddell's
都爹利會館

🍴🍴   🛋24 🍷🍴 🐾

HONG KONG 香港

Art and food have been inexorably linked since bison first appeared in Palaeolithic cave drawings. Here at Duddell's, art, culture and cuisine all come together over two bright, stylish floors which also host regular exhibitions, screenings and performances. In contrast to the contemporary look of the space, the Cantonese cooking is based on traditional methods, although the kitchen's skill is obvious and the quality of the ingredients palpable.

你或會驚歎鮮黃的長沙發、簡約時尚的硬木傢具和中國水墨畫,竟能如此協調和諧。由名廚主理的美食走的是樸實路線,以頂級材料配合傳統烹調技術與廚師那細緻的功夫製作食物,一點也不花巧。這間位於都爹利街的新餐館除了展現美食與藝術的結合外,亦是一種生活態度。

TEL. 2525 9191
Level 3, Shanghai Tang Mansion,
1 Duddell Street, Central
中環都爹利街 1 號上海灘 3 樓
www.duddells.co

■ PRICE 價錢
Lunch 午膳
set 套餐 $ 360
à la carte 點菜 $ 450-1,000
Dinner 晚膳
set 套餐 $ 1,280
à la carte 點菜 $ 450-1,000

■ OPENING HOURS 營業時間
Lunch 午膳 12:00-14:30 (L.O.)
Dinner 晚膳 18:00-22:30 (L.O.)

Épure

✗✗✗   ⪡ 🅿 ⊖18 ☏▯ ⠿

If you can avoid the temptations in the patisserie by the entrance you'll find yourself in a very comfortable French restaurant. Gold and greens combine with woods to create quite a striking look. The French chef uses his considerable expertise to produce classic French food with a few modern twists, such as vol-au-vent with langoustine and Brittany scallops. The outstanding wine list features an impressive selection of Burgundies and Clarets.

印上巴黎舊街道圖的金色大閘,為美食之旅揭開序幕。穿過第二道大門,是長弧形主餐室:綠色、金色與橡木交織出一份奢華時尚。法籍大廚以精湛的烹調功夫,選用法國時令食材,製作細膩味美的菜式。餐酒單內含超過四百款餐酒,當中有不少罕有的布根地垂直年份佳釀。半圓廂座,給你更多私人空間。

TEL. 3185 8338
Shop 403, Level 4,
Ocean Centre Harbour City,
Canton Road, Tsim Sha Tsui
尖沙咀廣東道海港城海洋中心 4樓 403號舖
www.epure.hk

■ PRICE 價錢
Lunch 午膳
set 套餐 $ 498-548
Dinner 晚膳
set 套餐 $ 1,388-1,588
à la carte 點菜 $ 900-1,400

■ OPENING HOURS 營業時間
Lunch 午膳 12:00-14:30 (L.O.)
Dinner 晚膳 18:30-21:30 (L.O.)

■ ANNUAL AND WEEKLY CLOSING 休息日期
Closed Sunday dinner 週日晚餐休息

Cantonese 粵菜

Farm House
農圃

✕ ✕   🍽24 📞🍴

Set in a sleek business building, this contemporary dining room has private rooms leading off it as well as an eye-catching aquarium running the entire length of one wall. A highlight of the Cantonese menu is the deep-fried chicken wing stuffed with glutinous rice, while other specialities include the baked sea whelk with goose liver, and steamed rice with abalone and dried chicken. Many of the ingredients are also available to buy.

飯店裝潢時尚，進門便可看到數間貴賓房和一個延伸整道牆的巨型水族箱，非常引人注目。農圃的粵菜選用特級新鮮材料炮製而成，著名菜式有古法糯米雞翼、鵝肝焗釀響螺和瑤柱鮑魚雞粒飯。飯店亦出售一些難於家中烹調的食物如鮑魚及海參。

TEL. 2881 1331
1F, China Taiping Tower,
8 Sunning Road, Causeway Bay
銅鑼灣新寧道 8 號中國太平大廈 1 樓
www.farmhouse.com.hk

■ PRICE 價錢
Lunch 午膳
à la carte 點菜 $ 200-900
Dinner 晚膳
à la carte 點菜 $ 200-900

■ OPENING HOURS 營業時間
Lunch 午膳 11:00-15:00 L.O. 14:45
Dinner 晚膳 18:00-00:00 L.O. 22:45

Felix

The unmistakeable hand of designer Philippe Starck has been at work at the top of The Peninsula, creating a striking restaurant with an ethereal quality. The kitchen matches the surroundings by using modern techniques to create inventive dishes; prices may be as vertiginous as the hotel but there is a reasonably priced early dinner menu. Competing with the theatrical design are some of the best views you'll find in any restaurant in the world.

著名設計師 Philippe Starck 匠心獨運，讓半島酒店的頂樓餐廳盡顯不凡。廚房配合整體環境，運用現代技巧創作新穎精緻的佳餚。餐廳收費大概如酒店的裝潢令人目眩，但亦有提供收費合理的特惠晚餐時段菜單。全球只有少數餐廳能與之匹敵的醉人景色，與舞台般的室內設計完美配合。

TEL. 2696 6778
28F, The Peninsula Hotel,
Salisbury Road, Tsim Sha Tsui
尖沙咀梳士巴利道半島酒店 28樓
www.peninsula.com

■ PRICE 價錢
set 套餐 $ 1,588
à la carte 點菜 $ 700-1,500

■ OPENING HOURS 營業時間
Dinner 晚膳 18:00-22:30 (L.O.)

FoFo by el Willy

Fofo means 'chubby' and, judging by the look on the faces of the plump pig and penguin figures dotted around the room, therein lies contentment. For those eating here, three of the authentic Spanish dishes for each person, plus a little rice, should bring equal joy. The appealing tapas range from the popular suckling pig, which is slow-roasted overnight, to fried croquettes of Iberian ham and fried gambas with garlic and chilli. Try the roof terrace for even better views.

Fofo是圓胖之意。小豬與企鵝裝飾臉上滿足的表情，與店名非常相配。在這兒，每位食客能享用三道傳統西班牙菜和少許飯，那份滿足，非筆墨能形容。從以慢火通宵烤製的脆皮乳豬，到脆炸伊比利亞火腿丸子和蒜椒炸蝦等，全是令人垂涎的西班牙小菜。可選擇在屋頂露台用餐。

TEL. 2900 2009
20F, M88 2-8 Wellington Street, Central
中環威靈頓街 2-8號 M88 20樓
www.fofo.hk

■ PRICE 價錢
Lunch 午膳
set 套餐 $238-285
à la carte 點菜 $300-600

Dinner 晚膳
à la carte 點菜 $300-600

■ OPENING HOURS 營業時間
Lunch 午膳　12:00-14:30 (L.O.)
Dinner 晚膳　18:00-22:30 (L.O.)

■ ANNUAL AND WEEKLY CLOSING 休息日期
Closed 3 days Lunar New Year and Sunday 農曆新年 3 天及週日休息

Cantonese 粵菜

MAP 地圖　19/C-1

Fook Lam Moon (Tsim Sha Tsui)
福臨門 (尖沙咀)

XXX　　　　　　　　　　　　　　&. 🍽 ⛶100 ◎♔

This Kowloon branch may have fewer corporate customers than the one in Wan Chai but it shares the same principles: fresh ingredients treated with the utmost care. The result is that this refined Cantonese cooking has been attracting a loyal following since the restaurant opened in 1972. Along with their signature crispy chicken are specialities like aged abalone braised with oyster sauce, and braised bird's nest in bamboo fungus.

與灣仔店相比，光顧九龍分店的商務人士可能較少，但兩店都秉承同一宗旨：以新鮮、時令材料精心炮製每道菜式。這種優良的粵菜烹調方法備受美食愛好者欣賞，難怪自1972年開業迄今吸引不少忠實捧場客。除招牌蠔皇乾鮑外，不妨也嘗嘗當紅炸子雞及官燕釀竹笙卷。

TEL. 2366 0286
53-59 Kimberley Road, Tsim Sha Tsui
尖沙咀金巴利道 53-59號
www.fooklammoon-grp.com

SPECIALITIES TO PRE-ORDER 預訂食物
Barbequed suckling pig (whole) 大紅片皮
乳豬全體 / Double-boiled whole chicken
stuffed with bird's nest 上湯鳳吞燕

■ PRICE 價錢
Lunch 午膳
à la carte 點菜 $ 300-2,000
Dinner 晚膳
à la carte 點菜 $ 400-2,000

■ OPENING HOURS 營業時間
Lunch 午膳　11:30-14:30 (L.O.)
Dinner 晚膳　18:00-22:30 (L.O.)

■ ANNUAL AND WEEKLY CLOSING 休息日期
Closed 2 days Lunar New Year
農曆新年休息 2 天

Cantonese 粵菜

Fook Lam Moon (Wan Chai)
福臨門 (灣仔)

&♿ ✋ 🍽150 🍷

Run with considerable passion by the third generation of the same family, Fook Lam Moon is one of the best known restaurants around and attracts many regulars. Decoration of the two large dining rooms is based around a colour scheme of gold, silver and bronze which seems appropriate as there are so many luxury items on the menu. The respect for the ingredients is palpable and signature dishes include baked stuffed crab shell and roast suckling pig.

福臨門意指好運來到你家門，現由創業家族的第三代經營，是城中享負盛名的酒家之一，深受一眾食家愛戴。店內兩個大堂以金、銀、銅色系裝潢，映襯着菜單上的珍饈百味。食材明顯經過精心處理，招牌菜包括釀焗鮮蟹蓋與大紅片皮乳豬。

TEL. 2866 0663
35-45 Johnston Road, Wan Chai
灣仔莊士敦道 35-45號
www.fooklammoon-grp.com

SPECIALITIES TO PRE-ORDER 預訂食物
Barbequed suckling pig (whole) 大紅片皮乳豬全體 / Double-boiled whole chicken stuffed with bird's nest 上湯鳳吞燕

■ PRICE 價錢
Lunch 午膳
à la carte 點菜 $ 300-2,000
Dinner 晚膳
à la carte 點菜 $ 400-2,000

■ OPENING HOURS 營業時間
Lunch 午膳　11:30-14:30 (L.O.)
Dinner 晚膳　18:00-22:30 (L.O.)

■ ANNUAL AND WEEKLY CLOSING 休息日期
Closed 2 days Lunar New Year
農曆新年休息 2 天

MAP 地圖 30/B-2

Forum
富臨飯店

❀❀

Everyone knows the name of Yeung Koon Yat, the owner chef of Forum; indeed, his signature dish of Ah Yat abalone has rapidly acquired iconic status and some have even been known to travel to Hong Kong from overseas just to try his delicacy. The new premises are more comfortable and contemporary than the old address and thankfully all the kitchen team made the move too. As well as abalone, you can try other options like pan-fried star garoupa.

各位對餐廳老闆楊貫一的大名一定不會陌生。多年來他的客由本地食客到世界知名人士，全是他的座上客，其招牌菜阿一鮑魚更是天下聞名。此店搬至現址後，面積更廣、裝潢更豪華兼具時代感。滿有默契的幕後團隊聚首一堂為食客炮製美食。日本乾鮑製作的砂鍋鮑魚和海鮮類如生煎東星斑等均不可錯過。

TEL. 2869 8282
1F, Sino Plaza,
255-257 Gloucester Road,
Causeway Bay
銅鑼灣告士打道 255-257號信和廣場 1樓

■ PRICE 價錢
Lunch 午膳
à la carte 點菜 $ 200-600
Dinner 晚膳
à la carte 點菜 $ 500-2,000

■ OPENING HOURS 營業時間
Lunch 午膳 11:00-14:45 (L.O.)
Sunday lunch 週日午膳
10:30-14:45 (L.O.)
Dinner 晚膳 17:30-22:30 (L.O.)

Fu Ho (Tsim Sha Tsui)
富豪 (尖沙咀)

🍴36 ⓒ🍴

Thanks to its authentic cooking, diners have been coming to this Cantonese restaurant on a hidden floor of the Miramar shopping centre for over a decade. Among the specialities that appeal to these scores of regulars are the signature abalone dishes, the bird's nest with almond cream and the fried rice 'Ah Yung'. The most recent refurbishment gave this comfortable and relaxing restaurant a contemporary and elegant look.

這家粵菜酒家憑着正宗的烹調方式打響名堂，即使位於美麗華商場不太起眼的一層，十多年來依然吸引無數饕客。招牌菜有阿翁鮑魚、杏汁官燕、阿翁炒飯。酒家於近年重新裝修後，不但時尚優雅，且予人舒適悠閒感覺。

TEL. 2736 2228
4F, Miramar Shopping Centre,
132 Nathan Road, Tsim Sha Tsui
尖沙咀彌敦道 132 號美麗華商場 4 樓

■ PRICE 價錢
Lunch 午膳
à la carte 點菜 $ 250-1,500
Dinner 晚膳
à la carte 點菜 $ 400-1,500

■ OPENING HOURS 營業時間
11:00-00:00 L.O. 22:30

HONG KONG 香港

Fu Sing (Causeway Bay)
富聲 (銅鑼灣)

XXX　　　　　　　　　　　　　　　　　　🚪32　◐🍴

With its modern interior, attentive service and accessible location, it is little wonder that this large second Fu Sing restaurant has proved so successful. The dim sum selection is comprehensive and the prices are suitably appealing to allow for much over-ordering. Specialities include steamed crab in Chinese wine and soy sauce chicken in Fu Sing style, but we also recommend the garoupa with preserved vegetables and fish head soup in Shun Tak style.

富現代感的裝潢，細心的服務，加上地點便利，難怪這間富聲第二分店會如此成功！點心選擇多且價錢合理，客人總忍不住多點幾道菜。招牌菜包括富聲花雕蒸蟹和鮑汁豉油雞。甜菜三葱炒斑球及順德無骨魚雲羹同樣值得一試。

TEL. 2504 4228
1F, 68 Yee Wo Street, Causeway Bay
銅鑼灣怡和街 68號 1樓

■ PRICE 價錢
Lunch 午膳
à la carte 點菜 $ 130-600
Dinner 晚膳
à la carte 點菜 $ 200-600

■ OPENING HOURS 營業時間
Lunch 午膳　11:00-14:30 (L.O.)
Weekend lunch 週末午膳　11:00-15:30 (L.O.)
Dinner 晚膳　18:00-22:30 (L.O.)

■ ANNUAL AND WEEKLY CLOSING 休息日期
Closed 2 days Lunar New Year
農曆新年休息 2 天

Fu Sing (Wan Chai)
富聲 (灣仔)

🍴🍴　　　　　　　　　　　　　　🛋36 ◑🍽

Located in a commercial building in Wan Chai, the dining room of Fu Sing is modern and benefits from having a glass roof. The service team are attentive and the cooking, with its broad repertoire of Cantonese dishes, is undertaken with equal care. Dim sum is recommended, as is fresh garoupa fillet with preserved cabbage, fish head soup in Shun Tak style, soy sauce chicken Fu Sing style, and steamed crab in Chinese wine.

富聲位處時尚大樓之中，升降機可帶你直達這富麗堂皇、佔地寬廣的酒家，採用玻璃天花的餐室設計風格富現代感。侍應服務非常周到，選擇多元化的粵菜餐單，全屬精心炮製之作。除了點心以外，推介菜式包括胡椒豬骨湯、富聲鮑汁豉油雞及花雕蒸蟹。

TEL. 2893 2228
3F, 353 Lockhart Road, Sunshine Plaza, Wan Chai
灣仔駱克道 353號三湘大廈 3樓

■ PRICE 價錢
Lunch 午膳
à la carte 點菜　$ 130-600
Dinner 晚膳
à la carte 點菜　$ 200-600

■ OPENING HOURS 營業時間
Lunch 午膳　11:00-15:00 (L.O.)
Dinner 晚膳　18:00-23:00 (L.O.)

■ ANNUAL AND WEEKLY CLOSING 休息日期
Closed 2 days Lunar New Year
農曆新年休息 2 天

Don't confuse the rating X with the Stars ✿! The first defines comfort and service, while Stars are awarded for the best cuisine.

千萬別混淆了餐具 X 和星星 ✿ 標誌！餐具標誌表示該餐廳的舒適程度和服務質素，而星星代表的是食物質素與味道非常出色而獲授為米芝蓮星級餐廳的餐館。

Read 'How to use this guide' for an explanation of our symbols, classifications and abbreviations.

請細閱「如何使用餐廳／酒店指南」，當中的標誌、分類等簡介助你掌握使用本指南的訣竅，作出智慧選擇。

Fung Lum
楓林小館

   40

Set opposite Tai Wai station and known for its striking façade is the original Fung Lum; the famed replica in Los Angeles was a hit in the 1980s. The recipes remain untarnished to this day, with the seafood being highly recommended, particularly the deep-fried shrimp on toast and the baked crab with black beans; many of the regulars believe that the pigeon is also a must. If ordering several dishes, ask for them to be paced accordingly.

位於大圍火車站對面的楓林小館，門面設計讓人印象深刻，店內裝潢充滿懷舊色彩；仿照這裡的原裝設計—著名的洛杉磯贗品—在一九八零年代曾瘋靡一時。傳統粵菜單依然深受歡迎，海鮮尤其出色，如窩貼蝦球及豉汁焗蟹，乳鴿是常客必吃之選。

TEL. 2692 1175
45-47 Tsuen Nam Road, Tai Wai,
Sha Tin
沙田大圍村南道 45-47號

■ PRICE 價錢
Lunch 午膳
à la carte 點菜 $ 100-200
Dinner 晚膳
à la carte 點菜 $ 150-500

■ OPENING HOURS 營業時間
Lunch 午膳 11:00-15:00 (L.O.)
Dinner 晚膳 17:30-22:30 L.O. 22:00

■ ANNUAL AND WEEKLY CLOSING 休息日期
Closed 4 days Lunar New Year
農曆新年休息 4 天

Fung Shing (Mong Kok)
鳳城 (旺角)

Owner-chef Mr Tam looks to the region of Shun Tak for inspiration for his tasty Cantonese cooking – must try dishes are stir-fried milk with egg whites and roasted suckling pig. This family business has been going since 1954; they have a second branch in North Point and their story has been published along with assorted recipes. The two-storey restaurant is always busy, so it's well worth booking in advance.

鳳城酒家的歷史與部分食譜已輯錄成書出版。主廚兼老闆譚國景從順德菜中尋找烹調美味廣東菜的靈感,大良炒鮮奶及馳名燒乳豬絕對值得一試。這個由家族經營的生意始於1954年,另外一間店位於北角。位於旺角的這家總店共有兩層。這裡門庭若市,建議預早訂座。

TEL. 2381 5261
1-2F, 749 Nathan Road, Mong Kok
旺角彌敦道 749號 1-2樓

■ PRICE 價錢
Lunch 午膳
à la carte 點菜 $ 100-350
Dinner 晚膳
à la carte 點菜 $ 150-350

■ OPENING HOURS 營業時間
Lunch 午膳　09:00-15:00 (L.O.)
Dinner 晚膳　18:00-22:30 (L.O.)

■ ANNUAL AND WEEKLY CLOSING 休息日期
Closed 4 days Lunar New Year
農曆新年休息 4 天

Gaddi's
吉地士

Gaddi's is something of an institution. A private lift whisks you to this 'fine dining' legend, which opened its doors in 1953. Live music and old-style British formality accompany the French cuisine, which is mostly classic but with a light, modern twist – try the Tasting menu. Gaddi's harks back to a bygone age where the act of dining was taken somewhat seriously and, as such, gentlemen are required to wear a jacket.

吉地士可說是城內有名的食府。專用電梯把你帶到這個享譽五十載的優質餐飲傳奇食店。現場音樂和古老英國禮儀配襯着傳統法國菜結合現代元素，Tasting menu值得一試。餐廳保留着昔日的典雅氣派，餐飲的真正意義得到尊重。男士們，謹記帶上一件西裝外套。

TEL. 2696 6763
1F, The Peninsula Hotel,
Salisbury Road, Tsim Sha Tsui
尖沙咀梳士巴利道半島酒店 1 樓
www.peninsula.com

■ PRICE 價錢
Lunch 午膳
à la carte 點菜 $ 1,200-1,700
Dinner 晚膳
set 套餐 $ 1,688-1,988
à la carte 點菜 $ 1,200-1,700

■ OPENING HOURS 營業時間
Lunch 午膳　12:00-14:30 (L.O.)
Dinner 晚膳　19:00-22:30 (L.O.)

HONG KONG 香港

Gainmore Cuisine
桂寶雞窩米線

🍲 10 ⏰🍴

It's all about Yunnan Cross Bridge rice noodles at lunch and chicken hotpot for dinner at this simple and clean two storey restaurant. The tasty hotpot uses a secret family recipe supplemented by assorted Chinese herbs and condiments. Lovers of spicier food can opt for the Sichuan hotpot which is available with differing levels of heat. The speciality is the chicken hotpot with abalone. Ask for a seat on the airier ground floor.

白天供應雲南過橋米線，晚上以雞鍋為主。用鐵鍋盛載，以中國香料、香草加自製秘料經數小時熬製而成的醬汁是其靈魂，加上鮮雞，實在是香氣誘人、滋味十足。嗜辣的你，還可選擇不同程度的麻辣味。最特別的首推以古法扣鮑魚作材料的鮑魚雞鍋。餐廳設計簡撲，環境整潔。地舖餐室的空氣較流通。

TEL. 2792 8388
77 Lion Rock Road, Kowloon City
九龍城獅子石道 77號

■ PRICE 價錢
Lunch 午膳
à la carte 點菜 $ 80-130
Dinner 晚膳
à la carte 點菜 $ 130-200

■ OPENING HOURS 營業時間
12:00-24:00 (L.O.)

Gin Sai
吟彩

✗　 ♿ 🛁 🍴24 🚇 🕐🍴 🎱

Whether your preference is for oden, tempura, sukiyaki, shabu-shabu, sushi, obatayaki or yakitori, you'll find fulfilment here. Indeed, such is the amount of choice on offer, you may be better simply ordering their 'special course'. The Japanese head chef makes very good use of seiro steamers so do try the steamed Wagyu or the Kurobuta pork as they are juicy and delicious. The sake selection is pretty good too!

用多采多姿形容吟彩提供的菜式種類實不為過。由日本大廚領導的團隊為你獻上刺身、關東煮、天婦羅、壽喜燒、爐端燒、串燒和涮鍋等美食。特色食物還包括蒸籠蒸，如籠蒸和牛或黑豚肉，肉汁鮮美。花多眼亂，難以取捨？可點選套餐。清酒單內的酒品是精選中的精選。

TEL. 2574 1118
GF, Oak Hill, 32-38 Cross Lane,
Wan Chai
灣仔交加里 32-38 號萃峯地下
www.ginsai.com.hk

■ PRICE 價錢
Lunch 午膳
set 套餐 $ 100-300
à la carte 點菜 $ 400-1,500
Dinner 晚膳
set 套餐 $ 580-880
à la carte 點菜 $ 400-1,500

■ OPENING HOURS 營業時間
Lunch 午膳　12:00-14:15 (L.O.)
Dinner 晚膳　18:00-22:30 (L.O.)

■ ANNUAL AND WEEKLY CLOSING 休息日期
Closed 3 days Lunar New Year and Sunday
農曆新年休息 3 天及週日休息

Go Ya
五谷

🍲 || ⟳10   �"

Owned and operated by the same team as No.5 Italian is this equally cosy yakitori restaurant. The dark colours and wood furnishing add to the intimate atmosphere. The skewers are cooked over traditional Japanese binchotan and the ones certainly worth trying include chicken with cartilage, crispy chicken skin, and high grade beef tongue. Nothing goes with yakitori quite like a beer and here it comes from a small Japanese brewery.

以黑色作主調的餐室內的手繪壁畫，出自五位東主之手，展現別樹一幟的東瀛味道。以備長炭燒烤的美食選擇豐富：雞肉棒、整塊燒烤的脆雞皮及只選用最佳部分的牛舌等是推介之選。店內還供應數款日本小型啤酒廠出品的啤酒，自家浸製果酒如荔枝和菊花酒，必為女士所愛。

TEL. 2504 2000
21 Brown Street, Tai Hang
大坑布朗街 21 號

■ PRICE 價錢
à la carte 點菜 $ 200-400

■ OPENING HOURS 營業時間
18:00-23:30 (L.O.)
Sunday lunch 週日午膳
12:00-14:30 (L.O.)
Sunday dinner 週日晚膳
18:00-23:30 (L.O.)

Golden Leaf
金葉庭

✗✗✗　　　　　　　　🤚 ⌂12 ◑🍴

The ever popular Golden Leaf restaurant is elegantly dressed with panels, sculptured wood, antique art pieces and chandeliers. It is to this cosy oriental environment that customers come to enjoy the chef's recommendations, such as the barbecued pork glazed with honey, poached prawns with preserved peel and diced vegetables, steamed fresh crab claw with minced ginger and rice wine, and poached chicken with chicken essence.

備受歡迎的金葉庭裝潢高貴典雅，以屏風、木雕、古董藝術品及吊燈裝飾。客人能在舒適且具東方情調的環境下，享受廚師的推介菜式：蜜糖汁叉燒、陳皮頭菜上湯浸鮮蝦、蒸薑米酒鮮蟹鉗或貴妃雞。此外，午市還提供套餐及一系列令人垂涎的點心。

TEL. 2822 8870
5F, Conrad Hotel, Pacific Place,
88 Queensway, Admiralty
金鐘道 88號太古廣場港麗酒店 5樓
www.conraddining.com

___

SPECIALITIES TO PRE-ORDER 預訂食物
Beggar's chicken 杭州富貴雞 / Poached whole pigeon with soya sauce 豉油皇浸乳鴿

■ PRICE 價錢
Lunch 午膳
à la carte 點菜 $ 400-2,000
Dinner 晚膳
à la carte 點菜 $ 400-2,000

■ OPENING HOURS 營業時間
Lunch 午膳　11:30-15:00 (L.O.)
Dinner 晚膳　18:00-23:00 (L.O.)

HONG KONG 香港

Golden Valley
駿景軒

The Emperor hotel is a regular haunt of many a famous face and avid race-goer at the celebrated course nearby. The hotel's traditional but fresh looking restaurant serves classic Cantonese and Sichuan cuisines but it is also known for its hotpots, which account for around 80% of its business in the winter months. Deep-fried crispy chicken is a must-have dish, while fish simmered with chilli is another of the kitchen's signature dishes.

英皇駿景酒店鄰近快活谷馬場，常有城中名人及賽馬愛好者在此出入。位於酒店一樓的中菜廳，裝潢極具中國傳統色彩。店內供應傳統廣東菜和四川菜；其四川麻辣火鍋頗受歡迎。必試之選為駿景脆皮炸雞，而麻辣水煮鮮魚片亦是其代表作。

TEL. 2961 3330
1F, The Emperor Hotel,
1 Wang Tak Street, Happy Valley
跑馬地宏德街 1 號英皇駿景酒店 1 樓
www.emperorhotel.com.hk

■ PRICE 價錢
Lunch 午膳
à la carte 點菜 $ 200-700
Dinner 晚膳
à la carte 點菜 $ 300-700

■ OPENING HOURS 營業時間
Lunch 午膳　11:00-15:30 (L.O.)
Dinner 晚膳　18:00-22:30 (L.O.)

Gonpachi
權八

P　💺16　�"ⓘ

Gonpachi in Tokyo became famous when it was used as the backdrop for a fight scene in Tarantino's 'Kill Bill'. Now there's a branch in Lee Gardens One, where lanterns and wooden architecture add to the Japanese feel. A wide selection of dishes is offered, from high-quality Miyazaki beef to assorted skewers and hand-made soba noodles. There are also over 80 types of sake available, along with a variety of Japanese whiskies and shochu cocktails.

日本甚具名氣的居酒屋落戶利園，古典和風裝潢與傳統日式廂座別有韻味。餐單選擇豐富：高級宮崎和牛、炭燒鵝肝、豆味濃郁的手作豆腐，甚至每天以人手打製的蕎麥麵配熱法國鴨肉湯等均十分美味。酒單涵蓋88款清酒及多款酒品如日本威士忌、葡萄酒及燒酎雞尾酒等。

TEL. 2787 3688
4F, Lee Gardens One,
33 Hysan Avenue, Causeway Bay
銅鑼灣希慎道 33號利園一期 4樓
www.gonpachi.com.hk

■ PRICE 價錢
Lunch 午膳
set 套餐 $ 168-388
à la carte 點菜 $ 250-700
Dinner 晚膳
à la carte 點菜 $ 250-700

■ OPENING HOURS 營業時間
Monday - Thursday 週一至週四
11:30-01:00 L.O. 24:00
Friday & Weekends 週五及週末
11:30-02:00 L.O. 01:00

■ ANNUAL AND WEEKLY CLOSING 休息日期
Closed Lunar New Year 農曆新年休息

HONG KONG 香港

Good Hope Noodle (Fa Yuen Street)
好旺角麵家 (花園街)

Mong Kok residents will know the name, as Good Hope Noodle has been around for over 40 years, but now they have a more comfortable spot in which to enjoy their favourite dishes. The brightly lit dining room is neatly furnished with booths and tiles. Food is prepared in the open kitchen, with noodles, congee and snacks served all day. Try the distinctive flavour of Zha Jiang Mian (fried noodles).

好旺角麵家在旺角區開業至今逾四十載，街坊對這名字一定不會陌生。新店以卡座為主，開放式廚房、光潔的牆身、地磚和明亮的燈光，為顧客提供了一個整潔的環境。店家全日供應粥品、粉麵和各式小吃。這兒的炸醬麵別具風格，不容錯過。

TEL. 2384 6898
18 Fa Yuen Street, Mong Kok
旺角花園街 18號

■ PRICE 價錢
à la carte 點菜 $ 40-80

■ OPENING HOURS 營業時間
11:00-00:45 (L.O.)

■ ANNUAL AND WEEKLY CLOSING 休息日期
Closed 3 days Lunar New Year
農曆新年休息 3 天

Shanghainese 滬菜 MAP 地圖 35/B-1

HONG KONG 香港

Grand Cuisine Shanghai Kitchen
君頤上海小廚

✗ ⊡14

Come at lunch during the week and you'll not only have to queue outside for a while but will probably also find yourself sharing your table. The reason for the popularity of this bright restaurant is the traditional Shanghainese cooking; you can watch the chefs prepare the dim sum and La Mian noodles in the open kitchen. Try the steamed prawn with egg white and yellow wine, and La Mian with minced meat in spicy sauce.

這家上海菜館供應的小菜全部以傳統上海菜烹調方式製作,非常受食客歡迎,午餐時段,不光要排隊輪候,甚至可能要與其他食客共用一桌。透過開放式廚房,你可以看見師傅製作點心和拉麵的情形。芙蓉花彫蒸蝦球和炸醬拉麵均值得一試。

TEL. 2568 9989
Shop G510-511, Po On Mansion, Taikoo Shing
太古城寶安閣地下 G510-511號舖

■ PRICE 價錢
Dinner 晚膳
à la carte 點菜 $ 100-300

■ OPENING HOURS 營業時間
11:00-22:30 (L.O.)

Grand Hyatt Steakhouse

XX　　　　　🍽 ⊟32 ⇌ ◑⁈ 🔗

As with most steakhouses around the world, this one comes with a decidedly masculine feel. Accessed via its own elevator, it's divided into three areas; the best spot is the moodily lit bar which has both counter seats and small tables for two by the windows. The prime cuts of beef are sourced from Canada, Nebraska and Japan; be sure to add the chunky chips cooked in duck fat to your order. There are elegant private rooms upstairs.

牛扒屋帶着剛陽味。顧客需乘搭專屬升降機，餐廳分為三個區，最佳位置在富情調的酒吧區，設吧枱座位及靠窗的二人桌。廚師深諳烹調肉類的法門，且以來自加拿大、內布拉斯加和日本的特級牛扒作材料。別忘了點鴨油炮製的厚切薯條作配菜。餐廳於上層備有多間設計優雅的私人宴會廳。

TEL. 2584 7722
MF, Grand Hyatt Hotel,
1 Harbour Road, Wan Chai
灣仔港灣道 1 號君悅酒店閣樓
www.hongkong.grand.hyatt.com

■ PRICE 價錢
Dinner 晚膳
à la carte 點菜 $ 700-2,000

■ OPENING HOURS 營業時間
Dinner 晚膳　18:00-22:30 (L.O.)

Grissini

Looking for a romantic dinner spot with views to match? Then this smart, candlelit Italian restaurant may just fit the bill. The range of authentic dishes comes from the length and breadth of Italy's regions and there's a good balance struck between tradition and innovation. Specialities include braised veal cheek; you can also expect an excellent cheeseboard. And, as the name suggests, the grissini are rather good too.

假如你嚮往在醉人夜景下享受燭光晚餐,這家時尚餐廳是必然之選。真材實料的菜式涵蓋意大利不同地域的風味,傳統特色與創意兼備。特色菜包括燴牛仔面頰肉及美味芝士拼盤,而作為店名的 Grissini 長條麵包亦別具水準。

TEL. 2584 7722
2F, Grand Hyatt Hotel,
1 Harbour Road, Wan Chai
灣仔港灣道 1 號君悅酒店 2 樓
www.hongkong.grand.hyatt.com

■ PRICE 價錢
Lunch 午膳
set 套餐 $458 à la carte 點菜 $540-650
Dinner 晚膳
set 套餐 $800 à la carte 點菜 $800-1,000

■ OPENING HOURS 營業時間
Lunch 午膳 12:00-14:30 (L.O.)
Dinner 晚膳 19:00-22:30 (L.O.)

■ ANNUAL AND WEEKLY CLOSING 休息日期
Closed Saturday lunch
週六午膳休息

Guo Fu Lou
國福樓

✕✕   ♿ ♨ 🍽16 ◑🍴

Moving from the 31st floor of iSquare TST to the basement of a hotel in Wan Chai may have resulted in more space for the restaurant's celebrity clientele but there's been no change in the quality of the cooking. The chef demonstrates his respect for Cantonese cuisine by adopting traditional cooking methods as well as by using top quality ingredients. Try the baked stuffed crab shell or the fried lobster with black bean chilli sauce.

從尖沙咀iSquare遷至灣仔，國福樓或許不像昔日受關注，然而卻為一眾低調的名人食客帶來方便。環境雖稱不上瑰麗豪華，卻不失優雅舒適，設有多間廂房供私人宴會之用。廚師堅守以頂級食材精心烹調傳統粵菜的宗旨。釀焗鮮蟹蓋及豉椒炒龍蝦球是其得意之作。

TEL. 2861 2060
LG2, The Empire Hotel,
33 Hennessy Road, Wan Chai
灣仔軒尼詩道 33號皇悅酒店 LG2

SPECIALITIES TO PRE-ORDER 預訂食物
Roasted crispy goose 明爐燒鵝 / Deep-fried stuffed crab claw with shrimp paste 百花炸釀蟹鉗 / BBQ suckling pig 大紅袍乳豬 / Traditional baked chicken in rock salt 正宗鹽焗雞

■ PRICE 價錢
Lunch 午膳
à la carte 點菜 $ 200-1,800
Dinner 晚膳
à la carte 點菜 $ 500-1,800

■ OPENING HOURS 營業時間
Lunch 午膳 11:00-15:00 (L.O.)
Dinner 晚膳 18:00-22:30 (L.O.)

■ ANNUAL AND WEEKLY CLOSING 休息日期
Closed 2 days Lunar New Year
農曆新年休息 2 天

Hing Kee
避風塘興記

☎❙❙

Originating in Causeway Bay two generations ago, the family moved their business to Tsim Sha Tsui, where they've made a name for themselves with their Boat People style cuisine; further testimony comes from the celebrity signatures lining the walls. Elder sister heads the serving team; younger brother takes charge in the kitchen. They are famous for their stir-fry crabs with black beans and chilli, roast duck and rice noodles in soup and congee.

此店由祖父輩於銅鑼灣開業經營，其後家族將餐廳移往尖沙咀，由家中大姐領導服務團隊、弟弟掌廚，建立了避風塘特色菜，牆上貼滿明星簽名，是此店名聞遐爾的明證。招牌菜包括避風塘炒蟹、燒鴨湯河及艇仔粥。

TEL. 2722 0022
1F, Bowa House, 180 Nathan Road,
Tsim Sha Tsui
尖沙咀彌敦道 180號寶華商業大廈 1樓

■ PRICE 價錢
Dinner 晚膳
à la carte 點菜 $ 300-700

■ OPENING HOURS 營業時間
Dinner 晚膳　18:00-04:00 (L.O.)

■ ANNUAL AND WEEKLY CLOSING 休息日期
Closed 2 days Lunar New Year
農曆新年休息 2 天

Ho Hung Kee
何洪記

No discussion about Hong Kong's historic noodle shops would be complete without mentioning Ho Hung Kee, which originally opened in Wan Chai in the 1940s and is famed for its springy wonton noodles and fresh, sweet soup. More elements have been added here at its new address – dim sum and some Cantonese dishes are now served too. For the interior, they've adopted a more contemporary, western style aesthetic.

要數香港歷史悠久的麵家，怎少得何洪記?此店自四十年代起在灣仔區營業，多年來其招牌雲吞麵憑着麵條彈牙、湯底鮮甜而口碑載道；其粥品也很出色。遷至現址後的新店，設計加入了不少現代西方元素，華麗而舒適。為滿足食客需求，增加了食物種類，除粥麵外，還供應點心和廣式小菜。

TEL. 2577 6028
Level 12, Hysan Place,
500 Hennessy Road, Causeway Bay
銅鑼灣軒尼詩道 500 號希慎廣場 12 樓

■ PRICE 價錢
à la carte 點菜 $ 100-200

■ OPENING HOURS 營業時間
11:30-22:45 (L.O.)
Weekends & Public Holidays
週末及公眾假期
11:00-22:45 (L.O.)

Ho To Tai
好到底

The atmosphere at this simple, two storey noodle shop is somewhat reminiscent of a bygone era. It's still run by the Chan family, who opened it in 1946. The most popular dishes are the wonton noodles, dried shrimp's roe with noodles, and homemade dumplings stuffed with fish skin. They also have their own noodle factory a few blocks away so as well as enjoying the noodles in the shop you can also buy the un-cooked noodles to take home.

這家麵店於1946年開業，樓高兩層的店鋪內是濃濃的懷舊氣氛。蝦子撈麵和特製魚皮水餃向來是此店最受歡迎的食物，還有雲吞，更是非試不可!麵店附近設有製麵工場，店主同時在市區設立多個麵食銷售店，出售自製乾麵。

TEL. 2476 2495
67 Fau Tsoi Street, Yuen Long
元朗阜財街 67號

■ PRICE 價錢
à la carte 點菜 $30-70

■ OPENING HOURS 營業時間
08:00-20:00 (L.O.)

■ ANNUAL AND WEEKLY CLOSING 休息日期
Closed 10 days Lunar New Year
農曆新年休息 10 天

Hong Zhou
杭州酒家

XX

🍱30 ◐🍴

The owner-chef has many of his fresh ingredients delivered from from Hong Zhou directly every afternoon and you certainly can tell when you bite into those delicious fried river prawns with Longjing tea leaves; the braised pork belly is also worth trying. The chef inherited his obvious passion for food and the delicate cuisine of Hong Zhou from his father (who was also a famous chef in town) and strives to keep his cooking authentic.

餐廳主廚兼老闆從同為城中名廚的父親身上遺傳了對食物及杭州美食的熱愛，努力維持正宗烹調方法，堅持每天下午由杭州運來新鮮食材。食材是優是劣，絕對騙不了人。建議嘗嘗鮮美的龍井河蝦仁，東坡肉亦值得一試。

TEL. 2591 1898
1F, Chinachem Johnston Plaza,
178-186 Johnston Road, Wan Chai
灣仔莊士敦道 178-186號
華懋莊士敦廣場 1樓

SPECIALITIES TO PRE-ORDER 預訂食物
Steamed chicken with stuffing 富貴雞

■ PRICE 價錢
Lunch 午膳
à la carte 點菜 $ 100-200
Dinner 晚膳
à la carte 點菜 $ 250-300

■ OPENING HOURS 營業時間
Lunch 午膳　11:30-14:30 (L.O.)
Dinner 晚膳　17:30-22:30 (L.O.)

■ ANNUAL AND WEEKLY CLOSING 休息日期
Closed 3 days Lunar New Year
農曆新年休息 3 天

Hugo's
希戈

The original Hugo's was founded back in 1969 and this new version remains true to its origins by offering the charms of a bygone age. That means there's everything from suits of armour to silver Christofle trolleys being wheeled around the room. The chef and his team prepare traditional European cuisine with pronounced French influences. Expect escargots, lobster bisque, steak au poivre and soufflés, along with grilled meats.

希戈本店創立於1969年，新店延續其懷舊感覺，這意味着店裡的一切 — 完整的銀鎧甲、Christofle品牌的頭盤餐車，全部原汁原味重現眼前。主廚與他的團隊為客人準備具濃厚法國特色的傳統歐洲菜。你可在這裡找到法國焗田螺、龍蝦湯、法式黑胡椒牛柳、梳乎厘與多款烤肉。

TEL. 3721 7733
Lobby F, Hyatt Regency Tsim Sha Tsui,
18 Hanoi Road, Tsim Sha Tsui
尖沙咀河內道18號凱悅酒店 - 尖沙咀大堂
www.hongkong.tsimshatsui.hyatt.com

■ PRICE 價錢
Lunch 午膳
à la carte 點菜 ＄750-1,700
Dinner 晚膳
set 套餐 ＄1,288
à la carte 點菜 ＄750-1,700

■ OPENING HOURS 營業時間
Lunch 午膳　12:00-14:30 (L.O.)
Dinner 晚膳　18:30-22:30 (L.O.)

HONG KONG 香港

IM Teppanyaki & Wine

🍴   🚪8 🚃 🕐🍴

Less a meal, more a full multi-sensory experience. Sit at the teppanyaki bar, admire the cooking show and enjoy contemporary Japanese flavours that make great use of prime ingredients like lobster and premium quality Wagyu. You also get to hear all about owner-chef Lawrence Mok's extraordinary triathlon experiences straight from his own mouth while he prepares your food. There is a private room available for small groups.

到這兒光顧的客人，十有八九是慕主廚莫師傅之名而來。坐在鐵板燒桌前，欣賞莫師傅用精湛廚藝為你炮製龍蝦和頂級和牛等美食，確是賞心樂事!莫師傅偶爾會與客人分享其參加鐵人賽的體驗，令你在一頓飯的時間得到多重感觀享受。餐室設計揉合了和風與時尚概念。小廂房適合私人聚會之用。

TEL. 2570 7088
134 Tung Lo Wan Road, Tai Hang
大坑銅鑼灣道 134號
www.imteppanyaki.com

■ PRICE 價錢
Lunch 午膳
set 套餐 $ 250-320
à la carte 點菜 $ 1,000-2,000
Dinner 晚膳
set 套餐 $ 1,280-1,680
à la carte 點菜 $ 1,000-2,000

■ OPENING HOURS 營業時間
Lunch 午膳 12:00-14:30 (L.O.)
Dinner 晚膳 18:00-22:30 (L.O.)

Inakaya
田舍家

XX　　　　　　　　　　　⟨ P ⊡36 ⊶ ☾⟨

As it sits on the 101st floor of the ICC, it will come as no surprise to learn that Inakaya provides stunning and unobstructed views of the harbour and Hong Kong Island. Apart from the kaiseki, the robatayaki is the highlight of this stylish Japanese eatery. Much of the produce, which is airfreighted from Japan on a daily basis, is on display – just pick what you fancy and the chefs will prepare it. There are six private rooms for groups.

田舍家進駐環球貿易廣場101樓最佳位置，大部分位置都能觀覽維港景色。除了懷石料理，還設有壽司吧及鐵板燒專枱。自成一角的爐端燒也是餐廳焦點所在，一如傳統居酒屋，每天從日本空運到來的新鮮食材鋪滿兩張吧枱，任君挑選，廚師還會即席為你炮製美食。店內有六間廂房，適合各種聚會。

TEL. 2972 2666
101F, International Commerce Centre,
1 Austin Road West, Tsim Sha Tsui
尖沙咀柯士甸道西1號環球貿易廣場101樓
www.jcgroup.hk

■ PRICE 價錢
Lunch 午膳
set 套餐 $280-790
　à la carte 點菜 $300-800
Dinner 晚膳
set 套餐 $900-1,980
　à la carte 點菜 $600-1,800

■ OPENING HOURS 營業時間
Lunch 午膳　12:00-14:30 (L.O.)
Dinner 晚膳　18:00-22:30 (L.O.)

■ ANNUAL AND WEEKLY CLOSING 休息日期
Closed Lunar New Year 年初一休息

HONG KONG 香港

Ippoh NEW
一宝

Ippoh has been a familiar name in Japan for over three generations and now these experts in tempura have a branch in Hong Kong. They use safflower oil to ensure that the natural taste of ingredients is not overpowered, and gas rather than electric stoves. All the seafood is flown in daily from Tokyo's Tsukiji Market and the sauce is made to a special secret recipe. The omakase is the best way to experience the seasonal ingredients.

大廚兼東主的家族在日本已有五代人經營天婦羅餐館，而一宝這個店名亦已經沿用了三代。這裡的天婦羅選用時令的日本海產和蔬菜，放在較輕純的紅花油中以明火烹調，進食時再配上每天鮮製的醬汁。要盡嘗最時令美食，建議點選廚師套餐。

TEL. 2468 0641
39 Aberdeen Street, Central
中環鴨巴甸街 39號
www.ippoh.com.hk

■ PRICE 價錢
Lunch 午膳
set 套餐 $ 480-1,100
Dinner 晚膳
set 套餐 $ 900-1,500

■ OPENING HOURS 營業時間
Lunch 午膳   12:00-14:00 (L.O.)
Dinner 晚膳   18:00-21:30 (L.O.)

■ ANNUAL AND WEEKLY CLOSING 休息日期
Closed mid-August, late December to early January and Wednesday
八月中、十二月尾至一月初及週三休息

Island Tang
港島廳

XXX   🛋40 ☏🍴

Sir David Tang's elegant art deco inspired room, with its chandeliers, rich wood panelling and mirrors, is reminiscent of 1940s Hong Kong. The menu offers a range of sophisticated and delicious Cantonese dishes, such as baked crab, sea cucumber with leeks, terrific roasted pigeon leg stuffed with liver sausage and many other classics. As befits the sophisticated surroundings, service is slick, well-organised and professional.

由鄧永鏘爵士設計，靈感源自裝飾藝術的高雅房間配有吊燈、厚木鑲板及鏡子，重現四十年代香港的風采。菜單上提供一系列獨特美味的廣東菜：焗蟹肉、蔥燒遼參到出色的潤腸燒釀鴿腿等。悉心專業的服務與出色的環境相得益彰。

TEL. 2526 8798
Shop 222, The Galleria,
9 Queen's Road Central
皇后大道中 9號嘉軒廣場 222號舖
www.islandtang.com

■ PRICE 價錢
Lunch 午膳
set 套餐 $ 368-468
à la carte 點菜 $ 500-2,000
Dinner 晚膳
à la carte 點菜 $ 500-2,000

■ OPENING HOURS 營業時間
Lunch 午膳   12:00-14:30 (L.O.)
Dinner 晚膳   18:00-22:30 (L.O.)

■ ANNUAL AND WEEKLY CLOSING 休息日期
Closed 3 days Lunar New Year and Sunday
農曆新年休息 3 天及週日休息

HONG KONG 香港

Isono NEW

🍴   🍽10 🚃 🍇

Bring plenty of friends or family to this charming and colourful café-style restaurant as its dishes are meant for sharing – some between 4 or 5 people. The menu takes its influence from a union of France, Italy and Spain, so expect everything from charcuterie to cheese, pasta to paella, and shoulder of pork to côte de boeuf. The atmosphere is warm, the wine list is perfectly suited to the food, and there's a terrace for al fresco cocktails.

這兒的菜單靈感源自西班牙、意大利和法國：尼斯沙律、西班牙鍋飯及選自三國的芝士等均有供應；每道菜式一般為二至三人分量和四至五人分量，適宜一家老少或與好友共聚。餐酒單上供應的意、法、西三國餐酒，全經過精心挑選，與店內的食物能完美配搭。

TEL. 2156 0688
6F, PMQ, 35 Aberdeen Street, Central
中環鴨巴甸街 35號 6樓
www.isono.com.hk

■ PRICE 價錢
Lunch 午膳
set 套餐 $ 189
à la carte 點菜 $ 250-350
Dinner 晚膳
à la carte 點菜 $ 250-350

■ OPENING HOURS 營業時間
Lunch 午膳 12:00-15:00 (L.O.)
Dinner 晚膳 18:00-23:00 (L.O.)

Iwanami NEW
岩浪

✗   🍴12   🚏   ◎🍴

The building hosts quite a number of Japanese restaurants but it's worth seeking out the tempura and sashimi served at Iwanami. The head chef is a local and he adds his own creative touches while at the same time using techniques based on traditional Japanese methods – ask for a counter seat so you can chat with him while he prepares something special for you. Signature dishes include Hokkaido milk tempura, abalone tempura and tuna toll.

各式天婦羅和新鮮高質的刺身均非常受歡迎，熟客都會點選炸鮮奶、天婦羅鮑魚和吞拿魚油卷（以混和吞拿魚油脂烤香的飯糰所製）等招牌菜式。大廚擅於運用不同食材，巧妙配搭製成一系列創意壽司。建議訂座時選擇壽司吧，可直接與廚師溝通，讓他為你度身製作特別美食。

TEL. 2591 1159
9F, Macau Yat Yuen Centre,
525 Hennessy Road, Causeway Bay
銅鑼灣軒尼詩道 525號澳門逸園中心 9樓

■ PRICE 價錢
Lunch 午膳
set 套餐 $ 130-390
à la carte 點菜 $ 300-800
Dinner 晚膳
set 套餐 $ 1,080-1,180
à la carte 點菜 $ 300-800

■ OPENING HOURS 營業時間
Lunch 午膳　12:00-14:30 (L.O.)
Dinner 晚膳　18:00-22:30 (L.O.)

■ ANNUAL AND WEEKLY CLOSING 休息日期
Closed 3 days Lunar New Year
農曆新年休息 3 天

Jardin de Jade
蘇浙滙

XXX   P ⊖16 ℃¶

The first Hong Kong venture from this renowned Shanghai restaurant group is certainly not lacking in grandeur, thanks to its double-height ceiling and striking chandelier. The kitchen naturally focuses on Shanghainese cooking and makes good use of traditional recipes but presents the dishes in a more modern style. High quality ingredients are sourced from the mainland for delicious dishes like steamed reeves shad and braised whole sea cucumber.

作為上海著名餐飲集團落戶香港的首家分店,餐廳的裝潢雅致,特高樓底配上引人注目的吊燈,別具氣派。餐館以時尚包裝演繹傳統上海菜式,味美且外型精緻。集團從內地搜羅優質食材,炮製出多款如清蒸鯽魚及葱燒大烏參等美食。

TEL. 3528 0228
GF, Sun Hung Kai Centre,
30 Harbour Road, Wan Chai
灣仔港灣道 30 號新鴻基中心地下
www.jade388.com

SPECIALITIES TO PRE-ORDER 預訂食物
Eight-treasure duck with spicy salt
椒鹽八寶鴨

■ PRICE 價錢
Lunch 午膳
à la carte 點菜 $ 200-800
Dinner 晚膳
à la carte 點菜 $ 200-800

■ OPENING HOURS 營業時間
Lunch 午膳   11:30-15:00 (L.O.)
Dinner 晚膳   17:30-22:30 (L.O.)

Jin Cuisine
晉薈

✗✗　　　　　　　　　　　　👐 ⊡24 ◐🍽

Having previously served Shanghainese food, Jin Cuisine now specialises in Cantonese cuisine. The highlight of the menu is the double-boiled soups, which are well worth ordering in advance. Other signature dishes include steamed winter melon with shredded mushrooms and roasted crispy chicken. The décor of the restaurant, which is located at the Holiday Inn Express but is run by the Royal Garden Hotel, remains unchanged.

由帝苑酒店經營管理的晉薈，位於將軍澳鐵路站旁的大樓中，地點便利。餐廳設計時尚，佈置簡潔舒適，自然光穿過玻璃窗滲進屋內，為店子帶來了點點生氣；供應當代粵菜，午市點心和小食選擇豐富，多款燉湯也相當出色。建議預訂及查詢當日廚師精選。

TEL. 2623 2333
2F Holiday Inn Express, Tower 4,
3 Tong Tak Street, Tseung Kwan O
將軍澳唐德街 3號
香港九龍東智選假日酒店 2樓
www.rghk.com.hk

SPECIALITIES TO PRE-ORDER 預訂食物
Steamed whole shrimp dumpling
原隻海中蝦餃

■ PRICE 價錢
Lunch 午膳
set 套餐 $198
à la carte 點菜 $150-400
Dinner 晚膳
set 套餐 $368
à la carte 點菜 $250-400

■ OPENING HOURS 營業時間
Lunch 午膳　11:00-15:00 (L.O.)
Dinner 晚膳　18:00-23:00 (L.O.)

Joi Hing
再興

The Chow family have had many barbecue shops but this one has been a feature here in Stewart Road since 1975 and is run very capably by the affable Mrs Chow. Her special recipe for the marinade is an integral part of the appeal. Pork, duck and goose are the primary meats, with BBQ pork being highly recommended. There's no menu – just cards stuck on the walls. If barbecue is not your thing then their curry sauce is pretty legendary too.

這家在1975年開業的燒臘店，在區內一直備受矚目。店家秘製的滷汁深受食客歡迎，叉燒、燒鵝及切雞等配上白飯或瀨粉，是地地道道的美食，令人食指大動。除了堂吃外，還提供外賣燒味，門外經常出現買外賣的人龍。

TEL. 2519 6639
1C Stewart Road, Wan Chai
灣仔史剑域道 1 號 C

■ PRICE 價錢
à la carte 點菜 $30-60

■ OPENING HOURS 營業時間
10:00-22:00 (L.O.)

■ ANNUAL AND WEEKLY CLOSING 休息日期
Closed 2 weeks Lunar New Year, Sunday and Public Holidays
農曆新年兩星期、週日及公眾假期休息

Kam's Kitchen
甘飯館

This little shop in Tin Hau's residential area is more generalist than its sister operation, Kam's Roast Goose. The small menu is very much geared to the local community and specialises in reassuringly traditional Cantonese dishes. It includes soups, seafood, clay pot dishes and, of course, the family forte - roast meats. There are also dishes, like prawns stuffed with crab's roe, requiring quite a lot of preparation time.

由鏞記甘氏家族第三代夥同共事多年的老伙計，在天后經營這間小菜館。餐牌上只有數十款選項，主打懷舊粵菜。富經驗的經理會向客人介紹特別推介如頗花功夫炮製的四、五十年代菜式禮雲子金龍之類。當然，家族馳名的燒鵝，肉汁豐腴，令人再三回味。餐廳座位不多，建議預先訂座。

TEL. 3568 2832
5 Mercury Street, Tin Hau
天后水星街 5 號

■ PRICE 價錢
Lunch 午膳
set 套餐 $ 40-60
à la carte 點菜 $ 150-300
Dinner 晚膳
à la carte 點菜 $ 150-300

■ OPENING HOURS 營業時間
Lunch 午膳   11:30-15:00 (L.O.)
Dinner 晚膳   18:00-22:30 (L.O.)

Kam's Roast Goose
甘牌燒鵝

The Kam family name is synonymous with their famous roast goose restaurant. This little place is owned by the third generation of the family and he wisely hired his father's former chef to ensure the goose is as crisp and succulent as ever. There's also suckling pig, goose neck and head, and goose blood pudding available. With only 30 seats, don't be surprised to see a queue.

從祖父輩創業至今歷七十多年，甘氏出品的燒鵝早已遠近馳名，現由第三代傳人在灣仔開設全新餐館，承傳父輩廚藝。與父輩共事多年的老師傅以甘氏家傳秘方炮製的燒鵝，掛在窗前令人垂涎欲滴。燒乳豬、鵝頭和鵝紅也非常美味。小店僅有30個座位，故常見輪位或買外賣的人龍。

TEL. 2520 1110
226 Hennessy Road, Wan Chai
灣仔軒尼詩道 226號
www.krg.com.hk

■ PRICE 價錢
Lunch 午膳
set 套餐 $ 60-80
à la carte 點菜 $ 50-150
Dinner 晚膳
à la carte 點菜 $ 50-150

■ OPENING HOURS 營業時間
11:30-21:15 (L.O.)

Kau Kee
九記

You'll probably have to line up in the street first to eat here: Kau Kee has been trading since the 1930s and has consequently built up a huge following which includes some well known faces from show business and politics. It's all very basic and you'll have to share your table but the food is delicious. Beef noodles are the speciality; different cuts of meat with a variety of noodles in a tasty broth or spicy sauce. Try the iced milk tea too.

要在九記用膳，你或許要在街上排隊等候：九記自三零年代開始營業，聚集了大量支持者，包括部分政商名人。其陳設回歸基本，進餐時要和其他人共用餐桌，但食物極具水準。牛腩麵是九記的特色；不同部位的肉塊配以各式粉麵，再加上清湯或辣醬，滋味無窮。奶茶亦值得一試。

TEL. N/A
21 Gough Street, Central
中環歌賦街 21 號

■ PRICE 價錢
à la carte 點菜 $40-90

■ OPENING HOURS 營業時間
12:30-22:30 (L.O.)

■ ANNUAL AND WEEKLY CLOSING 休息日期
Closed 10 days Lunar New Year, Sunday and Public Holidays
農曆新年 10 天、週日及公眾假期休息

An important business lunch? The symbol ⇄ indicates restaurants with private rooms.

需要一個合適的地點享用商務午餐？可從注有這個 ⇄ 標誌的餐廳中選一間有私人廂房又合你心意的餐館。

The symbol 🍸 denotes a particularly interesting wine list.

🍸 這個標誌表示該餐廳提供一系列優質餐酒。

Kazuo Okada
岡田和生

Harbourfront Landmark is a 25,000 sq.ft restaurant complex offering three distinct operations, one of which is this crisply decorated and elegant Japanese restaurant. Kaiseki is the main attraction and the seasonal ingredients are purchased directly from Japan, having been carefully sourced from all regions of the country. You will also be impressed by the antique crockery collection of over 400 pieces, many of which are more than 200 years old.

座落於海名軒的綜合餐飲場所，設有三家各具特色的餐廳。其中一家是裝潢精緻優雅的日本料理，主打懷石料理；廚師直接從日本十多個地方採購最新鮮的蔬菜、海鮮及肉類，質素無庸置疑，且全是最時令的食材。餐廳擁有四百多件具二、三百年歷史的古董餐具作盛器，令進餐體驗生色不少！

TEL. 3746 2722
5F, Harbourfront Landmark,
11 Wan Hoi Street, Hung Hom
紅磡環海街 11 號海名軒 5 樓
www.KOdining.com

■ PRICE 價錢
Lunch 午膳
set 套餐 $ 480
Dinner 晚膳
set 套餐 $ 1,280-3,500

■ OPENING HOURS 營業時間
Weekend lunch 週末午膳
12:00-15:00 (L.O.)
Dinner 晚膳 18:00-22:30 (L.O.)

■ ANNUAL AND WEEKLY CLOSING 休息日期
Closed Monday 週一休息

King's Garden
東來居

Unlike many hotpot restaurants, the environment here within the King's hotel is both contemporary and intimate. What also stands out is the food, particularly the pork bone soup base which takes more than 14 hours to prepare. Specialities to look out for include flaming king crab soup and chicken soup with coconut. The restaurant uses quality beef and seafood and dumplings are made to order.

有別於一般火鍋店，這間位於王子酒店內的餐廳，環境親切且有時代感。同樣與別不同的，是這裡的美食及湯底，特別是熬製十四個小時以上的豬骨湯底，另外還有火焰蟹皇湯、椰子雞湯等十數款湯底。餐廳採用上等牛肉和海鮮，餃子更是即點即製。

TEL. 2244 3355
1F, King's Hotel, 303 Jaffe Road,
Wan Chai
灣仔謝斐道 303 號王子酒店 1 樓

■ PRICE 價錢
Dinner 晚膳
à la carte 點菜 $280-600

■ OPENING HOURS 營業時間
Dinner 晚膳　18:00-00:30 (L.O.)

Kung Tak Lam (Causeway Bay)
功德林 (銅鑼灣)

    🍴🍴   🛗30   🕐🍴

As befits a vegetarian restaurant, Kung Tak Lam boasts a fresh, green look. Based on traditional Shanghainese cuisine but with less salt and oil, the dishes are not only healthy and good looking but also deliver some punchy flavours. Don't be alarmed to see words like 'pork' and 'chicken'– they merely show what can be done with soy bean products. Standout dishes include braised vegetarian 'meatball' in casserole and cold noodles.

翠綠配上淺色系的裝潢，予人清新自然的感覺，功德林素食菜館，為食客帶來印象深刻的綠色體驗。店家以傳統上海菜作藍本，配合少鹽少油的烹調方式製作出外型精緻且風味獨特的健康素食。雖然菜單上出現豬、雞等菜式，但其實全是大豆製品。特別推介菜式有砂鍋獅子頭及上海冷麵。

TEL. 2881 9966
10F, World Trade Centre,
280 Gloucester Road, Causeway Bay
銅鑼灣告士打道 280號世貿中心 10樓

■ PRICE 價錢
à la carte 點菜 $ 150-500

■ OPENING HOURS 營業時間
11:00-22:15 (L.O.)

Kwan Kee Bamboo Noodles (Cheung Sha Wan)
坤記竹昇麵 (長沙灣)

It's inside a local market but easy to spot, thanks to the big yellow sign above the entrance. All the noodles here are made using the traditional bamboo method, which may be labour intensive but leaves them tasting great as the noodles are freshly made each day; don't miss the signature dried shrimp roe mix with noodles. A glass wall allows you to watch each step of the noodle making process.

麵店位處住宅區的市集內，大門上的黃色招牌顯眼易認。與店東在廣州的家族麵店一脈相承，這裏的麵條均於店門旁的小工房中經人手以傳統竹昇法打製，每日鮮製、新鮮彈牙。蝦子撈麵是招牌菜式，萬不可錯過。

TEL. 3484 9126
1 Wing Lung Street, Cheung Sha Wan
長沙灣永隆街 1 號

■ PRICE 價錢
à la carte 點菜 $ 30-70

■ OPENING HOURS 營業時間
10:00-22:45 (L.O.)

Cantonese 粵菜

HONG KONG 香港

Lan Yuen Chee Koon
蘭苑饎館

The Chan's first place opened back in '84; they moved here in '97 to premises with a proper kitchen and now offer Cantonese claypots, healthy home-style steamed dishes, noodles and deliciously sweet puddings. Fine Chinese furniture is a feature of the small dining room, where Mrs Chan does the cooking and her husband the serving. The set menus at dinner prove particularly popular so be prepared to queue outside.

陳氏夫婦創辦的這家食館，原店在1984年開業，並於1997年遷到有正規廚房的現址；雅致的中式家具是餐廳的特色。廚房由陳太掌舵，供應各種粵式煲仔菜、健康家常蒸煮菜式、麵食、美味糕點和糖水。陳先生則負責招呼客人。晚飯時間的套餐特別受歡迎。顧客或需排隊輪候入座。

TEL. 2381 1369
318 Sai Yeung Choi Street North,
Prince Edward
太子西洋菜北街 318號

■ PRICE 價錢
set 套餐 $ 80-95
à la carte 點菜 $ 40-80

■ OPENING HOURS 營業時間
12:00-22:00 (L.O.)

■ ANNUAL AND WEEKLY CLOSING 休息日期
Closed 9 days Lunar New Year and Monday
農曆新年休息 9 天及週一休息

L'Atelier de Joël Robuchon

XX

Sit at the counter if you want to be at the centre of the operation, but if perching on a high chair is not for you or you want a little more formality, then Le Jardin is the better choice. The red and black colours marry perfectly, while the highly skilled kitchen uses prime ingredients to produce deceptively simple looking, contemporary dishes that display exquisite depth, balance and flavour. The superb wine list offers around 3,000 labels.

如欲觀賞開放式廚房的運作，建議坐在吧枱旁邊，但若不喜歡高腳椅，或希望正式一點，那麼Le　Jardin也許更佳。紅色與黑色的裝潢配搭得天衣無縫，烹調技術精湛的廚師選用上等食材，炮製出外觀漂亮吸引的菜式。酒牌包羅超過三千款佳釀。

TEL. 2166 9000
Shop 401, 4F, The Landmark,
15 Queen's Road Central
皇后大道中 15號置地廣場 4樓 401號舖
www.robuchon.hk

■ PRICE 價錢
Lunch 午膳
set 套餐 $478-2,080
à la carte 點菜 $800-2,000
Dinner 晚膳
set 套餐 $1,080-2,080
à la carte 點菜 $800-2,000

■ OPENING HOURS 營業時間
Lunch 午膳　12:00-14:30 (L.O.)
Dinner 晚膳　18:30-22:30 (L.O.)

Lau Sum Kee (Fuk Wing Street)
劉森記麵家 (福榮街)

This is one noodle shop that is not afraid of the competition. In a street overflowing with alternatives, Lau Sum Kee (and its sister shop around the corner) are packed with customers buzzing in and out. It is run by the third generation of the family, the noodles are pressed by bamboo and the wontons are freshly made at the shop. Recommendations include wonton noodles, dry prawn roe mix with noodles and pork knuckles mixed with noodles.

這家麵店可謂競爭力強勁!在滿是麵店的街道上，劉森記麵家（及其轉角位的姊妹店）仍然擠滿食客。此家由家族經營的麵店已傳到第三代，全部竹昇麵及雲吞均在店內新鮮人手製造。推薦麵食包括雲吞麵、蝦子撈麵及豬手撈麵。

TEL. 2386 3583
82 Fuk Wing Street, Sham Shui Po
深水埗福榮街 82號

■ PRICE 價錢
à la carte 點菜 $ 30-50

■ OPENING HOURS 營業時間
12:30-22:00 (L.O.)

■ ANNUAL AND WEEKLY CLOSING 休息日期
Closed 3 days Lunar New Year
農曆新年休息 3 天

HONG KONG 香港

Le Dôme de Cristal　NEW

✗✗✗

As the name suggests, this is a restaurant not short on luxury. Under a high domed ceiling is an elegant and beautifully lit circular room, with a long bar counter and a striking display of wines in a glass cellar – the list contains around 400 labels including much Roederer champagne. The contemporary French food comes with discreet Asian influences, with dishes such as foie gras ravioli with soy milk, ginger flavours and Chinese cabbage.

擺放在入口處的馬格南瓶路易王妃水晶香檳1999、玻璃餐酒窖走廊與米白色調設計成就了時尚華麗的格調。法籍主廚在祖家的烹調基礎上悄悄滲入了亞洲和現代烹調元素，法式鵝肝餛飩配椰菜及法國白鴿配紅菜頭薯蓉酸果汁是其拿手菜。酒單除供應約四百款餐酒，大部分為路易王妃香檳。

TEL. 2116 4688
3F, The Galleria,
9 Queen's Road Central
中環皇后大道中 9號嘉軒廣場 3樓
www.cristal-hk.com

■ PRICE 價錢
Lunch 午膳
set 套餐 $ 398-1,580
à la carte 點菜 $ 1,000-1,200

Dinner 晚膳
set 套餐 $ 1,280-1,580
à la carte 點菜 $ 1,000-1,200

■ OPENING HOURS 營業時間
Lunch 午膳　12:00-14:30 L.O. 13:30
Dinner 晚膳　18:00-22:30 (L.O.)

■ ANNUAL AND WEEKLY CLOSING 休息日期
Closed Sunday 週日休息

Le Soleil

Le Soleil shines a light on Vietnamese cooking, with specialities such as green mango and tripe salad, pork knuckle casserole with tamarind, and Vietnamese-style noodles. The menu also includes dishes boasting a more imprecise provenance, best described as 'Asian fusion'. The restaurant sits on the 3rd floor of the Royal Garden in the shadow of the hotel's atrium. While its decorative style is a little incongruous, it is well run and comfortable.

青芒果牛肚沙律、酸子汁豬手煲和各款越式河粉，Le Soleil 帶你走進越南美食的世界。然而菜牌上的菜式並不局限於傳統越南菜，還有滲入了亞洲風味的越南菜和法式越南菜。店子位於帝苑酒店3樓，能觀賞酒店中庭全景。裝潢清簡得來予人舒適之感。

TEL. 2733 2033
3F, The Royal Garden Hotel,
69 Mody Road, East Tsim Sha Tsui
尖沙咀麼地道69號帝苑酒店3樓
www.rghk.com.hk

■ PRICE 價錢
Lunch 午膳
à la carte 點菜 $ 250-650
Dinner 晚膳
à la carte 點菜 $ 250-650

■ OPENING HOURS 營業時間
Lunch 午膳　12:00-14:30 (L.O.)
Dinner 晚膳　18:00 -22:30 (L.O.)

Le Souk

✗   ☏ ❢

Le Souk brings a little exotic spice to the streets of SoHo and is owned by two friendly and hospitable Egyptian brothers who make time to ensure that everyone is having a good time. Trinkets, jewels and lanterns add plenty of colour to the intimate room, while the kitchen prepares Moroccan and Middle Eastern cuisine with care and attention. Tender and aromatic lamb tagine is a standout dish, as is the roasted fig salad.

由兩位友善好客的埃及兄弟開設的 Le Souk 座落於蘇豪內，為區內帶來一點獨特的中東味道。餐廳內的空間以色彩繽紛的小飾物、珠寶和燈籠點綴；大廚則在廚房精心烹調摩洛哥和中東美食。嫩滑又香氣洋溢的羊肉煲是出色之作，香燒無花果沙律亦不可錯過。

TEL. 2522 2128
4 Staunton Street, Central
中環士丹頓街 4 號

■ PRICE 價錢
Dinner 晚膳
à la carte 點菜 $ 200-400

■ OPENING HOURS 營業時間
Dinner 晚膳　17:00-00:00 (L.O.)

Lei Bistro
利小館

Providing healthy, appealingly priced cooking for everyone is the aim of this popular restaurant from the Lei Garden group. Along with northern and southern influenced dim sum are Cantonese dishes, as well as barbecued seafood. Specialities include steamed pork dumpling in Shanghai style, a daily Cantonese style soup, and chilled mango with grapefruit and sago. Despite a capacity of 150, it is still advisable to book.

為客人提供健康、價錢大眾化的美食，正是利苑集團開設這間餐館的概念。餐單選擇豐富，包括粵式小菜、燉湯、南北點心、麵食及甜品等，還有海鮮燒烤菜式。雖然餐館能容納一百五十名客人，但仍建議預先訂座。

TEL. 2602 8283
Shop B217-218, Basement 2,
Times Square, 1 Matheson Street,
Causeway Bay
銅鑼灣勿臣街 1 號
時代廣場地庫 2 樓 B217-B218號舖
www.leibistro.com

■ PRICE 價錢
à la carte 點菜 $80-170

■ OPENING HOURS 營業時間
11:00-23:00 L.O.22:15

■ ANNUAL AND WEEKLY CLOSING 休息日期
Closed 3 days Lunar New Year
農曆新年休息 3 天

HONG KONG 香港

Lei Garden (IFC)
利苑酒家 (國際金融中心)

🍴🍴   ♿ 🍽16 🕐🍴

Forward planning is advisable here – not only when booking but also when selecting certain roast meat dishes and some of their famous double-boiled soups which require advance notice. The extensive menu features specialist seafood dishes and the lunchtime favourites include shrimp and flaky pastries filled with shredded turnip. All this is served up by an efficient team, in clean, contemporary surroundings.

到這間利苑分店用餐，無論座位，還是食物如燒味或受歡迎的燉湯，均須提早預約。這裡菜式種類繁多，其中以海鮮炮製的佳餚最具特色，而午市時段的美食首推巧製點心如銀蘿千層酥。格局設計富時代氣息，潔淨雅致，服務效率亦十分高。

TEL. 2295 0238
Shop 3008-3011, Podium Level 3,
IFC Mall, 1 Harbour View Street, Central
中環港景街 1 號國際金融中心商場第 2 期
3樓 3008-3011號舖
www.leigarden.com.hk

SPECIALITIES TO PRE-ORDER 預訂食物
Dried abalone in oyster sauce 蠔皇乾鮑 /
Braised whole fish maw 蠔皇香扣原隻鮮肚公
/Braised goose web with Kanto spiky sea
cucumber 關東遼參扣玉掌 /Baked chicken
with sea salt in casserole 古仿鹽甂雞

■ PRICE 價錢
Lunch 午膳
à la carte 點菜 $ 150-800
Dinner 晚膳
à la carte 點菜 $ 200-800

■ OPENING HOURS 營業時間
Lunch 午膳　11:30-14:30 (L.O.)
Dinner 晚膳　17:30-22:30 (L.O.)

■ ANNUAL AND WEEKLY CLOSING 休息日期
Closed 3 days Lunar New Year
農曆新年休息 3 天

Lei Garden (Kowloon Bay)
利苑酒家 (九龍灣)

✕✕ 🍴 ⎙40 ◔🍴

Service is one of the strengths of this Lei Garden, located in a shopping mall near the MTR station. Signature dishes include the 10 different varieties of double-boiled tonic soups (to be ordered in advance), sautéed scallops with macadamia nuts and yellow fungus, and braised boneless spare-ribs with sweet and sour sauce. Those who like to eat lunch early or at pace are rewarded with a discount if they vacate their tables before 12:45pm.

這家利苑分店位於地鐵站附近的商場內，服務周到是其強項。招牌菜包括多款燉湯（須提前預訂）、米網黃耳夏果炒帶子、宮庭醬烤骨。中午12:45前離席有折扣優惠，對於喜歡提早吃午飯或能於短時間內吃畢午飯的顧客而言，確是佳音。

TEL. 2331 3306
Shop Unit F2, Telford Plaza 1,
33 Wai Yip Street, Kowloon Bay
九龍灣偉業街 33號德福廣場 F2號舖
www.leigarden.com.hk

SPECIALITIES TO PRE-ORDER 預訂食物
Dried abalone in oyster sauce 蠔皇乾鮑 /
Braised whole fish maw 蠔皇香扣原隻鰵肚公
/Braised goose web with Kanto spiky sea cucumber 關東遼參扣玉掌 /Baked chicken with sea salt in casserole 古仿鹽甆雞

■ PRICE 價錢
Lunch 午膳
à la carte 點菜 $ 100-750
Dinner 晚膳
à la carte 點菜 $ 150-750

■ OPENING HOURS 營業時間
Lunch 午膳　11:30-15:00 (L.O.)
Dinner 晚膳　18:00-23:00 (L.O.)

■ ANNUAL AND WEEKLY CLOSING 休息日期
Closed 3 days Lunar New Year
農曆新年休息 3 天

Lei Garden (Kwun Tong) 利苑酒家 (觀塘)

✕✕ ⊖20

Avoid the escalators and use the shuttle lift to get to the fifth floor in this confusingly arranged shopping mall. Once there, the set up will seem familiar if you've experienced other Lei Garden branches: dishes are standard Cantonese but are reliably cooked using fresh ingredients. The place is as frantic as the others but has been partitioned into different seating areas by smart trellises. Try not to sit near the entrance as it's noisy.

如欲更易找到和更快到達此酒家，請直接乘搭升降機到5樓。如你曾光顧其他利苑分店，對此店絕不會感到陌生：清一色的廣東菜與可靠的美食及新鮮的材料。當然，這裏同樣擠滿利苑的忠實顧客，簡潔的屏風巧妙地將餐廳分隔成不同用餐區。

TEL. 2365 3238
Level 5, apm, Millennium City 5,
418 Kwun Tong Road
觀塘道 418號創紀之城第 5 期 apm5樓
www.leigarden.com.hk

SPECIALITIES TO PRE-ORDER 預訂食物
Dried abalone in oyster sauce 蠔皇乾鮑 /
Braised whole fish maw 蠔皇香扣原隻繁肚公
/Braised goose web with Kanto spiky sea
cucumber 關東遼參扣玉掌 /Baked chicken
with sea salt in casserole 古仿鹽甑雞

■ PRICE 價錢
Lunch 午膳
à la carte 點菜 $ 100-750
Dinner 晚膳
à la carte 點菜 $ 150-750
■ OPENING HOURS 營業時間
Lunch 午膳　11:30-15:00 (L.O.)
Dinner 晚膳　18:00-23:30 (L.O.)
■ ANNUAL AND WEEKLY CLOSING 休息日期
Closed 3 days Lunar New Year
農曆新年休息 3 天

Lei Garden (Mong Kok)
利苑酒家 (旺角)

　　　　　　　　　　　　　　🍽 30　◐🍴

This is the original Lei Garden, which opened back in the 1970s; it's still as busy as ever so it's always worth booking ahead. The contemporary restaurant is spread over two floors and the upper space has views out onto the busy street. The long and varied Cantonese menu certainly represents good value; recommendations include tonic soups like double-boiled teal with Cordyceps militaris and fish maw.

由於這家餐廳實在太受歡迎，食客必須預先訂座。這家利苑總店開業於七十年代。富時代感的餐廳共分為兩層，樓上可看到旺角繁華的街景。以廣東菜為主的菜單花樣多變令人目不暇給，絕對物有所值。特別推薦各式燉品如蛹蟲草鬍燉花膠水鴨。

TEL. 2392 5184
121 Sai Yee Street, Mong Kok
旺角洗衣街 121 號
www.leigarden.com.hk

SPECIALITIES TO PRE-ORDER 預訂食物
Dried abalone in oyster sauce 蠔皇乾鮑 /
Braised whole fish maw 蠔皇香扣原隻繁肚公
/Braised goose web with Kanto spiky sea
cucumber 關東遼參扣玉掌 /Baked chicken
with sea salt in casserole 古仿鹽甑雞

■ PRICE 價錢
Lunch 午膳
à la carte 點菜 $ 100-750
Dinner 晚膳
à la carte 點菜 $ 150-750

■ OPENING HOURS 營業時間
Lunch 午膳　11:30-15:00 (L.O.)
Dinner 晚膳　18:00-23:30 (L.O.)

■ ANNUAL AND WEEKLY CLOSING 休息日期
Closed 3 days Lunar New Year
農曆新年休息 3 天

Lei Garden (North Point)
利苑酒家 (北角)

🍴 16 ⏰🍸

Discreetly tucked away on the first floor of a residential block and overlooking a pleasant courtyard garden is this branch of the popular chain. Things here can certainly get quite frenetic as it accommodates up to 200 people. The lengthy Cantonese menu mirrors what's available at other branches, but particular dishes worth noting here are the double-boiled soups and the daily seafood specialities.

這家深受歡迎的連鎖酒家分店,隱藏在住宅大廈一樓。從酒家外望是屋苑的翠綠庭園,寬敞的空間可容納多達二百人,氣氛往往極為熱鬧。這裏的菜單與其他利苑分店大致相同,除了各式燉湯之外,亦可嘗試每日海鮮精選。

TEL. 2806 0008
1F, Block 9-10, City Garden, North Point
北角城市花園 9-10 座 1 樓
www.leigarden.com.hk

SPECIALITIES TO PRE-ORDER 預訂食物
Dried abalone in oyster sauce 蠔皇乾鮑 /
Braised whole fish maw 蠔皇香扣原隻鰵肚公
/Braised goose web with Kanto spiky sea
cucumber 關東遼參扣玉掌 /Baked chicken
with sea salt in casserole 古仿鹽焗雞

■ PRICE 價錢
Lunch 午膳
à la carte 點菜 $ 100-750
Dinner 晚膳
à la carte 點菜 $ 150-750

■ OPENING HOURS 營業時間
Lunch 午膳　11:30-15:00 L.O.14:30
Dinner 晚膳　18:00-23:30 L.O.22:30

■ ANNUAL AND WEEKLY CLOSING 休息日期
Closed 3 days Lunar New Year
農曆新年休息 3 天

Lei Garden (Sha Tin)
利苑酒家 (沙田)

P ⏺60 ☎⏹

It may have been in town for over 20 years, however, refurbishment has kept this Lei Garden feeling fresh. It is located in New Town Plaza Sha Tin, which means that it can get especially busy at weekends when everyone needs refuelling after a day spent shopping. The menu largely follows the theme of others in the group; always ask for the daily special. Pre-ordering the seasonal double-boiled tonic soup is particularly recommended.

位於沙田新城市廣場的利苑分店已開業超過二十年，憑着精心烹調的正宗粵菜及舒適的室內環境，在區內蠻受食客歡迎，常常座無虛席。細心的服務員會在你致電訂座時提醒你預訂老火湯或時令特色小菜。

TEL. 2698 9111
6F, Phase I New Town Plaza, Sha Tin
沙田新城市廣場第 1 期 6 樓
www.leigarden.com.hk

SPECIALITIES TO PRE-ORDER 預訂食物
Dried abalone in oyster sauce 蠔皇乾鮑 /
Braised whole fish maw 蠔皇香扣原隻鰵肚公
/Braised goose web with Kanto spiky sea
cucumber 關東遼參扣玉掌 /Baked chicken
with sea salt in casserole 古仿鹽甂雞

■ PRICE 價錢
Lunch 午膳
à la carte 點菜 $ 100-750
Dinner 晚膳
à la carte 點菜 $ 150-750

■ OPENING HOURS 營業時間
Lunch 午膳 11:30-15:00 L.O. 14:45
Dinner 晚膳 18:00-23:30 L.O. 23:00

■ ANNUAL AND WEEKLY CLOSING 休息日期
Closed 3 days Lunar New Year
農曆新年休息 3 天

HONG KONG 香港

Lei Garden (Wan Chai)
利苑酒家 (灣仔)

XX ꟼ ⛫18 ☎⛾

An inventory of restaurants in Wan Chai wouldn't be complete without a Lei Garden. This branch is bigger than most and boasts a busy, bustling atmosphere, particularly at lunchtime. It follows the group's tried-and-tested formula by offering an extensive menu of dishes with luxurious dishes alongside less elaborate but classic Cantonese specialities. Seafood enthusiasts should consider pre-ordering the Alaskan king crab or Brittany blue lobster.

論灣仔區的出色食肆，當然少不了利苑的份兒。菜單包含珍饈百味與經典粵式小菜，種類繁多，加上巧手精製的點心和便利的地點，難怪總是座無虛席。食客可於訂位時跟店方預訂特別海鮮如亞拉斯加蟹和法國藍龍蝦等。

TEL. 2892 0333
1F, CNT Tower, 338 Hennessy Road, Wan Chai
灣仔軒尼詩道 338號北海中心 1樓
www.leigarden.com.hk

SPECIALITIES TO PRE-ORDER 預訂食物
Dried abalone in oyster sauce 蠔皇乾鮑 / Braised whole fish maw 蠔皇香扣原隻繁肚公 /Braised goose web with Kanto spiky sea cucumber 關東遼參扣玉掌 /Baked chicken with sea salt in casserole 古仿鹽甕雞

■ PRICE 價錢
Lunch 午膳
à la carte 點菜 $ 150-800
Dinner 晚膳
à la carte 點菜 $ 200-800

■ OPENING HOURS 營業時間
Lunch 午膳　11:30-14:45 (L.O.)
Dinner 晚膳　18:00-22:45 (L.O.)

■ ANNUAL AND WEEKLY CLOSING 休息日期
Closed 3 days Lunar New Year
農曆新年休息 3 天

Lin Heung Kui
蓮香居

This huge two-floor eatery opened in 2009 with the aim of building on the success of the famous Lin Heung Tea House in Wellington Street. It's modest inside but hugely popular and the dim sum trolley is a must, with customers keen to be the first to choose from its extensive offerings. The main menu offers classic Cantonese dishes with specialities such as Lin Heung special duck. The pastry shop below is worth a look on the way out.

佔地甚廣的蓮香居於2009年開幕，樓高兩層，延續威靈頓街蓮香樓的輝煌成績。樸素的內部裝潢掩不住鼎沸的人氣，點心車讓人急不及待從其各式各樣點心中選擇心頭好。菜單上羅列了傳統廣東菜及特色小菜，如蓮香霸王鴨。離開時路經樓下的中式餅店，不妨入內逛逛。

TEL. 2156 9328
2-3F, 40-50 Des Voeux Road West,
Sheung Wan
上環德輔道西 40-50號 2-3樓

■ PRICE 價錢
Lunch 午膳
à la carte 點菜 $ 50-150
Dinner 晚膳
à la carte 點菜 $ 100-400

■ OPENING HOURS 營業時間
06:00-22:30 (L.O.)

Liu Yuan Pavilion
留園雅敍

XX   ⊡16 ◎℞

Authentic Shanghainese specialities served in a room where you'll hear plenty of Shanghainese speakers really will make you think you're in Shanghai. Along with dim sum, you shouldn't miss the stir-fried shrimps, Mandarin fish with sweet and sour sauce, braised meatballs with vegetables or braised pig knuckle. A recent renovation has given the restaurant a look of understated elegance; the booths are the prized seats and it's worth pre-booking.

重新裝修後的留園雅敍素淨優雅，靠窗的卡座尤為舒適。開業多年的店子，擁有不少忠心擁躉。有趣的是，店內大部分食客和侍應，都會以上海話交談，當然，大家最關注的，還是這兒的正宗滬菜。不論是清炒蝦仁、松子桂魚、砂窩獅子頭或紅繞元蹄等經典小菜，還是點心均值得一試。

TEL. 2804 2000
3F, The Broadway,
54-62 Lockhart Road, Wan Chai
灣仔駱克道 54-62 號博匯大廈 3 樓

SPECIALITIES TO PRE-ORDER 預訂食物
Steamed Quarry fish with preserved melons 滷香瓜蒸鯽魚 / Smoked pomfret with tea leaves 煙燻倉魚

■ PRICE 價錢
Lunch 午膳
à la carte 點菜 $ 120-250
Dinner 晚膳
à la carte 點菜 $ 180-750

■ OPENING HOURS 營業時間
Lunch 午膳 12:00-15:00 L.O.14:30
Dinner 晚膳 18:00-23:00 L.O.22:30

■ ANNUAL AND WEEKLY CLOSING 休息日期
Closed 3 days Lunar New Year
農曆新年休息 3 天

Lo Chiu (Jordan)
老趙 (佐敦)

The Chinese owner had spent several years in Vietnam before arriving in Hong Kong and opening this Vietnamese restaurant back in 1978. He now has two other shops but this is his flagship. Steamed stuffed rice rolls, noodles in beef soup and cold vermicelli with pork, beef or chicken are some of the highlights, but the hotpot curry is also worth trying. The environment is basic but clean and the staff are helpful.

老闆是曾經在越南住過幾年的華僑，回香港後，在1978年開始經營這餐廳，現在已擁有兩家分店，但此店依然是他的旗艦店。越式蒸粉包、牛肉湯河，豬肉、牛肉或雞肉凍檬都是不錯的選擇，椰香咖喱也值得嘗試。餐廳裝修簡單整潔，侍應服務周到。

TEL. 2384 2143
25-27 Man Yuen Street, Jordan
佐敦文苑街 25-27號

■ PRICE 價錢
Lunch 午膳
set 套餐 $30-100　à la carte 點菜 $50-200
Dinner 晚膳
à la carte 點菜 $50-230
■ OPENING HOURS 營業時間
12:00-23:00 (L.O.)
■ ANNUAL AND WEEKLY CLOSING 休息日期
Closed 4 days Lunar New Year
農曆新年休息 4 天

Cantonese 粵菜

MAP 地圖   11/B-2

HONG KONG 香港

Loaf On
六福菜館

❀

🍴   ⊡36 ◖🍽

Spread over three floors and hidden behind a strip of seafood restaurants in Sai Kung is this neat little spot. The daily soup depends on what the owner buys from local fishermen; you can even bring your own fish and have it prepared by the kitchen. Besides seafood, Loaf On also offers simple but flavoursome Cantonese dishes like chilli and garlic bean curd, Loaf On-style chicken, and steamed sea fish with salt. The restaurant will relocate in 2016.

這家佔了三層樓的小菜館,藏身於西貢海鮮餐廳一帶後街。店主每天從當地漁民處搜購最新鮮的食材炮製是日魚湯,你亦可自行攜帶海鮮,交由廚師為你烹調。除了海鮮和魚湯,椒鹽奇脆豆腐和鹽蒸海魚也必須一試,別忘了預訂一客風沙雞。2016年將會遷址。

TEL. 2792 9966
49 See Cheung Street, Sai Kung
西貢市場街 49號

SPECIALITIES TO PRE-ORDER 預訂食物
Crispy skin chicken 脆 皮 風 沙 雞 /Fish soup 西 貢 地 道 魚 湯 /Minced fish in pumpkin soup 金湯魚蓉羹

■ PRICE 價錢
Lunch 午膳
à la carte 點菜 $ 200-500
Dinner 晚膳
à la carte 點菜 $ 200-500

■ OPENING HOURS 營業時間
11:00-23:00 L.O. 22:30

■ ANNUAL AND WEEKLY CLOSING 休息日期
Closed 3 days Lunar New Year
農曆新年休息 3 天

Lobster Bar and Grill
龍蝦吧

The big seller in this comfortable, clubby room is the seafood platter for two – it includes lobster, oysters, crab, tuna and abalone. Also popular are Maine and Spiny lobsters, the pasta dishes and specialities from the grill which come with a variety of accompaniments and sauces. Live music, a great drinks menu and a busy barman make for a fun, relaxing atmosphere in the evenings; lunch is more of a business affair.

令人垂涎的龍蝦吧海鮮拼盤，讓你一次過品嘗龍蝦、生蠔、阿拉斯加蟹腳、吞拿魚刺身和鮑魚的美味，實在是一大樂事。波士頓龍蝦、各款意大利麵條及提供多種配菜和醬汁伴吃選擇的烤肉菜式也是顧客喜愛的食品。現場樂隊演奏和豐富的餐酒選擇，帶來不一樣的悠閒晚膳。

TEL. 2820 8560
6F, Island Shangri-La Hotel, Pacific Place,
Supreme Court Road, Admiralty
金鐘法院道太古廣場港島香格里拉酒店 6樓
www.shangri-la.com

■ PRICE 價錢
Lunch 午膳
set 套餐 $ 598
à la carte 點菜 $ 600-1,400
Dinner 晚膳
set 套餐 $ 1,380-1,580
à la carte 點菜 $ 600-1,400

■ OPENING HOURS 營業時間
Lunch 午膳　12:00-14:30 (L.O.)
Dinner 晚膳　18:30-22:30 (L.O.)

Lucky Indonesia
好運印尼餐廳

One's first impression of this small dining room, with its wooden furniture and traditional wall hangings, is that it's a little dated, but you'll soon feel as though you have been transported to the Indonesian countryside. The Middle Java cuisine is not unlike the décor – there's no fancy presentation, just authentic and tasty flavours. Satay is charcoal roasted which creates a lovely aroma; also try the Nasi Kuming and Mee Goreng.

細小的用膳區、木製的家具及傳統的掛牆吊飾,室內裝潢予人點點懷舊感覺,令食客感到身處印尼郊區。一如其裝潢,此店的食物不賣弄花巧,只用真材實料炮製出正宗美味的爪哇中部菜式。炭燒沙嗲烤肉風味特別,而印尼黃薑飯和印尼炒麵更不容錯過。

TEL. 2389 3545
46 Tung Ming Street, Kwun Tong
觀塘通明街 46號

■ PRICE 價錢
à la carte 點菜 $ 40-80

■ OPENING HOURS 營業時間
11:00-21:00 (L.O.)

■ ANNUAL AND WEEKLY CLOSING 休息日期
Closed 3 days Lunar New Year
農曆新年休息 3 天

Luk Yu Tea House
陸羽茶室

✖   ⊟6   ◑⫪

Large numbers of both regulars and tourists come to Luk Yu Tea House for the traditionally prepared and flavoursome dim sum, and its three floors fill up quickly. The animated atmosphere and subtle colonial decoration are appealing but no one really stays too long; the serving team in white jackets have seen it all before and go about their work with alacrity. Popular dishes are fried prawns on toast and fried noodles with sliced beef.

陸羽茶室以傳統方法製作的美味點心，不光招來本地常客，更令不少外地遊客慕名而至，所以樓高三層的茶室經常滿座。生氣盎然的環境和帶點殖民地色彩的裝潢別具特色，穿着白色外套的侍應敏捷而專注地工作。除點心外其他菜式，如窩貼蝦及鼓椒牛肉炒麵也值得一試。

TEL. 2523 5464
24-26 Stanley Street, Central
中環士丹利街 24-26號

■ PRICE 價錢
Lunch 午膳
à la carte 點菜 $ 150-300
Dinner 晚膳
à la carte 點菜 $300-400

■ OPENING HOURS 營業時間
07:00-22:00 (L.O.)

■ ANNUAL AND WEEKLY CLOSING 休息日期
Closed 4 days Lunar New Year
農曆新年休息 4 天

Lung King Heen
龍景軒

XXXX

It's not just Chef Chan Yan Tak's dim sum that's gaining legendary status – every dish is delicately crafted and enticingly presented, and the quality of the ingredients is of the highest order. The delightful serving team describe dishes with care and obvious pride. Translated as 'view of the dragon', the restaurant offers a panorama of the harbour; its interior is smart and uncluttered, with hand-embroidered silk, columns and glass screens.

龍景軒名副其實，坐擁動人心弦的維港全景；餐廳內部時尚整潔，飾以手工刺繡絲綢、圓柱和玻璃屏幕。素負盛名的，絕不僅是美味點心，這裏每一度菜都採用最高級的食材並經過精心雕琢，賣相極其吸引。侍應團隊充滿朝氣，會向客人仔細介紹菜式，讓人感到他們以此餐廳為傲。

TEL. 3196 8880
4F, Four Seasons Hotel,
8 Finance Street, Central
中環金融街 8號四季酒店 4樓
www.fourseasons.com/hongkong

SPECIALITIES TO PRE-ORDER 預訂食物
Roast Peking duck 北京烤鴨

■ PRICE 價錢
Lunch 午膳
à la carte 點菜 $450-2,000
Dinner 晚膳
à la carte 點菜 $500-2,000

■ OPENING HOURS 營業時間
Lunch 午膳 12:00-14:30 (L.O.)
Dinner 晚膳 18:00-22:30 (L.O.)

Man Wah
文華廳

✿

🍴🍴🍴　　　　　　　　　⪡ 🖐 🪑14 🕐🍽 🎴

Ceiling lamps resembling birdcages; original, ornate silk paintings; and local rosewood combine to create the striking interior of this Cantonese restaurant on the 25th floor of the Mandarin Oriental hotel. Tsui Yin Ting is their private room for 14 people and is styled on an old Chinese pavilion. The chef's specialities include steamed garoupa with crispy ginger and crabmeat, and roast goose puff with yanmin sauce.

位於文華東方酒店25樓的文華廳裝潢華麗典雅，一盞盞仿鳥籠中式吊燈、牆上古色古香的絲綢畫與紫檀木的運用營造出雅致的古中國情調。裝飾一如中國古時涼亭的廂房聚賢亭能容納十四人。酥薑珊瑚蒸星斑球及仁稔燒鵝酥皆為這兒的名菜。

TEL. 2825 4003
25F, Mandarin Oriental Hotel,
5 Connaught Road, Central
中環干諾道中 5 號文華東方酒店 25樓
www.mandarinoriental.com/hongkong

■ PRICE 價錢
Lunch 午膳
set 套餐 $ 548-698
à la carte 點菜 $ 500-1,500
Dinner 晚膳
set 套餐 $ 988-1,488
à la carte 點菜 $ 500-1,500

■ OPENING HOURS 營業時間
Lunch 午膳　12:00-14:30 (L.O.)
Dinner 晚膳　18:30-22:30 (L.O.)

Mandarin Grill + Bar
文華扒房+酒吧

XXXX

♿ 🚱 🍽12 🚋 📞🍴 🍸

Designed by Sir Terence Conran, this is an elegant and luminous restaurant where the emphasis is on comfort and relaxation. If you want to add a little theatre then ask for a seat at the counter to watch the chefs preparing some of the many varieties of oysters that are available here. On the other side, behind a window, the kitchen team specialises in contemporary European cuisine; be sure to leave room for one of their soufflés.

這家典雅明亮的餐廳是著名室內設計師Sir Terence Conran 的作品，注重舒適與優閒。如果你想增添一點娛樂，可預訂吧枱位置，觀賞廚師準備餐廳提供的多種生蠔。選擇餐廳的另一邊，你可透過玻璃窗看到廚房團隊用心準備令人垂涎三尺的歐洲菜；切記預留空間品嘗梳乎厘甜品。

TEL. 2825 4004
1F, Mandarin Oriental Hotel,
5 Connaught Road, Central
中環干諾道中 5號文華東方酒店 1樓
www.mandarinoriental.com/hongkong

■ PRICE 價錢
Lunch 午膳
à la carte 點菜 $ 1,100-2,100
Dinner 晚膳
set 套餐 $ 1,688-1,888
à la carte 點菜 $ 1,100-2,100

■ OPENING HOURS 營業時間
Lunch 午膳 12:00-14:30 (L.O.)
Dinner 晚膳 18:30-22:30 (L.O.)
Sunday & Public Holidays 週日及公眾假期
18:30-21:30 (L.O.)

■ ANNUAL AND WEEKLY CLOSING 休息日期
Closed Weekend lunch
週末午膳休息

Sichuan 川菜

MAP 地圖 19/C-3

HONG KONG 香港

Mask of Sichuen & Beijing
面譜京川料理

Beijing opera masks hanging from the ceiling add to the atmosphere of this softly lit, contemporary dining room which has intimate booths as well as large tables. The menus offer a comprehensive selection of Sichuan and Pekingese dishes, along with some innovative offerings, like stir-fried shredded potato and mango. Diners can decide on their own level of spiciness and there's also a wide selection of vegetarian dishes available.

懸掛在天花上的京劇面譜，為柔和的燈光和富現代感的裝潢增添氣氛；這裡既提供私密的卡座，亦有大型餐桌。餐牌上的菜式種類繁多，既有齊全的川菜選擇，亦有京菜佳餚和多款素菜，更有創新之選，如香芒土豆絲。食客可自選辣度。

TEL. 2311 9233
Shop 33, GF,
KCR East Tsim Sha Tsui Station,
Tsim Sha Tsui
尖沙咀尖東站地下 33號鋪

■ PRICE 價錢
Lunch 午膳
set 套餐 $ 68
à la carte 點菜 $ 200-500
Dinner 晚膳
à la carte 點菜 $ 200-500

■ OPENING HOURS 營業時間
Lunch 午膳　12:00-15:30 (L.O.)
Dinner 晚膳　17:45-23:30 (L.O.)

May's Sawaddee Thailand
旺泰特食

On the ground floor of a residential building in the heart of Sai Kung sits this long, narrow, simply decorated but comfortable Thai restaurant. From the hospitable, all-female service team comes an extensive menu of authentic Thai dishes, whose highlights include yellow chicken curry in bread, fried crab with curry, Tom Yum Goong, and fried rice with minced meat and herbs, all made using fresh, good quality ingredients.

這家泰國餐廳位於西貢市中心的住宅大廈地下，店內空間既長且窄，裝修簡約但舒適。全女班的員工服務殷勤，店內提供多款正宗泰國菜，推介有黃咖喱雞配包、咖哩炒蟹、冬蔭功、肉碎香葉炒飯等。週末和假期或需要排隊輪候入座方能一嘗美食。

TEL. 2791 0522
24 Man Nin Street, Sai Kung
西貢萬年街24號

■ PRICE 價錢
Lunch 午膳
à la carte 點菜 $ 60-250
Dinner 晚膳
à la carte 點菜 $ 60-250

■ OPENING HOURS 營業時間
Lunch 午膳 12:00-15:00 (L.O.)
Dinner 晚膳 18:00-22:30 (L.O.)

Megan's Kitchen
美味廚

  ⊡32 ◎⫽

Can't decide between Cantonese or a hotpot? Or perhaps you'd like both? Megan's Kitchen can help as it offers a grand selection of Cantonese dishes, like steamed minced beef with dried mandarin peel and claypot rice, but is also known for its hotpots, which come with high quality ingredients like seafood or Japanese beef. The dining room has a warm, contemporary feel and there are several well-equipped private rooms.

廣東菜還是火鍋？還是想兩者兼得？美味廚讓你不再苦惱。這兒除了有各式廣東小菜如陳皮蒸手剁牛肉和美味煲仔飯外，火鍋亦同樣聞名，更有海鮮、和牛等高級火鍋配料。大廳設計溫馨時尚，並備有多個設備齊全的私人客房。

TEL. 2866 8305
5F, Lucky Centre,
165-171 Wan Chai Road, Wan Chai
灣仔灣仔道 165-171 號樂基中心 5 樓
www.meganskitchen.com

■ PRICE 價錢
Lunch 午膳
set 套餐 $ 60-150
à la carte 點菜 $ 200-500
Dinner 晚膳
à la carte 點菜 $ 200-500

■ OPENING HOURS 營業時間
Lunch 午膳　12:00-14:30 (L.O.)
Dinner 晚膳　18:00-23:00 (L.O.)

Don't confuse the rating ☓ with the Stars ✤! The first defines comfort and service, while Stars are awarded for the best cuisine.

千萬別混淆了餐具 ☓ 和星星 ✤ 標誌！餐具標誌表示該餐廳的舒適程度和服務質素，而星星代表的是食物質素與味道非常出色而獲授為米芝蓮星級餐廳的餐館。

Looking for a taste of local life? Check out our top street food picks.

到哪兒尋找本土特色小食？請翻閱本年度新增的街頭小吃推介。

l'itinéraire

MIC Kitchen

'Demon chef' Alvin Leung, of Bo Innovation fame, brings his innovative style of cooking to a new building in Kwun Tong. Here at MIC kitchen his team uses creative touches along with superlative cooking skills to mix and match Chinese and Western food – the resulting flavours are bound to surprise you. The interior is relaxed yet contemporary; ask for a seat at the counter if you want to watch the chefs work their magic while you eat.

廚魔Alvin Leung的新餐廳,他繼續發揮無窮創意,配合精湛廚藝和現代化的處理食物方法,揉合中西食材的特點,炮製出令人驚喜兼讚歡的美食。餐廳位於觀塘一棟新建成的大廈內,設計時尚簡約,感覺舒適。建議預訂開放式廚房前的座位,品嘗美食之餘能觀賞廚師的手藝。

TEL. 3758 2239
GF, AIA Kowloon Tower,
100 How Ming Street, Kwun Tong
觀塘巧明街100號友邦九龍大樓地下

■ PRICE 價錢
Lunch 午膳
set 套餐 $ 228
à la carte 點菜 $ 500-1,300
Dinner 晚膳
set 套餐 $ 438-988
à la carte 點菜 $ 500-1,300

■ OPENING HOURS 營業時間
Lunch 午膳   12:00-15:00 L.O. 14:30
Dinner 晚膳   18:30-22:30 (L.O.)

■ ANNUAL AND WEEKLY CLOSING 休息日期
Closed Sunday and Public Holiday lunch
週日及公眾假期午膳休息

Cantonese 粵菜 MAP 地圖 15/C-3

Ming Court
明閣

✕✕✕ ♿ 🧼 🅿 🍽36 🔔🍴 ❀

It's not just the expertly prepared Cantonese cooking that attracts diners to Ming Court – many also come here for the great wine list and thoughtfully suggested wine pairings, so expect plenty of expert advice on what wine to order with your garoupa or suckling pig. You also have a choice of dining room: Ming Sun is an elegantly dressed round room with a collection of Ming Dynasty bronzes; Ming Moon is a newer and more spacious room.

明閣吸引顧客之處，除了大廚的精湛粵菜廚藝，更因為此店提供多種餐酒，侍應還會協助顧客揀選適當的佳釀配合龍躉或脆皮乳豬佐吃。顧客還可選擇擺設着青銅器、充滿古風的明日或裝潢較現代時髦的明月用膳。

TEL. 3552 3300
6F, Langham Place Hotel,
555 Shanghai Street, Mong Kok
旺角上海街 555 號朗豪酒店 6 樓
www.hongkong.langhamplacehotels.com

SPECIALITIES TO PRE-ORDER 預訂食物
Drunken shrimp dumpling 貴妃醉蝦餃

■ PRICE 價錢
Lunch 午膳
à la carte 點菜 $ 450-1,200
Dinner 晚膳
à la carte 點菜 $ 450-1,500

■ OPENING HOURS 營業時間
Lunch 午膳　11:00-14:30 (L.O.)
Dinner 晚膳　18:00-22:30 (L.O.)

Moon Thai (Sheung Wan)

🍴　　　　　　　　　🛏 ⛱14 ◑🍴

Secreted on the second floor of the Holiday Inn Express, Moon Thai is led by an experienced Thai chef who insists on using the freshest ingredients. Seafood dishes are the ones that stand out and he is known particularly for his own creation of fried crab with tom yum paste. Get in the mood by beginning your evening with a lemongrass martini. There is also an Indian chef in the kitchen preparing some Indian specialities.

經驗老到的泰籍主廚統領的泰國廚師團隊，以本地新鮮食材與泰國進口香料、菜蔬，炮製正宗高級泰菜，尤擅長以海鮮入饌，主廚獨創的芭堤雅蟹逅是代表作。此店還提供小量印度菜如即烘印度酵餅和薄餅，由印裔廚師主理。泰籍調酒師調製的特飲如香茅馬天尼別具風味。

TEL. 2851 1288
2F, Holiday Inn Express,
83 Jervois Road, Sheung Wan
上環蘇杭街 83號
香港蘇豪智選假日酒店 2樓

■ PRICE 價錢
Lunch 午膳
set 套餐 $ 168-188
à la carte 點菜 $ 210-860
Dinner 晚膳
à la carte 點菜 $ 210-860

■ OPENING HOURS 營業時間
12:00-22:30 (L.O.)

Morton's of Chicago NEW

✗✗   ← ⊡12 ◎⫿

One longstanding feature of the Sheraton Hotel is this popular steakhouse in tones of white and grey. Regulars congregate in the bar after work before tucking into Morton's classic dishes: jumbo shrimp cocktail, whole baked Maine lobster and, of course, USDA and aged Australian beef. The wine list focuses largely on American labels and if you haven't got a window seat with an Island view you can instead watch the action in the open kitchen.

這家在2013年重新裝修過的餐廳，在本地食客及遊客中很有名。熟客喜歡下班後與三五知己在店中酒吧暢飲閒聊一會，再移步到設計時尚明亮、空間寬敞的餐室晚飯；欲一覽港島景色，可選擇窗門位置。這兒供應經典扒房菜式如西冷牛扒和心太軟等均見於餐單上。餐酒單主要供應美國餐酒及少量別國佳釀。

TEL. 2732 2343
4F, Sheraton Hotel, 20 Nathan Road,
Tsim Sha Tsui
尖沙咀彌敦道 20號喜來登酒店 4樓
www.mortons.com/hongkong

■ PRICE 價錢
Dinner 晚膳
à la carte 點菜 $ 600-1,200

■ OPENING HOURS 營業時間
Dinner 晚膳
17:30-23:00 (L.O.)

■ ANNUAL AND WEEKLY CLOSING 休息日期
Closed Lunar New Year 年初一休息

Mott 32
卅二公館

🍴🍴　　　　　　　　　　🪑20　◐🍴

Mott Street lies at the heart of Manhattan's Chinatown and number 32 was the address of the first Chinese grocery store to open in New York, back in the 19th century. This mix of old NYC and classic Chinese décor adds character to a room which already feels quite secretive as it's in the basement of the Standard Chartered Bank building. Apple wood-roasted Peking duck, and barbecue Spanish Teruel pork with yellow mountain honey are worth trying.

於渣打銀行大廈地庫內的卅二公館，宛如一間隱閉的會所，英文名字源於十九世紀紐約唐人街首家中式辦館的地址。店主花盡心思，揉合舊紐約與中國古典味道。為了品嘗粵菜而來的你，不仿試以蘋果木烤製的北京片皮鴨和蜜汁西班牙黑毛豬叉燒。你還可以隔着玻璃窗觀賞廚師炮製食物的過程。

TEL. 2885 8688
Basement Level,
Standard Chartered Bank Building,
4-4A Des Voeux Road, Central
中環德輔道中 4-4A號渣打銀行中心地庫
www.mott32.com

■ PRICE 價錢
Lunch 午膳
à la carte 點菜 $ 350-2,000
Dinner 晚膳
à la carte 點菜 $ 350-2,000

■ OPENING HOURS 營業時間
Lunch 午膳　12:00-14:30 (L.O.)
Dinner 晚膳　18:00-23:00 (L.O.)

HONG KONG 香港

Namo NEW

🍴　　　　　　　　　　　　　　🏠 ≤ ⬭10 ☎️🍽

A great harbour-facing terrace isn't the only attraction of this contemporary Thai restaurant in Empire Centre. The food, prepared by Thai chefs, brings together Thai and international ingredients as well as different cooking techniques. Try Iberico pork rib in northern Thai curry sauce, bouchot mussels in chili-galangal coconut broth, or Japanese tofu with crispy coconut coating. They also do interesting cocktails – sticky rice martini anyone?

海風、陽光和泰國菜往往是最佳配搭！坐在Namo的露天用餐區，邊欣賞對岸的港島景色，邊享用別具特色的泰式美食，的確十分寫意。這裡的菜式全由泰籍廚師按傳統方法烹調，配上國際化食材；試試西班牙豬肋骨伴清邁咖喱或椰香焗脆皮日本軟豆腐，必定令你感到驚喜。

TEL. 2739 1133
Shop G18, Empire Centre, 68 Mody Road,
Tsim Sha Tsui
尖沙咀麼地道 68號帝國中心 G18號舖

■ PRICE 價錢
Lunch 午膳
set 套餐 $ 88-238
à la carte 點菜 $ 200-300
Dinner 晚膳
à la carte 點菜 $ 200-300

■ OPENING HOURS 營業時間
12:00-01:00 (L.O.)

Nanxiang Steamed Bun (Causeway Bay)
南翔饅頭店 (銅鑼灣)

One reason for the popularity of this modern, intimate restaurant is their Xiao Long Bao which are slightly larger than usual and come with a thin, ivory-white wrapper and juicy filling. It also offers Shanghainese cuisine and dim sum; look out for braised minced pork ball and the jujube and egg yolk pastry which resembles a tiny handbag. The original Nanxiang Steamed Bun shop opened in Shanghai 100 years ago.

南翔饅頭店始於百年前的上海，銅鑼灣店是其在香港首家分店，既時尚又舒適。這裡的小籠包由從上海派駐香港的廚師監督製作，確保味道正宗，體積較一般的略大；象牙色薄嫩麵皮裡，是鮮美多汁的餡料。此外，一系列精製上海點心如小巧玲瓏的拎包酥也不容錯過。

TEL. 3690 2088
3F, Causeway Bay Plaza I,
489 Hennessy Road, Causeway Bay
銅鑼灣軒尼詩道 489號銅鑼灣廣場第一期 3樓
www.nanxiang.com.hk

■ PRICE 價錢
Lunch 午膳
set 套餐 $ 68
à la carte 點菜 $ 100-200
Dinner 晚膳
à la carte 點菜 $ 100-200

■ OPENING HOURS 營業時間
11:30-23:00 L.O. 22:30

■ ANNUAL AND WEEKLY CLOSING 休息日期
Closed Lunar New Year 年初一休息

HONG KONG 香港

New Shanghai
新滬坊

✕✕✕　　　　　　　　　　　　　　　　🛏14　◐🍴

Glass walls and exquisite Chinese art combine to create a strikingly contemporary interior here on the first floor of the Convention & Exhibition Centre. The menu offers a light, healthy style of Shanghainese cooking and mixes the traditional and the innovative, with dim sum coming from the open kitchen in the middle of the room. Specialities include stir-fried barley with air-dried pork and braised duck stuffed with glutinous rice.

玻璃牆結合精緻的中國藝術，為這家位於香港會議展覽中心一樓的餐廳，營造出極時尚的風格。新滬坊提供以輕盈健康為主、揉合傳統和創新意念的上海菜式，廚師在店中央的開放式廚房內為食客製作各款美味點心。馳名菜式包括豐年藏珍寶和江南八寶鴨。

TEL. 2582 7332
1F, Hong Kong Convention and
Exhibition Centre,
1 Harbour Road, Wan Chai
灣仔港灣道 1 號香港會議展覽中心 1 樓

■ PRICE 價錢
Lunch 午膳
set 套餐 $ 130-170
à la carte 點菜 $ 200-800
Dinner 晚膳
à la carte 點菜 $ 200-800

■ OPENING HOURS 營業時間
Lunch 午膳　12:00-15:00 (L.O.)
Dinner 晚膳　18:30-22:00 (L.O.)

■ ANNUAL AND WEEKLY CLOSING 休息日期
Closed 2 days Lunar New Year
農曆新年休息 2 天

Nicholini's
意寧谷

♿ 🔇 🍴 🍽18 🕐🍴 🍇

Not only does this Italian restaurant offer great views from its perch on the eighth floor of the Conrad Hotel, but it's also very handsome, thanks to the ornate ceiling, wood panelling and clever lighting. The menu keeps things classical and authentic, with a slight bias towards more northerly parts of Italy. The service is very professional and the wine list is impressive. There are two private rooms and brunch is served on Sundays.

這家風格獨特的意大利餐廳主要供應傳統、地道、正宗的意大利美食。專業細心的服務、醉人的美食、品質淳厚的佳釀，令食客為之動容!淺啡色系的簡約時尚設計，配合別樹一格的桂花葉型燈飾，置身其中，有一份說不出的從容自在。兩間私人廂房，適合十數人聚會。星期天還會供應早午拼餐。

TEL. 2822 8801
8F, Conrad Hotel, Pacific Place,
88 Queensway, Admirality
金鐘道 88 號太古廣場港麗酒店 8 樓
www.conraddining.com

■ PRICE 價錢
Lunch 午膳
set 套餐 $ 418-488
à la carte 點菜 $ 900-1,300

Dinner 晚膳
set 套餐 $ 1,138
à la carte 點菜 $ 900-1,300

■ OPENING HOURS 營業時間
Lunch 午膳　12:00-15:00 (L.O.)
Dinner 晚膳　18:00-23:00 (L.O.)

■ ANNUAL AND WEEKLY CLOSING 休息日期
Closed Saturday lunch
週末午膳休息

Nishiki

錦

Nishiki is concealed within the Regal Kowloon hotel but is owned and run by its Japanese chef. Tradition runs deep here, as demonstrated by the fact that the decorative style has remained largely unchanged for over 20 years. The atmosphere and the style of food are typical of an izakaya. Chicken meatball and tofu hotpot, BBQ eel and BBQ chicken are the recommendations. Booking is strongly advised – when doing so, ask for seats at the counter.

位於富豪九龍酒店內的這家餐廳，多年來見證着尖沙咀的變遷亦擁有一眾忠實追隨者，內部裝潢由始至今沒甚大變，很典型的居酒屋格局，氣氛總是熱鬧非常。食客最喜愛這裡的燒烤，如燒鰻、免治雞肉棒，而雞肉丸豆腐鍋亦美味非常。建議預先訂座，開放式廚房邊上的座位能觀賞廚師的技藝，氣氛更佳。

TEL. 2723 8660
Shop 103, 1F Regal Kowloon Hotel,
71 Mody Road, Tsim Sha Tsui
尖沙咀麼地道 71 號富豪九龍酒店 1 樓 103室

■ PRICE 價錢
Lunch 午膳
à la carte 點菜 $ 200-450
Dinner 晚膳
à la carte 點菜 $ 200-450

■ OPENING HOURS 營業時間
Lunch 午膳　12:00-14:00 (L.O.)
Dinner 晚膳　18:00-22:00 (L.O.)

No.5 Italian (Tai Hang)

HONG KONG 香港

Small, cosy and not without a little charm, No. 5 Italian is warmly run by five friends. The menu is equally diminutive with around five choices of starters, pastas and pizzas which are supplemented by a few daily specials on the blackboard. The thin-crust pizzas with homemade tomato sauce are the main attraction, and the owners have christened them after themselves, with names such as Pun's or Franco's. With only 30 seats, it's wise to book.

餐單內只有三十多款精選小菜，以脆薄餅底和特製番茄醬作賣點的五款薄餅分別以五位東主的名字命名，風味各異。每日限量供應四款鮮製意粉，當中以海膽扁長條麵配白松露汁最受歡迎。每日精選值得嘗試。座位有限，常常滿座，建議預訂座位。

TEL. 2504 2111
21 Brown Street, Tai Hang
大坑布朗街 21 號

■ PRICE 價錢
Lunch 午膳
à la carte 點菜 $ 250-400
Dinner 晚膳
à la carte 點菜 $ 250-400

■ OPENING HOURS 營業時間
Lunch 午膳　12:00-14:30 (L.O.)
Dinner 晚膳　18:00-22:30 (L.O.)

Japanese contemporary 時尚日本菜 MAP 地圖 19/C-3

HONG KONG 香港

Nobu

🍴🍴   ♿ ← 🖐 🪑16 🚇 ©🍴 🍇

This branch of the über-fashionable, international Nobu brand boasts an impressive ceiling fashioned from sea urchin spines and there are images of cherry blossom behind the bar. At lunch, bento boxes are the popular choice. At dinner, the kitchen's beguiling blend of Japanese and South American influences works its magic through a number of different styles which include sushi, sashimi and good quality seafood.

這家享譽國際的Nobu餐廳分店有着以海膽刺裝飾的天花，讓人印象深刻，背景更配有櫻花美景裝飾。午餐時間最受歡迎的是便當。而晚餐方面，主廚融合日本和美洲烹調風格炮製的嶄新口味更是迷人。菜式包括壽司、刺身和優質海鮮。

TEL. 2313 2340
2F, Intercontinental Hotel,
18 Salisbury Road, Tsim Sha Tsui
尖沙咀梳士巴利道18號洲際酒店2樓

■ PRICE 價錢
Lunch 午膳
à la carte 點菜 $ 400-1,400
Dinner 晚膳
à la carte 點菜 $ 500-1,600

■ OPENING HOURS 營業時間
Lunch 午膳　12:00-14:30 (L.O.)
Dinner 晚膳　18:00-23:00 (L.O.)

200

Noodlemi

It's easy to miss this little place and that would be a shame if you want fresh, healthy and contemporary-style Vietnamese food. It seats just 24 customers but thanks to some clever design they've managed to use every inch of space available so it never really feels too packed. The lunchtime crowd come mainly for the Vietnamese sandwiches made using French baguettes and the rice vermicelli dishes. All the food is gluten free and MSG free.

若不留心，便會錯過這家小店。店內只有二十四個座位，但特別設計的桌椅善用室內每一寸空間，因此並沒有壓逼感。精選餐單上的是清新健康的新派越式美食，各種用法國麵包做的越式三文治和一系列撈檬粉，頗受區內上班族歡迎。除麵包外，其他食物都不含味精和麩質。

TEL. 2253 1114
2 Bonham Strand, Sheung Wan
上環文咸東街 2號
www.noodle-mi.com

■ PRICE 價錢
à la carte 點菜 $ 50-100

■ OPENING HOURS 營業時間
11:30-21:45 (L.O.)

■ ANNUAL AND WEEKLY CLOSING 休息日期
Closed Public Holidays 公眾假期休息

Olé

XX

As the name somewhat suggests, both the decorative style and the menu of this Spanish restaurant have an unapologetically traditional look. The tiles, white walls and knick-knacks give it a certain charm and extra colour is provided by a plethora of paintings. The kitchen prepares the classics such as garlic shrimps, seafood paella and squid with ink sauce with aplomb; go for the churros with hot chocolate sauce for dessert.

單看店名就知道，無論裝修還是菜式都是地地道道的西班牙風味。瓷磚、白牆配以小擺設是魅力所在，無處不在的掛畫更為店子添幾分色彩。廚師從容地炮製蒜蓉蝦、海鮮炒飯和墨汁墨魚等傳統西班牙菜式。甜品建議一試西班牙小油條配熱朱古力醬。

TEL. 2523 8624
1F, Shun Ho Tower,
24-30 Ice House Street, Central
中環雪廠街 24-30 號順豪大廈 1 樓
www.olespanishrestaurant.com.hk

■ PRICE 價錢
Lunch 午膳
set 套餐 $ 190-260
à la carte 點菜 $ 400-900
Dinner 晚膳
à la carte 點菜 $ 400-900

■ OPENING HOURS 營業時間
Lunch 午膳　12:00-14:30 (L.O.)
Dinner 晚膳　18:30-23:00 (L.O.)

■ ANNUAL AND WEEKLY CLOSING 休息日期
Closed 4 days Lunar New Year and Sunday
農曆新年 4 天及週日休息

ON NEW

✿

🍴🍴   🏡   🍽12   🚋   🕐🍴   👥

With its panoramic terrace and floor to ceiling windows, the lounge makes you feel you're on a luxury cruise ship; a red carpeted staircase then brings you up to the soberly decorated restaurant which comes from the same team who brought you Upper Modern Bistro. From the open kitchen comes French cuisine with colourful Mediterranean influences. There are around 500 labels on the wine list and cheese lovers will want to check out the cheese room.

餐館於2014年12中開業,由Jéremy Evrard、Philippe Orrico和其他合伙人經營;Philippe Orrico負責領導廚師團隊,主要供應混合了地中海風味的法國菜;睡蟹龍蝦生蠔薯仔沙律、白汁帕爾瑪火腿雲吞均是招牌菜。食客還可到芝士房挑選喜歡的芝士。餐酒單上羅列約五百款餐酒,大部分源自法國和意大利。

TEL. 2174 8100
29F, 18 On Lan Street, Central
中環安蘭街 18號 29樓
www.ontop.hk

■ PRICE 價錢
Lunch 午膳
set 套餐 $328
à la carte 點菜 $400-950
Dinner 晚膳
à la carte 點菜 $400-950

■ OPENING HOURS 營業時間
Lunch 午膳　12:00-14:30 (L.O.)
Dinner 晚膳　18:00-22:30 (L.O.)

■ ANNUAL AND WEEKLY CLOSING 休息日期
Closed 4 days Lunar New Year and Sunday
農曆新年 4 天及週日休息

One Harbour Road
港灣壹號

One Harbour Road may be set in a hotel, but its graceful ambience will make you think you're on the terrace of an elegant 1930s Taipan mansion. Split-level dining adds to the airy feel, there are views of the harbour, and the sound of running water softens the bold statement of the huge pillars. Cantonese menus offer a wide variety of well-prepared meat and fish dishes. To see how they're created, consider booking the Chef's Table.

這裡的氣氛，令你仿如置身30年代的優雅大班府第。分層用餐，空間感較大，且能飽覽維港景色。大型蓮花池及潺潺的流水聲，使感覺硬朗的龐大柱子變得柔和。這裡的粵菜包括精心準備、種類繁多的肉類和魚類菜式。如想一睹烹調過程，可考慮預訂「廚師餐桌」。

TEL. 2584 7722
8F, Grand Hyatt Hotel,
1 Harbour Road, Wan Chai
灣仔港灣道一號君悅酒店 8樓
www.hongkong.grand.hyatt.com

■ PRICE 價錢
Lunch 午膳
à la carte 點菜　$ 300-800
Dinner 晚膳
à la carte 點菜　$ 450-800

■ OPENING HOURS 營業時間
Lunch 午膳　12:00-14:30 (L.O.)
Dinner 晚膳　18:30-22:30 (L.O.)

HONG KONG 香港

8 1/2 Otto e Mezzo - Bombana

❀ ❀ ❀

XXXX

🍽18 ◎🍴 ♨

Fellini's film about the search for inspiration provides the name for chef-owner Umberto Bombana's bright restaurant. It is an exquisitely framed and cleverly lit space, with a chic, urbane feel – check out the 'ageing cellar' for hams and cheeses. The Italian food is equally appealing: pappardelle with lamb and mushroom ragout; blue lobster and sea urchin with gnocchi; Tajima beef tongue and cheek braised in red wine; and, to finish, limoncello soufflé.

餐廳裝修色彩鮮艷，裝潢及照明充滿時尚都市感。命名源自費里尼那齣有關尋找靈感的電影。供應的意大利菜式惹人垂涎:迷迭香羊肚菌羊肉寬條麵、藍龍蝦海膽沙律配龍蝦汁、紅酒牛舌牛頰配糖漬水果、檸檬酒梳乎厘及意大利芝士蛋糕是必然之選。火腿與芝士的發酵窖是店內特色，餐酒選擇主要來自意大利 。

TEL. 2537 8859
Shop 202, 2F, Alexandra House,
18 Chater Road, Central
中環遮打 18號歷山大廈 2樓 202號舖
www.ottoemezzobombana.com

■ PRICE 價錢
Lunch 午膳
set 套餐 $ 520-1,380
à la carte 點菜 $ 760-1,060

Dinner 晚膳
set 套餐 $ 1,380
à la carte 點菜 $ 760-1,060

■ OPENING HOURS 營業時間
Lunch 午膳　12:00-14:30 (L.O.)
Dinner 晚膳　18:30-22:30 (L.O.)

■ ANNUAL AND WEEKLY CLOSING 休息日期
Closed Sunday 週日休息

HONG KONG 香港

Pak Loh Chiu Chow (Hysan Avenue) NEW
百樂潮州 (希慎道)

XX

🛗16 ◎🍴

There are now four branches of this Chiu Chow restaurant in Hong Kong, but this is the original – which was founded in 1967. For lunch try the baby oyster congee or the fried noodle with sugar and vinegar; in the evening you can go for something a little heavier like soyed goose liver. It's also worth pre-ordering a speciality, like deep-fried king prawn with bread noodles, and finishing with the classic Chiu Chow dessert of fried taro with sugar.

自1967年於銅鑼灣開業，發展至今已有多間分店，而希慎道這間老店的受歡迎程度始終如一。食客最愛的菜式包括各式鹵水食物如鵝肝及鵝，還有高質凍蟹，或者預訂特別菜式如子母龍鬚蝦、薑米乳鴿及荷包豬肚雞湯等等。

TEL. 2576 8886
GF, 23-25 Hysan Avenue, Causeway Bay
銅鑼灣希慎道 23-25號

■ PRICE 價錢
Lunch 午膳
à la carte 點菜 $ 100-200
Dinner 晚膳
à la carte 點菜 $ 200-400

■ OPENING HOURS 營業時間
11:00-23:00 (L.O.)

Pak Loh Chiu Chow (Times Square) NEW
百樂潮州 (時代廣場)

🍴🍴🍴   🛗12   🕐🍴

A vaulted ceiling, clever lighting, woods and leather all combine to create a striking contemporary restaurant on the 10th floor of Times Square. The chiu chow cuisine is prepared in a traditional way using authentic ingredients, although the presentation – like the room – is modern. For lunch try dim sum or something light, such as sliced pomfret or baby oyster congee; for dinner the stewed, dried Oma abalone is a must.

由本地年輕設計師操刀的室內設計，燈光、線條和空間構成出色的視覺效果，令人留下深刻印象。百樂這家分店提供一眾傳統潮州美食，配以精美外型，且份量較小巧容你可嘗味更多。煎鯧魚和鹵水鵝當然不能少，想試點特別的食物可預先通知店家，讓大廚為你炮製潮州燒盞。

TEL. 2577 1163
10F, Times Square, 1 Matheson Street, Causeway Bay
銅鑼灣勿地臣街 1 號時代廣場 10 樓

■ PRICE 價錢
Lunch 午膳
à la carte 點菜 $ 200-300
Dinner 晚膳
à la carte 點菜 $ 300-400

■ OPENING HOURS 營業時間
11:00-22:30 (L.O.)

■ ANNUAL AND WEEKLY CLOSING 休息日期
Closed Lunar New Year 農曆新年休息

Pang's Kitchen
彭慶記

Anyone living in Happy Valley will be familiar with Pang's Kitchen as it has been packing them in since it opened back in 2001. Its reputation is largely down to its Cantonese cuisine which comes in a decidedly homestyle, traditional style, with dishes such as baked fish intestines in a clay pot, whole superior abalone in oyster sauce, and seasonal dishes like snake soup. It is not a huge place so it's worth booking ahead.

跑馬地的街坊必定不會對彭慶記感到陌生,店舖自2001年開業以來一直服務該區。其馳名粵式佳餚主要是家常小菜和傳統菜式,如砵仔焗魚腸、蠔皇原隻吉品鮑及季節性菜式如太史五蛇羹。由於食店面積不大,食客宜預先訂座。

TEL. 2838 5462
25 Yik Yam Street, Happy Valley
跑馬地奕蔭街 25號

■ PRICE 價錢
Lunch 午膳
set 套餐 $ 68
à la carte 點菜 $ 250-500
Dinner 晚膳
à la carte 點菜 $ 250-500

■ OPENING HOURS 營業時間
11:00-22:45 (L.O.)

HONG KONG 香港

Peking Garden (Central)
北京樓 (中環)

🍴🍴🍴   🔔48   🕐🍴

Divided into two large and warmly lit rooms; one more traditionally decorated, the other better suited for bigger family groups. Be sure to time your visit for the noodle-making demonstration, performed by a chef every evening in the restaurant at 8:30pm. The signature dish is, of course, the Peking duck, which is prepared with great care. Also look out for the deep-fried prawns in chilli sauce, and diced steak with walnuts.

餐廳劃分為兩個大廳；一邊風格較為傳統,另一邊則較為適合大家族聚餐。緊記要算準時間,欣賞每晚8時30分的師傅即席拉麵表演。這裡的招牌菜當然是經過精心炮製的北京填鴨。其他值得一試的小菜有宮爆明蝦及琥珀牛柳粒。

TEL. 2526 6456
BF, Alexandra House, 18 Chater Road, Central
中環遮打道 18號歷山大廈地庫
www.maxims.com.hk

■ PRICE 價錢
Lunch 午膳
à la carte 點菜 $ 200-1,000
Dinner 晚膳
à la carte 點菜 $ 200-1,000

■ OPENING HOURS 營業時間
Lunch 午膳   11:30-15:00 L.O.14:45
Dinner 晚膳   18:00-23:30 L.O.22:30

Penthouse

Perched on the 30th floor – hence its name – is a restaurant with a New York loft-style look and an ersatz industrial feel. The menu keeps its influences largely within Europe and there are two main specialities that merit your attention: the homemade pastas and the juicy and tender meats cooked in the Josper grill oven. The lunchtime set menu includes appetisers and desserts from the 5m long buffet counter.

木地板、黑金屬架、水泥磚及鎢絲燈造出紐約風空間。採自世界各地的食材，以時尚烹調方式與歐陸風格炮製。每日鮮製的手造意粉頗受歡迎；以Josper炭爐烤煮的肉鮮嫩多汁，連骨美國肉眼扒絕不會讓你失望。

TEL. 2970 0828
30F, Soundwill Plaza 2 Midtown,
1-29 Tang Lung Street, Causeway Bay
銅鑼灣登龍街 1-29號金朝陽中心 2期 30樓
www.penthouse-dining.com

■ PRICE 價錢
Lunch 午膳
set 套餐 $258-420
à la carte 點菜 $400-900
Dinner 晚膳
à la carte 點菜 $400-900

■ OPENING HOURS 營業時間
Lunch 午膳　12:00-14:30 (L.O.)
Dinner 晚膳　18:00-22:30 (L.O.)

Petrus
珀翠

XXXXX   ふ ⟨ 🍽 ⎓20 ◐ 🍴 🍇

Petrus is firmly in the classical European style, with moulded ceilings, chandeliers, elaborately draped curtains and fine table settings; it also offers great views from its perch on the 56th floor. The service is very professional and at dinner you'll be accompanied by a harpist. All this is matched by very proficient French cooking that relies on a roll-call of top quality ingredients. The wine list has over 20,000 bottles, including Pétrus!

珀翠的經典歐陸格調，充分表現在其雕刻天花、吊燈、高雅的窗簾及排列優雅的餐桌上。餐廳座落於56樓，可飽覽海港美景，其服務專業之餘，晚飯時段更有現場豎琴演奏。這一切配上一流的法式烹調，與新鮮的食材可謂無與倫比。此外，餐酒選擇逾一千二百款，當中包括顯貴的珀翠！

TEL. 2820 8590
56F, Island Shangri-La Hotel, Pacific Place,
Supreme Court Road, Admiralty
金鐘法院道太古廣場
港島香格里拉酒店 56樓
www.shangri-la.com

■ PRICE 價錢
Lunch 午膳
à la carte 點菜 $900-1,400
Dinner 晚膳
à la carte 點菜 $1,000-1,400

■ OPENING HOURS 營業時間
Lunch 午膳   12:00-14:30 (L.O.)
Dinner 晚膳   18:30-22:30 (L.O.)

Pierre

✿ ✿

XXXX

♿ ⟨ 🖐 📺16 🍴 🎴

The top floor of the Mandarin Oriental provides suitably chic surroundings for celebrated French chef Pierre Gagnaire's culinary pyrotechnics. The intricate and innovative dishes and their component parts arrive in a number of vessels, all carefully explained by the charming staff. The views are absolutely terrific and the room itself is stylish, moodily lit and very comfortable. The focus here is on enjoyment with an atmosphere free from pomposity.

文華東方酒店頂樓的環境，與法國名廚Pierre Gagnaire讓人驚歎的美味菜式非常合襯。精緻創新的菜式與配菜以不同容器盛載着，殷勤細心的侍應會仔細為你講解每道菜式。餐廳景觀迷人，裝潢也甚有現代感，配合富情調的燈光，非常舒適。

TEL. 2825 4001
25F, Mandarin Oriental Hotel,
5 Connaught Road, Central
中環干諾道中 5號文華東方酒店 25樓
www.mandarinoriental.com/hongkong

■ PRICE 價錢
Lunch 午膳
set 套餐 $ 498-1,088
à la carte 點菜 $ 1,600-2,000

Dinner 晚膳
set 套餐 $ 1,088-1,688
à la carte 點菜 $ 1,600-2,000

■ OPENING HOURS 營業時間
Lunch 午膳　12:00-14:30 (L.O.)
Dinner 晚膳　18:30-22:30 (L.O.)

■ ANNUAL AND WEEKLY CLOSING 休息日期
Closed Saturday lunch, Sunday and Public
Holidays 週六午膳、週日及公眾假期休息

Po Kee
波記

Po Kee is familiar to anyone who's lived in Western District as it's been a feature here for over 40 years and for many local residents a bowl of rice noodles (Lai Fan) with roasted duck leg remains a cherished childhood memory. To prepare his own roast meats, the owner built a factory behind the shop when he moved it to the current address. Regulars know to come before 2pm which is about the time the pork sells out each day.

西環的居民對波記一定不會陌生，此店在區內已有逾四十年歷史，一碗美味的燒鴨腿瀨粉是許多人的童年回憶。遷至現址後，店主在店舖後自設工場，炮製多款燒味。區內居民對店內各款美食了若指掌，燒肉往往在下午二時前售罄，欲試其燒鵝，最好在四時前到達。

TEL. N/A
425 Queen's Road West,
Western District
西環皇后大道西 425號

■ PRICE 價錢
à la carte 點菜 $ 30-90

■ OPENING HOURS 營業時間
11:30-22:30 (L.O.)

■ ANNUAL AND WEEKLY CLOSING 休息日期
Closed Sunday 週日休息

HONG KONG 香港

Putien (Causeway Bay) NEW
莆田 (銅鑼灣)

🍴🍴   🅿   🛋14   ©🍴

The original restaurant was founded in Singapore in 2000 and named after a coastal city in Fujian province – the owner's home town. This branch comes with an easy-going atmosphere and its Fujian cuisine is respectful of tradition, with the focus on natural flavours. There's much to recommend, like stewed yellow crocker, seaweed with shrimps, and braised pig intestine; and don't miss their homemade chilli sauce – a perfect match for fried bean curd.

莆田於2000年在星加坡開業，後擴展至香港，老闆以其家鄉福建內的城市為餐廳命名，堅守忠於原味、鮮味自然的原則，做出一道道美味菜式；無論是清鮮嫩滑的燜黃花魚、回味悠長的九轉小腸，以至香酥的炒芋頭等都令人留下深刻印象，自家秘製的辣椒醬辣媽更是非試不可。

TEL. 2111 8080
Shop A, 7F, Lee Theatre Plaza,
99 Percival Street, Causeway Bay
銅鑼灣波斯富街99號利舞臺廣場7樓A號舖

■ PRICE 價錢
Lunch 午膳
à la carte 點菜 $ 100-300
Dinner 晚膳
à la carte 點菜 $ 100-300

■ OPENING HOURS 營業時間
Lunch 午膳　11:30-14:30 (L.O.)
Dinner 晚膳　17:30-22:00 (L.O.)

Qi
呇

 10

The word 'Qi' means 'shining star' and the idea for the name was inspired by the shape of star anise – an important component of Sichuan cooking. This is a hip, moody and atmospherically lit restaurant where the coolness of the look contrasts with the heat of the food. Blacks and reds and opera-inspired paintings help create the striking room while in the kitchen sauces, herbs and chillies from Sichuan are used to prepare hot, spicy dishes.

呇意謂明亮的星星，餐廳以此命名意在比喻四川菜常用的香料八角。室內裝潢別具一格，紅與黑的鮮明對比，昏暗的燈光配上川劇壁畫，時尚中蘊含中式韻味。廚師採用自四川運來的醬汁、香料和辣椒，以傳統烹調方法做出正宗的麻、辣、鮮和香的四川風味，配合不同地區的食材，令人驚喜。

TEL. 2527 7117
2F, J Senses , 60 Johnston Road,
Wan Chai
灣仔莊士敦道 60號 2樓
www.qi-sichuan.hk

SPECIALITIES TO PRE-ORDER 預訂食物
Chili Dungeness crab 霸王辣蟹

■ PRICE 價錢
Lunch 午膳
set 套餐 $ 130-180
à la carte 點菜 $ 200-750
Dinner 晚膳
à la carte 點菜 $ 200-750

■ OPENING HOURS 營業時間
Lunch 午膳　12:00-14:15 (L.O.)
Dinner 晚膳　18:00-22:30 (L.O.)

Qĭao Cuisine NEW
巧饍坊

🅿 ⌑12 ◑⊪

There's nothing quite like a culinary remedy when you're feeling down. From the same owner and management as Wing Lai Yuen – famous for dandan noodles – comes this restaurant guided by theories of Chinese medicine. The food is mostly Shanghainese and vegetarian and the menu explains which dish is good for what ails you. For example, vegetarian sweet and sour is great for those suffering from indigestion yet unsuitable for anyone with gout.

有着奪目的綠色門面巧饍坊，與隔壁的詠藜園源自同一集團。主要供應上海菜及素菜，更結合中醫藥知識傳承藥食同源的中醫理論，餐單上甚至列出個別菜式的食用宜忌。此外餐廳更聘有國家級廚師，為預訂國宴菜的客人籌備多達二十三道菜的套餐。

TEL. 3152 2162
Shop 106-107, 1F, Site 8,
Whampoa Garden, Hung Hom
紅磡黃埔花園第 8 期 1 樓 106-107 號舖

■ PRICE 價錢
Lunch 午膳
set 套餐 $ 55-80
à la carte 點菜 $ 150-400
Dinner 晚膳
à la carte 點菜 $ 150-400

■ OPENING HOURS 營業時間
Lunch 午膳　11:00-15:30　(L.O.)
Dinner 晚膳　18:00-22:30　(L.O.)

Ramen Jo (Causeway Bay)
拉麵Jo (銅鑼灣)

There are four kinds of ramen here, along with the seasonal special. The miso ramen is good but those who like a stronger taste should try the spicy ramen with pork char siu. The pork rib soup is cooked over 16 hours and the taste is rich and strong but never thick or greasy. The owner named his shop after his favourite Japanese animated character and he runs it with an energetic team of servers who help create a lively atmosphere.

東主以心愛的漫畫人物名字為店子命名，並與充滿朝氣的服務團隊把這間拉麵店打理得井井有條。餐單內提供四款拉麵及時令推介，花上十六個小時精心熬製的豬骨湯底是此店拉麵的精髓所在，味濃而不膩，再配上特製的麵條和醬汁，令人回味無窮。

TEL. 2885 0638
3 Caroline Hill Road, Causeway Bay
銅鑼灣加路連山道 3號

■ PRICE 價錢
Lunch 午膳
à la carte 點菜 $ 80-100
Dinner 晚膳
à la carte 點菜 $ 80-100

■ OPENING HOURS 營業時間
Lunch 午膳　12:00-14:30 (L.O.)
Dinner 晚膳　18:00-22:00 (L.O.)

Read 'How to use this guide' for an explanation of our symbols, classifications and abbreviations.

請細閱「如何使用餐廳／酒店指南」，當中的標誌、分類等簡介助你掌握使用本指南的訣竅，作出智慧選擇。

Enjoy good food without spending a fortune! Look out for the Bib Gourmand symbol ⊕ to find restaurants offering good food at great prices!

既想省錢又想品嘗美食，便要留心注有這個 ⊕ 車胎人標誌的餐廳，她們提供的是價錢實惠且高質素的美食。

les bonnes étapes

Restoran Indonesia 1968
印尼餐廳1968

Having been a fixture in Causeway Bay since 1968, this Indonesian restaurant is now run by the owners' sons. In 2011 they moved it to these more striking surroundings in Central, which are proving a hit with a hip young crowd. It comes divided into two rooms: one side with simple wooden tables, the other more intimate and connected to the bar. Street food specialities include satay cooked over charcoal, Lidah Semur and Ikan Asam.

早於1968年已在銅鑼灣開業的印尼餐廳，現時由東主的兒子接手經營，並於2011年搬到中環，成功吸引年輕食客。餐廳劃分為兩個區域，一邊簡單地放置5張木桌，另一邊則較為舒適，並連接酒吧。店內提供多種印尼街頭食品，包括碳燒沙爹、醬燒牛舌和亞參酸辣魚。

TEL. 2577 9981
5F, The L Place,
139 Queen's Road Central , Central
中環皇后大道中 139號 The L Place 5樓
www.ir1968.com

■ PRICE 價錢
Lunch 午膳
set 套餐 $ 98-158
à la carte 點菜 $ 180-500
Dinner 晚膳
à la carte 點菜 $ 180-500

■ OPENING HOURS 營業時間
12:00-23:30 (L.O.)

Robatayaki NEW
爐端燒

Run by the Harbour Grand Kowloon hotel and set on the ground floor of an office building opposite is, as the name tells you, a restaurant specialising in robatayaki. This busy spot has counter seats on three sides of the grills, and dishes are passed from chefs to diner via long paddles. The ingredients include seasonal vegetables and seafood from Japan, and Wagyu from Kobe and Australia. The snacks, like the crispy chicken wing, are excellent.

餐廳由九龍海逸君綽酒店營運，位處酒店正門對面。兩個爐端燒燒爐佔去餐室大部分空間，櫃台中陳列了琳瑯滿目的時令蔬菜和海產，廚師就坐在當中為你燒煮食物，由蔬菜、海鮮到和牛，選擇豐富。除爐端燒外還提供魚生、壽司和天婦羅。

TEL. 2996 8438
GF, Harbourfront Two,
22 Tak Fung Street, Whampoa Garden,
Hung Hom
紅磡黃埔花園德豐街22號海濱廣場2期地下

■ PRICE 價錢
Lunch 午膳
à la carte 點菜 $ 400-1,500
Dinner 晚膳
à la carte 點菜 $ 400-1,500

■ OPENING HOURS 營業時間
Lunch 午膳   12:00-14:00(L.O.)
Dinner 晚膳   18:00-22:30 (L.O.)

Japanese 日本菜

Japanese 日本菜

Japanese 日本菜

MAP 地圖   16/A-3

Ryu Gin
天空龍吟

♿ ≼ ⛶ 12 ◑🍽

Seiji Yamamoto, owner-chef of the celebrated Ryugin in Tokyo, chose Hong Kong and the 101st floor of the ICC tower as the location for his first overseas branch. The only menu is the 10 course kaiseki and it uses high quality ingredients imported from Japan. The food is a mix of traditional flavours, modern influences and personal touches. Wood and silver combine to create an elegant space and the views are spectacular.

東京著名食府龍吟的主廚兼東主山本征治先生，選擇了環球貿易廣場101樓作首家海外分店的地址，景觀極其壯麗，融合木材與銀色的裝潢，營造出高雅的空間。精緻的十道菜懷石料理採用來自日本的上等食材，並巧妙地融合了傳統與現代風味及創意配搭。

TEL. 2302 0222
101F, International Commerce Centre,
1 Austin Road West, Tsim Sha Tsui
尖沙咀柯士甸道西 1 號環球貿易廣場 101 樓
www.ryugin.com.hk

■ PRICE 價錢
Dinner 晚膳
set 套餐 $ 2,180

■ OPENING HOURS 營業時間
Dinner 晚膳   18:00-21:30 (L.O.)

■ ANNUAL AND WEEKLY CLOSING 休息日期
Closed 2 days Lunar New Year
農曆新年休息 2 天

HONG KONG 香港

Sabah (Wan Chai)
莎巴 (灣仔)

Sabah is one of the few Malaysian restaurants to have served authentic Malaysian food for many years. It may have an unremarkable façade, but at least it's easy to find thanks to the huge horizontal neon sign. The kitchen staff are all Malaysian and the care they take is palpable, as is the skill they show in preparing the dishes. Satay, king prawns with butter and deep-fried egg yolk, beef Rendang and Hainanese chicken rice are some of the highlights.

這家餐廳的外觀也許毫不起眼,但是靠着巨大的霓虹燈招牌,我們可輕易找到它。內部裝潢與外觀一樣平凡,但吸引眾多食客的並不是餐廳的室內設計,而是正宗的馬拉菜。精選菜式包括沙嗲、金絲奶油大蝦、巴東牛肉與海南雞飯。主廚秘方炮製的炸香蕉也十分惹味。

TEL. 2143 6626
98-102 Jaffe Road, Wan Chai
灣仔謝菲道 98-102號

■ PRICE 價錢
Lunch 午膳
set 套餐 $ 75
à la carte 點菜 $ 150-350
Dinner 晚膳
à la carte 點菜 $ 150-350

■ OPENING HOURS 營業時間
11:00-23:00 (L.O.)

■ ANNUAL AND WEEKLY CLOSING 休息日期
Closed 3 days Lunar New Year
農曆新年休息 3 天

HONG KONG 香港

Sai Kung Sing Kee
勝記

❀

✗　　　　　　　　　　　　　　　　　　🍽36 ◑🍴

At first sight, this brightly coloured seafood restaurant may not seem too dissimilar to others in Sai Kung. However, there is something special here and that's the abalone menu. The abalone are prepared in various ways, from deep-fried to steamed; try the stewed abalone in oyster sauce. The building has 12 variously sized dining rooms spread over its three floors, all differently decorated; the most contemporary are on the 1st and 2nd floors.

這棟建築物樓高三層，備有十二個大小不一、裝飾各異的房間，一樓和二樓的餐室裝潢較時尚，驟眼看來，跟西貢其他餐廳並沒兩樣。但是，它真正特別的地方，在於扣鮑魚菜式。這裡提供多種以不同方式烹調的鮑魚菜式，由酥炸到蒸煮式式俱備，特別推介古法扣兩頭鮑魚。

TEL. 2791 9887
39 Sai Kung Tai Street, Sai Kung
西貢西貢大街 39 號
www.singkee.ecomm.hk

SPECIALITIES TO PRE-ORDER 預訂食物
Crispy chicken 金牌炸子雞 / Stewed abalone in oyster sauce 古法扣鮑魚

■ PRICE 價錢
Lunch 午膳
à la carte 點菜 $ 100-950
Dinner 晚膳
à la carte 點菜 $ 180-950

■ OPENING HOURS 營業時間
11:00-22:30 (L.O.)

■ ANNUAL AND WEEKLY CLOSING 休息日期
Closed 2 days Lunar New Year
農曆新年休息 2 天

Sang Kee
生記

Having stood here proudly for over 30 years, Sang Kee is a true symbol of Wan Chai and remains refreshingly impervious to modernisation. The owner insists on buying the seafood herself each day and the Cantonese dishes are prepared using traditional methods. You'll find yourself thinking about their classic dishes like fried snapper, fried minced pork with cuttlefish, and braised fish with bitter melon long after you've sampled them.

現在許多粵菜餐廳都以雷同的裝潢和新派菜單作招徠，令生記這類傳統酒家讓人感到特別親切!開業三十多年，店主一直堅持每天親自採購優質海鮮，以傳統烹調方式製作一道道經典廣東菜：用時令材料炮製的乾煎海臘，家常菜如土魷煎肉餅和涼瓜炆魚等，令人回味無窮。

TEL. 2575 2236
1-2F, Hip Sang Building,
107-115 Hennessy Road, Wan Chai
灣仔軒尼詩道 107-115號協生大廈 1-2樓
www.sangkee.com.hk

■ PRICE 價錢
Lunch 午膳
set 套餐 $ 50-70
à la carte 點菜 $ 100-300
Dinner 晚膳
à la carte 點菜 $ 100-300

■ OPENING HOURS 營業時間
Lunch 午膳 12:00-14:30 (L.O.)
Dinner 晚膳 18:00-22:00 (L.O.)

■ ANNUAL AND WEEKLY CLOSING 休息日期
Closed first Monday of each month
每月第一個週一休息

French 法國菜   MAP 地圖 31/C-3

Seasons

HONG KONG 香港

The elegant Seasons restaurant occupies a huge space within Lee Gardens Two but it's split into four distinct areas, with each one representing one of the four seasons. Traditional French recipes are combined with the young chef's own ideas to create dishes that are full of verve and originality. Go for the Carte Blanche menu – a tasting menu designed for the whole table. The high quality ingredients are, appropriately enough, also very seasonal.

位於利園二期，面積寬敞，餐室分為四個部分，以四季為主題，各具特色與魅力。年輕大廚憑出色技藝與創意，將個人烹調風格應用於法國各地美食內，配合上等時令食材，製作別出心裁的小菜。Carte Blanche套餐是按食客的喜好特別設計的套餐。酒單選擇豐富，有不少由廚師親自引入的特別推介。

TEL. 2505 6228
Shop 308, 3F, Lee Gardens Two,
28 Yun Ping Road, Causeway Bay
銅鑼灣恩平道 28號利園 2期 3樓 308號舖
www.seasonsbyolivier.com

■ PRICE 價錢
Lunch 午膳
set 套餐 $318-478
à la carte 點菜 $650-900
Dinner 晚膳
set 套餐 $628-1,488
à la carte 點菜 $650-900

■ OPENING HOURS 營業時間
Lunch 午膳   12:00-14:30 (L.O.)
Dinner 晚膳   18:00-22:30 (L.O.)

225

Ser Wong Fun
蛇王芬

Regulars flock here for the snake soup and snake banquets in winter. No less than 15 varieties of double-boiled soups and a vast array of seasonal pot dishes are also offered, along with traditional Cantonese dishes and roast meats. The restaurant was established over 70 years ago and is under the stewardship of the fourth generation, so it is little wonder that a book has been published celebrating the family history and their cherished recipes.

七十年前開店的蛇王芬如今由第四代傳人主理,更出版了書籍介紹家族歷史及著名菜式。熟客經常來此品嘗蛇羹,冬天甚至會共享蛇宴。超過十五種老火燉湯任君選擇,此外亦提供一系列煲仔飯、傳統廣東菜式及燒味。

TEL. 2543 1032
30 Cochrane Street, Central
中環閣麟街 30號

■ PRICE 價錢
à la carte 點菜 $ 120-250

■ OPENING HOURS 營業時間
11:00-22:30 (L.O.)

■ ANNUAL AND WEEKLY CLOSING 休息日期
Closed 4 days Lunar New Year
農曆新年休息 4 天

French contemporary 時尚法國菜

MAP 地圖 29/C-3

Serge et le Phoque

Thanks to its large glass façade, discreet sign and understated, faux industrial interior, it's pretty apparent that the refreshingly relaxed Serge and The Seal is unlike many of the city's French restaurants. The appealingly minimalist surroundings contrast somewhat with the cooking, which is detailed and innovative. The set menus can change daily, depending on what's in the market, and are made up of small, elaborately constructed dishes.

小巧精緻的賣相和配搭創新的烹調，讓這家餐廳的食物有別於一般法國菜館，不光每道菜式都經過主廚精心設計和鑽研，餐單亦按每天市場上供應的食材更新。店內裝潢與時尚創新的烹調風格貫徹如一，落地玻璃窗與工業風陳設，透出一分灑脫，錯落有致的圓吊燈透着抽象表現主義，不羈中帶點藝術色彩。

TEL. 5465 2000
GF, Shop B2, The Zenith,
3 Wan Chai Road, Wan Chai
灣仔道 3號尚翹峰地下 B2號舖

■ PRICE 價錢
Dinner 晚膳
set 套餐 $ 650-850

■ OPENING HOURS 營業時間
Dinner 晚膳　18:00-22:30 (L.O.)

Seventh Son
家全七福

🍴🍴   🍽️ ⏲20 ◐🍴

The owner-chef named his restaurant in honour of his father who taught his seventh son how to cook when he was 14 years old. In the kitchen he insists on using the freshest seasonal ingredients and his technical skills in preparing the traditional Cantonese food are obvious. He uses less seasoning than many, so that his customers can appreciate the true flavour of the food. Barbecued suckling pig and crispy chicken are his specialities.

餐廳名稱含了東主父親的名字，英文名是他在家中的排行輩份，也表示傳承父親廚藝之意。東主自十四歲起隨父習廚，擅長高級功夫粵菜。他堅持用時令食材、以最小的調味料及精細的烹調，帶出食材的真味。大紅片皮乳豬和炸子雞是招牌菜。餐室設計簡潔高雅，服務周到。

TEL. 2892 2888
5-6F, Kwan Chart Tower,
6 Tonnochy Road, Wan Chai
灣仔杜老誌道 6號羣策大廈 5-6樓
www.seventhson.hk

■ PRICE 價錢
Lunch 午膳
à la carte 點菜 $ 200-3,000
Dinner 晚膳
à la carte 點菜 $350-3,000

■ OPENING HOURS 營業時間
Lunch 午膳　11:30-15:00 (L.O.)
Dinner 晚膳　18:00-22:30 (L.O.)

■ ANNUAL AND WEEKLY CLOSING 休息日期
Closed 2 days Lunar New Year
農曆新年休息 2 天

Sha Tin 18
沙田18

Dongguan and Cantonese specialities, like Houjie fish cakes with Chinese dry sausage and wok-fried goose with preserved soya bean sauce, are the draw at this contemporary restaurant. Enthusiastic amateur chefs will appreciate the four separate show kitchens, allowing them the chance to enjoy an insider's view of a culinary team in action. There are private dining rooms as well as a large outside terrace. Have a drink first in the Tin Tin bar.

這家時尚中菜餐廳提供東莞及粵式名菜，如厚街臘味煎魚餅和寮步薑葱爆炒塘鵝，令不少食客慕名而來。熱衷烹飪的食客必定欣賞餐廳內4個開放式廚房，讓他們近距離欣賞廚師的精湛廚藝。餐廳亦設有獨立房間和寬敞的露台。食客可於用餐前到毗鄰的天天吧暢飲一番。

TEL. 3723 7932
4F, Hyatt Regency Sha Tin,
18 Chak Cheung Street, University,
Sha Tin
沙田大學站澤祥街18號沙田凱悅酒店4樓
www.hongkong.shatin.hyatt.com

■ PRICE 價錢
Lunch 午膳
à la carte 點菜 $200-650
Dinner 晚膳
à la carte 點菜 $300-650

■ OPENING HOURS 營業時間
Lunch 午膳　11:30-15:00 (L.O.)
Dinner 晚膳　17:30-22:30 (L.O.)

Shang Palace
香宮

Antique Chinese window frames, lanterns and Sung style paintings evoke the grandeur of an ancient Chinese palace. Headed by celebrity Chef Mok Kit Keung, Shang Palace offers traditional and authentic Cantonese dishes with a nod to contemporary presentation. The care and attention shown by the service team is exemplary and highlights of the Cantonese menu include crispy lobster with oatmeal and braised spare rib with Chinkiang vinegar.

外型西化時尚，風味正宗傳統，是香宮供應的粵菜特色。店內裝潢由紅色漆牆、古董國畫及傳統燈籠組成，予人古色古香之感。服務團隊殷勤周到，烹調精巧的粵菜推介有麥片乳龍蝦球及稻草骨。

TEL. 2733 8754
Lower level, Kowloon Shangri-La Hotel,
64 Mody Road, East Tsim Sha Tsui
尖東麼地道 64號九龍香格里拉酒店地庫 1樓
www.shangri-la.com

SPECIALITIES TO PRE-ORDER 預訂食物
Beggar's chicken 富貴雞

■ PRICE 價錢
Lunch 午膳
set 套餐 $ 338-498
à la carte 點菜 $ 300-1,000
Dinner 晚膳
set 套餐 $ 598-1,188
à la carte 點菜 $ 400-1,000

■ OPENING HOURS 營業時間
Lunch 午膳　12:00-15:00 L.O. 14:45
Dinner 晚膳　18:30-23:00 L.O. 22:45

Shanghai Garden
紫玉蘭

🍴🍴   🍽15   ◷🍴

Local fans of Shanghai Garden needn't have panicked when they heard it was moving because it didn't go far – in fact, it remained in the same building. The new premises are smaller but infinitely better looking. Along with the traditional Shanghainese dishes you can expect some Beijing and Sichuan specialities. Try the juicy pan-fried beef cake and pork dumpling or more traditional offerings like braised sea cucumber with spring onion.

搬遷後的紫玉蘭，仍然在和記大廈內，只換了另一個舖位。此店提供傳統滬菜及小量京川菜。各款上海涼菜及鹹點最適合午飯享用，美味多汁的牛肉館餅和鮮肉鍋貼是最佳選擇。晚餐時可按上海人傳統，先嘗點涼菜後再進食熱菜如葱燒海參和滋味的紅燒八寶鴨。

TEL. 2524 8181
Shop 203, 2F, Hutchison House,
10 Harcourt Road, Admiralty
金鐘夏慤道10號和記大廈2樓203室

■ PRICE 價錢
Lunch 午膳
à la carte 點菜 $ 200-650
Dinner 晚膳
à la carte 點菜 $ 200-650

■ OPENING HOURS 營業時間
Lunch 午膳　11:30-14:45 (L.O.)
Dinner 晚膳　18:00-22:45 (L.O.)

She Wong Yee
蛇王二

Their signature snake soup has long been renowned and on a typical winter's day over 1,000 bowls are served. Regulars are quick to occupy one of the few tables for this memorable experience and it is no surprise that the recipe has remained unchanged for years. These days, those regulars come also for the famed barbecued meats and homemade liver sausages; the roast goose and double-boiled soups are good too.

此店位於銅鑼灣的中心地帶，以傳統方法烹調的蛇羹多年來口碑載道，秋冬高峰期更每日出售逾千碗。除此之外，其自製潤腸也同樣令食客趨之若鶩，而盅頭滋補燉湯是不少本地市民的最愛。店內氣氛熱鬧，需與其他人拼桌用膳。

TEL. 2831 0163
24 Percival Street, Causeway Bay
銅鑼灣波斯富街 24 號

■ PRICE 價錢
à la carte 點菜 $ 60-160

■ OPENING HOURS 營業時間
11:30-22:45 (L.O.)

■ ANNUAL AND WEEKLY CLOSING 休息日期
Closed 3 days Lunar New Year
農曆新年休息 3 天

Shek Kee Kitchen
石記廚房

🍲‖　　　　　　　　　　　　　🪑8

During the day, the shop sells Cha Chan Tang dishes, but we recommend it for the traditional, home-style Cantonese cooking it serves in the evening. The owner-chef goes to market each day in search of the freshest ingredients and some of his regulars even call him directly to order specific dishes for that night. Specialities are the salt-baked chicken, fried frogs' legs with garlic and chilli, and steamed egg white with crabmeat and asparagus.

餐廳在日間供應普通茶餐廳食物,而我們要推介的是其晚間供應的家庭式廣東小菜。大廚兼車主每天會親自往街市選購最新鮮的食材,部分熟客更會直接致電預訂當晚的菜式。菜單經常更新,確保所用的是最當造的時令食材。

TEL. 2571 3348
GF, 15-17 Ngan Mok Street, Tin Hau
天后銀幕街 17 號地下

■ PRICE 價錢
Lunch 午膳
à la carte 點菜 $ 100-300
Dinner 晚膳
à la carte 點菜 $ 100-300

■ OPENING HOURS 營業時間
Lunch 午膳　07:00-15:00 (L.O.)
Dinner 晚膳　18:00-23:00 (L.O.)

Shiba NEW

On a quiet street not far from the sea, and hidden behind a modest façade, is this intimate izakaya-style dining room – a good choice if you're meeting up with friends. It serves mainly yakitori and barbecued seafood; with shiso minced chicken, and minced pork with Sakura shrimps being two popular dishes. Most of the produce is imported from Japan, along with about 50 different sake, as well as shochu, fruit liqueurs and Japanese beers.

這小店子位於士美非路靠海一帶，離新啟用的港鐵堅尼地城站並不遠。低調的門面，十分平易近人的居酒屋餐室，最適宜和朋友邊吃燒肉串，邊品嘗清酒。這裡的清酒有五十種之多，而食物方面除燒雞肉之外，尚有其他肉類和多種海鮮；自家製的櫻花蝦免治豬肉和燒帆立貝最受歡迎。

TEL. 3568 2425
11 Smithfield, Kennedy Town
堅尼地城士美菲路 11 號

■ PRICE 價錢
à la carte 點菜 $ 300-550

■ OPENING HOURS 營業時間
18:00-24:00 (L.O.)

Shugetsu Ramen (Central)
麵鮮醬油房周月(中環)

The queues form early for the ramen here, with many of the customers coming for the Tsukemen ramen, as well as the Abura and special soup ramen. The shop makes its own noodles – which you can have thick or thin – but it is the sauce at the base of the slow-cooked soup that really makes the difference: it's fermented for 18 months in a 100 year old wooden basket and adds richness and depth.

周月與別不同之處，在其以醬油為湯底的神髓：採用有逾一百四十年歷史的愛媛縣梶田商店特製的醬油，配入沙丁魚粉、鯖魚粉及海帶長時間慢火熬製，味道更醇厚豐富。與日本店一樣，香港店設有製麵房，每天新鮮製造兩款粗幼不同的麵條。除了湯拉麵外，還供應沾麵。

TEL. 2850 6009
5 Gough Street, Central
中環歌賦街 5號
www.shugetsu.com.hk

■ PRICE 價錢
à la carte 點菜 $ 88-100

■ OPENING HOURS 營業時間
Weekdays 週一至週五 11:30-21:00 (L.O.)
Saturday 週六   12:00-21:00 (L.O.)
Sunday 週日   12:00-19:00 (L.O.)

Shugetsu Ramen (Quarry Bay)
麵鮮醬油房周月(鰂魚涌)

This was the second branch of Shugetsu to open in Hong Kong. It's the freshly made noodles and the soy sauce base that make them so popular. The broth is prepared with sardines, mackerel and kelp, and soy sauce that is produced by a longstanding factory in Ehime. The popular choice is Tsukemen, for which they use thick noodles to absorb the sauce's taste more easily – you decide how large a portion you want.

這是周月在香港的第二間分店，以鮮製麵條和醬油湯為賣點的拉麵店，湯底用放在百年木桶內經十八個月發酵而成的醬油，加上沙丁魚粉、鯖魚粉及海帶煮成，美味且味道特別。除了湯拉麵外，沾麵也頗受歡迎，選用的麵條較粗但掛湯力強，能盡吸醬汁精華。食客可選擇麵的份量。

TEL. 2854 9985
30 Hoi Kwong Street, Quarry Bay
鰂魚涌海光街 30 號
www.shugetsu.com.hk

■ PRICE 價錢
à la carte 點菜 $ 88-100

■ OPENING HOURS 營業時間
Weekdays 週一至週五 11:45-21:15 (L.O.)
Saturday 週六　12:00-21:00 (L.O.)
Sunday 週日　12:00-19:00 (L.O.)

■ ANNUAL AND WEEKLY CLOSING 休息日期
Closed Public Holidays 公眾假期休息

Sing Kee (Central) NEW
星記 (中環)

🍴   🗔12 🕒🍴

The second branch of Sing Kee is a bright, tidy spot serving classic Cantonese food – something that's proving increasingly hard to find in Central. You'll find only traditional recipes using chicken, pork and seafood here, free of gimmicks or fancy presentation. Many specialities need pre-ordering, like chicken with ginger in clam sauce, or apricot juice with fish maw and pig's lung. Come at lunch to take advantage of some reasonable prices.

想在中環區找到提供樸實高質的傳統粵菜且環境乾淨整潔的餐館，星記便是你的選擇。選用新鮮肉類如豬、雞及生猛海鮮等食材加上扎實的烹調技術，自然不乏支持者。午市提供一系列價錢實惠的小菜，甚得中環人士歡心。建議預訂燉湯如杏汁花膠燉豬肺。

TEL. 2970 0988
2F, 1 Lyndhurst Tower,
1 Lyndhurst Terrace, Central
中環擺花街 1 號一號廣場 2 樓

■ PRICE 價錢
Lunch 午膳
à la carte 點菜 $ 100-200
Dinner 晚膳
à la carte 點菜 $ 200-400

■ OPENING HOURS 營業時間
Lunch 午膳　11:30-14:15 (L.O.)
Dinner 晚膳　18:00-22:15 (L.O.)

■ ANNUAL AND WEEKLY CLOSING 休息日期
Closed Sunday lunch 週日午膳休息

Sing Kee (Wan Chai)
星記 (灣仔)

🍴 🛏36 ⏱🍽

Sing Kee stands out from its neighbours thanks to its eye-catching red and yellow sign but its main attraction is its authentic and traditional Cantonese cooking, which is prepared by a kitchen team who came from Sang Kee. The unremarkable interior doesn't matter to the regulars – they're all here for the skilful cooking and, in particular, the day's fresh fish. The pomelo skin dishes and the double-steamed soups are worth pre-ordering.

在酒吧林立的街道不遠處的一幢大廈內，有這間傳統廣東小菜館。鮮黃大紅的招牌非常搶眼，與其供應的菜餚一樣，令人印象深刻，雖沒有華麗包裝，卻憑扎實的烹調功夫和高質素食物贏得食客歡心。廚師每天在市場搜羅最生猛新鮮的海魚；柚皮菜式及燉湯需預訂。

TEL. 2528 9028
3F, The Phoenix, 23 Luard Road, Wan Chai
灣仔盧押道 23號 The Phoenix 3樓

SPECIALITIES TO PRE-ORDER 預訂食物
Double boiled soup 燉湯

■ PRICE 價錢
Lunch 午膳
à la carte 點菜 $ 150-300
Dinner 晚膳
à la carte 點菜 $ 150-300

■ OPENING HOURS 營業時間
Lunch 午膳　12:00-14:15 (L.O.)
Dinner 晚膳　18:00-22:15 (L.O.)

■ ANNUAL AND WEEKLY CLOSING 休息日期
Closed Sunday lunch 週日午膳休息

Sister Wah (Tin Hau)
華姐清湯腩 (天后)

With just six round tables, Sister Wah's diminutive dimensions are in direct contrast to the size of its reputation – this is one of the most famous beef brisket noodle shops. This family-run shop is always full and it is easy to see why: there are around 20 items on the menu which include Dan Dan noodles and Drunken chicken, but chief among them is the beef brisket in a clear soup.

只有六張圓桌的華姐清湯腩，規模與其名氣形成鮮明對比 — 這裡是最馳名的牛腩麵家之一。正因如此，這間家庭式經營的小店經常滿座，餐牌上約有二十種食品，包括擔擔麵和醉雞，但招牌菜當然是清湯牛坑腩。

TEL. 2807 0181
Shop A1, 13 Electric Road, Tin Hau
天后電氣道 13 號 A1 號舖

■ PRICE 價錢
à la carte 點菜 $ 30-60

■ OPENING HOURS 營業時間
11:00-23:00 (L.O.)

■ ANNUAL AND WEEKLY CLOSING 休息日期
Closed 6 days Lunar New Year
農曆新年休息 6 天

Siu Shun Village Cuisine (Kowloon Bay)
肇順名匯河鮮專門店 (九龍灣)

🍴   🍽32

Imitation bamboo and birdcage lampshades add to the somewhat eccentric decorative style of this restaurant that specialises in Shun Tak cuisine. It's in a shopping mall and is always crowded – so expect noise levels at the lively end of the scale. Customers come for various river fish dishes and specialities like stir-fried freshwater lobster with ginger and shallots, fresh prawns in XO sauce, and fish lips casserole.

這裡的著名菜式包括薑葱龍蝦球、XO醬炒花枝鮮蝦球、瓦罉煎焗魚咀，吸引很多本地食客到此品嘗順德菜及其河鮮菜式。餐廳位於商場內，經常座無虛席，店內鼎沸的人聲足以反映其熱鬧氣氛。仿竹及雀籠燈罩令這裡的裝潢風格更顯特色。

TEL. 2798 9738
7F, MegaBox, 38 Wang Chiu Road, Kowloon Bay
九龍灣宏照道 38號 MegaBox 7樓

■ PRICE 價錢
Lunch 午膳
à la carte 點菜 $ 100-300
Dinner 晚膳
à la carte 點菜 $ 150-300

■ OPENING HOURS 營業時間
Lunch 午膳   09:00-16:30 (L.O.)
Dinner 晚膳   18:00-23:30 (L.O.)

■ ANNUAL AND WEEKLY CLOSING 休息日期
Closed 3 days Lunar New Year
農曆新年休息 3 天

Snow Garden
雪園

🍴🍴 　　　　　　　🍱16 🍽

Established in 1992 at this sleek business address and known for its traditional Shanghainese cuisine, this is a restaurant that operates like clockwork and whose staff are warm and attentive. The long-standing chef's specialities are steamed herring and deep-fried chicken skin with four spices; braised sea cucumber with shrimp roe; and yellow fish with sweet and sour sauce. Dishes arrive carefully prepared and bursting with flavour.

餐廳於1992年於此商業區熱點開始營業，以精心烹調的上海菜馳名，人流絡繹不絕，員工態度親切熱誠。清蒸鰣魚、四寶片皮雞、蝦子大烏參及糖醋黃魚都是歷久不衰的廚師精選。每道菜式都經過精心製作，色香味俱全。

TEL. 2881 6837
2F, China Taiping Tower,
8 Sunning Road, Causeway Bay
銅鑼灣新寧道 8號中國太平大廈 2樓
www.snow-garden.com

■ PRICE 價錢
Lunch 午膳
set 套餐 $ 130
à la carte 點菜 $ 150-250
Dinner 晚膳
à la carte 點菜 $ 250-700

■ OPENING HOURS 營業時間
Lunch 午膳　11:30-14:45 (L.O.)
Dinner 晚膳　18:00-22:45 (L.O.)

■ ANNUAL AND WEEKLY CLOSING 休息日期
Closed 3 days Lunar New Year
農曆新年休息 3 天

Sorabol (Causeway Bay)
新羅寶 (銅鑼灣)

🍴🍴   🛋40   ◑🍴

This branch of the successful restaurant group opened here in 2011. Its aesthetic is based on a traditional and elegant Korean house and uses lotus flower patterned doors, wood carvings and brick walls to good effect. The authentic cuisine is prepared using quality ingredients and includes a special menu of Jeonju dishes, which is the owner's homeland. Beef is the popular choice for barbecuing but do also try the duck.

這個韓國餐廳集團於2011年在銅鑼灣開設此分店，店內裝潢取材自傳統韓國的精緻房舍，採用蓮花圖案的門、木雕和磚牆以塑造最佳的效果。食店選用優質食材製作正宗韓式料理。牛肉是韓式燒烤的最佳選擇，鴨肉及時令特別餐單也值得一試。

TEL. 2881 6823
Shop B, 18F, Lee Theatre Plaza,
99 Percival Street, Causeway Bay
銅鑼灣波斯富街 99號利舞臺廣場 18樓 B號舖
www.sorabol.com.hk

■ PRICE 價錢
Lunch 午膳
set 套餐 $ 72-98
à la carte 點菜 $ 200-650
Dinner 晚膳
à la carte 點菜 $ 200-650

■ OPENING HOURS 營業時間
Lunch 午膳   11:30-14:30 (L.O.)
Dinner 晚膳   17:30-22:30 (L.O.)

■ ANNUAL AND WEEKLY CLOSING 休息日期
Closed Lunar New Year 年初一休息

Spoon by Alain Ducasse

 ✤ 𝄖 🍽14 🚇 ☎🍴 ᯿

A ceiling lined, appropriately enough, with spoons; an impressive glass cellar holding around 600 wines; stylish surroundings; and fantastic views – all characteristics of this fashionable member of Alain Ducasse's global empire. The carefully prepared French cuisine is the ideal match for this environment, with such dishes as spit-roasted Bresse chicken with Swiss chard gratin, and baba with the Armagnac of your choice.

美妙景觀、時尚雅座、排列着匙羹的天花板,加上擺放了接近六百瓶佳釀令人嘆為觀止的玻璃酒櫃,打造成名廚艾倫杜卡斯美食王國的香港分部,為潮流時尚之選。推薦菜式包括布雷斯雞配奶油焗瑞士甜菜及法式自蘭地蛋糕。

TEL. 2313 2256
GF, Intercontinental Hotel,
18 Salisbury Road, Tsim Sha Tsui
尖沙咀梳士巴利道 18號洲際酒店地下
www.hongkong-ic.intercontinental.com

■ PRICE 價錢
Sunday lunch 週日午膳
set 套餐 $ 888
à la carte 點菜 $ 1,000-1,700
Dinner 晚膳
set 套餐 $ 1,688
à la carte 點菜 $ 1,000-1,700

■ OPENING HOURS 營業時間
Sunday lunch 週日午膳　12:00-14:30
Dinner 晚膳　18:00-23:00 (L.O.)

■ ANNUAL AND WEEKLY CLOSING 休息日期
Closed Tuesday to Saturday lunch and
Monday 週二至週六午膳及週一休息

Cantonese 粵菜 MAP 地圖 18/B-3

Spring Moon
嘉麟樓

  48

An integral part of The Peninsula hotel is this elegant Cantonese restaurant. Admire the tropical hardwood or the bamboo flower arrangements while sipping tea at the tea bar and then dine in the restaurant or on the more intimate mezzanine floor. Dishes are authentic and flavoursome – the lunch dim sum is very popular. There are 25 different teas available; feel free to ask questions as staff are regularly sent to China for in-depth training.

嘉麟樓是半島酒店不可或缺的部分，裝潢優雅豪華。食客可以邊在茶檔茗茶，邊欣賞餐廳內的熱帶硬木和竹花。你可以選擇在餐廳或較隱蔽的私家房內用餐，完善的服務配合美味的傳統菜餚。午餐時段的點心很受歡迎。店內提供二十五種茶，你可以隨意向侍應發問茗茶知識。

TEL. 2696 6760
1F, The Peninsula Hotel, Salisbury Road, Tsim Sha Tsui
尖沙咀梳士巴利道半島酒店 1 樓
www.peninsula.com

SPECIALITIES TO PRE-ORDER 預訂食物
Hangzhou beggar's fortune chicken
杭州富貴雞

■ PRICE 價錢
Lunch 午膳
à la carte 點菜 $ 300-500
Dinner 晚膳
à la carte 點菜 $ 500-1,500

■ OPENING HOURS 營業時間
Lunch 午膳　11:30-14:30 (L.O.)
Dinner 晚膳　18:00-22:30 (L.O.)

Summer Palace
夏宮

They've created a charming environment here in this 5th floor room, with its crystal chandeliers, traditional Chinese screens and well-spaced tables. The Cantonese menu features all the true classics and the kitchen uses carefully chosen ingredients to prepare dishes free from over-elaboration; double boiled soups are a speciality. To drink, there's a varied selection of wines by the glass, assorted Chinese liquors and exquisite teas.

營運者在這位於五樓的空間營造了迷人的環境，配上水晶吊燈、傳統中國屏風及悉心編排的餐桌擺放，為食客帶來舒適的用膳空間。粵菜菜譜羅列各款傳統名菜，廚師精心挑選食材，烹調時井井有條，毫不過火，燉湯更是其專長。

TEL. 2820 8553
5F, Island Shangri-La Hotel, Pacific Place,
Supreme Court Road, Admiralty
金鐘法院道太古廣場港島香格里拉酒店 5樓
www.shangri-la.com

SPECIALITIES TO PRE-ORDER 預訂食物
Double-boiled soups 燉 湯 /Eight treasure duck 夏 宮 八 寶 鴨 /Beggar's chicken 富貴雞

■ PRICE 價錢
Lunch 午膳
à la carte 點菜 $350-1,500
Dinner 晚膳
à la carte 點菜 $350-1,500

■ OPENING HOURS 營業時間
Lunch 午膳   11:30-14:30 (L.O.)
Dinner 晚膳   18:30-22:30 (L.O.)

Sun Tung Lok (Central)
新同樂 (中環)

XXX　　　　　　　　　　　　　　　　　　　　　　🛋36　📞🍽

The original Sun Tung Lok opened in 1969 in Causeway Bay; now fans of its Cantonese cuisine can choose between the branch in Tsim Sha Tsui and this newer one in Central. It's just as comfortable and well run and its private room is ideal for a business meal. Those who come for lunch are rewarded with exquisite handmade dim sum. The signature dishes are roast suckling pig with minced shrimp, and braised prime rib of beef with house gravy.

自1969年創業至今，新同樂的高級粵菜一直備受食客推崇，繼尖沙咀店後，於中環開設了分店。手工精細的點心是午飯聚餐必不能少的美食，馳名菜式如百花脆皮乳豬件和燒汁乾焗牛肋骨，令人回味無窮。裝潢精緻的廂房適合商務宴會。

TEL. 2807 2290
13 Stanley Street, Central
中環士丹利街13號
www.suntunglok.com.hk

■ PRICE 價錢
Lunch 午膳
set 套餐 $ 338
à la carte 點菜 $ 200-5,000
Dinner 晚膳
set 套餐 $ 1,280
à la carte 點菜 $ 400-5,000

■ OPENING HOURS 營業時間
Lunch 午膳　11:00-15:00 (L.O.)
Dinner 晚膳　18:00-22:00 (L.O.)

Sun Tung Lok (Tsim Sha Tsui)
新同樂 (尖沙咀)

☺☺

🍴🍴🍴

🍽48 🕐🍴

After 40 years in Happy Valley, Sun Tung Lok is now comfortably ensconced on the fourth floor of the Miramar shopping centre. A contemporary colour palette of grey, brown and beige is used to good effect in this stylish restaurant; ask for one of the three booths for extra privacy. The majority of the menu is Cantonese and dishes include rib of beef with house gravy, stuffed crab shell, and roast suckling pig; the abalone is a must.

在跑馬地駐紮四十年後，新同樂現在於美麗華商場4樓繼續營業。充滿時代感的灰色、咖啡色與米色的巧妙配搭讓店子看起來較摩登。店內設有三個廂座，以滿足需要私人空間的客人。八成菜式是粵菜，包括燒汁乾爝牛肋骨、鮮蘑菇焗釀蟹蓋及燒乳豬件。這裡的鮑魚是必試之選。

TEL. 2152 1417
4F, Miramar Shopping Centre,
132 Nathan Road, Tsim Sha Tsui
尖沙咀彌敦道 132號美麗華商場 4樓
www.suntunglok.com.hk

■ PRICE 價錢
Lunch 午膳
set 套餐 $ 298-428
à la carte 點菜 $ 300-500
Dinner 晚膳
à la carte 點菜 $ 500-800

■ OPENING HOURS 營業時間
Lunch 午膳　11:30-15:00 (L.O.)
Dinner 晚膳　18:00-22:30 (L.O.)

Cantonese Roast Meats 燒味

Sun Yuen Hing Kee
新園興記

Located next to Sheung Wan market, this traditionally styled, simple but well maintained barbecue shop has been run by the same family since the mid-1970s. Over the years they've built up an appreciative following so the small place fills quickly. The appetising looking suckling pigs are not the only draw: roast pork, duck and pigeon all have their followers, as do the soft-boiled chicken, the homemade sausages and the preserved meats.

位於上環街市旁邊，這間格調傳統簡單的燒味店自70年代中一直由同一家族經營。多年來，累積了不少忠實顧客，小小的地方往往座無虛席。這裡受歡迎的不僅是掛在廚房旁邊，賣相令人垂涎欲滴的乳豬，燒肉、烤鴨和乳鴿都各有忠實擁躉。白切雞、臘腸及臘肉亦十分吸引。

TEL. 2541 2207
327-329 Queen's Road Central,
Sheung Wan
上環皇后大道中 327-329號

■ PRICE 價錢
Dinner 晚膳
à la carte 點菜 $ 40-150

■ OPENING HOURS 營業時間
08:00-19:45 (L.O.)

■ ANNUAL AND WEEKLY CLOSING 休息日期
Closed 3 days Lunar New Year
農曆新年休息 3 天

HONG KONG 香港

Sushi Ginza Iwa

✺

🍴 🛏8 🕐🍴

There are views of Central through the small windows and the room is authentically uncluttered and calm, but frankly everyone's here for just one thing – sushi. To ensure each customer receives the same experience, the selection process for the ingredients is undertaken with great rigour, with all fish and seafood flown in daily from Tsukiji. And just like the original shop in Tokyo's Ginza district, the sushi is presented on a silver plate.

到達29樓後，要先經過一道木樓梯才能進到這間以日式原木裝潢、非常傳統的餐廳。壽司桌是餐廳焦點。與銀座總店一脈相承的銀色壽司盛器，給你一絲熟悉感覺。店東嚴格限定海產種類和來源地，鮮魚和海產每天由築地運送抵港，確保食客享受到跟總店一樣的味道。

TEL. 2619 0199
30F, Asia Pacific Centre,
8 Wyndham Street, Central
中環雲咸街 8號亞洲太平洋中心 30樓

■ PRICE 價錢
Lunch 午膳
set 套餐 $ 480-1,350
Dinner 晚膳
set 套餐 $ 1,650-3,000

■ OPENING HOURS 營業時間
Lunch 午膳　12:00-14:30 (L.O.)
Dinner 晚膳　18:30-22:30 (L.O.)

An important business lunch? The symbol ⇔ indicates restaurants with private rooms.

需要一個合適的地點享用商務午餐？可從注有這個 ⇔ 標誌的餐廳中選一間有私人廂房又合你心意的餐館。

The symbol 🍷 denotes a particularly interesting wine list.

🍷 這個標誌表示該餐廳提供一系列優質餐酒。

Sushi Mori Tomoaki NEW

🍴 　　　　　　　　🍽6 🚇 ☎🍴

The daily delivery of seafood at this sushi restaurant comes from Kyushu and Hokkaido. The rice is seasoned with red vinegar and each sushi has its own unique seasoning – for example nodoguro comes with yuzu pepper, and engawa with garlic soy sauce. For dinner it's best to go for the omakase which includes sashimi and assorted small dishes before the nigiri. At lunch there are set menus offering other Japanese cuisines such a sukiyaki and tempura.

這家餐廳貫通兩個單位，兩個壽司吧相面對，環境雅淨。中日混血的主廚年紀輕輕卻具多年製作傳統壽司經驗，且喜愛鑽研烹調技法，其壽司以每日由日本運到之新鮮食材，加上混和紅醋的米飯製成。午市提供逾十款定食；晚上可嘗嘗由十六道不同款壽司和魚生組合而成，梅花間竹式上菜的廚師套餐。

TEL. 2979 5877
GF, 9-23 Shell Street, Tin Hou
天后蜆殼街 9-23號地下
www.sushimoritomoaki.com.hk

■ PRICE 價錢
Lunch 午膳
set 套餐 $ 250-900
Dinner 晚膳
set 套餐 $ 1,500-2,000

■ OPENING HOURS 營業時間
Lunch 午膳　12:00-14:00 (L.O.)
Dinner 晚膳　18:30-22:30 (L.O.)

■ ANNUAL AND WEEKLY CLOSING 休息日期
Closed Mid-August, late December
to early January and Sunday
八月中、十二月尾至一月初及週日休息

HONG KONG 香港

Sushi Rozan
鮨魯山

With just 12 seats at its L-shaped counter, this small and elegant Japanese restaurant certainly looks authentic. Only a daily-changing omakase menu is served, which means the chef will decide everything for you, albeit after talking to you about preferences. He then prepares all the dishes in front of you, using top quality produce flown in daily from Japan, such as golden-eye snapper, white sea urchin and Ohmi Wagyu.

這家優雅傳統的壽司店。小小的店內只有依附着壽司吧枱的十二個座位和一個卡座。這裡只供應廚師套餐，日籍廚師在客人面前炮製食物，餐單和份量會按客人的飲食習慣調整。頂級食材如金目鯛、近江和牛及白海膽等每天由日本即日空運到港。

TEL. 2574 1333
GF Oak Hill, 18 Wood Road, Wan Chai
灣仔活道18號萃峯地下
www.ginsai.com.hk

■ PRICE 價錢
Lunch 午膳
set 套餐 $ 580-1,380
Dinner 晚膳
set 套餐 $ 1,580-2,880

■ OPENING HOURS 營業時間
Lunch 午膳　12:00-14:30 (L.O.)
Dinner 晚膳　18:30-21:30 (L.O.)

■ ANNUAL AND WEEKLY CLOSING 休息日期
Closed 3 days Lunar New Year and Monday
農曆新年3天及週一休息

Sushi Shikon
志魂

✗

🍴6 ⛓ ☏🍴

The name may have changed from Sushi Yoshitake to Sushi Shikon but the owner's aim remains the same: he wants his Hong Kong customers to enjoy the same superb quality sushi that he serves in his Tokyo restaurant – thus, the fish arrives daily from Tsukiji market and the rice comes from Niigata. The secret is in the vinegar which "creates harmony between the fish and the rice": it is made from two kinds of sake sediment and aged for four years.

Sushi Yoshitake易名Sushi Shikon後，提供優質食物的宗旨仍然不變，繼續堅持每天由築地漁市場運來鮮魚及選用由新潟運來頂級日本米。這兒的壽司烹調秘訣是以兩種成熟度達四年的清酒糟製造的醋入饌，鮮魚的鮮與米飯的醋香配搭出完美的味道。

TEL. 2643 6800
The Mercer Hotel, 29 Jervois Street,
Sheung Wan
上環蘇杭街29號尚圜酒店

■ PRICE 價錢
Dinner 晚膳
set 套餐 $ 3,500

■ OPENING HOURS 營業時間
Dinner 晚膳 18:00-20:00, 20:30-22:30

■ ANNUAL AND WEEKLY CLOSING 休息日期
Closed Sunday 週日休息

HONG KONG 香港

Sushi Ta-ke
竹 寿司

🍴   🚇10 🚆 🕐🍴

Sushi Ta-ke presents traditional Edomae sushi using the freshest ingredients. Along with sashimi, it also serves hot dishes like grilled swordfish and Wagyu beef – try too the Japanese pickle salad and boiled golden-eye snapper. The striking and artfully lit interior comes as no surprise when one considers the expertise of the three owners: one is an interior designer, one a lighting designer and the third a restaurateur.

竹寿司的室內設計突出且具藝術氣息，這跟三位東主的背景不無關係：一個室內設計師、一個燈光設計師，一個飲食業專家。餐廳以正宗傳統方式製作的壽司作賣點，魚生均每天由日本空運到港。除壽司外，還供應各款煮物和燒酒。可供選擇的清酒款色也很多。

TEL. 2577 0611
12F, Cubus, 1 Hoi Ping Road,
Causeway Bay
銅鑼灣開平道 1號 Cubus12樓
www.sushitake.com.hk

■ PRICE 價錢
Lunch 午膳
set 套餐 $ 238-1,500
à la carte 點菜 $ 300-1,800

Dinner 晚膳
set 套餐 $ 1,200-1,500
à la carte 點菜 $ 300-1,800

■ OPENING HOURS 營業時間
Lunch 午膳   12:00-15:00 L.O. 14:30
Dinner 晚膳   18:30-00:00 L.O.22:30

■ ANNUAL AND WEEKLY CLOSING 休息日期
Closed Lunar New Year 年初一休息

Ta Vie NEW
旅

🍴6 🕐⚟

After three years at Ryu Gin, Chef Sato Hideaki now displays his skills on the 2nd floor of the Pottinger Hotel. In an elegantly dressed restaurant he serves his own unique style of cuisine which fuses together Japanese and French techniques while using Asian ingredients. He serves an 8 course tasting menu, with most of the seafood coming directly from Tokyo. Along with French wine, Japanese wine and sake are three specially selected teas.

在龍吟工作數年後，日籍大廚佐藤秀明在中環石板街酒店開店再度獻藝，以其純熟的法日混合烹調技術，將從日本及其他亞洲地區精心搜購的食材炮製成佳餚；一些被濫用的熱門食材一定不會出現在套餐之中，保證給你一個不平凡的美食之旅。除葡萄酒及清酒外，店方更精選了三款清茶以供佐餐。

TEL. 2668 6488
2F, The Pottinger Hotel,
74 Queen's Road Central
中環皇后大道中 74號石板街酒店 2樓

■ PRICE 價錢
Dinner 晚膳
set 套餐 $ 1,880

■ OPENING HOURS 營業時間
Dinner 晚膳　18:00-21:30 (L.O.)

■ ANNUAL AND WEEKLY CLOSING 休息日期
Closed Sunday 週日休息

Tai Wing Wah
大榮華

🍴　　　　　　　　　　　　　　　　　　🍽20

Anyone travelling all the way to Yuen Long (in the north of New Territories) can seek reward for doing so by visiting this restaurant. It's above its own cake shop, which specialises in moon cakes and Chinese sausages, and serves dim sum and 'Walled Village' cuisine, alongside classic Cantonese dishes. Try the roast duck with bean paste and coriander; claypot rice with lard and premium soy sauce; and, above all, the steamed sponge cake.

很多人長途跋涉來到元朗，只有一個原因：光顧大榮華。此酒家除了供應點心外，還提供近百款圍村小菜及經典粵式名菜。香茜燒米鴨及砵仔豬油頭抽撈飯絕對不容錯過，當然少不了奶黃馬拉糕。入口旁的餅店，專門售賣月餅和臘腸，也是大榮華出品的著名食品。

TEL. 2476 9888
2F, 2-6 On Ning Road, Yuen Long
元朗安寧路 2-6號 2樓

■ PRICE 價錢
à la carte 點菜 $80-300

■ OPENING HOURS 營業時間
06:30-23:30 (L.O.)

Cantonese 粵菜

Cantonese 粵菜　　　　　　　　　　　　　　　　MAP 地圖　30/B-2

Tai Woo (Causeway Bay)
太湖海鮮城 (銅鑼灣)

🍴🍴　　　　　　　　　　　　　　　　　　　🛏24　◎🍴

One of the district's most famous names, Tai Woo moved to these newer, more comfortable surroundings in 2011 and, while the restaurant may be smaller than before, business is better than ever, with over 1,000 customers served every day. What hasn't changed is the quality of the cooking: along with a large menu of Cantonese seafood dishes, such as crunchy shrimp ball and mini lobster casserole, are favourites like sesame chicken baked in salt.

於八十年代開業的太湖是區內馳名酒家，尤擅海鮮菜式，2011年才搬遷到更新更舒適的現址。多年來食物質素維持不變，生意昌旺每天服務逾千名食客，提供多款廣東菜式，招牌菜有芝麻鹽焗雞、奇脆明珠伴金龍及薑米鮮魚炒飯等。

TEL. 2893 0822
9F, Causeway Bay Plaza 2,
463-483 Lockhart Road, Causeway Bay
銅鑼灣駱克道 463-483號
銅鑼灣廣場第二期 9樓
www.taiwoorestaurant.com

■ PRICE 價錢
Lunch 午膳
à la carte 點菜 $ 100-600
Dinner 晚膳
à la carte 點菜 $ 200-600

■ OPENING HOURS 營業時間
10:30-02:30 (L.O.)

■ ANNUAL AND WEEKLY CLOSING 休息日期
Closed Lunar New Year 年初一休息

HONG KONG 香港

Takeya
竹家

The Japanese owner-chef was originally posted to Hong Kong as an engineer but, having settled here and married a local girl, he switched careers and together they opened this little yakitori shop in Hung Hom. Seating just 15, it's an intimate spot, made warmer with lots of bamboo. There's extensive choice, with seasonal specialities available. Try the special selections of Japanese wine or the high quality homemade umeshu.

日籍店主兼大廚在香港工作多年，其後與太太定居香港並展開新生活，一起經營這間以竹子為主題的串燒小店，小小的店子只有十五個座位卻予人親密溫暖的感覺。店內串燒種類繁多，時有特別食物推介。供應的日本酒較別的店子獨特，尤以自家浸製的梅酒更是不俗。

TEL. 2365 8878
Shop 1, On Wah Building,
31C1 Tak Man Street, Whampoa Estate,
Hung Hom
紅磡黃埔新村德民街 31C1 安華樓 1號舖

■ PRICE 價錢
Dinner 晚膳
à la carte 點菜 $150-400

■ OPENING HOURS 營業時間
Dinner 晚膳　18:00-22:30 (L.O.)

■ ANNUAL AND WEEKLY CLOSING 休息日期
Closed 14 days Lunar New Year and
Monday 農曆新年 14 天及週一休息

Cantonese 粵菜

T'ang Court

唐閣

🅿 ⏸24

Rich silks and contemporary art line the walls of the lavishly furnished main dining room, on the first floor above the hotel's grand lobby. There's also a dramatic staircase leading up to a second floor of tables and exclusive private dining rooms named after famous Tang Dynasty poets. The cooking displays considerable skill; try sautéed prawns with deep-fried taro puffs or crispy, salty chicken. Service is polished and well-structured.

位於酒店大堂樓上的主菜廳,以優質絲緞配合富時代氣息的牆身,裝潢豪華。一道華麗的樓梯連上二樓的餐桌,更設有以唐代著名詩人命名的貴賓廳。菜餚極具水準,荔茸寶盒或脆香芋茸伴蝦球、秘製鹽焗雞均不容錯過。服務也經過精心編排。

TEL. 2132 7898
1F, The Langham Hotel, 8 Peking Road,
Tsim Sha Tsui
尖沙咀北京道 8 號朗廷酒店 1 樓
www.hongkong.langhamhotels.com

SPECIALITIES TO PRE-ORDER 預訂食物
Baked Blue Point oysters with port wine
砵酒焗美國蠔

■ PRICE 價錢
Lunch 午膳
à la carte 點菜 $ 400-1,700
Dinner 晚膳
à la carte 點菜 $ 400-1,700

■ OPENING HOURS 營業時間
Lunch 午膳　12:00-15:00 L.O. 14:30
Dinner 晚膳　18:00-23:00 L.O. 22:30

HONG KONG 香港

Tasty (IFC)
正斗粥麵專家 (國際金融中心)

Over 1,000 customers a day, many of whom work in IFC, crowd into this Tasty, so be prepared to queue and share a table before tucking into the hallmark shrimp wonton or the much-loved beef and rice noodle stir fry. Also recommended from the vast choice is congee with prawns. The interior has been redecorated and is now more contemporary.

這裡每日有逾千名顧客，當中大部分在IFC工作，繁忙時間到訪，便要做好排隊和拼桌的準備。熱門食品包括招牌鮮蝦雲吞麵和極受歡迎的干炒牛河。此外，我們亦向你推介生猛大蝦粥。重新裝修後的餐室更見時尚華麗。

TEL. 2295 0101
Shop 3016, Podium Level 3, IFC Mall,
1 Harbour View Street, Central
中環港景街1號國際金融中心商場 3樓
3016號舖
www.tasty.com.hk

■ PRICE 價錢
à la carte 點菜 $ 90-200

■ OPENING HOURS 營業時間
11:00-22:45 (L.O.)

Tate

HONG KONG 香港

Vicky Lau is the young owner-chef of this contemporary yet also quite intimate restaurant. Her cooking is an eclectic mix of French and Japanese influences and each dish is beautifully presented – a reflection, perhaps, of her previous career as a graphic designer. Two set menus, which change seasonally, are offered; opt for the nine-courses.

年青的劉小姐是這家時尚又親切的餐廳的大廚兼東主。她的烹調風格融合了法國和日本特色，每道菜式都設計得十分精美，與她是前平面設計師的身份不無關係。此店每晚只供應兩款套餐，共計九道菜，並以優質時令食材入饌，因此會隨季節更換餐單。

TEL. 2555 2172
59 Elgin Street, Central
中環伊利近街 59號

■ PRICE 價錢
Dinner 晚膳
set 套餐 $ 980-1,280

■ OPENING HOURS 營業時間
Dinner 晚膳 18:30-22:00 (L.O.)

■ ANNUAL AND WEEKLY CLOSING 休息日期
Closed Sunday 週日休息

Thai Chiu (Sham Shui Po)
泰潮 (深水埗)

Hainanese chicken; tom yum kung with seafood; fried egg with herbs and the various different styles of curry are just some of the highlights from an extensive menu prepared by native Thai chefs at this simple little restaurant. It's made up of two modest dining rooms, both decorated in bright green and yellow, with plastic tables and small stools. Simple it may be, but the food is good and the prices are competitive.

海南雞、冬蔭功海鮮湯、香草煎蛋及一系列咖喱只是種類繁多的菜單的一部分，全店食物一律由這家簡樸小餐廳的泰籍廚師主理，味道美味，價錢相宜。餐廳由兩個餐室組成，兩間房都以亮綠及黃色裝潢，配以膠桌和小板凳，感覺樸實自然。

TEL. 2314 3333
101-103 Fuk Wing Street, Sham Shui Po
深水埗福榮街 101-103號

■ PRICE 價錢
set 套餐 $ 40-60
à la carte 點菜 $ 60-150

■ OPENING HOURS 營業時間
11:30-23:00 (L.O.)

■ ANNUAL AND WEEKLY CLOSING 休息日期
Closed 3 days Lunar New Year
農曆新年休息 3 天

Cantonese 粵菜

MAP 地圖　26/B-1

The Boss
波士廳

🍴🍴　　　　　　　　　　　　　　🍽14　☎🍴

HONG KONG 香港

The Boss may operate out of a basement location but enthusiastic lighting and a cool colour palette keep things feeling bright and fresh. Top quality Cantonese cooking is the attraction here; the bird's nest with abalone is a very popular dish and seafood lovers will appreciate that they can have their favourite fish cooked the way they like. Try the more innovative dishes like pan-fried Kobe beef and sautéed prawn with wasabi.

乍聽名字，誰會想到這是一家裝潢時尚的粵菜館?具時代感的冷色系與玻璃牆身和鏡子的配搭，非常明亮光潔。菜式方面，提供傳統高級粵菜，鮑魚燕窩是焦點所在。食客亦可從十種烹調方式中擇其一，讓廚師為你炮製心愛的游水海鮮。

TEL. 2155 0552
Basement, Peter Building,
58-62 Queen's Road, Central
皇后大道中 58-62號振邦大廈地庫

■ PRICE 價錢
Lunch 午膳
à la carte 點菜 $ 200-250
Dinner 晚膳
set 套餐 $ 680
à la carte 點菜 $ 300-900

■ OPENING HOURS 營業時間
Lunch 午膳　11:30-16:30 (L.O.)
Dinner 晚膳　17:30-22:30 (L.O.)

The Bostonian
美岸海鮮廳

XX　　　　　　　　　　　　　　　　　　　　　　

The self-assured Bostonian is a handsome and sophisticated restaurant offering all the things you'd expect from an American restaurant: plenty of hearty salads, lots of lobster, oysters, assorted seafood and, of course, a huge choice of prime beef from the grill. The set lunch with the seafood buffet is particularly popular, as is brunch on a Sunday. It's unlikely anyone has ever left here still feeling hungry.

美岸海鮮廳的高水準美食令人印象深刻，店內供應的菜式完全符合你對美式餐廳的期望：豐富的沙律和大量龍蝦、蠔及各類海鮮，種類多樣的特級烤牛肉當然不會或缺。在這裡進餐，沒人會空肚而回。這裡的半自助海鮮午市套餐及週日早午合餐非常受食客歡迎。

TEL. 2132 7898
BF, The Langham Hotel, 8 Peking Road,
Tsim Sha Tsui
尖沙咀北京道 8號朗廷酒店地庫
www.hongkong.langhamhotels.com

■ PRICE 價錢
Lunch 午膳
set 套餐 $ 378
à la carte 點菜 $ 400-1,000
Dinner 晚膳
à la carte 點菜 $ 400-1,000

■ OPENING HOURS 營業時間
Lunch 午膳　12:00-14:30 (L.O.)
Dinner 晚膳　18:30-23:00 (L.O.)

The Chairman
大班樓

☖20 ◷🍴

The Chairman looks to small suppliers and local fishermen for its ingredients and much of the produce used is also organic. Showing respect for the provenance of ingredients, and using them in homemade sauces and flavoursome dishes such as steamed crab with aged Shaoxing, crispy chicken stuffed with shrimp paste and almond sweet soup, has attracted a loyal following. The restaurant is divided into four different sections and service is pleasant and reassuringly experienced.

大班樓的食材來自小型供應商和本地漁民，大部分都是有機材料，且將精挑細選的材料用來製作醬料和烹調美味菜式，如雞油花雕蒸大花蟹、香煎百花雞件配魚露、生磨杏仁菜等，吸引不少忠實擁躉。餐廳分成四個不同用餐區，服務令人賓至如歸。

TEL. 2555 2202
18 Kau U Fong, Central
中環九如坊 18號
www.thechairmangroup.com

■ PRICE 價錢
Lunch 午膳
set 套餐 $ 198-218
à la carte 點菜 $ 500-800
Dinner 晚膳
à la carte 點菜 $ 500-800

■ OPENING HOURS 營業時間
Lunch 午膳　12:00-14:00 (L.O.)
Dinner 晚膳　18:00-22:00 (L.O.)

■ ANNUAL AND WEEKLY CLOSING 休息日期
Closed 3 days Lunar New Year
農曆新年休息 3 天

The Continental NEW

HONG KONG 香港

You feel you're in a grand European café, albeit one with 21st century additions – it's bright, comfortable and chic. Under the management of the Swire Group and British chef Rowley Leigh, it is open for breakfast, lunch, afternoon tea and dinner and the menu's an intriguing mix of British and French cuisine, with a little Italian in there too. Try Dingley Dell pork chops with Swiss chard, veal kidneys with mustard sauce, and chocolate soufflé.

餐廳由太古集團及英籍廚師Rowley Leigh共同營運。波浪型天花、琉璃球吊燈、綠色軟座椅、栗子色木地板，令人猶如置身於一間既時尚且貴氣的傳統歐洲咖啡館中。這兒供應的菜式混合了英、法、意三國的元素，招牌菜包括瑞士甜菜菜Dingley Dell走地豬扒、朱古力梳乎厘及雞肉羊奶芝士慕絲。

TEL. 2704 5211
Shop 6, 4F, Pacific Place, 88 Queensway,
Admiralty
金鐘道 88號太古廣場 4樓 406室
www.thecontinentalhongkong.com

■ PRICE 價錢
Lunch 午膳
set 套餐 $ 265
à la carte 點菜 $ 290-850
Dinner 晚膳
à la carte 點菜 $ 290-850

■ OPENING HOURS 營業時間
Lunch 午膳　12:00-14:30 (L.O.)
Dinner 晚膳　18:00-22:30 (L.O.)

The Pawn　NEW

　　　　　　　　　　　　　　　🚇 ⭘ 10

The building, which dates from the late C19 and was used as a pawn shop, is a must-see: soak up the Wan Chai atmosphere from the 1st floor bar before heading up to the restaurant which is split between a number of rooms blending modern design with a Chinese period feel. The modern British cooking uses herbs grown on the roof; expect the likes of fish pie, roast cod with celeriac, and dishes to share like braised short rib and Baked Alaska.

餐廳在一幢建於19世紀晚期的建築物內，室內保留了部分古舊裝飾。一樓名為植物園，是酒吧和休憩處；二樓是餐室，有數間小廂房及可欣賞舊區景致的露台；頂樓天台稱為農莊，種植了許多花卉和烹調用的香草。餐廳主要供應時尚英國菜如烤鱈魚焦糖洋蔥及火焰雪山等均值得一試。

TEL. 2866 3444
2F, 62 Johnston Road, Wan Chai
灣仔莊士敦道 62號 2樓
www.thepawn.com.hk

■ PRICE 價錢
Lunch 午膳
set 套餐 $ 220
à la carte 點菜 $ 370-950
Dinner 晚膳
à la carte 點菜 $ 370-950

■ OPENING HOURS 營業時間
Lunch 午膳　12:00-14:30 (L.O.)
Dinner 晚膳　18:00-22:30 (L.O.)

The Square
翠玉軒

XXX   ☐48 ☏�ℙ

To retain the food's natural flavour, the chef insists on using fresh, seasonal produce – he also cooks in a healthy way. Delicacies such as poached spotted garoupa in soya milk broth, and crispy fried boneless chicken stuffed with minced prawn purée are worth a try. Climbing the small staircase up to The Square always adds to the sense of anticipation and this is all the greater these days as the last makeover left the room looking very handsome.

每次踏上往翠玉軒的梯級，內心總會惦念着其美味佳餚和貼心服務，不期然便加快了步伐。這兒的粵菜烹調甚具心思。大廚選用當造食材，加上細膩健康的烹調方式，保留並特出了食材原味。美食包括鮮豆漿浸海星石斑及脆皮江南百花雞等。

TEL. 2525 1163
Shop 401, 4F, Exchange Square Podium, Central
中環交易廣場平臺 4樓 401號舖
www.maxims.com.hk

■ PRICE 價錢
Lunch 午膳
set 套餐 $ 228
à la carte 點菜 $ 250-300
Dinner 晚膳
à la carte 點菜 $ 300-800

■ OPENING HOURS 營業時間
Lunch 午膳   11:00-14:30 (L.O.)
Dinner 晚膳   18:00-22:30 (L.O.)

The Steak House Wine bar + grill

One of the most sophisticated grill rooms in town comes with its own colourful wine bar and an impressive wine list – it's 70% American and includes an impressive number of top Californian wines. The ingredients used here are unimpeachable: beef sourced from Australia, the U.S. and Canada is supplemented by great seafood. You even get to choose your knife from 10 different models. Service is professional but also has personality.

作為城中最著名的扒房之一，它擁有出色的酒吧及令人眼花繚亂的餐酒名單，當中70%產自美國，更包括了許多頂級加州葡萄酒。這裡採用的全是一流食材：來自澳洲、美國與日本的牛肉，配合鮮美的海鮮。你還可以從十種餐刀中挑選最心儀的款式作餐具！服務專業友善。

TEL. 2313 2405
LF, Intercontinental Hotel,
18 Salisbury Road, Tsim Sha Tsui
尖沙咀梳士巴利道18號洲際酒店地庫1樓

■ PRICE 價錢
Weekends lunch 週末午膳
set 套餐 $ 698-898
Dinner 晚膳
à la carte 點菜 $1,000-2,500

■ OPENING HOURS 營業時間
Weekends lunch 週末午膳　12:00-14:30 (L.O.)
Dinner 晚膳　18:00-23:00 (L.O.)

The Swiss Chalet
瑞士餐廳

When considering where to eat in Hong Kong, one's thoughts wouldn't necessarily include a Swiss restaurant but step inside and you'll be instantly transported 6,000 miles to an Alpine chalet full of conviviality. The Swiss chef concentrates on the familiar so along with the hearty meat dishes is the famous cheese fondue, made with five different types of cheese together with kirsch. Cheeses are a big deal here, with over 20 varieties on offer.

在香港，可選擇的瑞士餐廳不多，位於赫德道的這家卻值得推介。木傢俱、小窗戶和別的裝飾物，予人置身瑞士小木屋之感。店東兼主廚將家鄉正宗口味帶給食客。牛面沙律、炸牛仔肉和五種芝士混合櫻桃酒而成的芝士火鍋必不可錯過。超過二十種瑞士芝士及多款瑞士飲品和餐酒供選擇。

TEL. 2191 9197
12-14 Hart Avenue, Tsim Sha Tsui
尖沙咀赫德道 12-14號

■ PRICE 價錢
Lunch 午膳
set 套餐 $ 210
à la carte 點菜 $ 250-650
Dinner 晚膳
set 套餐 $ 480
à la carte 點菜 $ 250-650

■ OPENING HOURS 營業時間
Lunch 午膳　12:00-15:00 (L.O.)
Dinner 晚膳　18:00-22:45 (L.O.)

The Vietnam Woods
悅木

🍴   🛋8

The latest branch from Lo Chiu is perhaps the most comfortable, with its attractive façade, modern interior, cosy seating and chic, white private room. You'll find various Vietnamese dishes on the menu here, along with an extensive selection of appetisers. The cooking is traditional but the presentation modern; deluxe beef noodles in soup is a highlight. The popular set lunch menu ensures it's particularly busy at midday.

作為老趙集團的一員，餐廳外觀吸引，室內舒適的雅座和白色主調的獨立廂房，裝潢時尚。在菜單中會見到所有老趙招牌越南菜及多款餐前特色小吃。悅木牛肉粉是其中一道招牌菜，牛肉與上湯會分開奉上，盛載上湯的小鍋會放在小爐上加熱。午市套餐極受歡迎，因此午市經常座無虛席。

TEL. 2866 0013
Shop 1, York Place, 22 Johnston Road,
Wan Chai
灣仔莊士敦道 22號 York Place1號鋪

■ PRICE 價錢
Lunch 午膳
set 套餐 $ 98-118
à la carte 點菜 $ 90-205
Dinner 晚膳
set 套餐 $ 120-200
à la carte 點菜 $ 90-205

■ OPENING HOURS 營業時間
Lunch 午膳 12:00-15:00 (L.O.)
Dinner 晚膳 18:00-22:30 (L.O.)
Weekends 週末 12:00-22:30 (L.O.)

■ ANNUAL AND WEEKLY CLOSING 休息日期
Closed 3 days Lunar New Year
農曆新年休息 3 天

Tim Ho Wan (North Point)
添好運 (北角)

The residents of North Point appear mighty glad that Tim Ho Wan finally opened a branch on Hong Kong Island. The soberly furnished dining room is always packed and at peak hours there'll even be a queue outside. The atmosphere is typical of a local tea house and hums with general contentment. There are over twenty different dim sum choices, along with a few desserts, and the menu changes each month.

添好運自從在港島區開設分店以來，一直深受北角區街坊喜愛；裝修雖簡約但客源不絕，每逢繁忙時段更會大排長龍；店內氣氛與一般本地茶樓無異，熱鬧而略嫌擠逼。餐牌上雖只列有二十多款點心及數款甜品，但餐單上的食物款式會每月更新一次。

TEL. 2979 5608
2-8 Wharf Road, North Point
北角和富道 2-8號

■ PRICE 價錢
à la carte 點菜 $30-50

■ OPENING HOURS 營業時間
10:00-21:30 (L.O.)

■ ANNUAL AND WEEKLY CLOSING 休息日期
Closed 3 days Lunar New Year
農曆新年休息 3 天

HONG KONG 香港

Tim Ho Wan (Sham Shui Po)
添好運 (深水埗)

⑤　♨24　🚫🍴

The second branch of Tim Ho Wan is able to accommodate a few more customers than the original and is located in a more residential area; but don't be surprised to find a queue of expectant diners outside here too. The 25 different dim sum choices are reasonably priced and carefully prepared. Highlights include steamed shrimp dumpling, baked bun with barbecue pork and steamed beef balls. There are four small private rooms on the first floor.

這家添好運的第二分店，座落於人口稠密的住宅區內，儘管能容納更多人客，但若看到店外等候入座的人龍，你不需要感到意外。供應二十五款由廚師巧手製作、價錢實惠的點心，不可不試的包括蝦餃、酥皮焗叉燒包和陳皮牛肉球。一樓設有四間小型貴賓房。

TEL. 2788 1226
9-11 Fuk Wing Street, Sham Shui Po
深水埗福榮街 9-11號

■ PRICE 價錢
à la carte 點菜 $30-50

■ OPENING HOURS 營業時間
08:00-21:30 (L.O.)

■ ANNUAL AND WEEKLY CLOSING 休息日期
Closed 3 days Lunar New Year
農曆新年休息 3 天

Tim Ho Wan (Tai Kwok Tsui)
添好運 (大角咀)

Mention dim sum and many people will instantly think of the bustling Tim Ho Wan shop in Mong Kok. Here, at their new place, the crowds still flock in but the place is more spacious and feels even bigger, thanks to the high ceilings and bright lights. The reason for its popularity is the twenty different kinds of traditional Cantonese dim sum – made by hand with fresh ingredients – and the reasonable prices charged.

想到添好運的美味點心時，便會想起旺角舊店的擁擠。新店位於大角咀一個大型屋苑內，比舊店寬敞，高樓底配搭白色主調的裝潢，舒適明淨。然而，主角還是那二十多款廣式點心。沒有花巧的外型、創新的配搭，有的是傳統手工藝加上新鮮食材，價廉味美，難怪經常座無虛席。

TEL. 2332 2896
Shop G, 72A-B, Olympian City2,
18 Hoi Ting Road, Tai Kwok Tsui
大角咀海庭道 18號奧海城 2期 G72A-B舖

■ PRICE 價錢
à la carte 點菜 $30-50

■ OPENING HOURS 營業時間
10:00-21:30 (L.O.)

■ ANNUAL AND WEEKLY CLOSING 休息日期
Closed 3 days Lunar New Year
農曆新年休息 3 天

Tim's Kitchen (Sheung Wan)
桃花源小廚 (上環)

XXX   ⬡26 ☎🍴

Success lead to Tim's Kitchen moving to these premises in 2010 – it's in the same area as before but, with two floors and a capacity of 100, is much larger; chef-owner Tim's son designed the colourful, modern room. Plenty of choice is offered, including popular specialities like Crystal prawn, pomelo skin and pork stomach, which showcase the kitchen's respect for the ingredients. There are now branches in Shanghai and Macau.

桃花源小廚遷至現址後，共有兩層，可容納一百人。店主兼廚師黎先生的兒子設計了色彩豐富兼時尚的房間。新店比舊店提供更多粵菜，當然，鎮店菜如玻璃蝦球、柚皮及豬肚仍然羅列在菜單上，每款食品都證明廚房對優質材料的高度重視。業務已擴展至澳門及上海。

TEL. 2543 5919
84-90 Bonham Strand, Sheung Wan
上環文咸東街 84-90號
www.timskitchen.com.hk

SPECIALITIES TO PRE-ORDER 預訂食物
Steamed whole fresh crab claw with winter melon 冬瓜蒸原隻鮮蟹鉗 / Deep-fried whole fresh crab claw with peppercorn salt 椒鹽炸原隻鮮蟹鉗

■ PRICE 價錢
Lunch 午膳
à la carte 點菜 $ 150-300
Dinner 晚膳
à la carte 點菜 $ 300-1,000

■ OPENING HOURS 營業時間
Lunch 午膳   11:30-14:30 (L.O.)
Dinner 晚膳   18:00-22:30 (L.O.)

■ ANNUAL AND WEEKLY CLOSING 休息日期
Closed 4 days Lunar New Year
農曆新年休息 4 天

Tin Lung Heen
天龍軒

⚜️⚜️

XXXXX   ♿ ⬅ 🥢 🍽️36 🍷 🎐

Occupying a large section of the 102nd floor of the Ritz-Carlton is this striking Cantonese restaurant, appropriately named 'Dragon in the sky'. Filling such a dramatic space could be daunting but the pleasant staff make it feel more intimate. The menu focuses on traditional, familiar dishes; the chefs, unlike in Tosca next door, are mere shadows glimpsed occasionally through the lattice screens. There are several charming private rooms.

位於香港麗思卡爾頓酒店102樓，這間極具氣派的粵菜餐館以氣勢十足的天龍命名。空間感之大幾乎讓人無所適從，但殷勤的服務人員讓你倍感親切。菜單着重傳統菜式。與相鄰的Tosca相反，你只能在屏風後隱約看見大廚的身影。另設有多個精緻的私人包廂。

TEL. 2263 2270
102F, The Ritz-Carlton Hotel,
1 Austin Road West, TST
尖沙咀柯士甸道西 1 號
麗思卡爾頓酒店 102 樓
www.ritzcarlton.com/hongkong

■ PRICE 價錢
Lunch 午膳
à la carte 點菜 $450-1,300
Dinner 晚膳
à la carte 點菜 $450-1,300

■ OPENING HOURS 營業時間
Lunch 午膳　12:00-14:30 (L.O.)
Dinner 晚膳　18:00-22:30 (L.O.)

Tosca

    🏻 ← 🍽 ⏲18 ☎🍴 🍇

It is not just the incomparable views from its lofty location within the Ritz-Carlton hotel that set Tosca apart - its striking interior, with its huge Murano glass chandelier and open kitchen, is as dramatic as any production of Puccini's opera. There's a pleasing southern Italian accent to the extensive menu; dishes to look out for include tagliolini with prawns and chilli, and mountain lamb chops with roast potatoes and black olives.

座落於麗思卡爾頓酒店高層位置，能俯瞰全景，但它的獨特之處是富麗堂皇的內部裝修、巨型慕拉諾玻璃吊燈和開放式廚房，加起來比普契尼的歌劇還要扣人心弦。豐富的菜單帶着讓人喜悅的南意情調。推介美食有香辣大蝦意粉及山羊扒伴焗薯黑橄欖。

TEL. 2263 2270
102F, The Ritz-Carlton Hotel,
1 Austin Road West, TST
尖沙咀柯士甸道西 1號麗思卡爾頓酒店 102樓
www.ritzcarlton.com/hongkong

■ PRICE 價錢
Lunch 午膳
à la carte 點菜 $ 1,000-1,500
Dinner 晚膳
set 套餐 $ 1,280-2,180
à la carte 點菜 $ 1,000-1,500

■ OPENING HOURS 營業時間
Lunch 午膳　12:00-14:30 (L.O.)
Dinner 晚膳　18:00-22:30 (L.O.)

Town NEW

🍴🍴   🛋8

Bryan Nagao, the chef-owner of this chic yet relaxed urban eatery, is a name familiar to Hong Kong food lovers. Here he has created a menu that reflects his international background by using Japanese and Hawaiian influences along with French and Italian flavours, in dishes like suckling pig with clams and miso broth, and black ink udon with prawns and scallops. Lunch is a simpler affair and includes an hors d'oeuvres buffet.

混凝土和紅磚牆、櫟木地板、藍或淺咖啡色靠背椅與面向繁忙街道的落地玻璃窗塑造出活潑、現代的感覺。主廚兼東主Bryan Nagao設計的菜單帶有日本、夏威夷、法國和意大利風格；其拿手菜包括西西里蝦配黑松露魚子醬薄肉片及自製墨汁烏冬配紫蘇葉西班牙大蝦帶子等。午餐供應較簡約的餐單和自助頭盆。

TEL. 2568 8708
10F, Cubus, 1 Hoi Ping Road,
Causeway Bay
銅鑼灣開平道 1號 Cubus10樓

■ PRICE 價錢
Lunch 午膳
set 套餐 $ 198-248
à la carte 點菜 $460-800
Dinner 晚膳
à la carte 點菜 $460-800

■ OPENING HOURS 營業時間
Lunch 午膳 12:00-14:30 (L.O.)
Dinner 晚膳 18:30-22:30 (L.O.)

Trusty Congee King (Wan Chai)
靠得住 (灣仔)

The owner, Mr Lam, opened his first shop after his friends were so impressed by his ability to throw together a quick congee meal that they suggested he should start selling it. His was purported to be the first congee shop in Hong Kong to use a fish soup base for congee. These days, his specialities are salted meat rice dumpling and poached fresh fish skin. With a name that includes the words 'trusty' and 'king', how can you go wrong?

靠得住的出品一如其名，從不令人失望。店主林先生的巧手粥品備受親友讚賞，因此在2000年他開辦了首間粥店，據說這是全港首家採用魚湯作粥底的粥店。其他招牌食品有鹹肉粽及皇牌魚皮。

TEL. 2882 3268
7 Heard Street, Wan Chai
灣仔克街 7號

■ PRICE 價錢
à la carte 點菜 $30-110

■ OPENING HOURS 營業時間
11:00-22:45 (L.O.)

■ ANNUAL AND WEEKLY CLOSING 休息日期
Closed 2 days Lunar New Year
農曆新年休息 2 天

Looking for a taste of local life? Check out our top street food picks.

到哪兒尋找本土特色小食？請翻閱本年度新增的街頭小吃推介。

Symbols shown in red indicate particularly charming establishments .

紅色標誌　　　　表示酒店和餐館在同級別的舒適程度中較優秀。

Tsim Chai Kee (Wellington Street)
沾仔記 (威靈頓街)

This highly regarded, simple noodle shop has been here since 1998 and is easy to spot – just look for the lunchtime queues. The staff are as bright as their aprons; the popular side booths are quickly snapped up; and the regulars know to eat outside peak times when the pace is less frenetic. The attraction is the handmade fish balls, the generously filled wontons and the beef; ordering a three topping noodle is the way to go.

享負盛名的沾仔記於1998年開業，裝修簡單但整潔舒適。侍應制服明亮潔淨，設有卡位卻經常滿座；熟客會在非繁忙時間光顧，因氣氛較悠閒。著名食品包括自製鮮鯪魚球、餡料豐富的招牌雲吞及鮮牛肉麵；你可以來一碗三拼湯麵，一次過品嘗以上三種美食。

TEL. 2850 6471
98 Wellington Street, Central
中環威靈頓街 98號

- PRICE 價錢
à la carte 點菜 $25-50

- OPENING HOURS 營業時間
09:00-22:00 (L.O.)

- ANNUAL AND WEEKLY CLOSING 休息日期
Closed 4 days Lunar New Year
農曆新年休息 4 天

HONG KONG 香港

Tsui Hang Village (Tsim Sha Tsui)
翠亨邨(尖沙咀)

XX   P ⇦60 ☺¶

Many in Tsim Sha Tsui will recognise the name, as Tsui Hang Village opened in this shopping mall in the 1970s, before moving upstairs in 2011 into more contemporary surroundings. The menu is largely traditional Cantonese, supplemented by the head chef's own creations. Through the large window watch the chefs prepare specialities like braised beef ribs, shredded chicken and honey-glazed barbecued pork – their best seller; the dim sum is also good.

尖沙咀坊眾大都會認識翠亨邨,因為它早在1970年代已經在這個購物商場開業。菜式以傳統粵菜為主,再加上一些大廚自家創作。透過大玻璃窗,你可以看到廚師烹調各式佳餚,如醬燒牛肋排、翠亨邨靚一雞及最暢銷的蜜汁叉燒;這兒的點心也非常出色。

TEL. 2376 2882
5F, Miramar Shopping Centre,
132 Nathan Road, Tsim Sha Tsui
尖沙咀彌敦道132號美麗華商場5樓
www.tsuihangvillage.hk

■ PRICE 價錢
Lunch 午膳
à la carte 點菜 $130-300
Dinner 晚膳
à la carte 點菜 $200-500

■ OPENING HOURS 營業時間
Lunch 午膳   11:30-14:45 (L.O.)
Dinner 晚膳   18:15-23:00 (L.O.)

Tulsi (North Point)
羅勒 (北角)

The baby sister to Tulsi in Quarry Bay is next to North Point MTR's Exit B4 and comes with tightly packed tables that ensure there's always a warm, convivial atmosphere. You'll find the aromas coming from the clean, compact kitchen will quickly stimulate your appetite. The colourful, tasty Indian specialities are made using quality ingredients; signature dishes are butter chicken using marinated and barbecued chicken, and rogan josh.

Tulsi在北角港鐵站附近開設了這家分店。小小的店子內，牆壁懸着油畫、天花上的吊燈帶有古典味，簡約的設計風格營造出和諧溫馨的氣氛。友善親切的服務和香氣四溢、令人垂涎的亞洲風味美食如牛油雞、印度烤雞和咖喱羊肉等，讓食客賓至如歸。

TEL. 2568 3806
Fairview Court, 5-13 Tsat Tze Mui Road,
North Point
北角七姊妹道 7號昌輝閣後座地下
www.tulsi.com.hk

■ PRICE 價錢
Lunch 午膳
à la carte 點菜 $ 200-250
Dinner 晚膳
à la carte 點菜 $ 200-250

■ OPENING HOURS 營業時間
Lunch 午膳　11:30-14:45 (L.O.)
Dinner 晚膳　18:00-23:00 (L.O.)

HONG KONG 香港

Tulsi (Quarry Bay)
羅勒 (鰂魚涌)

🍴   📞🍽

Those in Quarry Bay who are partial to Indian food have but one place to choose. Fortunately that place is Tulsi, a warm and cosy restaurant, opened in 2009, which also represents good value for money. The experienced chef looks to northern India for most of his influences and the specialities include Nawabi chicken and Jheenga Shola. The appealing set lunch explains the full house most weekdays.

鰂魚涌區的老饕想一嘗印度菜，大抵只有一個選擇，它就是2009年開業的 Tulsi，環境舒適親切而且價廉物美。經驗豐富的大廚尤其精於印度北部菜餚，特色菜包括印式帝皇雞和醉酒炭燒蝦。午餐廣受歡迎，平日午市大多數座無虛席。

TEL. 2561 2968
Shop 1, GF, Hoi Kwong Court,
13-15 Hoi Kwong Street, Quarry Bay
鰂魚涌海光街 13-15號海光苑地下 1號舖
www.tulsi.com.hk

■ PRICE 價錢
Lunch 午膳
set 套餐 $ 68
à la carte 點菜 $ 120-260
Dinner 晚膳
à la carte 點菜 $ 120-260

■ OPENING HOURS 營業時間
Lunch 午膳   11:00-14:30(L.O.)
Dinner 晚膳   18:00-22:30 (L.O.)

Tze Yuet Heen
紫粵軒

        ⊡16

HONG KONG 香港

The main restaurant of the Crowne Plaza Kowloon East hotel is this smart Cantonese restaurant. It uses a water theme as the inspiration behind its design and its painted screens and artwork are brought to life by judicious lighting. Over 100 Cantonese dishes are on offer, including plenty of vegetarian options and healthy delicacies, and preparation methods are largely traditional. The set menus are particularly appealing.

紫粵軒提供過百款依照傳統烹調方法炮製的廣東菜，還有一系列美味健康素菜。選擇午、晚市套餐，可一次過品嘗多款廚師推介。裝潢以流水作主題，融入中國傳統繪畫藝術：涓涓流水般的地氈、半透明水墨畫屏風和獨特的天花燈飾等，顯示出設計者的巧思。

TEL. 3983 0628
2F, Crowne Plaza Kowloon East,
3 Tong Tak Street, Tseung Kwan O
將軍澳唐德街 3號
香港九龍東皇冠假日酒店 2樓
www.crowneplaza.com

SPECIALITIES TO PRE-ORDER 預訂食物
Double boiled caterpillar fungus with sea
cucumber 冬蟲夏草燉燉參

■ PRICE 價錢
Lunch 午膳
set 套餐 $ 98
à la carte 點菜 $ 180-700
Dinner 晚膳
à la carte 點菜 $ 180-700

■ OPENING HOURS 營業時間
Lunch 午膳   11:30-14:30 (L.O.)
Dinner 晚膳   18:00-22:30 (L.O.)

Upper Modern Bistro

✗✗   ☎🍴

HONG KONG 香港

The owner-chef at this warm, bright and contemporary bistro is Philippe Orrico, who made his name at Hullett House – watch him and his hard-working brigade going about their business in the raised open kitchen. Their creativity is most evident in the starters and the small bites which come with touches of Asian influence; the main courses tend to be more traditionally French in their makeup. There's a great choice of over 30 French cheeses.

落地玻璃牆配以淡灰色裝潢，感覺舒適隨意。開放式廚房設在高了一級的位置，主廚就在當中發揮才華。簡單的菜單上，主菜較傳統，融入了東方色彩的前菜及佐酒小吃則較有創意，當中以偏向日本風味的小吃最為精彩。超過三十款法國芝士必能滿足喜歡芝士的你。

TEL. 2517 0977
6-14 Upper Station Street,
Sheung Wan
上環差館上街 6-14 號
www.upper-bistro.com

■ PRICE 價錢
Lunch 午膳
set 套餐 $ 228-368
à la carte 點菜 $ 460-800
Dinner 晚膳
à la carte 點菜 $ 460-800

■ OPENING HOURS 營業時間
12:00-22:30 (L.O.)
Weekends & Public Holidays
週末及公眾假期   11:00-23:00 (L.O.)

Japanese 日本菜

Wa-En NEW
和宴

XX   🍽20 ◐🍴

Its prime cuts of Wagyu beef from Saga and Kagoshima have made this Japanese barbecue and grill restaurant a popular place, especially with groups out for a fun night because customers can grill the meats themselves. The seafood and pork, which are also imported from Japan, are well worth trying too. Service is helpful and the extraction fan is reassuringly efficient!

和宴可能是最早在香港營業的日式烤肉店，吸引處在其高品質且經細心處理的食材和體貼的服務。你可從餐單選擇來自鹿兒島或佐賀等地的頂級和牛肉及多種日本海產與肉類，跟朋友圍爐燒烤自得其樂。餐廳還提供多款熱食。抽風設備良好，不必擔心油煙問題。

TEL. 3428 3345
12F, The Toy House, 100 Canton Road, Tsim Sha Tsui
尖沙咀廣東道 100 號彩星集團大廈 12 樓

■ PRICE 價錢
Lunch 午膳
set 套餐 $ 110-180
à la carte 點菜 $ 400-800
Dinner 晚膳
set 套餐 $ 430
à la carte 點菜 $ 400-800

■ OPENING HOURS 營業時間
Lunch 午膳   12:00-14:30 (L.O.)
Dinner 晚膳   18:00-22:30 (L.O.)

■ ANNUAL AND WEEKLY CLOSING 休息日期
Closed 2 days Lunar New Year
農曆新年休息 2 天

Wagyu Kaiseki Den

🍴🍴🍴   ♿ 🈂 🏮24 🚇 🕐🍴 🎎

Don't let the name confuse you - Wagyu beef is not the only ingredient. In fact, it's just one of numerous imported items that appear on the daily changing Kaiseki menu, where some modern touches sit alongside more traditional elements. Seasonality and freshness are fundamental to the passionate Japanese chef here; watch Hiroyuki Saotome and his team perform by reserving at the counter. Expect a comprehensive sake list too.

看店名便知頂級和牛是這兒的主角。主廚對食材要求嚴謹，只用時令和最新鮮的材料。每天更新的懷石餐單，除了和牛外，還包羅多種即日進口的新鮮食材，再以傳統與現代兼容的烹調方式炮製。店內提供的清酒從日本各地搜羅而得，選擇豐富。

TEL. 2851 2820
263 Hollywood Road, Sheung Wan
上環荷李活道 263號

■ PRICE 價錢
Dinner 晚膳
set 套餐 $ 1,980

■ OPENING HOURS 營業時間
Dinner 晚膳 19:00-21:30 (L.O.)

■ ANNUAL AND WEEKLY CLOSING 休息日期
Closed 3 days Lunar New Year and Sunday
農曆新年休息 3 天及週日休息

Wagyu Takumi

There's something appealing about a restaurant that's hidden away: this small, elegant Japanese restaurant is secreted behind wooden doors at the back of a skyscraper. Once you've found it you'll find yourself sitting at one of 12 counter seats arranged around an open kitchen. The Japanese chef uses high quality ingredients and mixes French and Japanese cooking styles to create a daily changing 9-course dinner menu, with Omi Wagyu the speciality.

兩道隱蔽卻又似曾相識的拉門，藏身其後的是這間優雅的小餐廳，全店只有圍着中央開放式廚房的十二個座位。日籍大廚融會法日兩國的烹調技巧和飲食傳統，配上頂級時令食材，炮製出九道菜的法日晚餐，當中的重點菜是炭燒近江和牛。晚餐菜單會每天更新。店內供應的清酒質素非常好。

TEL. 2574 1299
GF, Oak Hill, 16 Wood Road, Wan Chai
灣仔活道 16號萃峯地下
www.ginsai.com.hk

■ PRICE 價錢
Lunch 午膳
set 套餐 $ 988-1,380
Dinner 晚膳
set 套餐 $ 1,980

■ OPENING HOURS 營業時間
Lunch 午膳　12:00-14:30 (L.O.)
Dinner 晚膳　18:00-22:30 (L.O.)

■ ANNUAL AND WEEKLY CLOSING 休息日期
Closed 3 days Lunar New Year and Sunday
農曆新年休息 3 天及週日休息

HONG KONG 香港

Wang Fu (Central)
王府 (中環)

Wang Fu was one of the first shops to open on Wellington Street and its Pekingese dumplings are renowned. Over ten kinds of freshly hand-made dumplings with different fillings are on offer each day. Don't miss the green onion mutton dumpling or the vegetarian dumpling – the tomato and egg dumpling, which is only available after 2pm, is also good. As well as the dumplings and noodles, assorted hot Sichuan dishes are also offered.

王府是威靈頓街最早期開業的水餃店,其北京水餃遠近馳名,供應的餃子款色超過十種,每天均由人手新鮮包製,羊肉京葱餃和花素餃不可不試。除水餃麵食外,還供應多款京川熱食小菜。

TEL. 2121 8006
65 Wellington Street, Central
中環威靈頓街 65號

■ PRICE 價錢
à la carte 點菜 $ 40-100

■ OPENING HOURS 營業時間
11:00-22:00 (L.O.)

■ ANNUAL AND WEEKLY CLOSING 休息日期
Closed 4 days Lunar New Year
農曆新年休息 4 天

Whisk

  　　　　　 ♿ 🍽 🕛24 ☎🍴 🍇

Contemporary European cooking techniques and the finest seasonal ingredients from around the world are used here at Whisk to create satisfying dishes with appealing combinations of flavours. Try the tagliolini with Bretagne lobster or suckling pig with pickled vegetables. The restaurant has a relaxed yet comfortable feel; there are over 200 wines available and you can also have drinks on the adjoining terrace.

採用當代歐洲烹調技巧，融合全球時令精選食材的Whisk，創造出多款獨特菜式，為食客的味覺帶來新享受。推介菜式包括布列塔尼龍蝦意粉和烤乳豬配醃製蔬菜。此店提供超過二百款全球精選佳釀，愛酒之士可與良朋在此品酒談心，在露台享用另有一番風情!

TEL. 2315 5999
5F, The Mira Hotel, 118 Nathan Road, Tsim Sha Tsui
尖沙咀彌敦道 118號 The Mira 5樓
www.themirahotel.com

■ PRICE 價錢
Lunch 午膳
set 套餐 $ 318-368
à la carte 點菜 $ 900-1,200

Dinner 晚膳
set 套餐 $ 920-1,480
à la carte 點菜 $ 900-1,200

■ OPENING HOURS 營業時間
Lunch 午膳　12:00-14:30 (L.O.)
Dinner 晚膳　18:00-22:30 (L.O.)

■ ANNUAL AND WEEKLY CLOSING 休息日期
Closed Sunday dinner and Monday
週日晚膳及週一休息

Wing Lai Yuen
詠藜園

♿ **P** 🛇12 ✆🍴

The film business glitterati used to flock to the original shop in San Po Kong for the authentic Sichuan Dan Dan noodles. A decade ago the Yeung family moved it to its current address in Whampoa Garden, where the Dan Dan noodles are still the main attraction, although these days you can decide whether or not you want them spicy. Along with other Sichuan dishes are a few Shanghainese specialities too.

新蒲崗原舖吸引了無數影星名人，全為了一嘗正宗四川擔擔麵蜂擁而至。隨着社區的發展，楊氏家族決定把店子遷址到現在的黃埔花園。直至今日擔擔麵仍然是其主打麵食，不過，現在你還可以選擇辣或不辣的湯底。另外，店內同時供應多款川菜和上海美食。

TEL. 2320 6430
Shop 102-105, 1F, Whampoa Plaza,
Site 8, Hung Hom
紅磡黃埔花園第 8 期 1 樓 102-105號舖

■ PRICE 價錢
Lunch 午膳
à la carte 點菜 $ 100-150
Dinner 晚膳
à la carte 點菜 $ 100-150

■ OPENING HOURS 營業時間
Lunch 午膳　11:00-15:30 (L.O.)
Dinner 晚膳　18:00-22:30 (L.O.)

Wing Wah
永華雲吞麵家

This simple operation has been maintaining high standards for well over 50 years now, the secret being that they do everything from scratch upstairs, making their noodles by hand using bamboo. So proud are they of their skills that there's a photographic display of their craft on the walls. Finest offerings include shrimp wonton and barbecued pork noodle, a coconut milk dessert with honeydew melon and sago and drinks like sweet herbal tea.

這間麵家營運至今逾五十年，一直堅持在店舖樓上的小工房中，用傳統人工竹竿打製麵條方法製作麵條，店主以高水準的麵條深感自豪，牆上貼滿製麵過程的照片。招牌美食包括鮮蝦雲吞麵及炸醬麵等，亦有令人驚喜的蝦籽柚皮及自家磨製的合桃露。

TEL. 2527 7476
89 Hennessy Road, Wan Chai
灣仔軒尼詩道 89號

■ PRICE 價錢
à la carte 點菜 $40-150

■ OPENING HOURS 營業時間
12:00-02:00 (L.O.)
Sunday 週日　12:00-01:00 (L.O.)

■ ANNUAL AND WEEKLY CLOSING 休息日期
Closed 3 days Lunar New Year
農曆新年休息 3 天

HONG KONG 香港

Wonton Master
灃家

Those familiar with the Tasty Group will find the menu and style of food here reassuringly familiar – Cantonese-style congee and noodles, along with dim sum and other Cantonese specialities. It is the springy noodles that pull in the crowds – they're served with soup freshly made to a secret recipe handed down by the Ho family. Creative congee hotpots, made with a water-to-rice ratio of 9 to 1, are offered in winter and are worth trying.

似曾相識的餐單和熟悉的味道，這家餐廳其實是正斗集團一員，以提供廣式粥麵為主，再加點心和多款小菜。沿用家傳秘方烹製的湯底配上新鮮製作、質感彈牙的麵條，令人留下深刻印象。冬季更會供應以九比一米水比例熬煮的粥底火鍋，配合新鮮材料，也值得一試。餐廳設計時尚活潑。

TEL. 3148 9488
Shop 13, L3 APM Millennium City 5,
418 Kwun Tong Road, Kwun Tong
觀塘創紀之城第 5 期 APM商場 3樓 13號舖

■ PRICE 價錢
à la carte 點菜 $40-140

■ OPENING HOURS 營業時間
11:30-22:30 (L.O.)

Wu Kong (Causeway Bay)
滬江 (銅鑼灣)

🍴🍴   🪑36   🕐🍴

The many customers of this Shanghainese restaurant had reason to celebrate its relocation in 2011 to the upper level of Lee Theatre Plaza as it resulted in better views, more space and a nicer environment in which to eat. An experienced kitchen shows its practised hand in specialities such as braised pig's knuckle with brown sauce and honey ham and crispy bean curd in bread. Do try the hairy crab menu in the autumn season.

於2011年搬到利舞臺高層的滬江飯店，為顧客帶來更佳的景觀、更寬敞的空間和更舒適的環境，讓他們更盡情享用美食。廚藝精湛的廚師是顧客炮製多款巧手小菜，如紅燒元蹄和響鈴火腿夾。於秋季期間，肥美的大閘蟹是必吃的時令佳餚。

TEL. 2506 1018
Shop B, 17F, Lee Theatre Plaza,
99 Percival Street, Causeway Bay
銅鑼灣波斯富街 99號利舞臺廣場 17樓 B號舖
www.wukong.com.hk

■ PRICE 價錢
Lunch 午膳
set 套餐 $ 88
à la carte 點菜 $ 150-450
Dinner 晚膳
à la carte 點菜 $ 150-450

■ OPENING HOURS 營業時間
Lunch 午膳   11:45-14:45 (L.O.)
Dinner 晚膳   17:45-22:45 (L.O.)

■ ANNUAL AND WEEKLY CLOSING 休息日期
Closed 3 days Lunar New Year
農曆新年休息 3 天

HONG KONG 香港

Xuan Sushi
玄鮨

✗   ⚏ ☎♙

Whilst there are tables in this gracefully decorated and surprisingly spacious dining room, the best place to sit is at the long, wave-shaped counter. From here you can watch the action as the four sushi chefs prepare the omakase menu – they use Niigata rice and two different types of vinegar for the sushi. There are other hot dishes available and many of the ingredients are flown in daily from Japan.

棕色木材與黃銅管的配搭，予人時尚優雅的感覺。壽司吧佔了大部分空間，大廚就在吧枱後為你準備各款美味壽司。這裡的壽司飯是用新潟米按特定比例加入兩種醋煮成，其餘材料均每日由日本新鮮運到。坐在吧枱前享用廚師套餐是最好選擇。此店亦供應燒物及天婦羅等熱食。

TEL. 2537 5555
3F, Parekh House,
61-63 Wyndham Street, Central
中環雲咸街 61-63號巴力大廈 3樓

■ PRICE 價錢
Lunch 午膳
set 套餐 $ 300-500
Dinner 晚膳
set 套餐 $ 1,200-2,000

■ OPENING HOURS 營業時間
Lunch 午膳 12:00-14:30 (L.O.)
Dinner 晚膳 18:00-22:30 (L.O.)

■ ANNUAL AND WEEKLY CLOSING 休息日期
Closed Sunday 週日休息

Yan Toh Heen
欣圖軒

Its location on the ground floor of the Intercontinental hotel may be somewhat concealed but it's well worth seeking out this elegant Cantonese restaurant and that's not just because of the lovely views of Hong Kong Island. The authentic, carefully prepared specialities include golden frogs' legs with spicy salt; scallops with minced shrimp and pear; double-boiled fish maw and sea whelk; and wok-fried lobster with crab roe and milk.

這家優雅的粵菜酒家座落於洲際酒店地下，所處位置可能較為隱閉，但十分值得去尋找，而這裡的魅力，絕不止於能夠觀賞香港島的美景，更因其供應多款精心炮製的傳統粵式佳餚，包括：黃金椒鹽田雞腿、龍帶玉梨香、花膠響螺燉湯及龍皇炒鮮奶等。

TEL. 2313 2243
GF, Intercontinental Hotel,
18 Salisbury Road, Tsim Sha Tsui
尖沙咀梳士巴利道18號洲際酒店地下

SPECIALITIES TO PRE-ORDER 預訂食物
Braised fish maw with sea cucumber in oyster jus 蠔皇厚花膠扣遼參 / Barbecued whole suckling pig 金陵脆皮乳豬 / Peking duck 北京片皮鴨 / Hangzhou beggar's fortune chicken 杭州富貴雞

■ PRICE 價錢
Lunch 午膳
à la carte 點菜 $350-2,000
Dinner 晚膳
set 套餐 $2,000-3,288
à la carte 點菜 $500-2,000

■ OPENING HOURS 營業時間
Lunch 午膳   12:00-14:30 (L.O.)
Dinner 晚膳   18:00-23:00 (L.O.)

Yat Lok
一樂燒鵝

If you're after delicious roast goose then Yat Lok may fit the bill. This family business has been going since 1957 but moved to its current location in 2011. The owner-chef prepares his roast meats using a secret family recipe; his chicken in soy sauce and rose wine is well worth ordering. The place is basic and space limited – you'll be sharing your table with others – but the owner's wife and her team create a pleasant atmosphere.

一樂早於1957年開始營業，其後在2011年遷至現址。每次經過其門前，總會被掛在窗前的燒鵝吸引而垂涎三尺。以家族秘方醃製、經過二十多道工序炮製而成的燒鵝，色香味俱佳，蠻受街坊歡迎，其他食物如玫瑰油雞也做得不錯。

TEL. 2524 3882
34-38 Stanley Street, Central
中環士丹利街 34-38號

■ PRICE 價錢
à la carte 點菜 $30-360

■ OPENING HOURS 營業時間
10:00-21:00 (L.O.)
Sunday & Public Holidays 週日及公眾假期
10:00-17:00 (L.O.)

■ ANNUAL AND WEEKLY CLOSING 休息日期
Closed 3 days Lunar New Year
農曆新年休息 3 天

Yau Yuen Siu Tsui
有緣小敍

The owner's wife works alone in this shop, serving authentic Shaanxi dishes and snacks from her hometown, like dumplings and baked buns with meat. The most impressive dish is Biang Biang noodles – these long, flat, handmade noodles come with a spicy chilli sauce and are full of flavour. Other specialities include Shaanxi-style noodles with vegetables and pork in spicy and sour soup, and Shaanxi-style bread with stewed pork.

由原來位於西貢街的小店搬至現址後，環境較為舒適且能招待更多客人。來自陝西的店東太太為食客奉上風味獨特的家鄉小食如哨子麵、肉夾饃等，其中最令人難忘的莫過於Biang Biang麵。這款由人手製作，麵身寬長的麵食配上特製醬料，香辣味濃，令人再三回味。店內還提供多款熱葷小菜。

TEL. 5300 2682
GF, 36 Man Yuen Street, Jordan
佐敦文苑街 36號地下

■ PRICE 價錢
à la carte 點菜 $30-100

■ OPENING HOURS 營業時間
12:00-22:00 (L.O.)

Yè Shanghai (Tsim Sha Tsui)
夜上海 (尖沙咀)

XXX

  ♿ 🍽 ⛴80 📞🍴

Drawing not only on Shanghai but also on the neighbouring provinces of Jiangsu and Zhejiang, the cooking here is subtle and expertly balanced. Specialities include sautéed shredded Mandarin fish, baked stuffed crab shell and Ningbo-style baby ribs glazed with Zhejiang black vinegar. The contemporary décor recalls 1930s Shanghai in its use of dark woods, subdued lighting and semi-private alcoves. This is a busy, sophisticated operation.

這裡的烹調水準專業，技術精湛，不但提供上海菜，還供應江蘇及浙江菜。特色美食包括龍鬚桂魚絲，蟹粉釀蟹蓋及寧波肋骨。餐廳以當代風格設計，採用昏暗的燈光，深色的木材，加上半私家餐桌，散發着三十年代上海的味道。餐廳生氣勃勃，營運順暢，服務非常周到。

TEL. 2376 3322
6F, Marco Polo Hotel, Harbour City,
Canton Road, Tsim Sha Tsui
尖沙咀廣東道海運大廈馬哥孛羅酒店 6樓
www.elite-concepts.com

■ PRICE 價錢
Lunch 午膳
à la carte 點菜 $ 150-300
Dinner 晚膳
à la carte 點菜 $ 250-600

■ OPENING HOURS 營業時間
Lunch 午膳　11:30-15:00 L.O. 14:30
Dinner 晚膳　18:00-23:00 L.O. 22:30

Yee Tung Heen
怡東軒

XXX   🦽 🅿 ⇔60 ◐♨

The first thing you'll notice is the Chinese ornaments and the second is how well Chinese screens and contemporary lighting go together. This elegant restaurant not only offers traditional Cantonese favourites but also serves specialities of a more creative persuasion. The enthusiastic chef and his team spend much time seeking out the best quality seasonal ingredients, whether that's from local markets or overseas.

踏入怡東酒店內的怡東軒中菜廳，馬上便會給精緻的中式擺設吸引。往內走，會發現四周的中式屏風與現代天花燈，配搭得十分別致。餐廳供應傳統粵菜，廚師及營運團隊充滿熱誠，專程由本地及世界各地搜羅各種高質素及時令食材，時有創新菜式或特別餐單推出。

TEL. 2837 6790
2F, The Excelsior Hotel,
28 Gloucester Road, Causeway Bay
銅鑼灣告士打道 281號怡東酒店 2樓

SPECIALITIES TO PRE-ORDER 預訂食物
Baked traditional salt-crusted chicken with
Chinese wine 古法酒香鹽焗雞

■ PRICE 價錢
Lunch 午膳
à la carte 點菜 $ 200-500
Dinner 晚膳
à la carte 點菜 $ 400-800

■ OPENING HOURS 營業時間
Lunch 午膳   12:00-14:30 (L.O.)
Dinner 晚膳   18:00-22:30 (L.O.)

HONG KONG 香港

Yin Yue
殷悅

XX   🚻 P ☎️🍴

Yin Yue provides a warm and relaxing space; its large windows letting in lots of light and providing great views of Tsuen Wan from its perch on the top floor of a hotel. The cooking is undertaken by an experienced chef who prepares the attractively presented dishes in a traditional but healthy way, using secret recipes, quality ingredients and a lesser amount of oil. Try suckling pig with dried mullet roe, or stir-fried beef with black truffle.

位於酒店頂樓，以淡色系作裝潢的餐廳，格調輕鬆。兩邊的落地玻璃窗除了引入自然光外，還讓你一覽舊社區景色。店內粵菜由富數十年經驗的大廚主理，結合了健康少油的烹調方式與傳統秘方，再配上世界各地食材和日本美學，型味俱佳。推介菜式有用台灣烏魚子製作的烏金麒麟乳豬和黑松露牛柳粒。

TEL. 2409 3182
30F, Panda Hotel, 3 Tsuen Wah Street, Tsuen Wan
荃灣荃華街 3號悅來酒店 30樓
www.pandahotel.com.hk

■ PRICE 價錢
Lunch 午膳
à la carte 點菜 $ 120-400
Dinner 晚膳
à la carte 點菜 $ 300-900

■ OPENING HOURS 營業時間
Lunch 午膳   11:00-14:30 (L.O.)
Sunday & Public Holidays
週日及公眾假期   10:00-15:00 (L.O.)
Dinner 晚膳   18:00-22:00 (L.O.)

Yixin NEW
益新

🍴🍴   ⌂ 20   ☎🍴

North Point was the original location for this family-run restaurant when it opened in the 1950s. It's moved a few times since then but is now firmly ensconced here in Wan Chai. Run by the 3rd generation of the family, a sense of continuity also comes from the head chef who has been with the company over 50 years! The Cantonese food is traditional, with quite a few Shun Tak dishes; specialities include roasted duck Pipa-style, and smoked pomfret.

早於五十年代於港島區開業，輾轉搬至灣仔現址，現由第三代經營。益新一向以傳統粵菜馳名，餐單上不乏耗功夫製作的懷舊菜式，吸引不少客人在此舉行宴會。琵琶鴨、金錢雞及煙焗鯧魚等都是常客所愛。除了地面的主廳和客房外，地庫還有一個裝潢時尚的餐室。

TEL. 2834 9963
50 Hennessy Road, Wan Chai
灣仔軒尼詩道 50 號

■ PRICE 價錢
Lunch 午膳
à la carte 點菜 $ 150-200
Dinner 晚膳
à la carte 點菜 $ 250-350

■ OPENING HOURS 營業時間
Lunch 午膳   11:30-15:30 (L.O.)
Dinner 晚膳   17:30-22:30 (L.O.)

■ ANNUAL AND WEEKLY CLOSING 休息日期
Closed 2 days Lunar New Year and 1st July lunch 農曆新年 2 天及 7 月 1 日午膳休息

Japanese 日本菜

HONG KONG 香港

MAP 地圖 28/B-3

Youka
八日

The chocolate box façade gives little away but step inside and you'll find yourself in a simple, cosy and contemporary space with a genuine Japanese flavour. Those who are curious to learn more about the cooking process should sit in front of the open kitchen to take advantage of the live cookery show. The chef's unequivocal commitment to using only the best ingredients means that much of the produce is flown in daily from Japan.

餐廳的黑色外牆十分引人注目。室內面積不大，簡單時尚的裝潢隱隱滲出一絲日本韻味。最佳的位置莫過於開放式廚房前的座位，你可以一邊品嘗美食、一邊欣賞廚師出色的廚藝。廚師最着重食材的時令性，因此，美味的和食套餐只選用每天即日由日本運到的新鮮材料炮製。這兒的壽司頗受食客歡迎。

TEL. 2833 5188
35-45 Johnston Road, Wan Chai
灣仔莊士敦道 35-45號
www.youka.hk

■ PRICE 價錢
Lunch 午膳
set 套餐 $ 180-338
à la carte 點菜 $ 250-900
Dinner 晚膳
set 套餐 $ 550-1,280
à la carte 點菜 $ 400-900

■ OPENING HOURS 營業時間
Lunch 午膳　12:00-14:30 (L.O.)
Dinner 晚膳　18:00-22:30 (L.O.)

Yù Lěi
玉蕾

⟨ 🧼 ⬭18 ◎🍴

The strikingly decorated Yù Lěi is part of a harbourside restaurant complex, and specialises in Shanghainese cuisine; look out for creatively presented dishes like Drunken Kyu Shu crab, stir-fried sliced abalone with seasonal vegetables, and stir-fried seaweed and water bamboo. At lunch the restaurant also serves Cantonese dim sum and assorted roast meats. The main dining room comes in vivid green and the five private rooms are named after flowers.

裝潢耀目的玉蕾是此區海傍飲食綜合場所的一部份，主要供應上海菜。此店提供的創意菜式包括九州醉蟹、生炒鮮鮑片及苔條茭白。餐廳於午市期間供應廣東點心和燒味併盤；主用餐區以鮮明的綠色為主題，五個私人廂房則分別以花卉命名。

TEL. 3746 2788
5F, Harbourfront Landmark,
11 Wan Hoi Street, Hung Hom
紅磡環海街 11 號海名軒 5 樓
www.KOdining.com

SPECIALITIES TO PRE-ORDER 預訂食物
Drunken Kyu Shu crab 醉蟹 (10 days 日)

■ PRICE 價錢
Lunch 午膳
set 套餐 $ 398
à la carte 點菜 $ 250-1,000
Dinner 晚膳
à la carte 點菜 $ 350-1,500

■ OPENING HOURS 營業時間
Lunch 午膳　12:00-15:00 (L.O.)
Dinner 晚膳　18:00-22:30 (L.O.)

■ ANNUAL AND WEEKLY CLOSING 休息日期
Closed Monday 週一休息

HONG KONG 香港

Yuè (Gold Coast)
粵 (黃金海岸)

✗✗   👋 🍽24 ☎🍴

It's not often one can enjoy Cantonese food surrounded by verdant scenery but here on the ground floor of the Gold Coast hotel that's exactly what you get as this comfortable restaurant looks out onto a delightful garden. The menu includes both traditional and more contemporary dishes and it's worth seeking out the chef's specialities such as barbecued pork and chicken liver with honey, and deep-fried chicken with shrimp paste.

位於黃金海岸酒店的地面層，優雅舒適的室內環境，與大型玻璃窗外的園林景致巧妙地配合起來。選擇豐富的餐單提供傳統懷舊及較創新的粵菜，廚師精選菜式如蜜餞金錢雞和星洲蝦醬炸雞件等，值得一試。邊品嘗美味的廣式點心邊欣賞怡人的園林美景，實在是賞心樂事。

TEL. 2452 8668
LG/F, Gold Coast Hotel,
1 Castle Peak Road, Gold Coast
黃金海岸青山公路 1號黃金海岸酒店低層
www.goldcoasthotel.com.hk

■ PRICE 價錢
Lunch 午膳
à la carte 點菜 $ 200-500
Dinner 晚膳
à la carte 點菜 $ 250-700

■ OPENING HOURS 營業時間
Lunch 午膳   11:30-15:30 L.O. 15:15
Sunday & Public Holidays 週日及公眾假期
09:00-16:00 (L.O.)
Dinner 晚膳   18:30-23:00 L.O. 22:45

Yuè (North Point)
粵 (北角)

　　　　　 🖐 **P** 🍽100 ⓞ

It may seem like nothing more than a mezzanine area of the City Garden hotel but it's well worth coming up here for the Cantonese food. The experienced chef's respect for the traditions of Cantonese cuisine is clearly demonstrated in dishes like double-boiled jus of almonds with fish maw, fried rice with prawns and barbecue pork, and seared garoupa with layered egg white. There are a number of different sized private rooms.

看起來只是城市花園酒店的間層，並不特別，定讓不少人忽略了這間中菜廳，但絕對值得前來一嘗這兒的粵菜。資深大廚對傳統粵菜的尊重完全反映在其製作的各樣菜式上，例如杏汁花膠燉蹄筋、師傅炒飯和雪嶺紅梅映松露等。餐廳設有不同大小的廂房供各類宴會之用。

TEL. 2806 4918
1F, City Garden Hotel,
9 City Garden Road, North Point
北角城市花園道 9號城市花園酒店 1樓
www.citygarden.com.hk

■ PRICE 價錢
Lunch 午膳
à la carte 點菜 $ 150-650
Dinner 晚膳
à la carte 點菜 $ 200-650

■ OPENING HOURS 營業時間
Lunch 午膳　11:30-14:30 (L.O.)
Dinner 晚膳　18:00-22:30 (L.O.)

Yue Kee
裕記

Over 40,000 geese are needed each year to satisfy demand at this large, second-generation family business, which opened back in 1958. The geese are sourced from eight different farms in Mainland China and if contentment is indicated by the amount of noise generated, then clearly these roasted geese are much appreciated by the customers. The restaurant has 50 tables, which are divided between eight simply decorated rooms. It's worth booking ahead.

這家家族經營的餐館於1958年開業，現在由第二代打理。食店每年分別在中國內地八個農場購入超過四萬隻鵝以確保供應充足，店主多年來一直堅持按家傳秘方以炭火烤製燒鵝，味道特佳。店內共有五十桌，分佈於八間房內。建議預訂座位。

TEL. 2491 0105
9 Sham Hong Road, Sham Tseng
深井深康路 9號
www.yuekee.com.hk

■ PRICE 價錢
à la carte 點菜 $ 150-550

■ OPENING HOURS 營業時間
11:00-23:00 (L.O.)

■ ANNUAL AND WEEKLY CLOSING 休息日期
Closed 3 days Lunar New Year
農曆新年休息 3 天

Sichuan 川菜

Yun Yan
雲陽

X　　　　　　　　　　　　　　　P　⇥12　◎ⅈ

Yun Yan began life in the 1990s in Tsim Sha Tsui but has now firmly established itself in Causeway Bay. It wasn't just its appearance and atmosphere that changed when it moved – the kitchen also played its part. Whilst the Sichuan specialities are still prepared to the same high standard, it puts its own spin on some dishes and presents them in a very modern style. Try the translucent beef slices and hand-cut noodles in supreme soup.

早於九十年代在尖沙咀開業，遷至現址後，室內裝潢以淡素色調配合時尚設計，予人耳目一新之感。傳統川菜亦以新形象示人，外觀雖變味道卻不變。經典菜式如燈影牛肉和幼如髮絲的大刀金絲麵均不能錯過。自由調味的豆腦創作趣味十足。門前湘竹上的斑點寓意的應是因辣而出的汗水而非淚痕吧!

TEL. 2375 0800
10F, Time Square, 1 Matheson Street,
Causeway Bay
銅鑼灣勿地臣街 1 號時代廣場 10 樓
www.yunyan.hk

■ PRICE 價錢
Lunch 午膳
set 套餐 $ 88
à la carte 點菜 $ 100-150
Dinner 晚膳
à la carte 點菜 $ 200-250

■ OPENING HOURS 營業時間
Lunch 午膳　12:00-15:45 (L.O.)
Dinner 晚膳　18:00-22:00 (L.O.)

Zenpachi NEW
禪八

✗✗   ⏷20 ☎↹

It's all about sukiyaki and shabu shabu at this Japanese restaurant. The high quality ingredients include Saga beef and assorted seafood from Japan, along with Australian Wagyu. The soup base of the shabu shabu is nicely concentrated and using a paper pot ensures that the stock is never oily. For the sukiyaki, you can choose either Kansai or Kanto style and can either do the cooking yourself or ask the staff to do it for you.

店內餐單毫不複雜，提供日式火鍋及汁燒會席料理，配以佐賀5A和牛、澳洲和牛及各種日本海鮮等食材。火鍋使用日本紙鍋，能吸走油脂和雜質，味道更清鮮。顧客可選擇關東或關西兩種不同做法的汁燒鍋，更可請店員協助烹調。靠窗有數張榻榻米餐桌，適合二人用餐，別具情調。

TEL. 3428 3615
6F, The Toy House, 100 Canton Road, Tsim Sha Tsui
尖沙咀廣東道100號彩星集團大廈6樓

■ PRICE 價錢
Lunch 午膳
set 套餐 $ 110-750
à la carte 點菜 $ 400-800
Dinner 晚膳
set 套餐 $ 400-900
à la carte 點菜 $ 400-800

■ OPENING HOURS 營業時間
Lunch 午膳   12:00-14:30 (L.O.)
Dinner 晚膳   18:00-22:30 (L.O.)

■ ANNUAL AND WEEKLY CLOSING 休息日期
Closed 2 days Lunar New Year
農曆新年休息2天

Zhejiang Heen
浙江軒

At what must be one of the easiest restaurants to find – just look for the huge Zhejiang landscape on the outside of the building – you'll find authentic Zhejiang and Shanghainese specialities made from top quality ingredients, such as smoked fish, shrimps with seaweed, and steamed chou tofu. Run by a Zhejiang Fraternity Association, the dining room is spread over two floors and while it may not be particularly lavish, it is comfortable.

要數最容易找的酒家，這家必定榜上有名，因為它的外牆有一大幅浙江風景圖。你可在這裏品嘗到採用上等食材烹調的傳統浙江及上海美食，如長江燻魚、苔條蝦仁及紹興蒸臭豆腐。這裡由香港浙江省同鄉會聯合會經營，樓高兩層，雖然裝修並不豪華，但感覺十分舒適。

TEL. 2877 9011
2-3F, 300-306 Lockhart Road,
Wan Chai
灣仔駱克道 300-306號 2-3樓

SPECIALITIES TO PRE-ORDER 預訂食物
Crispy deep-fried chicken with 4 treasures
四寶片皮雞 / Braised duck stuffed with 8
treasures 蠔燒八寶鴨

■ PRICE 價錢
Lunch 午膳
à la carte 點菜 $180-600
Dinner 晚膳
à la carte 點菜 $180-600

■ OPENING HOURS 營業時間
Lunch 午膳　11:00-14:30 (L.O.)
Dinner 晚膳　18:00-22:30 (L.O.)

■ ANNUAL AND WEEKLY CLOSING 休息日期
Closed 3 days Lunar New Year
農曆新年休息 3 天

Street Food 街頭小吃
Popular places for snack food
馳名小食店

Block 18 Doggie's Noodle 十八座 狗仔粉

Fried pork fat noodles.
狗仔粉(豬油渣麵)及豬皮蘿蔔。

$ 20-30   12:00-04:00

MAP 地圖   17/C-2
GF, 27A Ning Po Street, Jordan
佐敦寧波街 27A地下

Butchers Club

Burgers and duck fat fries.
漢保包及鴨油薯條。

$ 100-150   12:00-23:00

MAP 地圖   28/A-2
GF, 2 Landale Street, Wan Chai
灣仔蘭杜街 2號

Canaan Thai Snack 迦南泰國小食

Thai rice noodles and snacks.
泰國米粉及小食。

$ 25-50   11:00-21:00

MAP 地圖   34/B-1
GF, 72 Java Road, North Point
北角渣華道 72號地下

Cheung Hing Kee (Tsuen Wan) 祥興記 (荃灣)

Shanghainese pan-fried pork buns; beancurd and rice vermicelle soup.

上海生煎包及油豆腐粉絲湯。

$ 30-50   10:00-22:00

MAP 地圖 5/B-1
13 Chuen Lung Street, Tsuen Wan
荃灣川龍街 13號

Chin Sik 千色車仔麵

Choose your own selection of noodles and toppings.

車仔麵。

$ 25-50   11:30-01:00

MAP 地圖 5/B-1
49 Shiu Wo Street, Tsuen Wan
荃灣兆和街 49號

Fat Boy 第三代肥仔

Octopus and duck's stomach marinated in soy sauce.

墨魚及鴨胗。

$ 20-40   13:00-24:00

MAP 地圖 19/C-2
3 Hau Fook Street, Tsim Sha Tsui
尖沙咀厚福街 3號

Hop Yik Tai 合益泰小食

Rice rolls; fish balls and radish.

豬腸粉、魚蛋、豬皮及蘿蔔。

$ 30-50   06:30-20:30

MAP 地圖 7/B-2
121 Kweilin Street, Sham Shui Po
深水埗桂林街 121號

Joyful Dessert House

Western desserts like mango Napoleon, pineapple sherbet.

西式甜品如黑糖芭菲、芒果拿破崙及燒菠蘿雪芭。

$ 30-60   14:00-02:00

MAP 地圖   15/D-3
74 Hak Po Street, Mong Kok
旺角黑布街74號

Kai Kai 佳佳甜品

Glutinous rice dumplings in ginger sweet soup; stew papaya with rock sugar.

寧波薑汁湯丸、冰糖燉木瓜。

$ 20-30   12:00-04:00

MAP 地圖   17/C-2
121-123 Parkes Street, Jordan
佐敦白加士街121-123號

Kei Tsui 奇趣餅家

Cantonese puddings and pastries like Xiaofeng cake and walnut cookies.

雞仔餅、合桃酥及香蕉糕等。

$ 20-40   08:00-20:00

MAP 地圖   15/D-2
135 Fa Yuen Street, Mong Kok
旺角花園街135號

Kelly's Cape Bop

Korean fried chicken; tteokbokki; kimbap.

韓國炸雞、辣年糕、飯卷。

$ 50-150   11:00-21:00

MAP 地圖   28/B-3
57 Johnston Road, Wan Chai
灣仔莊士敦道57號

Keung Kee 強記

Glutinous rice; rice rolls and sweet soup.

糯米飯、腸粉及糖水。

$ 20-40   12:00-01:00

MAP 地圖   29/D-2
382 Lockhart Road, Wan Chai
灣仔駱克道 382號

Kung Wo Tofu 公和荳品廠

Tofu pudding, pan-fried tofu snacks and homemade sugar-free soy milk.

豆腐花、煎釀豆腐及無糖豆漿。

$ 30-50   07:00-21:00

MAP 地圖   7/B-2
118 Pei Ho Street, Sham Shui Po
深水埗北河街 118號

Kwan Kee Store 坤記糕品

Chinese rice pudding; white sugar cake and black sesame rolls.

砵仔糕、芝麻糕、白糖糕、馬蹄糕等。

$ 30-50   08:00-23:00

MAP 地圖   7/B-2
115-117 Fuk Wa Street, Sham Shui Po
深水埗福華街 115-117號

Lan Ying 蘭英印尼小食

Satay and nasi rendang.

沙爹串燒及巴東牛肉飯。

$ 20-50   11:00-24:00

MAP 地圖   13/D-1
92-94 Fuk Lo Tsun Road, Kowloon City
九龍城福佬村道 92-94號

Lei Keung Kee (North Point) 利強記 (利強記)

Egg waffles.

雞蛋仔及格仔餅。

$ 30-50   07:00-23:00

MAP 地圖 34/C-1
492 King's Road, North Point
北角英皇道 492號

Mak Kee 麥記美食

Xiao Lung Bao, pan-fried pork dumplings, pan-fried pork buns and fish balls.

小籠包、鍋貼、生煎包、魚蛋及蔥油餅。

$ 30-50   11:00-23:00

MAP 地圖 34/B-2
21-23 Fort Street, North Point
北角堡壘街 21-23號

Mammy Pancake 媽咪雞蛋仔

Classic street food cooked in a special egg waffle pan.

雞蛋仔。

$ 15-30   12:30-21:00

MAP 地圖 19/C-2
8-12 Carnarvon Road, Tsim Sha Tsui
尖沙咀加拿芬道 8-12號

Soupreme 湯品小棧

Cantonese double-boiled soups like matsutake soup.

粤式燉湯如牛肝菌湯、松茸湯。

$ 30-50   12:00-21:00

MAP 地圖 14/B-3
20 Beech Street, Tai Kwok Tsui
大角咀櫸樹街 20號

Three Potatoes 叁薯

Baked potatoes, fries and potato hash.

焗薯、炸薯及薯餅。

$ 25-40   12:00-21:00

MAP 地圖   15/C-2
Shop 5, 6F, 30-32A Nullah Road, Mong Kok
旺角水渠道 30-32A號地下 5號舖

Wah Yuan 華園甜品

Cantonese sweet soup.

廣東糖水。

$ 20-40   11:00-20:00

MAP 地圖   8/A-2
GF, 38 Shung Ling Street, San Po Kong
新蒲崗崇齡街 38號地下

Wing On 榮安小食

Cart noodles and chicken wing tips.

車仔麵及雞翼尖。

$ 25-50   11:00-20:00

MAP 地圖   5/B-1
24 Tai Ho Road, Tsuen Wan
荃灣大河道 24號

Ying Kee 英記美點小食

Cantonese wonton noodles.

雲吞麵。

$ 25-40   11:00-01:00

MAP 地圖   8/A-2
GF, 10 Hong Keung Street, San Po Kong
新蒲崗康強街 10號地下

HOTELS
酒店

HOTELS IN ORDER OF COMFORT
酒店 — 以舒適程度分類

City Garden
城市花園

You'll find the City Garden in a largely residential area, a short walk from Fortress Hill MTR. The bedrooms would not necessarily win any design awards but they are fair in both size and price. The Garden Café offers an extensive international buffet; Satay Inn on the basement level provides Asian specialities; and Yuè serves authentic Cantonese dishes.

城市花園酒店座落於寧靜的住宅區內，與炮台山港鐵站只有咫尺，交通網絡非常便利。除了佔盡港島區的優越地勢外，客房空間充裕且收費合理；附屬的綠茵閣餐廳提供豐富的午、晚市環球美食自助餐，開設在一樓的粵中菜廳則提供傳統廣東佳餚。

TEL. 2887 2888
FAX. 28871111
9 City Garden Road, North Point
北角城市花園道 9號
www.citygarden.com.hk

RECOMMENDED RESTAURANTS 餐廳推薦
Yuè (North Point) 粵（北角）⚹ XX

🛉 = $ 2,800-4,200
🛉🛉 = $ 2,800-4,200
Suites 套房 = $5,900
☕ = $178

Rooms 客房　598
Suites 套房　15

Conrad
港麗

Sitting above the Pacific Place complex is the Conrad, deftly mixing the traditional with the modern. The vast oval lobby showcases Chinese vases and bronze sculptures. Bedrooms are between the 40th and 61st floors, ensuring sweeping views; suites are particularly spacious and have elegant marble bathrooms. An outdoor swimming pool offers an equally dramatic panorama.

酒店位處集購物娛樂於一身的太古廣場之上。寬闊的橢圓形大堂擺放着中式花瓶及銅像，設計融合了傳統和現代元素，優雅而壯麗；寢室設在40至61樓，坐擁遼闊美景，而套房則特別寬敞，設有雲石浴室。室外游泳池讓你飽覽香港全景。

TEL. 2521 3838
FAX. 2521 3888
Pacific Place, 88 Queensway,
Admiralty
金鐘道 88號太古廣場
www.conradhotels.com

RECOMMENDED RESTAURANTS 餐廳推薦
Golden Leaf 金葉庭　XxX

🛉 = $ 5,300-6,850
🛉🛉 = $5,400-6,950
Suites 套房 = $ 8,600-38,000
☕ = $ 280

Rooms 客房　467
Suites 套房　46

Cordis
康思得

Chinese modern art is showcased at this 42-storey glass tower – there are over 1,500 paintings, sculptures and installations spread around the hotel, which is located in a vibrant and bustling neighbourhood. Bedrooms come in a sober yet contemporary style, there's a pool on the roof and guests can choose from a wide selection of restaurants and bars. The hotel was previously called Langham Place.

酒店座落於行人如鯽的旺角中心地帶的朗豪現易名為康得思。琉璃塔般的大樓高42層，不僅有科技發燒友夢寐以求的電子產品，還有超過1,500幅畫作、雕塑與裝置藝術品分佈於整棟大樓內，是一個中國現代美術展覽館。客房的設計含蓄而時髦，天台設有游泳池，並有多間餐廳供客人選擇。

TEL. 3552 3388
FAX. 3552 3322
555 Shanghai Street, Mong Kok
旺角上海街 555號
www.cordishotels.com/en/hong-kong/

RECOMMENDED RESTAURANTS 餐廳推薦
Ming Court 明閣　❀❀　XxX

👤 = $ 1,900-3,700
👥 = $ 1,900-3,700
Suites 套房 = $ 3,400-11,000
☕ = $ 218

Rooms 客房　632
Suites 套房　34

Crowne Plaza
皇冠假日

Upper level bedrooms at this modern, corporate-minded hotel have the best outlooks, which include views of the Happy Valley racetrack on the south side. All of the bedrooms are decently sized and come with glass-walled bathrooms and impressive extras such as a wide choice of pillows. On the top floor you'll find Club@28: a chic bar with a terrace.

這家精心設計的時尚酒店，高層客房坐擁最美麗的港島景觀，南邊客房可飽覽跑馬地馬場全景。所有房間都寬敞舒適，浴室牆壁以玻璃砌成，擴闊了視覺上的空間，設施應有盡有，包括不同款色的枕頭。酒店頂層有為時尚人士而設的Club@28 酒吧，還有小型泳池和健身室。

TEL. 3980 3980
FAX. 3980 3900
8 Leighton Road, Causeway Bay
銅鑼灣禮頓道 8 號
www.cphongkong.com

👤 = $ 2,300-2,800
👤👤 = $ 2,300-2,800
Suites 套房 = $ 5,000
☕ = $ 210

Rooms 客房　253
Suites 套房　10

Crowne Plaza Kowloon East
九龍東皇冠假日

A comfortable, well-equipped hotel in a busy commercial district with good transport links. It boasts one of the largest ballrooms around and dining options include a buffet, a Chinese restaurant and an Italian on the roof-top, along with a bar with great views. The contemporary bedrooms are warm and stylish and come with glass-walled bathrooms and a host of extras.

由著名酒店集團管理，座落於將軍澳鐵路站上蓋，交通便捷。客房設計時尚，色調柔和、簡單的線條和善用空間的設計，平實卻不失優雅。大型多用途宴會廳和會議設施是其一大特色。綠草如茵的露天花園可作婚禮場地。酒店頂層的露天酒吧是一個能讓人放鬆心情的好去處。

TEL. 3983 0388
FAX. 3983 0503
3 Tong Tak Street, Tseung Kwan O
將軍澳唐德街 3號
www.crowneplaza.cn

RECOMMENDED RESTAURANTS 餐廳推薦
Tze Yuet Heen 紫粵軒 ✗✗

♦ = $ 1,700-8,100
♦♦ = $ 1,700-8,100
Suites 套房 = $ 9,100-11,000
☕ = $ 198

Rooms 客房 354
Suites 套房 5

East
東隅

East is a modern business hotel designed for those who, like the hotel staff, can wear a pair of Converse with their suit. It has an uncluttered lobby, a bright, open plan restaurant serving international cuisine, and a great rooftop terrace bar named 'Sugar', as this was once a sugar factory. Bedrooms are minimalist but well-kept; corner rooms are especially light.

標榜為品味商務酒店。整潔的大堂、時尚的酒吧、提供國際美食的餐廳,加上可觀看迷人維港景色的天台酒吧Sugar——名字靈感源自酒店前身的糖廠,絕對切合你的需要。客房佈置簡約優雅,以大量玻璃與木材塑造出溫暖感覺與品味。位處轉角的客房景觀尤佳。

TEL. 3968 3968
FAX. 3968 3988
29 Taikoo Shing Road, Island East
港島東太古城道 29號
www.east-hongkong.com

♂ = $ 2,800-3,650
♂♂ = $ 2,800-3,650
Suites 套房 = $ 4,300-7,000
☕ = $ 218

Rooms 客房　339
Suites 套房　6

Four Seasons
四季

Four Seasons hotel not only offers some of the most spacious accommodation in Hong Kong but the bedrooms, which have wall-to-wall windows, also feature an impressive array of extras. Choose between a Western style room and one with a more Asian feel; all have large and luxurious bathrooms. The hotel also boasts two bars, two swimming pools and two world class restaurants.

四季酒店與維港毗鄰，景色壯麗，提供香港最寬敞時尚的客房。客房佈置分為現代風格和東方情調兩種，且設有大型豪華浴室。Blue Bar專為享受雞尾酒和現場音樂演奏而設。水療設施令人印象難忘，更設有兩個溫度不同的泳池。舒適的環境與高質素服務兩者俱備。

TEL. 3196 8888
FAX. 3196 8899
8 Finance Street, Central
中環金融街 8號
www.fourseasons.com/hongkong

ⵔ = $ 4,500-9,200
ⵔⵔ = $4,500-9,200
Suites 套房 = $ 9,500-75,000
☕ = $ 280

Rooms 客房　399
Suites 套房　54

RECOMMENDED RESTAURANTS 餐廳推薦
Caprice ✿✿ ✗✗✗✗✗
Lung King Heen 龍景軒 ✿✿✿ ✗✗✗✗

Gold Coast
黃金海岸

Travel 20 or so minutes from the city centre and you could find yourself relaxing in a hotel on the shoreline surrounded by 10 acres of landscaped garden. Next to the Marina and Yacht Club, the hotel offers extensive recreational facilities and, while the bedrooms are not particularly modern, they are bright, decently proportioned and offer pleasant sea views.

黃金海岸座落於海岸邊，毗鄰泳灘及遊艇會，有多項戶外康樂設施及面積甚廣的園林，與繁囂的市中心有一段距離，是一間理想渡假酒店。客房裝潢稱不上豪華新穎，卻寬敞明亮，且能欣賞怡人海景，部分房間附設露台。酒店的餐飲設施完善，花園旁的粵提供美味廣東菜。

TEL. 2452 8888
FAX. 2440 7368
1 Castle Peak Road, Gold Coast
黃金海岸青山公路 1號
www.goldcoasthotel.com.hk

RECOMMENDED RESTAURANTS 餐廳推薦
Yuè (Gold Coast) 粵（黃金海岸）XX

👤 = $ 2,600-3,800
👥 = $ 2,600-3,800
Suites 套房 = $ 5,500-19,000
☕ = $ 218

Rooms 客房 444
Suites 套房 9

Grand Hyatt
君悅

The hotel, with its striking lobby, has been a fixture here in Wan Chai since 1998 and is perfectly located for the Convention and Exhibition Centre. Most of the bedrooms have recently been refurbished and are now more contemporary. The hotel offers impressive views, a large outdoor pool, and a wide selection of restaurants along with a new champagne bar.

酒店鄰近香港會議展覽中心，維港兩岸景色盡收於眼底。富麗堂皇的大堂早於1998年酒店開業時便已落成，全面修葺後的客房裝潢更時尚。酒店設有多家餐館分別提供中外菜式及附設有大型室外泳池。

TEL. 2588 1234
FAX. 2802 0677
1 Harbour Road, Wan Chai
灣仔港灣道 1 號
www.hongkong.grand.hyatt.com

RECOMMENDED RESTAURANTS 餐廳推薦
Grand Hyatt Steakhouse　XX
Grissini　XxX
One Harbour Road 港灣壹號　XxX

♦ = $ 6,000-7,600
♦♦ = $ 6,000-7,600
Suites 套房 = $ 10,000-55,000
☕ = $ 318

Rooms 客房　499
Suites 套房　46

Harbour Grand Kowloon
九龍海逸君綽

This shimmering glass structure is right on the waterfront and offers superb views across Victoria Harbour. It boasts a spectacularly grand lobby with an impressive white marble staircase and, although the bedrooms are bright, comfortable and well-equipped, they are sober by comparison to other areas. Do visit the dramatic rooftop pool with its glass walls.

這座位於紅磡海濱、閃閃發亮的玻璃建築物與維港相毗鄰，金碧輝煌的大堂設有白色雲石階梯。房間光潔舒適，設備齊全，相比酒店內其他設施或有點樸實。住客可於天台上的玻璃幕牆泳池內盡情暢泳及享用頂樓健身中心設施及蒸氣浴。

TEL. 2621 3188
FAX. 2621 3311
20 Tak Fung Street, Whampoa Garden,
Hung Hom
紅磡黃埔花園德豐街 20號
www.harbourgrand.com/kowloon

RECOMMENDED RESTAURANTS 餐廳推薦
Robatayaki 爐端燒 ❌

- = $ 2,900-4,200
- = $ 3,100-4,500
Suites 套房 = $ 5,800-35,000
- = $218

Rooms 客房 506
Suites 套房 48

Harbour Plaza 8 Degrees
8度海逸

An eight degree incline is this tall and contemporary hotel's unique selling point, from the lobby ceiling and walls to the glasses in the restaurant. Bedrooms may be quite compact but they are thoughtfully laid out and come in warm hues; the higher the floor, the brighter the room. The hotel should benefit from the huge development project that's upgrading this area.

這家酒店的最大特色是，從大堂天花到牆身以至餐廳玻璃都傾斜了八度。以暖色系裝潢的睡房，面積雖然不算寬敞，但絕對經過精心佈置。層數愈高，房間愈光亮開揚。泳池雖然四面被牆圍繞，但環境依然清幽宜人。

TEL. 2126 1988
FAX. 2126 1900
199 Kowloon City Road, To Kwa Wan
土瓜灣九龍城道 199號
www.harbour-plaza.com/hp8d

👤 = $ 2,300-3,550
👥 = $ 2,300-3,550
Suites 套房 = $ 4,200-5,200
☕ = $ 145

Rooms 客房　678
Suites 套房　24

Harbour Plaza North Point
北角海逸

Those doing business in North Point or Quarry Bay will find this hotel a useful address. It's spread over 32 floors and everything feels contemporary, right from the moment you enter the lobby with its unusual water feature. Bedrooms are a fair size and well soundproofed. There are also 180 serviced suites available for long-stay clients (a minimum of one month).

樓高32層的北角海逸酒店地點便利，對在北角或鰂魚涌洽談商務的人士來說，是短暫停留的好住處。大堂水池的設計盡顯時尚氣派。客房寬敞而寧靜：大部分房間只有淋浴設備，如需泡浴，須於訂房時提出。酒店另設有180間為長期住客而設的服務式套房，租期最短為一個月。

TEL. 2187 8888
FAX. 2187 8899
665 King's Road, North Point
北角英皇道665號
www.harbour-plaza.com

👤 = $ 2,150-3,500
👥 = $ 2,150-3,500
Suites 套房 = $ 3,950-6,950
☕ = $ 158

Rooms 客房　548
Suites 套房　121

Hyatt Regency Sha Tin
沙田凱悅

Just a minute's walk from University Station is this 26 floor hotel, whose large, well-equipped bedrooms have either harbour or mountain views. It makes clever use of neutral colours and natural materials like stone and wood to create a soothing ambience. It's business-orientated during the week; the impressive leisure facilities appeal to families at weekends.

沙田凱悅於2009年開幕，從港鐵大學站前往僅需步行兩分鐘。酒店設計充滿時代感，巧妙運用中性色彩及天然物料如石材及木材製造出柔和融洽的感覺。酒店平日以接待商務旅客為主，到週末則以出色的休閒設施吸引家庭顧客。

TEL. 3723 1234
FAX. 3723 1235
18 Chak Cheung Street, University, Sha Tin
沙田大學站澤祥街18號
www.hongkong.shatin.hyatt.com

👤 = $ 1,200-4,150
👥 = $ 1,200-4,150
Suites 套房 = $ 3,150-19,200
☕ = $ 218

Rooms 客房　434
Suites 套房　133

RECOMMENDED RESTAURANTS 餐廳推薦
Sha Tin 18 沙田 18　✗✗

Hyatt Regency Tsim Sha Tsui
尖沙咀凱悅

Occupying floors 3-24 of the impressive K11 skyscraper means that bedrooms here at the Hyatt Regency benefit from impressive views of the city or harbour. The rooms are decorated in a crisp, modern style; anyone choosing the Regency Club level has access to a private lounge. There are dining options galore and an impressive selection of whiskies in the Chin Chin Bar.

尖沙咀凱悅佔據K11摩天大樓的3至24層，並與K11購物藝術館相連，酒店房間能看到城市的繁華景色，或是醉人的維港景致。房間風格清新時尚，選擇嘉賓軒樓層的住客更可享受專用酒廊服務。酒店提供多種餐飲選擇，請請吧內的威士忌種類之多更是令人歎為觀止。

TEL. 2311 1234
FAX. 3721 1235
18 Hanoi Road, Tsim Sha Tsui
尖沙咀河內道 18號
www.hongkong.tsimshatsui.hyatt.com

RECOMMENDED RESTAURANTS 餐廳推薦
Hugo's 希戈 ✗✗

👤 = $ 1,750-5,600
👥 = $1,750-5,600
Suites 套房 = $ 3,550-22,200
☕ = $ 228

Rooms 客房 348
Suites 套房 33

Symbols shown in red indicate particularly charming establishments 🏠🏠 XxX.

紅色標誌 🏠🏠 XxX 表示酒店和餐館在同級別的舒適程度中較優秀。

If you are looking for particularly pleasant accommodation, book a hotel shown in red: 🏠…🏠🏠🏠.

欲享受特別舒適的留宿體驗,請參考注有此 🏠……🏠🏠🏠 紅色酒店標誌的推介酒店。

Icon
唯港薈

Rocco Yim, Sir Terence Conran and William Lim were among the celebrated designers brought together to create this chic hotel, which is owned and run by the Hong Kong Polytechnic University. Its style credentials are clear, from the works by local artists to the modern staircase and 'vertical garden'. Market is a buffet restaurant; formal dining in Above and Beyond.

著名設計師嚴迅奇、泰倫斯‧康藍爵士和林偉而等攜手打造出這間由香港理工大學營運、最新最潮的酒店。它的設計風格鮮明，可欣賞本地藝術家的精彩作品，亦有令人驚歎的現代化樓梯和垂直花園。The Market是廣受歡迎的自助餐廳，天外天則供應傳統粵菜。

TEL. 3400 1000
FAX. 3400 1001
17 Science Museum Road,
East Tsim Sha Tsui
尖東科學館道 17號
www.hotel-icon.com

RECOMMENDED RESTAURANTS 餐廳推薦
Above & Beyond 天外天　✗✗✗

🧍 = $ 2,700-5,000
🧍🧍 = $ 2,700-5,000
Suites 套房 = $ 5,300-10,000
☕ = $ 218

Rooms 客房　236
Suites 套房　26

Indigo
英迪格

Bordering Tai Yuen Street and its market, so ideally placed for discovering old Hong Kong, Indigo is also a good choice for those who've come to shop – there's even a shopping bag placed in every room! For others, there's always the rooftop bar and infinity pool. The bedrooms come with floor-to-ceiling windows and boast some cute design touches.

這幢外觀獨特的建築物座落於灣仔商業區及住宅區交界，不光擁有完善的交通網絡，更與有濃厚地區色彩的市集毗鄰，讓你深入了解本區生活脈搏。全部房間設有落地玻璃窗，傢俱擺設均經過精心設計，設施亦十分齊全，文具、購物袋一應俱全。天台玻璃底泳池，前臨山巒，感覺開揚，是放鬆身心的好地方。

TEL. 3926 3888
FAX. 3926 3926
246 Queen's Road East, Wan Chai
灣仔皇后大道東 246號
www.hotelindigo.com/hongkong

🧍 = $ 1,700-2,700
🧍🧍 = $ 1,700-2,700
Suites 套房 = $ 3,000-4,600
🛏 = $ 198

Rooms 客房　132
Suites 套房　6

Intercontinental
洲際

It may be unremarkable from the outside, but this hotel is decidedly impressive once you're in the lobby with its magnificent harbour views. All bedrooms are well-equipped, with spacious marble bathrooms. Relax in either the swimming pool or spa pool, or enjoy a massage in an outside cabana. Options for dining are excellent (see separate entries) and service is exemplary.

踏入富麗堂皇的酒店大堂,望着一流海景,絕對令你印象深刻。客房非常寬敞,淺色調的設計予人寧靜感覺,更設有寬闊的雲石浴室。你可以在優雅的游泳池或水療池鬆弛身心;戶外的池邊小室內有按摩服務。酒店內的餐飲服務非常出色,服務水準一流。

TEL. 2721 1211
FAX. 2739 4546
18 Salisbury Road, Tsim Sha Tsui
尖沙咀梳士巴利道 18號
www.intercontinental.com

RECOMMENDED RESTAURANTS 餐廳推薦
Nobu   XX
Spoon by Alain Ducasse   ✿   XxxX
The Steak House Wine bar + grill   XxX
Yan Toh Heen 欣圖軒 ✿✿   XxxX

♦ = $7,200-9,400
♦♦ = $7,200-9,400
Suites 套房 = $10,200-118,000
☕ = $320

Rooms 客房   478
Suites 套房   25

Intercontinental Grand Stanford
海景嘉福

After a comprehensive renovation programme, this 18-storey waterfront hotel, which opened back in 1981, is looking much more contemporary in style. The service is good and the bedrooms are a decent size – just be sure to ask for one with a harbour view. There are plenty of dining options and the heated outdoor swimming pool on the roof is nicely secluded.

這幢龐大的臨海建築物樓高18層，建於1981年並剛完成全面翻新工程。翻新後的寢室雅致時尚，因此訂房時謹記要選擇一間有海景並且經過翻新的房間。酒店頂層設有健身室及戶外溫水泳池。酒店內有數間食店供住客選擇。

TEL. 2721 5161
FAX. 2732 2233
70 Mody Road, East Tsim Sha Tsui
尖東麼地道 70號
www.hongkong.intercontinental.com

♂ = $ 4,700-6,200
♂♂ = $ 4,700-6,200
Suites 套房 = $ 10,000-25,000
☕ = $ 225

Rooms 客房　531
Suites 套房　39

Island Shangri-La
港島香格里拉

A vast, intricate Chinese silk painting towers over the glamorous atrium and rises up all of 16 storeys; more sparkle is provided by the dazzling array of chandeliers placed around the hotel. The bedrooms are thoughtfully laid out and comfortable; those rooms on the Horizon Club (52nd to 55th floor) are especially sumptuous and have access to a super rooftop terrace.

延伸至16樓、世上最大幅的中國絲綢畫，筆工細膩、構圖錯綜複雜，散發着迷人魅力，加上金光閃爍的吊燈，營造出五光十色的中庭，令人目眩神馳。樓上是華麗典雅的客房，尤以52至55樓豪華閣樓層的房間為甚，此樓層的住客可使用專屬會客廳和美不勝收的天台庭園。

TEL. 2877 3838
FAX. 2521 8742
Pacific Place, Supreme Court Road, Admiralty
中區法院道太古廣場
www.shangri-la.com

RECOMMENDED RESTAURANTS 餐廳推薦
Lobster Bar and Grill 龍蝦吧 XX
Petrus 珀翠 XXXXX
Summer Palace 夏宮 ❀❀ XXX

♦ = $4,600-6,000
♦♦ = $4,950-6,350
Suites 套房 = $10,400-31,600
☕ = $298

Rooms 客房 531
Suites 套房 34

JW Marriott
萬豪

Boasting 602 rooms spread over 35 storeys, this business hotel also offers a number of executive floors which have their own discreet lounge and meeting rooms. The bedrooms are functional but up-to-date and there's a pleasant outdoor pool and a well-equipped fitness centre. Dining options include Cantonese and seafood, along with a wine bar and tea room.

以商務住客為主的萬豪酒店樓高三十五層，客房數量達602間。位於頂樓的一列行政套房，附有素雅的休息室和會議室。房間設計富現代感且十分實用。戶外游泳池環境清幽、健身中心設備齊全，還網羅了各地餐飲美食，廣東菜、海鮮、酒吧、茶室等不同類別的餐室任君選擇。

TEL. 2810 8366
FAX. 2845 0737
Pacific Place, 88 Queensway, Admiralty
金鐘道88號太古廣場
www.jwmarriotthongkong.com

= $3,800-5,200
= $3,800-5,200
Suites 套房 = $6,800-7,300
= $298

Rooms 客房　577
Suites 套房　25

Kowloon Shangri-La
九龍香格里拉

The first thing to strike you will be the size and grandeur of the lobby, with its marble, sparkling chandeliers and tiered water fountain – it is certainly one of the most impressive aspects of this business-orientated hotel. The enthusiastic staff are another great strength. The bedrooms are larger than many of its competitors and come with a subtle Asian theme.

不僅是氣派宏偉的雲石酒店大堂，還是閃爍的吊燈與三層噴泉水池，都令你對這家以商務為主的酒店留下極深刻印象。全部客房都經過重新粉飾，跟其他同級酒店比較更見寬敞，服務水準更是無庸置疑。最佳的客房採用亞洲風情為主題作裝潢。

TEL. 2721 2111
FAX. 2723 8686
64 Mody Road, East Tsim Sha Tsui
尖東麼地道 64 號
www.shangri-la.com

RECOMMENDED RESTAURANTS 餐廳推薦
Shang Palace 香宮 ✿✿ XxxX

♦ = $ 2,600-3,200
♦♦ = $2,600-3,200
Suites 套房 = $ 4,380-22,480
☑ = $ 255

Rooms 客房　645
Suites 套房　43

Lan Kwai Fong
蘭桂坊

A hotel which feels part of the local area and mixes Chinese and contemporary furniture, neutral tones and dark wood veneers to create a relaxing environment. Try to secure one of the deluxe corner bedrooms or a suite with a balcony if you want more space; those higher than the 21st floor have the harbour views. Celebrity Cuisine offers accomplished Cantonese food.

融合了中國傳統與現代品味的傢俱，中性色調及深色木間隔，營造出舒適環境。如果你需要更寬敞的空間，建議預訂轉角位置的豪華客房或附設露台的套房。21樓以上的房間可飽覽維港景色。客人可借用房間內的流動電話，方便在外與朋友聯絡。

TEL. 3650 0000
FAX. 3650 0088
3 Kau U Fong, Central
中環九如坊 3號
www.lankwaifonghotel.com.hk

RECOMMENDED RESTAURANTS 餐廳推薦
Celebrity Cuisine 名人坊 ✿✿ XX

♦ = $ 1,200-4,000
♦♦ = $1,200-4,000
Suites 套房 = $ 3,000-7,000
☕ = $ 165

Rooms 客房　157
Suites 套房　5

Lanson Place

♿ ⚐ 🏊 🛗

This discreet and stylish boutique hotel comes with an air of calm exclusivity and an attractive European-influenced aesthetic. The cool lounge and bar allows the hotel to feel more intimate than the number of bedrooms would suggest. Those rooms come with small kitchenettes and have a clean and bright feel. The hotel is ideally located for those going to HK stadium.

擁有歐洲風格的典雅外觀，Lanson Place能稱為一間時尚精品酒店。古典與現代設計交織出酒店的獨特氣派，室內的藝術作品，營造溫暖寧靜的感覺。客房雅致明亮，設有大型窗戶，多家客房能眺望香港大球場。休閒舒適的休息室與酒吧也是入住期間值得蹓躂的地方。

TEL. 3477 6888
FAX. 3477 6999
133 Leighton Road, Causeway Bay
銅鑼灣禮頓道 133號
www.lansonplace.com

♦ = $ 1,800-4,000
♦♦ = $1,800-4,000
Suites 套房 = $ 4,800-12,000
☕ = $ 210

Rooms 客房 188
Suites 套房 6

LKF
蘭桂坊

LKF styles itself in the 'boutique' class and the wining and dining happens on the higher floors: Slash, on the 29th, is an intimate lounge bar and leads up to their restaurant and roof terrace. Contemporary bedrooms have been thoughtfully designed and come with espresso machines to give you a high, and comfortable beds with goose down pillows to bring you back down.

LKF屬於精品級酒店之列。酒店的樞紐安置在較高樓層：29樓的Slash是舒適時尚的酒廊；沿級而上便是酒店附設的餐廳及屋頂平台，客人可在此遠眺迷人景色。寬敞及時尚的客房設有蒸餾咖啡機，你可以邊呷着咖啡，邊靠着睡床上的鵝絨枕頭，享受一刻悠閒與安寧。

TEL. 3518 9688
FAX. 3518 9699
33 Wyndham Street, Lan Kwai Fong, Central
中環蘭桂坊雲咸街33號
www.hotel-LKF.com.hk

♦ = $ 1,800-8,000
♦♦ = $1,800-8,000
Suites 套房 = $ 3,500- 20,000
☕ = $200

Rooms 客房　86
Suites 套房　9

Mandarin Oriental
文華東方

Having celebrated its 50th birthday in 2013, this iconic hotel continues to update itself while remaining true to its heritage. Bedrooms may not be the largest but are charmingly decorated and are split between Tai Pan-style (woods and browns) and brighter Veranda-style. The spa is a spiritual haven and the dining and bar options are many and varied.

開業超過五十年，營運者在保留其優良傳統之餘，還致力提升其質素。和其他酒店相比，其客房並非最大，但無論是典雅的大班風格或陽台房間的裝潢均非常精緻，附設的水療設施令你如置身伊甸園；酒店還為客人提供多元化餐飲選擇。

TEL. 2522 0111
FAX. 2810 6190
5 Connaught Road, Central
中環干諾道中 5 號
www.mandarinoriental.com/hongkong

RECOMMENDED RESTAURANTS 餐廳推薦
Man Wah 文華廳 ✿ XxX
Mandarin Grill + Bar
文華扒房 + 酒吧 ✿ XxxX
Pierre ✿✿ XxxX

🛉 = $ 5,500-7,400
🛉🛉 = $ 5,500-7,400
Suites 套房 = $8,000-68,000
☕ = $288

Rooms 客房 430
Suites 套房 71

Metropark (Causeway Bay)
銅鑼灣維景

This 31-storey tower near Victoria is a popular choice for business travellers. Its bedrooms are not that large so it's worth booking one of the executive rooms, many of which have harbour views. The rooftop swimming pool is small but appealing and the views from the fitness centre help you deal with the pain of exercise. Café du Parc offers all-day buffet dining.

酒店大樓樓高三十一層，鄰近維多利亞公園，為商務旅客提供舒適環境及娛樂設施。這兒大部分房間的面積較小，因此選擇面積較大的行政套房絕對物有所值，而大部分房間可看到無敵海景。小型天台游泳池配備水底音樂，設計別出心裁。附設的繽紛維苑餐廳全日均有自助餐供應。

TEL. 2600 1000
FAX. 2600 1111
148 Tung Lo Wan Road, Causeway Bay
銅鑼灣道 148號
www.metroparkhotel.com

♦ = $ 2,500-5,900
♦♦ = $ 2,500-5,900
Suites 套房 = $ 6,900
☐ = $ 148

Rooms 客房 243
Suites 套房 23

New World Millennium
千禧新世界

The former Nikko hotel is now run by a different management company but little else has changed here. The hotel is known for its comprehensive banqueting and conference rooms and its impressive number of restaurants providing a wide range of different cuisines. The smart bedrooms come with up-to-the-minute comforts. The harbour-front location adds to the appeal.

日航酒店易名後，酒店完善的宴會及會議設施仍然保留，四間提供不同菜式的餐廳仍然為賓客提供多種選擇，令他們樂在其中；優越的海濱地段及設計現代化的智能客房，為顧客帶來舒適享受，上述種種條件均足以令它躋身國際級酒店之列。

TEL. 2739 1111
FAX. 2311 3122
72 Mody Road, East Tsim Sha Tsui
尖東麼地道 72號
www.newworldmillenniumhotel.com

♦ = $ 1,600-3,700
♦♦ = $ 1,600-3,700
Suites 套房 = $ 3,500-8,500
☕ = $ 270

Rooms 客房　445
Suites 套房　18

HONG KONG 香港

Ozo Wesley
遨舍衛蘭軒

⚐ ♿ ⚐ ⚐

You'll find Ozo Wesley sitting pretty between Wan Chai and Admiralty so it's ideally placed whether you're in town for business or just in the mood for shopping and dining. All of the guest rooms are crisply decorated in a bright, fresh and contemporary style and the effective soundproofing ensures a decent night's sleep however busy it is outside.

位於金鐘與灣仔交界，距金鐘的商業金融區只有數分鐘路程，附近的小街道滿佈食店，位置便利，適合商業旅客。大堂設計具時代感。251間客房，均以素色系配搭簡單時尚裝潢，舒適的感覺令你身心放鬆。全部房間都設有大玻璃窗和隔音設備，讓你既能欣賞灣仔的繁華景象又能享受片刻寧靜。

TEL. 2292 3000
FAX. 2292 3001
22 Hennessy Road, Wan Chai
灣仔軒尼詩道 22號
www.ozohotels.com

👤 = $ 3,850-4,850
👥 = $3,850-4,850
☕ = $ 145

Rooms 客房　235

Panorama
麗景

It will come as no great surprise to learn that the views from this well located hotel are rather impressive. The 324 bedrooms are divided into various categories that include Silver, Gold, Club Harbour and Suites. All benefit from having large windows but book a corner suite and you can even enjoy the terrific harbour vista from the bathtub!

麗景共有324間客房，按最新穎的意念，設計出三種房間類型：銀賓客房、黃金客房和尊貴海景客房。層數愈高，景觀愈發動人心弦。酒店最佳的客房位於角位，客人可以一邊享受泡浴，一邊欣賞迷人的維港美景。設於38樓的AVA餐廳佈置時尚，各式各樣的歐陸佳餚任君品嘗。

TEL. 3550 0388
FAX. 3550 0288
8A Hart Avenue, Tsim Sha Tsui
尖沙咀赫德道 8A號
www.hotelpanorama.com.hk

† = $ 4,000-7,200
†† = $4,000-7,200
Suites 套房 = $ 10,000-13,000
☕ = $ 198

Rooms 客房　312
Suites 套房　12

Royal Plaza
帝京

A comprehensive renovation has left the Royal Plaza looking stylish and contemporary. A new bar was created which provides striking views of Lion Rock, and the bedrooms, which were already a good size, now come with plenty of mod cons. The hotel is ideally placed in the heart of Kowloon and is surrounded by many of Hong Kong's traditional markets.

全新裝修的帝京酒店，時尚而富格調。新開設的Lion Rock酒吧，讓你飽覽獅子山美景。原本已稱得上寬敞的客房內，增設了不少現代化設備。酒店座落於繁盛的九龍中心位置，附近是最具本土氣息的街道市集。

TEL. 2928 8822
FAX. 2606 0088
193 Prince Edward Road West,
Mong Kok
旺角太子道西 193號
www.royalplaza.com.hk

♙ = $ 2,800-4,700
♙♙ = $3,200-5,100
Suites 套房 = $ 6,200-7,600
☕ = $ 148

Rooms 客房　659
Suites 套房　34

Sheraton
喜來登

One of Hong Kong's biggest hotels is a short walk from the Star Ferry Pier so you can expect some great views of Victoria Harbour. These can be best appreciated from the health club's rooftop pool, over a plate of oysters in the wine bar, or from a swish executive room on the 16th or 17th floor. The hotel also has a cigar room, a wine shop and an international café.

位於九龍半島的喜來登是香港最大的酒店之一，只需短短的步行距離便到達天星碼頭。客人可盡覽維多利亞港景色，最佳位置包括健身俱樂部的天台游泳池、16樓及17樓的高級面海行政套房，在蠔酒吧吃蠔時亦可欣賞美景。較為樸實但非常舒適的有雪茄廊、酒舖和國際咖啡廳。

TEL. 2369 1111
FAX. 2739 8707
20 Nathan Road, Tsim Sha Tsui
尖沙咀彌敦道 20號
www.sheraton.com/hongkong

RECOMMENDED RESTAURANTS 餐廳推薦
Celestial Court 天寶閣　XXX

♦ = $ 4,800-6,900
♦♦ = $ 4,800-6,900
Suites 套房 = $ 7,500-16,000
⌷ = $ 245

Rooms 客房　691
Suites 套房　91

The Fleming
芬名

An attractive, contemporary lobby draws you into this centrally located Wan Chai hotel. Bedrooms offer decent dimensions for such an urban environment, with standard rooms measuring 20 square metres. The hotel also acknowledges its varied clientele by offering 'Her Space' or 'His Space' rooms with differing amenities. The diminutive Cubix serves international cuisine.

酒店位於灣仔心臟地帶，充滿時尚氣息的大堂極具吸引力。其標準客房面積達20平方米，在擁擠的市區環境中，為你提供充裕的私人空間。為照顧不同客人需要，店內設有男士及女士專用客房，備有各具特色的用品。精巧的餐廳Cubix 供應多國美食。

TEL. 3607 2288
FAX. 3607 2299
41 Fleming Road, Wan Chai
灣仔菲林明道 41 號
www.thefleming.com

♦ = $ 1,100-4,280
♦♦ = $1,100-4,280
☐ = $ 158

Rooms 客房 66

The Landmark Mandarin Oriental
置地文華東方

From the personal airport pick-up to the endless spa choices, this is the hotel for those after a little pampering. Not only are the comfortable, smartly designed bedrooms big on luxury and size but they also come with stylish bathrooms attached; these feature either sunken or circular baths. MO is the cool ground floor bar for all-day dining or night time cocktails.

從專人機場接送服務到設備完善的水療設備，置地文華東方讓你盡享尊貴服務。令人讚歎的不光是設計型格獨特、面積達450至600呎的寬敞客房，還有房內豪華時尚的浴室設備，包括巨型下沈式或圓形浴缸。位於地下的MO Bar是解決一日三餐和品嘗雞尾酒的好去處。

TEL. 2132 0188
FAX. 2132 0199
15 Queen's Road, Central
中環皇后大道中 15號
www.mandarinoriental.com/landmark

RECOMMENDED RESTAURANTS 餐廳推薦
Amber ✿✿ ✗✗✗✗

👤 = $6,000-8,400
👤👤 = $6,000-8,400
Suites 套房 = $18,000
☕ = $240

Rooms 客房　101
Suites 套房　11

HONG KONG 香港

The Langham
朗廷

Once inside the hushed surroundings of this elegant hotel, the clamour of Peking Road feels like a distant memory. Its striking lobby, furnished in a classical European style, features some impressive contemporary art and sculptures. Bedrooms are quite traditional in style and comfortable. The charm of the hotel is underpinned by modern facilities and attentive service.

進入這棟優雅建築物,讓你立刻忘卻北京道熙來攘往的煩囂。大堂以傳統歐洲風格裝潢,配上當代藝術品及雕塑作點綴,奢華奪目。豪華客房融合了古典歐陸情調和當代中國風格兩種風味迥異的元素。迷人之處,盡見於其現代設施及細心服務。

TEL. 2375 1133
FAX. 2375 6611
8 Peking Road, Tsim Sha Tsui
尖沙咀北京道 8號
www.hongkong.langhamhotels.com

RECOMMENDED RESTAURANTS 餐廳推薦
T'ang Court 唐閣 ❀❀❀ 𝟀𝟀𝟀𝟀
The Bostonian 美岸海鮮廳 𝟀𝟀

🚹 = $ 3,000-4,500
🚹🚹 = $3,000-4,500
Suites 套房 = $ 5,200-19,500
☕ = $ 238

Rooms 客房　464
Suites 套房　25

The Mercer
尚圜

Those who need the convenience of a Central location but also want a little space should consider The Mercer. The narrow 31 storey building just has 15 standard bedrooms but 40 one-bedroom suites. Ubiquitous beige tones add to the up-to-date feel and rooms come with large writing desks and a host of free extras which include the minibar and local phone calls.

如果你既愛中環的便利，又需要較多私人空間，尚圜酒店絕對適合你。建築外型修長，樓高三十一層，只有十五間標準客房，卻有達四十間單人睡房套間。統一的米白色調營造出時尚感覺，房間設有大型書桌和附送多項免費服務，包括免費本地電話服務和迷你酒吧。

TEL. 2922 9988
FAX. 2922 9920
29 Jervois Street, Sheung Wan
上環蘇杭街29號
www.themercer.com.hk

👤 = $ 1,980-4,000
👤👤 = $1,980-4,000
Suites 套房 = $ 3,000-6,000

Rooms 客房　15
Suites 套房　40

RECOMMENDED RESTAURANTS 餐廳推薦
Sushi Shikon 志魂 ❀❀❀ 🍴

The Mira

Give every room an Arne Jacobsen 'Egg chair'; add a cool, urban aesthetic and all the hi-tech extras you'll ever need and you have The Mira – a stylish, vibrant and modern hotel. What the rooms may lack in size, they more than make up for in design and it's worth asking for one facing Kowloon Park. Bathrooms are equally impressive and suites even more spectacular.

型格、現代的設計，再加上高科技產品，你得到的就是The Mira－一家極為時尚、充滿活力的摩登酒店。房間面積略小，但出色的設計可彌補不足，浴室非常現代化；套房裝潢豪華。訂房時不妨要求面向九龍公園的客房。舒適豪華的水療設施值得一讚。

TEL. 2368 1111
FAX. 2369 1788
118 Nathan Road, Tsim Sha Tsui
尖沙咀彌敦道118號
www.themirahotel.com

RECOMMENDED RESTAURANTS 餐廳推薦
Cuisine Cuisine at The Mira 國金軒 XXX
Whisk XX

♂ = $ 3,600-4,500
♂♂ = $ 3,600-4,500
Suites 套房 = $ 7,000-48,000
☕ = $ 228

Rooms 客房 446
Suites 套房 46

The Peninsula
半島

2013 saw the grande dame of Hong Kong hotels celebrate her 85th birthday, just as the refurbishment of the bedrooms was completed – they now come with a contemporary elegance and clever touch-pad technology. The iconic lobby remains the place for afternoon tea; the spa boasts a Roman-style pool; and a host of dining choices range from the modern to the traditional.

酒店內部修葺已於2013年年初竣工，剛好趕及慶祝酒店開業85週年。經重新粉飾後的客房更時尚雅致，房內設備全部透過高科技觸控屏操作。作為酒店標誌的大堂保留原來樣式，供顧客享用下午茶；羅馬式泳池仍然是一貫的迷人；新派菜和傳統菜餐館一應俱全。

TEL. 2920 2888
FAX. 2722 4170
Salisbury Road, Tsim Sha Tsui
尖沙咀梳士巴利道
www.peninsula.com

RECOMMENDED RESTAURANTS 餐廳推薦
Chesa 瑞樵閣　XX
Felix　XX
Gaddi's 吉地士　XxxX
Spring Moon 嘉麟樓　XxX

† = $ 5,880-8,580
†† = $ 5,880-8,580
Suites 套房 = $10,800-128,000
☕ = $350

Rooms 客房　246
Suites 套房　54

The Pottinger
中環・石板街

Standing in the middle of Central, and on one of Hong Kong's oldest 'stone slab streets', is this elegant and stylish hotel. Its location is celebrated through its collection of iconic and historic photographs taken by award-winning artist Fan Ho. The 68 bedrooms are contemporary and graceful and boast all the amenities the modern traveller expects.

位於有過百年歷史的砵甸乍街(又名石板街)旁邊,故以此命名。斜斜的石板路見證了中環百多年來的故事,也為酒店增添了一分魅力。接待廳雖小卻流露着歐陸優雅格調,共有68間客房,面積適中、設備齊全。位處中環心臟地帶,無論往辦公、飲食、娛樂或乘搭交通工具都非常便利,是商務住宿的理想選擇。

TEL. 2308 3188
74 Queen's Road Central, Central
中環皇后大道中 74號
www.thepottinger.com

RECOMMENDED RESTAURANTS 餐廳推薦
Ta Vie 旅 ✿ XX

👤 = $ 1,300-3,800
👥 = $ 1,300-3,800
Suites 套房 = $ 4,000-8,000

Rooms 客房　61
Suites 套房　7

The Ritz-Carlton
麗思卡爾頓

The highest hotel in the world occupies the top 16 floors of Hong Kong's tallest building; to witness first-hand just how high this feels, head up to the cool Ozone bar on the 118th floor – it even comes with an outside terrace! Bedrooms are large and elegant and the suites are equipped with telescopes so guests can keep an eye on what's happening down on earth.

這家全球最高酒店佔據了香港最高建築物最頂的16層樓，部分人置身其中可能會感到暈眩。其位於118層的Ozone 酒吧設有戶外露台，而游泳池也設於海拔490米高處。酒店客房空間佫大、裝潢高雅，套房中還設有望遠鏡，讓住客居高臨下俯瞰香港景色。

TEL. 2263 2263
FAX. 2263 2260
International Commerce Centre,
1 Austin Road West, Tsim Sha Tsui
尖沙咀柯士甸道西 1號環球貿易廣場
www.ritzcarlton.com/hongkong

RECOMMENDED RESTAURANTS 餐廳推薦
Tin Lung Heen 天龍軒 ❀❀ XxxX
Tosca ❀ XxxX

♦ = $ 7,600-11,100
♦♦ = $ 7,600-11,100
Suites 套房 = $ 16,000-139,000
☖ = $ 318

Rooms 客房 262
Suites 套房 50

The Royal Garden
帝苑

The Royal Garden is a hotel that seems to exude class. One of its most notable features is its 110 foot atrium – guestrooms are accessed through corridors which overlook it. Those bedrooms are decorated to a good standard and come with an impressive array of modern facilities. Guests also have an impressive number of restaurants from which to choose.

帝苑酒店是一間與別不同的酒店，110呎高以繁茂的枝葉裝潢的中庭更是其最大特色，不論住宿在哪一個樓層，沿走廊進入客房時都能俯視庭內景況。客房設計具水準，且附有現代化設備。酒店內還設有多家不同種類的餐館，中外菜式應有盡有。

TEL. 2721 5215
FAX. 2369 9976
69 Mody Road, East Tsim Sha Tsui
尖東麼地道 69號
www.rghk.com.hk

RECOMMENDED RESTAURANTS 餐廳推薦
Dong Lai Shun (Tsim Sha Tsui)
東來順 （尖沙咀）✗✗
Le Soleil ✗✗

♦ = $ 4,000-6,000
♦♦ = $ 4,000-6,000
Suites 套房 = $ 6,800-68,800
☕ = $ 288

Rooms 客房　372
Suites 套房　48

The Upper House
奕居

This discreet and stylish hotel is on the wish-list of fashionistas everywhere. The clever use of art, sculpture and natural materials makes one feel one is in a private house, albeit one with a pervading sense of calm and luxury. Bedrooms are airy and uncluttered, with concealed hi-tech extras. The large bathrooms have great 'traveller's bags' and good views.

奕居早已成為潮流人士趨之若鶩的住宿熱點，是一家經過精心設計，細緻豪華的時尚酒店。藝術品、雕塑和天然物料帶來非凡效果，瀰漫着平和氣息，營造出私人居所的感覺。房間開揚而秩序井然，隱藏着不少高科技用品。大型浴室提供高級沐浴用品，更可觀賞美妙景色。

TEL. 2918 1838
FAX. 3968 1200
Pacific Place, 88 Queensway, Admiralty
金鐘道 88號太古廣場
www.upperhouse.com

RECOMMENDED RESTAURANTS 餐廳推薦
Café Gray Deluxe　XX

♦ = $4,500-6,000
♦♦ = $4,500-6,000
Suites 套房 = $12,000-17,000
☐ = $245

Rooms 客房　96
Suites 套房　21

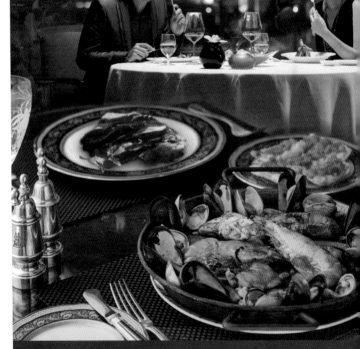

Tasteful Moments

*Enjoy the fusion between the brilliance of international and local cuisine,
savor the elegant contrast between the modern and the traditional.
Indulge in the city's living culture and treasure each tasteful moment.*

TOUCHING MOMENTS
EXPERIENCE MACAU

MACAU
澳門

RESTAURANTS
餐廳

STARRED RESTAURANTS
星級餐廳

Within this selection, we have highlighted a number of restaurants for their particularly good cooking. When awarding one, two or three Michelin Stars there are a number of factors we consider: the quality and compatibility of the ingredients, the technical skill and flair that goes into their preparation, the clarity and combination of flavours, the value for money and above all, the taste. Equally important is the ability to produce excellent cooking not once but time and time again. Our inspectors make as many visits as necessary, so that you can be sure of the quality and consistency.

A two or three star restaurant has to offer something very special that separates it from the rest. Three stars – our highest award – are given to the very best.

Cuisines in any style of restaurant and of any nationality are eligible for a star. The decoration, service and comfort levels have no bearing on the award.

在這系列的選擇裡，推薦的是食物質素特別出色的餐廳。給予一、二或三粒米芝蓮星時，我們考慮到以下因素：材料的質素和配搭、烹調技巧和特色、氣味濃度和組合、價錢是否相宜及味道層次。同樣重要的是該餐館的食物恆常保持在高水平。閣下對我們的推薦絕對可以放心！我們的評審員會因應需要多次到訪同一家餐館，以確認其食物品質能恆常保持高水準。

二或三星餐廳必有獨特之處，比同類型其他餐廳更出眾。最高評級 – 三星 – 只會給予最好的餐廳。

星級評定不會受到餐廳風格、菜式、裝潢陳設、服務及舒適程度影響。只要烹調技巧出色，食物品質特別優秀，都有機會獲得米芝蓮星星。

✿ ✿ ✿
Exceptional cuisine, worth a special journey.
卓越的烹調，值得專程到訪。

Our highest award is given for the superlative cooking of chefs at the peak of their profession. The ingredients are exemplary, the cooking is elevated to an art form and their dishes are often destined to become classics.

獲得最高級別的餐館，其廚師的烹調技巧卓絕，選用用料堪稱典範，並將烹飪提升至藝術層次，菜式大多會成為經典。

Robuchon au Dôme

Excellent cooking, worth a detour.
烹調出色,值得刻意造訪。

The personality and talent of the chef and their team is evident in the refined, expertly crafted dishes.

主廚的個人風格與烹飪天賦及其團隊的優秀手藝完全反映在精巧味美的菜式上。

Golden Flower 京花軒		XxxX	Chinese 中國菜	403
Jade Dragon 譽瓏軒	⅋	XxX	Cantonese 粵菜	410
The Tasting Room 御膳房	⅋	XxxX	French contemporary 時尚法國菜	440
Zi Yat Heen 紫逸軒		XxxX	Cantonese 粵菜	449

High quality cooking, worth a stop!
優質烹調,不妨一試!

Within their category, these establishments use quality ingredients and serve carefully prepared dishes with distinct flavours.

此名單上的餐館,在同類型餐館中,其食材較具質素,烹調細緻用心、味道出色。

Feng Wei Ju 風味居	NEW	XxX	Hunanese and Sichuan 湘川菜	401
King 帝皇樓		XX	Cantonese 粵菜	413
Mizumi 泓	NEW	XxX	Japanese 日本菜	422
8 1/2 Otto e Mezzo	NEW	XxX	Italian 意大利菜	428
Shinji 金坂	NEW	XX	Sushi 壽司	431
Terrazza 庭園	⅋	XxX	Italian 意大利菜	435
The Golden Peacock 皇雀		XX	Indian 印度菜	437
The Kitchen 大廚		XX	Steakhouse 扒房	438
Tim's Kitchen 桃花源小廚		XxX	Cantonese 粵菜	441
Wing Lei 永利軒		XxxX	Cantonese 粵菜	444

BIB GOURMAND RESTAURANTS
車胎人美食推介餐廳

TThis symbol indicates our inspectors' favourites for good value. These restaurants offer quality cooking for $300 or less (price of a 3 course meal excluding drinks).

這標誌表示評審員認為最超值的餐廳：費用在 300 元或以下（三道菜式但不包括飲料）

A Lorcha 船屋		X	Portuguese 葡國菜	380
Café Leon 利安咖啡屋		X	Portuguese 葡國菜	389
Chan Seng Kei 陳勝記		🍜	Cantonese 粵菜	394
Cheong Kei 祥記		🍜	Noodles 麵食	395
Din Tai Fung (COD) 鼎泰豐 (新濠天地)	NEW	X	Shanghainese 滬菜	397
Hou Kong Chi Kei 濠江志記美食		🍜	Cantonese 粵菜	406
IFT Educational Restaurant 旅遊學院教學餐廳		XX	Macanese 澳門菜	407
Lou Kei (Fai Chi Kei) 老記 (筷子基)		🍜	Cantonese 粵菜	417
Luk Kei Noodle 六記粥麵		🍜	Noodles and Congee 粥麵	418
Manuel Cozinha Portuguesa 阿曼諾葡國餐		X	Portuguese 葡國菜	420
Tou Tou Koi 陶陶居		X	Cantonese 粵菜	442

NEW : New entry in the guide 新增推介
🍜 : Restaurant promoted to a Bib Gourmand or Star 評級有所晉升的餐廳

RESTAURANTS BY AREA
餐廳 — 以地區分類

Coloane 路環

Macau 澳門

NEW ：New entry in the guide 新增推介

😋 ：Restaurant promoted to a Bib Gourmand or Star 評級有所晉升的餐廳

Taipa 氹仔

RESTAURANTS BY CUISINE TYPE
餐廳 — 以菜式分類

Cantonese 粵菜

Canton 喜粵			XxX	Taipa 氹仔	390
Chan Seng Kei 陳勝記		⊛	吕	Coloane 路環	394
Dynasty 8 朝			XxX	Taipa 氹仔	399
Hou Kong Chi Kei 濠江志記美食		⊛	吕	Macau 澳門	406
Imperial Court 金殿堂			XxX	Macau 澳門	409
Jade Dragon 譽瓏軒	⌣	❀❀	XxX	Taipa 氹仔	410
Kam Lai Heen 金麗軒	NEW		XX	Macau 澳門	411
King 帝皇樓		❀	XX	Macau 澳門	413
Lai Heen 麗軒	NEW		XxXxX	Taipa 氹仔	415
Lei Garden 利苑酒家			XX	Taipa 氹仔	416
Lou Kei (Fai Chi Kei) 老記(筷子基)		⊛	吕	Macau 澳門	417
Lung Wah Tea House 龍華茶樓			吕	Macau 澳門	419
San Tou Tou 新陶陶			X	Taipa 氹仔	430
Tim's Kitchen 桃花源小廚		❀	XxX	Macau 澳門	441
Tou Tou Koi 陶陶居		⊛	X	Macau 澳門	442
Wing Lei 永利軒		❀	XxxX	Macau 澳門	444
Ying 帝影樓			XxX	Taipa 氹仔	448
Zi Yat Heen 紫逸軒		❀❀	XxxX	Taipa 氹仔	449

Cantonese Roast Meats 燒味

Chan Kuong Kei (Rua do Dr. Pedro Jose Lobo) 陳光記(羅保博士街)		吕	Macau 澳門	393

Chinese 中國菜

Beijing Kitchen 滿堂彩		XX	Taipa 氹仔	386
Golden Flower 京花軒	❀❀	XxxX	Macau 澳門	403
Square Eight 食 · 八方		X	Macau 澳門	432
The Eight 8餐廳	❀❀❀	XxxX	Macau 澳門	436

NEW : New entry in the guide 新增推介
⌣ : Restaurant promoted to a Bib Gourmand or Star 評級有所晉升的餐廳

Tenmasa 天政	XX	Taipa 氹仔	434

Korean 韓國菜

Myung Ga 名家	X	Taipa 氹仔	423

Macanese 澳門菜

Café Encore 咖啡廷		XX	Macau 澳門	388
Carlos 加路		X	Macau 澳門	391
IFT Educational Restaurant 旅遊學院教學餐廳	🍴	XX	Macau 澳門	407

Noodles 麵食

Cheong Kei 祥記	🍴	🍜	Macau 澳門	395
99 Noodles 99麵		X	Macau 澳門	427

Noodles and Congee 粥麵

Luk Kei Noodle 六記粥麵	🍴	🍜	Macau 澳門	418
Ngao Kei Ka Lei Chon 牛記咖喱美食		🍜	Macau 澳門	425
Wong Kung Sio Kung 皇冠小館		🍜	Macau 澳門	445
Wong Kung Sio Kung (Broadway) 皇冠小館 (百老匯) NEW		🍜	Taipa 氹仔	446

Portuguese 葡國菜

A Lorcha 船屋	🍴	X	Macau 澳門	380
A Petisqueira 葡國美食天地		X	Taipa 氹仔	381
Antonio 安東尼奧		XX	Taipa 氹仔	382
Banza 百姓		X	Taipa 氹仔	385
Café Leon 利安咖啡屋	🍴	X	Taipa 氹仔	389
Castiço		X	Taipa 氹仔	392
Clube Militar de Macau 澳門陸軍俱樂部		XX	Macau 澳門	396
Espaço Lisboa 里斯本地帶		X	Coloane 路環	400
Gosto 葡軒		X	Taipa 氹仔	404
Guincho a Galera 葡國餐廳		XxxX	Macau 澳門	405
Manuel Cozinha Portuguesa 阿曼諾葡國餐	🍴	X	Taipa 氹仔	420

Shanghainese 滬菜

Din Tai Fung (COD)
鼎泰豐（新濠天地）   NEW   ⊛   ॸ   Taipa 氹仔   397

Singaporean and Malaysian 星馬菜

Katong Corner 咖東   NEW   🍜   Taipa 氹仔   412

Spanish 西班牙菜

La Paloma 芭朗瑪   ॸॸ   Macau 澳門   414

Steakhouse 扒房

The Kitchen 大廚   ✿   ॸॸ   Macau 澳門   438

Sushi 壽司

Shinji 金坂   NEW   ✿   ॸॸ   Taipa 氹仔   431

Thai 泰國菜

Naam 灆   NEW   ॸॸ   Macau 澳門   424

NEW : New entry in the guide 新增推介
⤷ : Restaurant promoted to a Bib Gourmand or Star 評級有所晉升的餐廳

STREET FOOD
街頭小吃

Popular places for snack food
馳名小食店

Aboong 韓國鯛魚燒乳酪雪糕	Macau 澳門	450
Chong Shing 昌盛	Macau 澳門	450
Dai Gwan 台灣帝鈞碳烤胡椒餅	Macau 澳門	450
Fong Kei 晃記餅家	Taipa 氹仔	451
Lei Ka Choi 李家菜	Taipa 氹仔	451
Lemon Cello 檸檬車露	Macau 澳門	451
Lord Stow's Bakery 安德魯餅店	Coloane 路環	451
Mok Yee Kei 莫義記	Taipa 氹仔	452
Neng Meng Wang 檸檬王	Macau 澳門	452
Sun Ying Kei 新英記	Macau 澳門	452
Ving Kei 榮記荳腐	Macau 澳門	452
Yi Shun 義順鮮奶	Macau 澳門	453

A Lorcha
船屋

🍴   ℂ🍴

Business is booming at this friendly Portuguese restaurant and that's not just because it's close to Barra Temple. The owner's mother still holds the most important role here – as head chef – and she makes sure the quality of the food remains high. A charcoal grill in the kitchen is used for the barbecue and grill dishes and carefully prepared specialities include Ameijoas "Bulhão Pato", Arroz de marisco à Portuguesa and Galinha à Africana.

這家服務親切殷勤的葡國餐廳，位於媽閣廟附近，但地點便利並非其成功的主要因素。餐廳總廚的要職由東主母親擔任，致力保持食品質素和正宗風味。燒烤菜式全部用炭爐烹調。餐廳精選推介包括橄欖油香蒜炒鮮蜆、葡式燴海鮮飯及非洲辣雞。

TEL. 2831 3193
289 Rua do Almirante Sérigo
河邊新街 289號

■ PRICE 價錢
Lunch 午膳
à la carte 點菜 MOP 200-350
Dinner 晚膳
à la carte 點菜 MOP 200-350

■ OPENING HOURS 營業時間
Lunch 午膳　12:30-15:00 L.O. 14:30
Dinner 晚膳　18:30-23:00 L.O. 22:30

■ ANNUAL AND WEEKLY CLOSING 休息日期
Closed Tuesday　週二休息

A Petisqueira
葡國美食天地

Step through the door and you'll instantly feel as though you've been transported to a cosy little restaurant in the Portuguese countryside. A small bar at the entrance leads you into a simple, rustic dining room where the focus is on classic Portuguese cuisine served in a friendly, unpretentious atmosphere. Authentic dishes include bacalhau prepared in five different ways, and fried clams; look out too for the daily specials.

甫踏進大門，你便會感到仿如置身葡萄牙鄉村中的小餐館內。入口設有小酒吧，緩緩而入便是設計淳樸且帶鄉村風味的餐室；這兒供應的傳統葡國美食做法正宗而不花巧，服務親切友善。推介食物為炒蜆及以五種不同方法烹調的馬介休；每日會提供六至七款是日精選，不妨一試。

TEL. 2882 5354
15 Rua S. Joao, Taipa
氹仔生央街 15號

■ PRICE 價錢
Lunch 午膳
à la carte 點菜 MOP 180-400
Dinner 晚膳
à la carte 點菜 MOP 180-400

■ OPENING HOURS 營業時間
Lunch 午膳　12:30-14:15 (L.O.)
Dinner 晚膳　18:45-22:00 (L.O.)

■ ANNUAL AND WEEKLY CLOSING 休息日期
Closed Monday 週一休息

Antonio
安東尼奧

🍴   🏠 📅12 📞

Antonio now occupies a three storey house, with dining rooms divided between the ground and first floors; it also has a charming little terrace. Wooden floors, Portuguese glazed tiles and leather seats help create a European look, while the paintings add a more contemporary note. The eponymous owner-chef provides friendly service and his specialities include gratinated goat's cheese with honey and olive oil, and seafood stew in a copper pot.

安東尼奧現址在離舊店不遠的一座三層高小屋中，餐室主要在地下和二樓，還附有小陽台。為了營造歐陸風情，店主選用了木地板、葡式瓷磚及皮椅，牆上的油畫替店子添了點現代氣息。店主的好客熱情和餐單卻保持不變，蜜糖橄欖油烤山羊芝士和海鮮雜燴當然仍在餐單上。

TEL. 2899 9998
7 Rua dos Clerigos
氹仔木鐸街 7號
www.antoniomacau.com

SPECIALITIES TO PRE-ORDER 預訂食物
Cabidela duck rice 血鴨飯 / Portuguese veal stew 葡萄牙燉牛仔肉

■ PRICE 價錢
à la carte 點菜 MOP 300-500

■ OPENING HOURS 營業時間
12:00-00:00 L.O. 22:30

Aruna's Maharaja Indian Curry
阿露娜印度皇室咖喱

Aruna opened one of the first Indian restaurants in Macau, back in 1983; this, her most recent branch, is her biggest. It's spread over two floors and, as the name suggests, there is something palatial about the look, with its marble floors and golden sculptures. The menu is not too big, with northern India providing the most popular specialities, such as samosa chaat and royal lamb curry; be sure to end with gulab jamum.

早於1983年，阿露娜就在澳門開設第一家印度餐廳，而這間店子是她旗下規模最大的分店。樓高兩層，全店鋪上雲石地板並飾以黃金雕塑，裝潢散發着宮廷氣派。其菜牌選擇不多，供應最受歡迎的乳酪咖喱角及皇牌咖喱羊肉等北印度美食，別忘記以甜蜜圓為完美一餐劃上句號。

TEL. 2877 2844
92 Avenida de Marciano Baptista
新口岸畢仕達大馬路 92號

■ PRICE 價錢
Lunch 午膳
à la carte 點菜 MOP 90-180
Dinner 晚膳
à la carte 點菜 MOP 90-180

■ OPENING HOURS 營業時間
Lunch 午膳　11:00-15:30 (L.O.)
Dinner 晚膳　18:00-23:00 (L.O.)

Aurora NEW
奧羅拉

🔾 ⟨ 🖐 **P** ⛉16 🚋 ☎🍴

Having a drink on the stunning terrace is a must before eating at this contemporary Italian restaurant – it's on the 10th floor of Altira Macau and provides terrific views of Macau. The restaurant has an elegant and sophisticated feel, which is helped along by the attentive and well-informed staff. There's an open kitchen and also some counter seating; the cuisine is creative and accomplished and there's an attractively priced set menu at lunch.

空間寬敞、設計時尚的奧羅拉位於新濠鋒酒店10樓，落地玻璃窗築成一道有形無色的城牆，將明亮的餐室與只供客人會飲、景色迷人的露台分隔；一到晚上，不論於室內室外均能欣賞到醉人夜色。侍應的服務貼心專注；還可讓侍酒師替你配搭餐點與美酒。午市套餐價錢甚具吸引力。

TEL. 8803 6678
10F, Altira Hotel, Avenida De Kwong Tung, Taipa
氹仔廣東大馬路新濠鋒酒店 10樓
www.altiramacau.com

■ PRICE 價錢
Lunch 午膳
set 套餐 MOP 188-368
à la carte 點菜 MOP 400-900

Dinner 晚膳
set 套餐 MOP 688-888
à la carte 點菜 MOP 400-900

■ OPENING HOURS 營業時間
Lunch 午膳   12:00-14:00 (L.O.)
Dinner 晚膳   18:30-22:15 (L.O.)

■ ANNUAL AND WEEKLY CLOSING 休息日期
Closed Sunday dinner & Monday
週日晚膳及週一休息

Banza
百姓

🍴　　　　　　　　　　　　　　　　　　　　　📞🍴

The Portuguese owner, whose nickname is Banza, visits local markets each morning to decide on the chef's frequently changing specials; fish dishes tend to be the most popular choice among his many regulars. The restaurant lies in the shadow of a huge apartment complex and comes in tones of green and white, with large paintings and a cosy mezzanine seating about six. Banza can also give you advice on his selection of Portuguese wines.

此店以店主的別名命名，他每天早上都會前往市場，為每日精選尋找靈感和挑選食材。眾多美食中以魚類最受歡迎。餐廳座落於氹仔的大型屋苑內，四周環境寧靜。裝潢以白、綠為主色，掛有大型畫作。Banza還會向你介紹他精選的葡萄牙美酒。

TEL. 2882 1519
Avenida de Kwong Tung, n°s 154A e 154B, Edf. Nam San Garden, Bl. 5, r/c "G" e "H", Taipa
氹仔廣東大馬路 154A及 154B號
南新花園第 5座地下 G,H座

■ PRICE 價錢
Lunch 午膳
à la carte 點菜 MOP 200-480
Dinner 晚膳
à la carte 點菜 MOP 200-480

■ OPENING HOURS 營業時間
Lunch 午膳　12:00-15:00 (L.O.)
Dinner 晚膳　18:30-22:30 (L.O.)

■ ANNUAL AND WEEKLY CLOSING 休息日期
Closed Monday 週一休息

Beijing Kitchen
滿堂彩

    ⬚12 ◔

'Dinner and a show' at Beijing Kitchen means one and the same, as the cooking is divided between four lively show kitchens which will hold your attention. There's a dim sum and noodle area; a duck section with two applewood-fired ovens; a wok station; and a dessert counter whose bounty is well worth leaving room for. Northern China provides many of the specialities. Ask for one of the tables under the birdcages suspended from the ceiling.

這家店子有四個開放式廚房：點心與粉麵區、烤鴨區、明爐小炒區和甜品區；食客在進餐之餘還能欣賞現場「直播」的烹飪表演，稱得上集用膳與娛樂於一身。烤鴨區廚房內懸掛着兩座燃木窯爐，甚具特色，因此絕不能錯過這兒的烤鴨。招牌菜以北方菜為主。建議選擇天花上懸着鳥籠的座位，別有趣味。

TEL. 8868 1930
GF, Grand Hyatt Hotel, Estrado do Istmo, Cotai
路氹連貫公路君悅酒店地下
www.macau.grand.hyatt.com

■ PRICE 價錢
à la carte 點菜 MOP 300-1,000

■ OPENING HOURS 營業時間
11:30-00:00 (L.O.)

Belcanção
鳴詩

Belcanção is a relaxing buffet restaurant and is ideal for anyone who fancies a quick culinary world tour that's easy on the wallet. Warm, natural colours of brown and beige decorate the elegant room, while chefs from different countries man the open kitchens. There are stations offering Portuguese, Chinese, Indian and international cuisines, along with a selection of mostly French pastries. Brunch at weekends is served from 12-3pm.

鳴詩氣氛閒適輕鬆，價錢實惠，適合喜歡於一頓飯內嘗遍全球美食的食客。餐室以暖色系、感覺自然的棕色和米白色裝飾，來自不同國家的廚師分別掌管各個開放式廚房。店內提供葡萄牙、國際、中國及印度美食和一系列法國糕點。周末早午併餐供應時間為中午十二時至下午三時。

TEL. 2881 8811
GF, Four Seasons Hotel, Estrada da Baia de N. Senhora da Esperanca, s/n, The Cotai Strip, Taipa
氹仔路氹金光大道 -望德聖母灣大馬路
四季酒店地下
www.fourseasons.com/macau/

■ PRICE 價錢
Lunch 午膳
set 套餐 MOP 198
Dinner 晚膳
set 套餐 MOP 498-588

■ OPENING HOURS 營業時間
Lunch 午膳   12:00-14:30 (L.O.)
Dinner 晚膳   18:00-22:30 (L.O.)

Café Encore
咖啡廷

Café Encore is an elegant restaurant on the ground floor of the Encore hotel. The look is that of a classic European café but one with a strong Italian accent. The menu offers a combination of Macanese and Portuguese cuisine, along with a separate menu of Cantonese dishes, but it is in the Macanese specialities that the kitchen particularly excels. Try dishes like curried crab and baked African chicken.

咖啡廷位於萬利酒店地下，格調高雅。餐廳設計以傳統歐洲餐館裝潢作藍本，並滲入大量意大利藝術元素。菜單以澳門菜與葡國菜為主，另設有粵菜菜單。不過這裡最出色的還是地道澳門菜，例如咖喱蟹與非洲雞。

TEL. 8986 3616
GF, Encore Hotel, Rua Cicade de Sintra, Nape
外港新填海區仙德麗街萬利酒店地下
www.wynnmacau.com

■ PRICE 價錢
à la carte 點菜 MOP 250-800

■ OPENING HOURS 營業時間
06:30-03:00 (L.O.)

Café Leon
利安咖啡屋

Many will have fond memories of Café Leon from the years it sat by Sai Van lake. It's now in Taipa and boasts a new and slightly more contemporary look, but what hasn't changed is the food which is prepared by the same kitchen team as before. Signature dishes include grilled Macau sole with butter sauce, braised prime beef rib in red wine, and roasted chicken stuffed with rice.

於1989年開業，座落於西灣湖邊的利安確令不少人留下美好回憶。在2013年遷至現址，環境轉變但美食不變，由原來的廚師團隊繼續為食客炮製一系列美味菜式，包括多道利安名菜如牛油扒金邊龍脷，原條牛肋骨和燒雞釀飯等。

TEL. 2830 1189
Na Taipa Rua Do Regedor No. 79
氹仔地堡街 79號

■ PRICE 價錢
Lunch 午膳
à la carte 點菜 MOP 180-600
Dinner 晚膳
à la carte 點菜 MOP 180-600

■ OPENING HOURS 營業時間
Lunch 午膳 11:30-14:30 (L.O.)
Dinner 晚膳 18:00-22:00 (L.O.)

■ ANNUAL AND WEEKLY CLOSING 休息日期
Closed Wednesday 週三休息

Canton
喜粵

🏷 ✗✗✗   ♿ 🍽 🛎24 ⏰

Modern in design and a deep sensual red in colour, Canton is a stylish restaurant with a sophisticated atmosphere – and is hidden away in a corner of the world's biggest indoor gaming floor. A Kouan-Chiau (gastronomic) version of Cantonese cooking is on offer, with dishes like steamed egg white topped with red birds nest, and deep-fried duck with almond flake in a lime sauce. Popular Sichuan dishes are also available.

喜粵位於世上最大室內娛樂場的一角，採用誘人的深紅色作主調，裝潢時尚。菜單以廣州粵菜如太極芙蓉紅燕及西檸杏香鴨片等為主。此外，店內亦有提供數款四川名菜，讓食客有更多美食選擇。

TEL. 8118 9930
Shop 1018, Casino level, The Venetian Resort, Estrada da Baia de N. Senhora da Esperanca, s/n, The Cotai Strip, Taipa
氹仔路氹金光大道 -望德聖母灣大馬路
威尼斯人酒店娛樂場地下 1018號舖
www.venetianmacao.com

■ PRICE 價錢
Lunch 午膳
à la carte 點菜 MOP 250-1,000
Dinner 晚膳
à la carte 點菜 MOP 400-1,000

■ OPENING HOURS 營業時間
Lunch 午膳　　11:00-15:00 L.O.14:45
Dinner 晚膳　　18:00-23:00 L.O.22:45

Carlos
加路

A wide choice of reasonably priced Macanese and Portuguese dishes attract plenty of customers to this relaxing, family-style restaurant. The hospitable Carlos is rightly proud of his secret recipe for marinated grilled chicken and bacalhau a bras. He goes to the market each day in search of the freshest seafood and it is always worth ordering the crab in advance; larger parties can also pre-order the whole roasted piglet or leg of lamb.

這家感覺溫馨舒適的家庭式餐廳，供應多款澳門和葡國美食，價格實惠，因此吸引大量食客慕名而來。熱情好客的加路先生，對其加路秘製燒雞及薯絲馬介休深以為傲。他每天會親自到市場搜購新鮮海產、海蟹等食材，嗜蟹者最好預訂海蟹。如人數多，可以考慮預訂原隻燒乳豬或燒羊肶。

TEL. 2875 1838
GF, Rua Cidade de Braga, Ed. Vista
Magnifica, Nape
新口岸填海區柏嘉街帝景苑地下

■ PRICE 價錢
Lunch 午膳
à la carte 點菜 MOP 150-300
Dinner 晚膳
à la carte 點菜 MOP 150-300

■ OPENING HOURS 營業時間
Lunch 午膳　12:00-14:30 (L.O.)
Dinner 晚膳　18:00-22:30 (L.O.)

■ ANNUAL AND WEEKLY CLOSING 休息日期
Closed Public Holidays 公眾假期休息

Castiço

Hidden a few blocks behind the main street of Taipa's old town is this simple, unassuming little place with just five tables. The Portuguese owner-chef, who came to Macau in 2004, treats his many local customers like family and operates from early morning until late evening, preparing home-style dishes in his small open kitchen. Recommended are the stewed pork with clams, oven roasted bacalhau with potatoes and duckling rice.

葡籍東主兼廚師於2004年移居澳門，後開設了這家隱藏於氹仔舊城區大街附近的小店。小店陳設簡約樸實，只有五張餐桌，他就在細小的開放式廚房烹調家庭式美食，待客人如親人。食店營業時間由清早到深夜，收費合理，推介菜有豬肉粒炒蜆、馬介休燴薯仔及鴨飯。

TEL. 2857 6505
65B Rua Direita Carlos Eugénio, Taipa
氹仔施督憲正街 65號 B

■ PRICE 價錢
à la carte 點菜 MOP 130-270

■ OPENING HOURS 營業時間
11:00-22:30 (L.O.)

■ ANNUAL AND WEEKLY CLOSING 休息日期
Closed Thursday 週四休息

Chan Kuong Kei (Rua do Dr. Pedro Jose Lobo)
陳光記(羅保博士街)

Red and yellow are the colours of this very clean shop, as well as the uniforms worn by the team of well-organised ladies who run it. Their barbecue meats and noodles attract an eclectic mix of customers, ensuring that it is always crowded and full of life. The roast goose and the barbecued pork are two of the most popular choices but it is also worth trying the double or triple rice plates.

此店位於澳門中心地點，以紅黃兩種顏色作主調，就是勤快的女店員身上的制服也不例外。這裡的燒味與粉麵吸引了各式各樣的客人，經常門庭若市，整間店子充滿活力。店內供應的食物中以燒鵝和叉燒最受歡迎，雙拼與三拼飯同樣值得一試。

TEL. 2831 4116
19 Rua Do Dr. Pedro Jose Lobo, Centro
羅保博士街 19號

■ PRICE 價錢
à la carte 點菜 MOP 40-100

■ OPENING HOURS 營業時間
10:30-21:30 (L.O.)

Chan Seng Kei
陳勝記

Chan Seng Kei has stood next to the ancient church for over 70 years and is now run by the 3rd generation of the family. It's well known for its traditional Cantonese food, with seafood supplied daily by local fishermen. The signature dish is stewed duck with tangerine peel but, as the cooking process takes more than 10 hours, only a few are available each day. It's a simple, semi open-air restaurant intertwined with several old banyan trees.

座落舊教堂旁的陳勝記開業至今已傳至第三代,向以傳統粵菜和海鮮菜式馳名。新鮮野生海鮮每天直接從漁民處採購;而製作工序繁複,需烹調十個小時的陳皮鴨是其招牌菜,每天限量供應。半開放式餐室非常樸實,當中數棵樹身粗壯的老榕樹,見證着飯店逾七十載歷史。

TEL. 2888 2021
Rua Caetano No21, Coloane
路環計單奴街 21號

■ PRICE 價錢
à la carte 點菜 MOP 150-350

■ OPENING HOURS 營業時間
12:00-22:30 (L.O.)

■ ANNUAL AND WEEKLY CLOSING 休息日期
Closed 2 days Lunar New Year
農曆新年休息 2 天

Noodles 麵食

MAP 地圖 36/A-3

Cheong Kei
祥記

MACAU 澳門

A family business since the '70s, this tiny noodle shop sticks to its roots and its thin, fine noodles are pressed by bamboo shoots in its own little factory nearby. Their soup uses dried prawns and bonito and is cooked for 8 hours. The noodles with dried shrimp roe are great, but also try the wonton and deep-fried fish ball. Although it's handily placed on Rua de Felicidade, you'll need to weave round shoppers and stalls to get here.

這間家族經營的小麵店於七十年代開業，且在鄰近自設小型廠房製造幼細竹昇面。湯底以蝦乾和柴魚熬製八小時；蝦籽撈麵非試不可，雲吞及鯪魚球亦不容錯過。

TEL. 2857 4310
68 Rua de Felicidade
福隆新街 68號

■ PRICE 價錢
Lunch 午膳
à la carte 點菜 MOP 25-50
Dinner 晚膳
à la carte 點菜 MOP 25-50

■ OPENING HOURS 營業時間
11:30-23:30 (L.O.)

■ ANNUAL AND WEEKLY CLOSING 休息日期
Closed 4 days each month 每月休息 4 天

Clube Militar de Macau
澳門陸軍俱樂部

🍴🍴   ♿ 🍽32 ☎🍽

Built in 1870 for the benefit of army officers, this striking pink-hued building was renovated in 1995 when its restaurant was opened to the public; but sadly the delightful sitting room and bar are reserved for its club members. The room has a charming colonial feel, thanks largely to the echoing teak floorboards, netted windows and ceiling fans. The kitchen focuses on traditional Portuguese flavours and hosts occasional food festivals.

這座最初為澳門陸軍軍官而設的粉紅色建築物建於1870年，在1995年完成翻新，並將餐廳對外開放，惟俱樂部內的雅致大廳及酒吧則只限會員使用。大廳內的柚木地板，配上窗紗的大窗及天花板上的吊扇，帶有濃厚的殖民地色彩。俱樂部供應傳統葡萄牙菜式，並會偶爾舉辦美食節。

TEL. 2871 4000
975 Avenida da Praia Grande
南灣大馬路 975號
www.clubemilitardemacau.net

■ PRICE 價錢
Lunch 午膳
à la carte 點菜 MOP 250-450
Dinner 晚膳
à la carte 點菜 MOP 250-450

■ OPENING HOURS 營業時間
Lunch 午膳　12:30-15:00 L.O. 14:30
Dinner 晚膳　19:00-23:00 L.O. 22:30

Din Tai Fung (COD) NEW
鼎泰豐（新濠天地）

The second floor of COD plays host to a plethora of casual eateries – and in the corner you'll find this sizeable branch of the international chain. Din Tai Fung is rightly known for its exquisite Xiao Long Bao but also special here is the steamed crab roe and pork dumpling. Other notables from the 70-odd Shanghainese dishes on offer include the excellent braised beef noodle soup. To finish, try the red bean glutinous rice cake.

這家鼎泰豐在澳門的第一間分店，位於新濠天地的蘇濠區內，特高的樓底搭配一貫的雅淨裝潢。菜單包羅逾七十款涼菜、麵食、小炒、湯品及甜點等，焦點自然是玲瓏的小籠包，香濃味美的紅燒牛肉麵會給你不少驚喜，正宗上海甜點如赤豆鬆糕亦不容錯過。

TEL. 8868 7348
Level 2, City of Dreams, Estrada do Istmo, Cotai
路氹連貫公路新濠天地 2樓
www.dintaifung.com

■ PRICE 價錢
Lunch 午膳
à la carte 點菜 MOP 120-250
Dinner 晚膳
à la carte 點菜 MOP 120-250

■ OPENING HOURS 營業時間
11:00-22:15 (L.O.)

■ ANNUAL AND WEEKLY CLOSING 休息日期
Closed Lunar New Year 農曆新年休息

Don Alfonso 1890
當奧豐素 1890

XXXX   ᕗ 🚲 **P** 🍽10 ☎🍴 ⅋

This opulent dining room features dozens of red Murano chandeliers and a huge fresco of the Italian coast divided into five parts. The somewhat dated feel and bright lights can detract a little from the experience but the Italian cuisine uses well-selected ingredients and flavours are clean and sharp. Service can be almost overly attentive. If you're lucky, you'll be here during one of the owner's quarterly visits when he prepares his own tasting menu.

這家豪華餐室的獨特之處是設有許多紅色穆拉諾穆琉璃吊燈，並懸了一幅將意大利海岸分為五個部分的巨型壁畫。古老的風格和明亮的光線配搭令人嚮往，此外，其意大利菜選材不俗，清新味美，服務更是周到得有點超乎常理。如果你運氣不俗，還有機會品嘗店主每季度的特備餐單。

TEL. 8803 7722
3F, Grand Lisboa Hotel, Avenida de Lisboa
葡京路新葡京酒店 3樓
www.grandlisboahotel.com

■ PRICE 價錢
Lunch 午膳
set 套餐 MOP 330-530
à la carte 點菜 MOP 600-1,100
Dinner 晚膳
à la carte 點菜 MOP 600-1,100

■ OPENING HOURS 營業時間
Lunch 午膳　12:00-14:30 (L.O.)
Dinner 晚膳　18:30-22:30 (L.O.)

Dynasty 8
朝

♿ 👆 ⛏20 ☏🍴

Old China is celebrated at this sophisticated and professionally run Chinese restaurant within the Conrad hotel. It takes its name and decorative styling from the eight dynasties of ancient China – Qin, Han, Sui, Tang, Song, Yuan, Ming and Qing – which are also used as the names of the private dining rooms. The traditional Cantonese food includes a varied choice of dim sum at lunch and the restaurant boasts an impressive wine cellar.

朝，顧名思義，其名字和室內裝潢意念源自中國古代八個皇朝：商、秦、漢、唐、宋、元、明、清。雕花木椅、木地板、紅燈籠和中式古典簷篷營造出強烈的中國古風。此店除供應以最新鮮的食材製作的傳統廣東小菜外，午市還有點心供應，還設有酒窖，適合愛酒人士。

TEL. 8113 8920
Level 1, Conrad Hotel, Estrada da Baia de N. Senhora da Esperanca, s/n, The Cotai Strip, Taipa
氹仔路氹金光大道望德聖母灣大馬路
康萊德酒店 1樓
www.conradmacao.com

■ PRICE 價錢
Lunch 午膳
à la carte 點菜 MOP 150-900
Dinner 晚膳
à la carte 點菜 MOP 250-900

■ OPENING HOURS 營業時間
Lunch 午膳　11:00-15:00 (L.O.)
Dinner 晚膳　18:00-23:00 (L.O.)

MACAU 澳門

Espaço Lisboa
里斯本地帶

The owner has created a homely 'Lisbon space' within this two-storey house in this Chinese village. The decorative style comes straight out of Portugal, as do the influences behind many of the home-style dishes. Don't miss the presunto pata negra and if you fancy something a little different then try the African chicken from Mozambique with its coconut flavour. Ask for a table on the veranda when the weather is right.

Espaço意謂空，店主有意在東方這臨海小鎮營造一個充滿葡國情調的空間。不論是鋪地板的石塊、擺設以至烹調用的陶缽，全部從葡國運抵。葡籍廚師用家鄉材料與傳統食譜炮製多款家常菜。源自莫桑比克食譜的非洲雞，咬咬椰汁香，美味無窮；風味絕佳的黑蹄火腿亦不能錯過。

TEL. 2888 2226
Rua das Gaivotas No8, Coloane
路環水鴨街 8號

SPECIALITIES TO PRE-ORDER 預訂食物
Lobster Rice 龍蝦飯／Suckling pig (whole)
乳豬

■ PRICE 價錢
Lunch 午膳
à la carte 點菜 MOP 250-500
Dinner 晚膳
à la carte 點菜 MOP 250-500

■ OPENING HOURS 營業時間
Lunch 午膳 12:00-15:00 (L.O.)
Dinner 晚膳 18:30-22:00 (L.O.)
Weekends 週末 12:00-22:30 (L.O.)

■ ANNUAL AND WEEKLY CLOSING 休息日期
Closed Wednesday 週三休息

Feng Wei Ju NEW
風味居

MACAU 澳門

🕸 🍽16 ☎🍴

A bright and shiny golden bar is the first thing you notice at this 5th floor restaurant at StarWorld. Gold is certainly used enthusiastically - so much so you may even need to keep your sunglasses on! There are three types of cuisine served: Sichuan, with dishes such as sautéed chicken with peanuts and red chili; Hunanese with specialities like steamed carp fish head; and handmade noodles, which you can watch being made in the open kitchen.

當大紅配上金，整個餐室都給映襯得金光閃爍；紅色就像與餐廳提供的湘川菜互相呼應似的。由剁椒魚頭到宮保雞丁，味道全都鮮辣刺激！此外，還有多款手製麵條和餃子。離開餐廳時你除了一定會帶着飽飽的肚子外，還可能會帶着一雙被金光刺得感到疲累的眼睛。

TEL. 8290 8668
5F, StarWorld Hotel, Avenida da Amizade
友誼大馬路星際酒店 5樓

■ PRICE 價錢
Lunch 午膳
à la carte 點菜 MOP 150-250
Dinner 晚膳
à la carte 點菜 MOP 250-500

■ OPENING HOURS 營業時間
11:00-23:00 (L.O.)

Read 'How to use this guide' for an explanation of our symbols, classifications and abbreviations.

請細閱「如何使用餐廳／酒店指南」，當中的標誌、分類等簡介助你掌握使用本指南的訣竅，作出智慧選擇。

Don't confuse the rating 𝕏 with the Stars ✿! The first defines comfort and service, while Stars are awarded for the best cuisine.

千萬別混淆了餐具 𝕏 和星星 ✿ 標誌！餐具標誌表示該餐廳的舒適程度和服務質素，而星星代表的是食物質素與味道非常出色而獲授為米芝蓮星級餐廳的餐館。

Golden Flower
京花軒

Within the Encore hotel is this elegant and sophisticated restaurant, whose kitchen is noted for its dextrous use of superb ingredients in the preparation of three different cuisines: Sichuan, Lu and Tan – along with a few Cantonese dishes. The room is adorned with the colours of gold and orange and the booths are the prized seats, but wherever you sit you'll receive charming service from the strikingly attired ladies, including the 'tea sommelier'.

京花軒座落於澳門萬利酒店內，以金色和橙色裝潢，既典雅又獨特。店內設有圓形白色皮卡座，不管安坐何處，都能享受端莊的女侍應的悉心服務，包括「調茶」服務。廚房最出色之處，除了選料上乘，還能俐落地烹調出川菜、魯菜、譚家菜三款不同菜系的菜式，同時供應少量廣東菜。

TEL. 8986 3689
GF, Encore Hotel, Rua Cicade de Sintra, Nape
外港新填海區仙德麗街萬利酒店地下
www.wynnmacau.com

■ PRICE 價錢
Weekend lunch 週末午膳
à la carte 點菜 MOP 450-2,100
Dinner 晚膳
à la carte 點菜 MOP 450-2,100
■ OPENING HOURS 營業時間
Weekend lunch 週末午膳   11:30-14:30 (L.O.)
Dinner 晚膳   18:00-23:00 L.O.22:30

■ ANNUAL AND WEEKLY CLOSING 休息日期
Closed Monday 週一休息

MACAU 澳門

Gosto
葡軒

   P ⊕ 12

The cupola ceiling and vintage photographs of old Portugal go some way to imbuing this restaurant within the Galaxy with something of a colonial atmosphere. The kitchen is headed up by a Portuguese chef and you can certainly taste the authenticity in specialities like deep-fried cod fish balls with chickpea salad and the classic Portuguese egg tarts. There are also a number of quality Portuguese wines on offer.

圓拱型的天花及充滿葡國風情的掛牆相片，這間在銀河渡假城內的餐館帶着濃厚的舊殖民地色彩。由葡萄牙籍主廚帶領廚房團隊為食客獻上一道道風味正宗的葡國菜。特色菜如炸馬介休球配雞心豆沙及傳統葡國蛋撻尤為滋味。多款葡萄牙餐酒可供選擇。

TEL. 8883 2221
G21, GF East Promenade, Galaxy Hotel,
Estrada da Baia de Nossa Senhora da
Esperança, Cotai
澳門銀河購物大道東地下 G21

■ PRICE 價錢
Lunch 午膳
à la carte 點菜 MOP 200-250
Dinner 晚膳
à la carte 點菜 MOP 250-300

■ OPENING HOURS 營業時間
Lunch 午膳 12:00-15:00 (L.O.)
Dinner 晚膳 18:00-23:00 (L.O.)
Weekends and Public Holidays
週末及公眾假期 12:00-23:00 (L.O.)

Guincho a Galera
葡國餐廳

🗡🗡🗡🗡 　　　　　　　　　♿ ⊟12 ☏🍴 🕸

Portuguese 'fine dining' comes to Macau in the form of this branch of Fortaleza do Guincho restaurant in Cascais, near Lisbon. It occupies the room in the Lisboa hotel that was formerly used by Joël Robuchon. The atmosphere is refined, the decoration vivid and the service attentive. The Portuguese food is refined and classical and is occasionally accompanied by subtle French notes; it is also complemented by a very impressive wine list.

來自鄰近里斯本的卡斯凱什，Fortaleza do Guincho餐廳的分店正式登陸澳門，帶來葡式高級餐飲享受。它位處葡京酒店內，餐廳格調高雅、裝潢精緻，服務亦十分周到。它供應的葡式佳餚製作精美、味道正宗，偶爾亦會滲入些許法國風味。餐廳還提供種類繁多的美酒。

TEL. 8803 7676
3F, Hotel Lisboa, 2-4 Avenida de Lisboa
葡京路 2-4號葡京酒店 3樓
www.hotelisboa.com

■ PRICE 價錢
Lunch 午膳
set 套餐 MOP 310-380
à la carte 點菜 MOP 530-1,500
Dinner 晚膳
set 套餐 MOP 630
à la carte 點菜 MOP 530-1,500

■ OPENING HOURS 營業時間
Lunch 午膳　12:00-14:30 (L.O.)
Dinner 晚膳　18:30-22:30 (L.O.)

Hou Kong Chi Kei
濠江志記美食

There are a couple of challenges to overcome – it'll take you a while to find this hidden little shop and the environment is not particularly striking – but the satisfying Cantonese dishes, which reflect owner-chef Mr. Chan's great enthusiasim for food, are well worth coming for. Call in advance to reserve the fresh seafood dishes like the steamed crab with sticky rice; also try the barbecued fish and the deep-fried taro fish ball.

要找到這家位置隱蔽的餐廳確是個小小的挑戰，其環境亦非十分出眾；但你所獲得的回報，就是一嘗東主兼廚師陳先生主理的廣式佳餚，並感受他對烹調美食的熱情。個別海鮮美食如蒸糯米蟹飯，需致電預訂；其他推介菜式還有燒魚及香芋炸魚球。

TEL. 2895 3098
GF, Block 3, Lai Hou Gardens, Rua Coelho do Amaral
白鴿巢前地麗豪花園第三座地舖
佳樂園石級上

SPECIALITIES TO PRE-ORDER 預訂食物
Steamed crab on sticky rice 蒸糯米蟹飯／
Grilled fish or prawns 燒魚或蝦

■ PRICE 價錢
Dinner 晚膳
à la carte 點菜 MOP 100-200

■ OPENING HOURS 營業時間
19:00-23:00 (L.O.)

■ ANNUAL AND WEEKLY CLOSING 休息日期
Closed the 15th & 16th of each month
每月 15 及 16 日休息

IFT Educational Restaurant
旅遊學院教學餐廳

🍴🍴   🍽12 🕐🍴

The kitchen is led by a professional chef but his brigade is made up of
students, as this restaurant is run by the Institute of Tourism Studies. It
offers a good selection of European and Portuguese dishes and uses
many herbs, salad leaves and vegetables grown in its own organic
garden; look out for African chicken with couscous and IFT seafood
rice. This is a good spot for dinner away from the bustle of the casinos.

這家旅遊學院教學餐廳的廚房由專業廚師主理,而團隊則由學生組成,供應多
款歐陸及葡國美食,其特色是採用多種自家種植的有機香草、沙律菜和蔬果作
食材。推介菜式有非洲雞及學院海鮮飯。遠離澳門喧囂的賭場,這裡是悠閒地
享用晚餐的好去處。

TEL. 8598 3077
Colina de Mong-Há, Rampe do Forte de
Mong-Há
望廈山
www.ift.edu.mo/pousada

■ PRICE 價錢
Lunch 午膳
set 套餐 MOP 200
à la carte 點菜 MOP 250-450
Dinner 晚膳
set 套餐 MOP 700
à la carte 點菜 MOP 250-450

■ OPENING HOURS 營業時間
Lunch 午膳   12:30-14:30 (L.O.)
Dinner 晚膳   19:00-22:00 (L.O.)

■ ANNUAL AND WEEKLY CLOSING 休息日期
Closed weekends and Public Holidays
週末及公眾假期休息

Il Teatro
帝雅廷

XXXX　　　　　　　　　　よ ← 🖐 P ⊟14 ◎🍴

To recommend a restaurant whose appeal lies beyond its cooking may be a little odd, but at Il Teatro it seems most diners turn up primarily to watch the stunning fountains; these are in a lake and are musically choreographed to change colour and appearance every few minutes. Ask for a table with a view and don't wear sneakers, or you won't get in. The cuisine is straightforward Italian fare, such as seafood risotto or pasta, served with style and élan.

大多數食客到來是為了觀賞噴泉美景。餐廳七成以上座位面向表演湖噴泉，每數分鐘音樂水柱交替、激光穿梭的震撼，盡收眼簾。因此，記着預訂面向噴泉的座位！此外，穿波鞋者不准內進。菜餚方面，主要提供簡約的意大利菜，如海鮮意大利飯或意大利粉，風味獨特且服務殷勤周到。

TEL. 8986 3663
GF, Wynn Hotel, Rua Cidade de Sintra, Nape
外港填海區仙德麗街永利酒店地下
www.wynnmacau.com

■ PRICE 價錢
Dinner 晚膳
set 套餐 MOP 728
à la carte 點菜 MOP 500-1,000

■ OPENING HOURS 營業時間
17:30-23:30 (L.O.)

■ ANNUAL AND WEEKLY CLOSING 休息日期
Closed Monday 週一休息

Imperial Court
金殿堂

   🦽 🤲 **P** 🍽36 𝟾𝟾

A massive marble pillar with a carved dragon dominates this elegant and contemporary restaurant, which is found on the same floor as the VIP lobby. The kitchen prepares classic Cantonese cuisine, with dishes such as scrambled organic egg whites with sea urchin and crabmeat, which is topped with caviar; braised boneless pork knuckle; and turtle rim in shrimp roe sauce. The impressive wine list includes over 1,000 labels.

金殿堂與貴賓大堂位於同一樓層，龐大的雕龍雲石柱是最矚目之處，設計風格高貴優雅中見時尚。餐廳主要供應廣東美食，如海膽鮮蟹肉炒蛋白及蝦子瑞裙邊扣豬肘等；餐酒選擇逾千種，令人印象深刻。

TEL. 8802 2361
GF, MGM Hotel, Avenida Dr. Sun Yat Sen, Nape
外港新填海區孫逸仙大馬路美高梅酒店地下
www.mgmmacau.com

■ PRICE 價錢
Lunch 午膳
set 套餐 MOP 188-320
à la carte 點菜 MOP 250-1,000
Dinner 晚膳
set 套餐 MOP 1,380
à la carte 點菜 MOP 500-2,000

■ OPENING HOURS 營業時間
Lunch 午膳　11:00-15:00 L.O. 14:30
Dinner 晚膳　18:00-23:00 L.O. 22:30

Jade Dragon
譽瓏軒

🍴🍴🍴   🍽20   🕐🍴   🎐

Traditional Chinese art, ebony, crystal, gold and silver converge with modern design to form this stunning and eminently comfortable Cantonese restaurant. Equal thought has gone into the details, such as the striking carved jade chopstick holder. The specialities to look out for are goose grilled over lychee wood, and barbecued Ibérico pork. Seafood is also a highlight, along with herbal soups and recipes based on traditional medicine.

譽瓏軒的瑰麗裝潢十分美輪美奐。烏木、金、銀和水晶的運用，揉合了現代設計與中國傳統美學的精髓，透明方柱酒窖、豪華廂房，或是餐桌上的玉雕筷子座，都給人留下深刻印象。食材均是高級用料。按中藥處方熬煮的老火湯和以荔枝柴烤製的燒鵝和黑毛豬叉燒值得一試。

TEL. 8868 2822
Level 2, The Boulevard, City of Dreams
Estrada do Istmo, Cotai
路氹連貫公路新濠天地新濠大道 2樓
www.cityofdreamsmacau.com/restaurant

SPECIALITIES TO PRE-ORDER 預訂食物
Steamed Herbal Chicken Wrap 藥膳紙包雞 /
Whole Supreme Fish Maw 原隻廣肚花膠公

■ PRICE 價錢
Lunch 午膳
à la carte 點菜 MOP 350-1,800
Dinner 晚膳
à la carte 點菜 MOP 500-1,800

■ OPENING HOURS 營業時間
Lunch 午膳   11:00-15:00 (L.O.)
Dinner 晚膳   18:00-23:00 (L.O.)

Kam Lai Heen NEW
金麗軒

  🖐 ⊟12 ◎🍴

Grand Lapa's Cantonese restaurant is an elegant space, with eye-catching ceiling lights and subtle Chinese design motifs. The long-standing chef and his team prepare traditional Cantonese cuisine which goes down well with their many local Macanese customers. Signature dishes include steamed silver cod in Oolong tea soup, and scallops and soft bean curd soup; it is also worth pre-ordering the Beggar's chicken.

金麗軒位於酒店大堂之上，裝潢並非十分豪華，卻有一種自然的寧靜與優雅。經驗十足的廚師團隊按傳統技法，炮製一系列富澳門特色的粵菜。凍頂銀鱈魚及茶壺豆腐海鮮湯均值得嘗試。

TEL. 8793 3821
2F, Grand Lapa Hotel, 956-1110 Avenida da Amizade, Macau
澳門友誼大馬路 956-1110號
金麗華酒店 2樓

■ PRICE 價錢
Lunch 午膳
set 套餐 MOP 388 -1,748
à la carte 點菜 MOP 250-500

Dinner 晚膳
set 套餐 MOP 388 -1,748
à la carte 點菜 MOP 350-800

■ OPENING HOURS 營業時間
Lunch 午膳   11:00-15:00 (L.O.)
Dinner 晚膳   18:00-22:00 (L.O.)

■ ANNUAL AND WEEKLY CLOSING 休息日期
Closed Tuesday 週二休息

MACAU 澳門

Katong Corner NEW
咖東

In amongst the many Asian brands and local eateries that populate this foodie street is a contemporary yet relaxed dining room serving Singaporean and Malaysian food. The laksa is a must – it's made using a special recipe that delivers complex yet balanced flavours. Another signature dish is the Black Pepper Crab: an aromatic and flavoursome dish where the sweetness of the crab meat works well with the black pepper from Sarawak.

百老匯酒店後面的食街，齊集數十間澳門本土和亞洲食店，實是遊澳旅客的一個新去處!咖東提供一系列星馬美食如海南雞和肉骨茶等，當中非試不可的是以重達一公斤的斯里蘭卡肉蟹，加上以沙撈越黑椒所製的黑胡椒炒蟹及湯底加入了蟛蜞、喇沙葉的招牌喇沙。

TEL. 8883 1876
Shop E-G031-G032, Broadway Macau, Cotai
路氹城澳門百老匯 E-G031-G032號舖

■ PRICE 價錢
Lunch 午膳
à la carte 點菜 MOP 100-200
Dinner 晚膳
à la carte 點菜 MOP 100-200

■ OPENING HOURS 營業時間
Sunday to Thursday 週日至週四
12:00-22:30 (L.O.)
Friday, Saturday and Public Holidays
週五、週六及公眾假期　12:00-01:00 (L.O.)

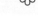
King
帝皇樓

Fans of Celebrity Cuisine in Hong Kong will recognise many of Chef Cheng's delicate and sophisticated specialities as he is one of the owners of this elegant and comfortable Cantonese restaurant. These signature dishes include braised abalone with goose web, and baked chicken with Shaoxing wine; the homemade dim sum also comes highly recommended. Being sufficiently removed from the casinos means the atmosphere is comparatively sedate.

香港名廚鄭錦富的擁躉定會覺得帝皇樓的精美菜式似曾相識，因為他正是這家廣東酒家的東主之一。此酒家的招牌菜有鵝掌扣吉品鮑魚及花雕焗飛天雞，自製點心亦十分值得一試。酒家位置與各大賭場之間有一段距離，環境較為寧靜。

TEL. 2875 7218
GF, AIA Tower, 251A-301 Avenida Comercial de Macau
澳門商業大馬路友邦廣場地下

■ PRICE 價錢
Lunch 午膳
à la carte 點菜 MOP 150-300
Dinner 晚膳
à la carte 點菜 MOP 250-500

■ OPENING HOURS 營業時間
Lunch 午膳 11:30-15:00 (L.O.)
Dinner 晚膳 17:30-23:00 (L.O.)

Spanish 西班牙菜 MAP 地圖 38/A-2

La Paloma
芭朗瑪

🏠 🅿 ⌖30 🍴 🐾

Secluded like hidden treasure from the rest of the city, La Paloma is a very appealing restaurant and bar, enhanced by a charming terrace, floor-to-ceiling glass and stone walls which are part of the original 17th century fortress foundations. A bold nouveau riche style of furniture lends it a chic yet casual air; it is wonderfully intimate and romantic at night. The refined Spanish cuisine offers a great assortment of tapas and exquisite paellas.

芭朗瑪餐廳及酒吧，位於一座十七世紀舊城堡改建而成的酒店內，遠離城市的煩囂。迷人的洋台、落地玻璃和古堡原來的石牆，塑造出獨特風采。傢具陳設時尚高雅，別具氣派且予人舒適感覺，晚上更是浪漫醉人。其西班牙菜精緻優雅，嘗味套餐是不錯的選擇。

TEL. 2896 8686
2F, Pousada de São Tiago Hotel, Avenida da República, Fortaleza de São Tiago da Barra
西灣民國大馬路聖地牙哥古堡酒店 2 樓
www.saotiago.com.mo

■ PRICE 價錢
Lunch 午膳
à la carte 點菜 MOP 500-900
Dinner 晚膳
à la carte 點菜 MOP 500 -900

■ OPENING HOURS 營業時間
Lunch 午膳   12:00-14:30 (L.O.)
Dinner 晚膳 18:30-22:30 (L.O.)

MACAU 澳門

Lai Heen NEW
麗軒

If you're looking to impress then you can't fail with this Cantonese restaurant on the top floor of the Ritz-Carlton hotel. The stunning room is richly decorated and supremely comfortable, as are the numerous private dining rooms which can be opened out and enlarged. The ambition of the kitchen is apparent in the Cantonese specialities – they are presented in a modern way and are a match for the sumptuous surroundings.

麗軒位處麗思卡爾頓酒店51樓，居高臨下，盡賞窗外秀麗景色。富麗堂皇的裝潢與造型時尚精緻的傳統粵菜，同時滿足視覺與味覺的需求。館內設有五間裝飾同樣華美，能隨時將木板牆移開騰出更多空間的私人廂房，適合舉行大小宴會。

TEL. 8886 6868
51F, The Ritz-Carlton, Galaxy, Estrada da Baia da N. Senhora da Esperanca, Cotai
氹仔路望德聖母灣大馬路麗思卡爾頓酒店51樓
www.theritzcarlton.com/macau

■ PRICE 價錢
Lunch 午膳
set 套餐 MOP 428
à la carte 點菜 MOP 250-1,000
Dinner 晚膳
à la carte 點菜 MOP 350-1,000

■ OPENING HOURS 營業時間
Lunch 午膳   11:30-14:30 (L.O.)
Dinner 晚膳   17:30-22:30 (L.O.)

■ ANNUAL AND WEEKLY CLOSING 休息日期
Closed Monday 週一休息

Lei Garden
利苑酒家

    🅿   🍽14   ☎🍴

A smart restaurant set amongst the canals of this vast hotel's third floor – arrive by gondola if you wish…Venetian guests predominate here; gamblers mostly give it a miss as it's too far from the gaming tables. Walls of marble provide the backdrop to a comprehensive range of traditional Cantonese dishes which are delivered by an efficient and well-organised team of servers. The best place to be seated is in one of the cosy booths.

餐廳設於三樓，佔據此大型酒店運河旁的位置，雄據地利，顧客可以乘坐貢朵拉前往這兒。由於離賭場較遠，娛樂場玩家通常會光顧其他餐廳，因此這裡的顧客以酒店住客為主。雲石牆壁與傳統廣東菜互相映襯。服務效率非常高。最好的座位是靠近前門的舒適卡位。

TEL. 2882 8689
Shop 2130, 3F Grand Canal Shoppes, The Venetian Resort, Estrada da Baia de N. Senhora de Esperança, Taipa
氹仔路望德聖母灣大馬路威尼斯人酒店
大運河購物中心 3樓 2130號舖
www.venetianmacao.com

■ PRICE 價錢
Lunch 午膳
à la carte 點菜 MOP 200-1,000
Dinner 晚膳
à la carte 點菜 MOP 250-1,000

■ OPENING HOURS 營業時間
Lunch 午膳　11:30-15:00 L.O. 14:30
Dinner 晚膳　18:00-23:00 L.O. 22:15

■ ANNUAL AND WEEKLY CLOSING 休息日期
Closed 3 days Lunar New Year
農曆新年休息 3 天

Lou Kei (Fai Chi Kei)
老記 (筷子基)

If you're looking for a simple, good value supper then Lou Kei may well fit the bill. Granted, it may not be in the centre of town, but every cab driver knows this lively place. It has been renowned for over 20 years for its sizeable selection of tasty noodles, congee and Cantonese dishes; frogs' legs in a clay pot and sea crab congee are both highly recommended. The interior is bright and neat while the service is polite and attentive.

若然你想品嘗價廉物美的美食，老記便是不二之選。儘管餐廳並非位於市中心，但是所有的士司機皆知這間馳名食府的所在地。老記二十多年來提供美味粥品麵食及廣東菜式，其田雞腿煲及水蟹粥更備受食客推崇，店內光猛潔淨，侍應親切有禮。

TEL. 2856 9494
Avenida Da Concórdia N, 12R/C E S/L
Loja H
和樂大馬路 12號宏基大廈第 4座 H及 M鋪

■ PRICE 價錢
à la carte 點菜 MOP 120-250

■ OPENING HOURS 營業時間
18:00-05:00 (L.O.)

MACAU 澳門

Luk Kei Noodle
六記粥麵

The second generation owner-chef insists on making his very popular noodles the traditional way: with a bamboo stick. The small menu provides photos of the specialities which include noodles with dried prawn roe; crunchy deep-fried wontons; crispy fish balls with soft centres served with either oyster or soy sauce; and the filling congee with crab. This is a small and busy shop, found on a lively street next to the pier.

第二代店主兼大廚堅持以傳統手法炮製極受歡迎的竹昇麵。小小的餐牌上附有特色食品的照片，包括蝦子撈麵、炸鴛鴦（炸雲吞及米通鯪魚球），還有水蟹粥。這家廣受食客歡迎的小店，就在碼頭旁邊的熱鬧街道上。

TEL. 2855 9627
1-D Travessa da Saudade
沙梨頭仁慕巷 1號 D

■ PRICE 價錢
à la carte 點菜 MOP 40-70

■ OPENING HOURS 營業時間
18:30-02:30 (L.O.)

■ ANNUAL AND WEEKLY CLOSING 休息日期
Closed 4 days Lunar New Year
農曆新年休息4天

Lung Wah Tea House
龍華茶樓

Little has changed from when this old-style Cantonese tea house, up a flight of stairs, opened in the 1960s: the large clock still works, the boss still uses an abacus to add the bill and you still have to refill your own pot of tea at the boiler. The owner buys fresh produce, including chicken for their most popular dish, from the market across the road. Get here early for the freshly made dim sum.

這家有一列樓梯的傳統廣東茶樓自一九六零年代開業以來，變化不大—古老大鐘依然在擺動，老闆依然用算盤結算帳單，你依然要自行到熱水器前沖茶。店主從對面街市選購新鮮食材烹調美食，包括茶樓名菜油雞。建議早上前來享用新鮮點心。

TEL. 2857 4456
3 Rua Norte do Mercado Aim-Lacerda
提督市北街 3號

■ PRICE 價錢
à la carte 點菜 MOP 25-140

■ OPENING HOURS 營業時間
07:00-14:00 (L.O.)

■ ANNUAL AND WEEKLY CLOSING 休息日期
Closed　4 days Lunar New Year, 4 days May and 4 days October 農曆新年、五月及十月各休息4天

Manuel Cozinha Portuguesa
阿曼諾葡國餐

Authenticity and hospitality are what draws customers to this cosy little corner restaurant. Newcomers will find themselves welcomed by the owner-chef just as warmly as if they were regulars. His traditional Portuguese cooking uses quality ingredients and many of the dishes are cooked in the old-fashioned barbecue way. He makes his own cheese and the two specialities of which he is most proud are stewed rabbit, and fried rice with squid ink.

離開氹仔舊城區的熱鬧街道，從施督憲正街向飛能便度街方向走，便會找到位於路口這家小店。在這兒你能吃到美味正宗的葡國菜。葡籍店東兼主廚親切好客。他堅持選用本地和葡國優質食材，且以碳火燒烤食物，還在店內自製芝士。炆兔肉和墨魚汁炒飯是他最引以為傲的菜式。

TEL. 2882 7571
Rua de Femão Mendes Pinto, Nº 90 R/C,
Taipa
氹仔飛能便度街 90號

SPECIALITIES TO PRE-ORDER 預訂食物
Roasted piglet "Manuel style" 原隻阿曼諾燒乳豬 / Baked lobster "Manuel style" 阿曼諾焗龍蝦 /Seafood rice 海鮮飯

■ PRICE 價錢
Lunch 午膳
à la carte 點菜 MOP 130-340
Dinner 晚膳
à la carte 點菜 MOP 130-340

■ OPENING HOURS 營業時間
Lunch 午膳 12:00-15:00 (L.O.)
Dinner 晚膳 18:00-22:00 (L.O.)

■ ANNUAL AND WEEKLY CLOSING 休息日期
Closed Wednesday 週三休息

Mezza9

Mezza9 is ideal for those who can never decide on what nationality of cuisine they fancy but who do like a little theatre with their food. The vast and quite striking interior comes with several show kitchens offering an impressive array of different cuisines: you can choose sushi, chargrilled meats, Cantonese wok dishes, Macanese specialities, South Asian noodles and even Sunday brunch. The vaulted wine cellar is the pick of the private rooms.

如果你是嗜吃一族，又經常無法決定享用哪一國的菜式，Mezza9是你理想之選。餐廳面積非常闊落，設有數個開放式廚房，供應多國菜式，包括壽司、烤肉、廣東小炒、澳門特色菜、南亞麵食等。假日還會提供早午合餐。二人套餐份量不少，且能一次過品嘗多國美食。

TEL. 8868 1920
3F, Grand Hyatt Hotel, City of Dreams,
Estrado do Istmo, Cotai
路氹連貫公路新濠天地君悅酒店 3樓
www.macau.grand.hyatt.com

■ PRICE 價錢
à la carte 點菜 MOP 300-1,200

■ OPENING HOURS 營業時間
Dinner 晚膳   17:30-23:00 (L.O.)

MACAU 澳門

Mizumi NEW
泓

🍴🍴🍴 　　　　　🛋8 　�‍ 　☎🍴

A comfortable Japanese restaurant run by an earnest young team, located in – and run by – the Wynn hotel. It uses two consultants – Chef Shimamiya from Sushiden in Hokkaido, and Chef Yoshida from Ishigaki Yoshida in Tokyo. They create the menus and pick the fish in Tokyo's Tsukiji market, along with the finest aged beef from a private ranch on Ishigaki Island, south of Okinawa. Try the kuruma ebi and anago sushi and end with tofu cheesecake.

永利酒店內的日本料理泓真給人渙然一新的感覺，所說的除了裝潢外，更多的是這裡的食物。選用高質食材，包括每週三次由築地市場運到的新鮮海產及精心搜購的沖繩和牛等，再加上精細的烹調，確令人回味無窮。除魚生、壽司外，也提供爐端燒、鐵板燒及天婦羅。

TEL. 8986 3663
GF, Wynn Hotel, Rua Cidade de Sintra, Nape
外港新填海區仙德麗街永利酒店地下
www.wynnmacau.com

■ PRICE 價錢
Dinner 晚膳
set 套餐　MOP 998-3,880
à la carte 點菜 MOP 500-1,600

■ OPENING HOURS 營業時間
Dinner 晚膳　17:30-23:30 (L.O.)

■ ANNUAL AND WEEKLY CLOSING 休息日期
Closed Tuesday 週二休息

Korean 韓國菜

Myung Ga
名家

      ♿ 🖐 🛋8 🔔🍴

Many ingredients are imported from Korea to ensure authenticity at this restaurant specialising in Korean classics and BBQ. If you opt for one of the large booths, instead of the cushioned seating on the floor, you'll get your own grill. The family set menu for up to six people is a popular way to sample dishes like homemade kimchi. Along with the contemporary cocktails, you can also try traditional Korean drinks like milky white makgeolli.

名家供應的食材全都是從韓國搜購回來,確保客人吃到原汁原味的韓國菜。食客除了可以以韓國傳統方式,以墊子墊着坐在地上進餐外,還可選擇坐在擁有獨立燒烤爐的卡座上。家庭套餐和自製泡菜非常受歡迎。餐酒選擇豐富,除了新派雞尾酒外,還提供乳白濁酒之類的傳統韓國餐酒。

TEL. 8883 2221
G27, GF East Promenade, Galaxy Hotel,
Estrada da Baia de Nossa Senhora da
Esperança, Cotai
澳門銀河購物大道東地下 G27
www.galaxymacau.com

■ PRICE 價錢
Lunch 午膳
à la carte 點菜 MOP 150-200
Dinner 晚膳
à la carte 點菜 MOP 300-350

■ OPENING HOURS 營業時間
12:00-23:00 (L.O.)

Naam NEW
灆

  ♿ ☎️

The name of Grand Lapa's Thai restaurant translates as 'water' which seems appropriate as it overlooks the pool and tropical garden and features a small fountain in the middle of the room, which all add to the calm and peaceful atmosphere. The majority of the kitchen and service teams are Thai and the food is attractively presented and the spicing is well-judged. The menu also features a section of Royal Thai cuisine dishes.

Naam在泰文中是水的意思。餐廳位於泳池旁邊，中央位置設有一口噴泉，天然光線從其頂上透射而下，整個環境寧靜而優雅。這兒的泰國菜味道較為柔諧，更設有一系列的宮廷菜式，友善的泰國侍應亦會給予客人合適的推介。

TEL. 8793 4818
GF, Grand Lapa Hotel, 956-1110 Avenida da Amizade, Macau
澳門友誼大馬路 956-1110號
金麗華酒店地下
www.wynnmacau.com

■ PRICE 價錢
Lunch 午膳
à la carte 點菜 MOP 350-750
Dinner 晚膳
à la carte 點菜 MOP 350-750

■ OPENING HOURS 營業時間
Lunch 午膳 12:00-15:00 (L.O.)
Dinner 晚膳 18:30-22:00 (L.O.)

■ ANNUAL AND WEEKLY CLOSING 休息日期
Closed Monday 週一休息

Ngao Kei Ka Lei Chon
牛記咖喱美食

Set at the corner of a main road and a narrow street full of industrious little shops. The broken neon lights outside may lessen its appeal but this is a friendly, well-run and well-staffed little noodle shop, with regulars popping in and out throughout the day. Bestsellers are the crab noodles and the crab congee but it's also worth trying the clear soup with beef flank and the spicy chicken or beef curry with noodles.

此店位於大街一角的小巷內，四周的小店均其門如市，常客往來不絕。四周老舊的建築物看似減弱了餐廳的吸引力，但小麵店職員的友善態度和管理有序彌補了這個不足，店內服務令人滿意。最暢銷的美食要算是水蟹、蟹黃炆伊麵和蟹粥，清湯牛腩和椰汁咖哩雞、牛筋麵也值得一試。

TEL. 2895 6129
GF, 1 Rua de Cinco de Outubro
十月初五街 1號地下

■ PRICE 價錢
à la carte 點菜 MOP 40-90

■ OPENING HOURS 營業時間
08:00-02:00 (L.O.)

An important business lunch? The symbol ⇔ indicates restaurants with private rooms.

需要一個合適的地點享用商務午餐？可從注有這個 ⇔ 標誌的餐廳中選一間有私人廂房又合你心意的餐館。

The symbol 🍷 denotes a particularly interesting wine list.

🍷 這個標誌表示該餐廳提供一系列優質餐酒。

99 Noodles
99麵

Noodle lovers will need a few visits to this stylish pit-stop at the Encore hotel to work their way through the huge choice of Chinese noodles – there's everything from Beijing la mian to Shanxi knife-shaved, tip-ended and one string noodles, all served with various broths and garnishes, along with specialities from Northern China. The colours of the room are vivid; the jumbo chopsticks on the walls are striking; and the atmosphere's buzzy.

細小的餐室以鮮艷的紅色作主調，牆上懸着一雙雙色彩繽紛的巨型筷子，華麗且充滿活力，與四周的賭場環境風格一致。顧名思義，這裡是嘗麵的好地方：北京拉麵、山西刀削麵、轉盤剔尖及一根麵等多款麵食，配以各式湯底和澆頭，令人食指大動。餃子和北方點心當然也不能錯過。

TEL. 8986 3663
GF, Encore Hotel, Rua Cicade de Sintra, Nape
外港新填海區仙德麗街萬利酒店地下
www.wynnmacau.com

■ PRICE 價錢
à la carte 點菜 MOP 180-1,000

■ OPENING HOURS 營業時間
11:00-01:00 (L.O.)

8 1/2 Otto e Mezzo NEW

✕✕✕   🍽12   🍴   ☺🍷   🏵

A handsome, well-dressed Italian restaurant with a striking central cocktail bar – this comfortable, elegant space certainly pays suitable homage to the Hong Kong original. Chef Umberto Bombana sensibly offers virtually the same menu and the wine list is of equal breadth and depth, with a focus on Italian and French wines. The entrance is from the Promenade Shopping Mall of the Galaxy but you can also enter from the lobby of the Ritz-Carlton.

美輪美奐的佈置和奪目的雞美酒吧，此家位於時尚匯內的 8 ½ Otto e Mezzo與香港店一脈相承，同由名廚Bombana帶領，不論是餐牌還是食物風格均與香港店無異。餐酒單羅列的美酒種類豐富，有不少來自意大利及法國的佳釀。此店有兩個入口，分別設在購物區內和麗思卡爾頓酒店大堂內，易於尋找。

TEL. 8886 2169
1F, Galaxy, The Promenade, Shop 1031,
Avenida de Cotai
澳門銀河綜合渡假城 1樓 1031號舖
www.ottoemezzobombana.com

OPRICE 價錢
set 套餐 MOP 1,380
à la carte 點菜 MOP 800-1,500

■ OPENING HOURS 營業時間
Dinner 晚膳 18:00-22:30 (L.O.)

■ ANNUAL AND WEEKLY CLOSING 休息日期
Closed Sunday 週日休息

French contemporary 時尚法國菜

Robuchon au Dôme
天巢法國餐廳

😋😋😋

🍴🍴🍴🍴🍴   ♿ 🥂 👔 🍽10 🕤 🎗

WACAU 澳門

Joël Robuchon's flagship restaurant sits majestically in the dome of the Grand Lisboa hotel, where a striking chandelier competes for your attention with 360° views of Macau. Impeccable service, immaculate table settings and a superb wine list all complement the superlative contemporary cuisine. Try roast guinea fowl with foie gras or Kagoshima beef with simmered shallots and potato soufflé, followed by egg soufflé or something from the dessert trolley.

Joël Robuchon 的旗艦店位於新葡京酒店內。矚目的大型水晶吊燈和令人屏息的360度澳門全景，餐桌亦佈置得十分細緻，實在是賞心悅目。這兒除了供應優質的當代菜式，還提供超過八千種餐酒。服務亦很周到。烤珍珠雞伴鵝肝及和牛紅酒燴幼葱都是推介之選。

TEL. 8803 7878
43F, Grand Lisboa Hotel, Avenida de Lisboa
葡京路新葡京酒店 43樓
www.grandlisboahotel.com

■ PRICE 價錢
Lunch 午膳
set 套餐 MOP 598-788
à la carte 點菜 MOP 1,300-2,500
Dinner 晚膳
set 套餐 MOP 1,588-2,688
à la carte 點菜 MOP 1,300-2,500

■ OPENING HOURS 營業時間
Lunch 午膳　12:00-14:30 (L.O.)
Dinner 晚膳　18:30-22:30 (L.O.)

San Tou Tou
新陶陶

🍴   ☏🍴

Found on a narrow street in the centre of Taipa is this Cantonese restaurant, run by the same family for three generations and now supervised by two brothers. The cooking is very traditional and it is the chicken soup served in very hot clay pots that attracts so many; but there are plenty of other, more affordable, specialities. The restaurant is spread over two floors and the air conditioning is most efficient!

這間家族經營的廣東菜餐廳位於氹仔中心地帶的小巷內，現時由第三代的兩兄弟主理。煮法非常傳統，燉雞湯用砂鍋盛載，吸引大量食客。除此之外，這裡還提供很多價錢相宜的小菜選擇。

TEL. 2882 7065
26 Rua Correia da Silva, Taipa
氹仔告利雅施利華街 26 號

SPECIALITIES TO PRE-ORDER 預訂食物
Salt-baked chicken 古法鹽焗雞 / Crispy chicken 脆皮炸子雞

■ PRICE 價錢
Lunch 午膳
à la carte 點菜 MOP 180-550
Dinner 晚膳
à la carte 點菜 MOP 180-550

■ OPENING HOURS 營業時間
Lunch 午膳 11:30-15:00 (L.O.)
Dinner 晚膳 17:30-22:00 (L.O.)

■ ANNUAL AND WEEKLY CLOSING 休息日期
Closed 1 week Lunar New Year, 2 days early May and 2 days early October 農曆新年 7 天、五月初及十月初各休息 2 天

Shinji NEW
金坂

♿ 🅿 🍽12 🚃 ☎🍴

MACAU 澳門

There's a real flavour of Japan at this sushi restaurant, from the kanji characters on the wall to the impressive counter, which uses 220 year old cypress wood. The fish comes from Tokyo's Tsukiji Market; the sushi is relatively small and delicate; and the vinegar is a pale red. Go for the 'Edomae 15 Sushi' menu if you just want sushi; if you'd prefer to start with appetisers and sashimi then choose the 'Wa' or 'Shin' menus.

步入金坂，即能感受到濃濃的日本風：由享齡二百二十歲的柏木打造的日式壽司枱、牆上的日本漢字、清一色的日籍服務員，頃刻讓你誤以為自己穿越到了日本。喜歡壽司的你可從江戶前壽司挑選心愛的手握紅醋飯壽司，欲先品嘗刺身請從真或和餐單上挑選從竹地市場直接運到的鮮魚。

TEL. 8868 7300
Level 1, Crown Towers, City of Dreams,
Estrada do Istmo, Cotai
路氹連貫公路新濠天地皇冠度假酒店 1樓
www.cityofdreamsmacau.com/dining/
asian/kanesaka

■ PRICE 價錢
Lunch 午膳
set 套餐 MOP 688-1,688
Dinner 晚膳
set 套餐 MOP 1,688-2,988

■ OPENING HOURS 營業時間
Lunch 午膳　12:00-14:30 (L.O.)
Dinner 晚膳　18:00-22:30 (L.O.)

■ ANNUAL AND WEEKLY CLOSING 休息日期
Closed Tuesday lunch and Monday
週二午膳及週一休息

Square Eight
食 · 八方

Square Eight's cuisine covers large swathes of China and includes Cantonese noodles, Northern specialities, Shanghainese recipes, Chiu Chow, Macanese rice meals, Hong Kong style noodle dishes and a few offerings from other Asian countries. You're given a large sheet of paper listing all the dishes; simply tick the ones you fancy. It's lively and busy, staff are swift but engaging and the long, open-plan kitchen adds to the bustle.

食 · 八方的餐牌羅列了中國各地菜式：廣東麵類、北方特色菜、上海美食、潮州佳餚、澳門飯餐及港式麵食等，還包羅數款其他亞洲國家的特色美食。食客只需在點菜單上隨意挑選心儀菜式。店內很熱鬧，服務快捷周到，長長的開放式廚房更為餐廳增添一份生氣。

TEL. 8802 2389
GF, MGM Hotel, Avenida Dr. Sun Yat Sen, Nape
外港新填海區逸仙大馬路美高梅酒店地下
www.mgmmacau.com

■ PRICE 價錢
Lunch 午膳
à la carte 點菜 MOP 120-350
Dinner 晚膳
à la carte 點菜 MOP 120-350

■ OPENING HOURS 營業時間
Open 24 hours 24 小時營業

Temptations
品味坊

XX

On the 16th floor atop the StarWorld hotel is a bright, airy restaurant serving a variety of cuisines from a number of European countries – your best bet is to go straight for the Portuguese and Macanese specialities. If you're undecided about dessert, then peek into the kitchen through the window and watch the effort that goes into their creation. This well-run restaurant is ideally suited for those wanting to relax with family or friends.

位於星際酒店16樓，室內設計以時尚簡約線條配合淺棕色調，淡雅輕鬆的環境氣氛與酒店內其他設施或店鋪截然不同，讓人眼前一亮。餐廳主要提供歐陸菜和葡國菜，半自助午餐包含多款前菜與甜品及精選燒烤美食，是不錯的休閒聚餐處。食客可透過開放式廚房的玻璃窗欣賞廚師製作甜品的過程。

TEL. 8290 8688
16F, StarWorld Hotel, Avenida da Amizade
友誼大馬路星際酒店 16樓
www.starworldmacau.com

■ PRICE 價錢
Lunch 午膳
set 套餐 MOP 178
à la carte 點菜 MOP 300-700
Dinner 晚膳
à la carte 點菜 MOP 300-700

■ OPENING HOURS 營業時間
12:00-22:00 (L.O.)

Tenmasa
天政

Taipa's own version of Tenmasa, which opened in Tokyo in 1937 and is still going strong, is a charmingly run restaurant that boasts a sushi bar, a tempura counter and a tatami floor, as well as decked walkways leading across golden pebble ponds to private rooms. Sit and watch the chef at work, as he uses quality ingredients to prepare well-balanced dishes. There are a variety of different menus available at lunch.

天政早於1937年在東京開業，至今仍廣受歡迎。澳門的天政設有壽司吧、天婦羅櫃枱及榻榻米地板，也有鋪板走廊、金石水池和私人餐室。食客可安坐座位上，觀看廚師大顯身手，將優質食材炮製成美味菜式。餐廳於午市時代提供多款精選美食。

TEL. 2886 8868
11F, Altira Hotel, Avenida de Kwong Tung, Taipa
氹仔廣東大馬路新濠鋒酒店 11樓
www.altiramacau.com

■ PRICE 價錢
Lunch 午膳
set 套餐 MOP 288-1,180
à la carte 點菜 MOP 400-1,200

Dinner 晚膳
set 套餐 MOP 488-1,950
à la carte 點菜 MOP 400-1,200

■ OPENING HOURS 營業時間
Lunch 午膳   12:00-14:15 (L.O.)
Dinner 晚膳   18:00-22:15 (L.O.)

■ ANNUAL AND WEEKLY CLOSING 休息日期
Closed Monday 週一休息

Terrazza
庭園

  ♿   🧼   **P**   🍽14   🍇

It is all about relaxation at this large, classically decorated Italian restaurant – thanks largely to the very comfortable chairs and the warm and welcoming service. The menu covers all parts of the country and there's something for everyone, whether you're after a pizza or a more elaborate dish. One thing definitely worth exploring is the wine list. There's a great glass-enclosed private room on the terrace which is surrounded by waterfalls.

古典優雅的設計、柔軟舒適的座椅、友善熱情的服務，讓你身心放鬆。這裡供應的菜式涵蓋意大利全國美食，不論是薄餅或是別的意大利菜，你總能挑選到合心意的美食。最使人驚喜的，是其種類繁多的酒單。露台上的玻璃屋私人廂房給瀑布重重圍着，置身其中猶如身處花果山下的水簾洞，令人嚮往。

TEL. 8883 2221
201, 2F Galaxy Hotel, Estrada da Baia de Nossa Senhora da Esperanca, Cotai
路氹望德聖母灣大馬路澳門銀河
銀河酒店 2樓 201號舖
www.galaxymacau.com

■ PRICE 價錢
Sunday lunch 週日午膳
à la carte 點菜 MOP 550-700
Dinner 晚膳
à la carte 點菜 MOP 550-700

■ OPENING HOURS 營業時間
18:00-23:00 (L.O.)
Sunday 週日
Lunch 午膳   11:00-16:00 (L.O.)
Dinner 晚膳   17:00-23:00 (L.O.)

The Eight
8餐廳

XXXX

 P ⊟24

The lavish interior uses the traditional Chinese elements of the goldfish and the number eight to ensure good fortune for all who dine here. The cuisine is a mix of Cantonese and Huaiyang, but the kitchen also adds its own innovative touches to some dishes. Specialities include steamed crab claw with ginger and Chinese wine, and stir-fried lobster with egg, minced pork and black bean. At lunchtime, over 40 kinds of dim sum are served.

豪華的內部裝潢採用了傳統中國元素，如金魚及數目字8，寓意所有到訪的客人都會遇上好運。菜式融合了廣東及淮揚風味，部份美食更滲入了創新點子。推介菜式有薑米酒蒸鮮蟹拑及廣東式炒龍蝦。午餐時段供應逾四十款點心。

TEL. 8803 7788
2F, Grand Lisboa Hotel, Avenida da Lisboa
葡京路新葡京酒店 2樓
www.grandlisboahotel.com

■ PRICE 價錢
Lunch 午膳
à la carte 點菜 MOP 200-1,000
Dinner 晚膳
à la carte 點菜 MOP 500-1,000

■ OPENING HOURS 營業時間
Lunch 午膳 11:30-14:30 (L.O.)
Sunday & Public Holidays
週日及公眾假期
Lunch 午膳 10:00-15:00 (L.O.)
Dinner 晚膳 18:30-22:30 (L.O.)

Indian 印度菜

The Golden Peacock
皇雀

✕✕   ♿ 🍽40 ◐🍴

MACAU 澳門

The peacock is India's national bird and is used for striking decorative effect at this contemporary Indian restaurant at The Venetian, along with copper, glass, screens and Sadeli mosaics. The chef hails from Kerala but his menu covers all parts of the country making good use of quality ingredients; through the window you can watch his team working with the tandoor oven. At lunch an appealing and good value buffet is provided.

態度嚴謹認真的印度主廚每天以新鮮食材炮製出多道色香味俱全的印度美食。除了主餐牌上的菜色，餐廳會在午市時段供應自助餐，價錢相宜。店內以簡約時尚的印度風格為主，並以印度國鳥孔雀作裝飾，帶着濃濃的印度風情。

TEL. 8118 9696
Shop 1037, 1F The Venetian Resort,
Estrada de Baia de N. Senhora da
Esperanca, Taipa
氹仔路望德聖母灣大馬路威尼斯人酒店
大運河購物中心 1樓 1037號舖

■ PRICE 價錢
Lunch 午膳
buffet 自助餐 MOP 158
Dinner 晚膳
à la carte 點菜 MOP 250-500

■ OPENING HOURS 營業時間
Lunch 午膳　11:00-15:00 (L.O.)
Dinner 晚膳　18:00-22:45 (L.O.)

The Kitchen
大廚

There's a handsome, masculine feel to this restaurant on the 3rd floor of the Grand Lisboa. It comes with a sushi bar, a salad counter and a live fish tank but the star of the show is undoubtedly the beef. Prime meat from the US, Japan and Australia is cooked on an open flame and you decide which cut you want and in what size. You're guaranteed to find something to go with your steak from the wine list of over 15,000 labels.

將西式扒房、日式壽司吧及海鮮魚缸融匯一室，這裡的設計確是匠心獨具，閃爍的天花燈飾、金牛形酒吧等，都給人留下深刻印象，更讓人難以忘懷的是其美食!食客可在肉櫃挑選來自美國、澳洲及日本等地的頂級牛肉，並選取不同部位與份量，亦可從魚缸中點選新鮮海產。逾萬款餐酒可供選擇。

TEL. 8803 7777
3F, Grand Lisboa Hotel, Avenida de Lisboa
葡京路新葡京酒店 3樓
www.grandlisboahotel.com

■ PRICE 價錢
Lunch 午膳
set 套餐 MOP 360-550
à la carte 點菜 MOP 480-1,700
Dinner 晚膳
à la carte 點菜 MOP 480-1,700

■ OPENING HOURS 營業時間
Lunch 午膳　12:00-14:30 (L.O.)
Dinner 晚膳　18:30-22:30 (L.O.)

The Ritz-Carlton Café NEW
麗思咖啡廳

Tiles, mirrors and marble have all been used to great effect to create a chic French brasserie here at the Ritz-Carlton. There's a Tasting menu along with the à la carte and set menus so, whether you're here for a full meal of classic French dishes or a quick bite or afternoon tea after shopping, you'll find there's plenty of choice. You can also expect live music, mime artists and even a caricaturist.

意大利白色雲石地、長長的真皮沙發和圓型雲石面餐桌、典雅的水滴型吊燈、精緻的長鏡，營造出高雅、舒適的環境。來自法國里昂的主廚擅長烹調法國住家菜，許多食客到此是為了品嘗帶有住家風味的法國菜。除了美食，餐廳內每天都有不同的表演藝術如音樂現奏、默劇等演出。

TEL. 8886 6868
GF, The Ritz-Carlton, Galaxy, Estrada da Baia da N. Senhora da Esperanca, Cotai
路氹望德聖母灣大馬路澳門銀河銀河綜合渡假城麗思卡爾頓酒店地下
www.ritzcarlton.com/macau

■ PRICE 價錢
Lunch 午膳
set 套餐 MOP 238-268
à la carte 點菜 MOP 500-900
Dinner 晚膳
set 套餐 MOP 488
à la carte 點菜 MOP 500-900

■ OPENING HOURS 營業時間
Lunch 午膳   11:30-14:30 (L.O.)
Dinner 晚膳   17:30-22:30 (L.O.)

The Tasting Room
御膳房

✗✗✗✗　　　　　　　　　　⅋ ⪡ 🍽 🍴14 ◎🍽 🅰

Finding respite on the Cotai Strip away from the lively casino vibe can be hard but this relaxing restaurant could help. It's an elegant circular room and offers discreet service. The food is largely French and the Bresse pigeon is the favoured dish of the locals. The chef adds his own unique touches, like onion ice cream to the onion soup. Be sure to have the Chef's Menu.

欲在金光大道賭場內找個地方歇歇，可以到這家氣氛輕鬆的餐廳。圓形的主餐室華麗優雅，侍應服務細心周到。以供應法國菜為主，最著名的是法國乳鴿。大廚喜歡將自己的創意融入菜式中，如洋蔥湯加上洋蔥雪糕。八道菜的總廚精選套餐絕對非試不可。

TEL. 8868 6681
3F, Crown Towers, City of Dreams,
Estrada do Istmo, Cotai
路氹連貫公路新濠天地皇冠度假酒店 3樓
www.cityofdreamsmacau.com/restaurant

■ PRICE 價錢
Lunch 午膳
set 套餐 MOP 388-528
à la carte 點菜 MOP 650-2,150
Dinner 晚膳
set 套餐 MOP 828-2,088
à la carte 點菜 MOP 650-2,150

■ OPENING HOURS 營業時間
Lunch 午膳　12:00-14:30 (L.O.)
Dinner 晚膳　18:00-22:30 (L.O.)

Tim's Kitchen
桃花源小廚

✕✕✕

🍽24 ⚬🍴 ⚮

Hong Kong foodies make special pilgrimages here and it's easy to see why: the Cantonese dishes may appear quite simple but they are very skilfully prepared. Among the highlights are poached and sliced pork stomach in wasabi sauce, and sweet & sour pork ribs. Do make sure you try the crystal prawn and, during the winter, the tasty snake ragout. The restaurant is decorated with a variety of operatic costumes and photos.

香港食家喜歡專程到此朝聖，原因十分簡單：此食店的廣東菜式看似簡單，卻實在是經過精心巧手炮製。推介菜式包括凉伴爽肚片及京都骨。此外，萬勿錯過玻璃蝦球，而冬天的重點推介則離不開美味的蛇羹。餐廳放滿戲曲照片和戲服裝飾，散發出淡淡的藝術氣息。

TEL. 8803 3682
Shop F25, GF, Hotel Lisboa, East Wing,
2-4 Avenida de Lisboa
葡京路 2-4號葡京酒店東翼地下 F25號鋪
www.hotelisboa.com

■ PRICE 價錢
Lunch 午膳
à la carte 點菜 MOP 200-700
Dinner 晚膳
à la carte 點菜 MOP 400-1,300

■ OPENING HOURS 營業時間
Lunch 午膳　12:00-15:00 L.O. 14:30
Dinner 晚膳　18:30-23:00 L.O. 22:30

Tou Tou Koi
陶陶居

🍴 　　　　　　　　　　🍽 24 📞🍴

As this 80 year old restaurant is always packed, it's vital to book ahead; at the same time why not also pre-order the duck? It's dim sum during the day and Cantonese cuisine at night and among the favourites are deep-fried crab, chicken soup and fish from the tank in the dining room. Service is sufficiently swift to accommodate the non-stop flow of customers. A refurbishment has left the restaurant looking much more contemporary.

有八十多年歷史的陶陶居總是賓客如雲，必須訂座，你亦可順道預訂八寶鴨。日間以點心為主，晚上則提供粵菜，受歡迎菜式包括金錢蟹盒和古法雞煲，還有新鮮烹調的海魚。為了應付絡繹不絕的客人，侍應生的工作效率十分高。酒家翻新後裝潢更見時尚。

TEL. 2857 2629
6-8 Travessa do Mastro
爐石塘巷 6-8號

■ PRICE 價錢
Lunch 午膳
à la carte 點菜 MOP 100-300
Dinner 晚膳
à la carte 點菜 MOP 250-800

■ OPENING HOURS 營業時間
Lunch 午膳　09:00-15:00 (L.O.)
Dinner 晚膳　17:00-00:00 L.O. 23:30

Vida Rica
御苑

🍴🍴   ♿ ← 🖐 💺24

Dark marble and Asian art combine to create a sophisticated yet relaxing spot here on the second floor of the Mandarin Oriental. The kitchen's plan is to make everyone's life a little richer by covering all bases: the large menu offers international cuisine with a French twist, and also some Cantonese dishes. There's also a simple lunchtime buffet in the bar on the same floor.

座落於文華東方酒店二樓，裝潢結合深色雲石和亞洲藝術的御苑，營造出既豪華又悠閒的氣氛。它的宗旨，是要做到面面俱圓，令所有顧客的生活都更見豐盛。豐富的菜單羅列多國菜式、法式糕點和廣東經典美食。同一樓層的酒吧，更提供簡便的午市自助餐。

TEL. 8805 8918
2F, Mandarin Oriental Hotel, Avenida Dr.
Sun Yat Sen, Nape
外港新填海區孫逸仙大馬路
文華東方酒店 2樓
www.mandarinoriental.com/macau

■ PRICE 價錢
Lunch 午膳
à la carte 點菜 MOP 450-1,100
Dinner 晚膳
à la carte 點菜 MOP 700-1,100

■ OPENING HOURS 營業時間
Lunch 午膳　12:00-14:30 (L.O.)
Dinner 晚膳　18:00-22:30 (L.O.)

Wing Lei
永利軒

An opulent, comfortable restaurant in vibrant red, characterised by vast lanterns at the entrance and a striking three-dimensional dragon made of ninety thousand pieces of crystal. As befits such sumptuous surroundings, the service is courteous and attentive. Tourists and a large number of families create a lively ambience as they tuck into the large menu of Cantonese classics.

這家紅彤彤的餐廳入口掛着一些大型燈籠，襯托一條以九萬片水晶製成的立體龍，盡展豪華氣派；舒適的紅色座椅讓人更添好感。餐廳的裝潢實屬一流，服務也親切周到。食客多是一家大小或娛樂場玩家，氣氛非常熱鬧。餐廳供應傳統粵菜，菜式選擇良多。

TEL. 8986 3688
GF, Wynn Hotel, Rua Cidade de Sintra, Nape
外港新填海區仙德麗街永利酒店地下
www.wynnmacau.com

■ PRICE 價錢
Lunch 午膳
à la carte 點菜 MOP 300-2,000
Dinner 晚膳
à la carte 點菜 MOP 500-2,000

■ OPENING HOURS 營業時間
Lunch 午膳   11:30-15:00 (L.O.)
Sunday and Public Holiday lunch
週日及公眾假期午膳   10:30-15:30 (L.O.)
Dinner 晚膳   18:00-23:00 (L.O.)

Wong Kung Sio Kung
皇冠小館

Owner Mr. Cheng, who is native Macanese, has over 30 years of experience when it comes to making noodles using the traditional bamboo pressing method. His shop opened back in 2000 but such was its popularity that he later expanded into next door. A selection of traditional Cantonese dishes is offered but most come here for the sea crab congee and the bamboo noodles with dried shrimp roe (which is also sold in bottles in the shop).

澳門土生土長的東主鄭先生，已有逾三十年以傳統竹竿手打方法製麵的經驗。餐廳早於2000年開業，大受歡迎下擴充至隔鄰舖位。他的店子提供一系列傳統廣東美食，但慕名而來的食客，通常會點遠近馳名的竹昇蝦子撈麵及海蟹粥。店內亦有出售瓶裝蝦子。

TEL. 2837 2248
308-310A Rua do Campo
水坑尾街 308-310號 A
www.wongkun.com.mo

■ PRICE 價錢
à la carte 點菜 MOP 30-120

■ OPENING HOURS 營業時間
10:00-02:00 (L.O.)
Weekends 週末 09:30-02:00 (L.O.)

■ ANNUAL AND WEEKLY CLOSING 休息日期
Closed 5 days Lunar New Year
農曆新年休息 5 天

MACAU 澳門

Wong Kung Sio Kung (Broadway) NEW
皇冠小館 (百老匯)

If you're looking for a quick bite after watching all the street entertainment on Broadway then try this simple noodle and congee shop. The menu is slightly smaller than the original branch but it still has the same focus on handmade noodles using the traditional bamboo method and served with dried shrimp roe. The congee is smooth and satisfying and has a delicate aftertaste and there are also a few other hot dishes available.

百老匯酒店後面的食街，雲集多間澳門當地知名食店，非常熱鬧。作為當地代表之一，皇冠小館以古法竹杆炮製的彈牙麵配大頭蝦子及以新鮮原隻海蟹及瑤柱熬製的蟹粥馳名。另外還有其他粥麵小食和數款小炒。環境簡樸乾淨。

TEL. 8883 3338
Shop A-G017, Broadway Macau, Cotai
路氹城澳門百老匯 E-G017

■ PRICE 價錢
Lunch 午膳
à la carte 點菜 MOP 80-150
Dinner 晚膳
à la carte 點菜 MOP 80-150

■ OPENING HOURS 營業時間
11:00-03:00 (L.O.)

Xin
鮮

The philosophy behind this restaurant is as simple as its name suggests – it's all about "freshness". On offer are hotpots, seafood and Asian-inspired dishes. You can make up your own hotpot using the superb ingredients from the buffet, along with seven different kinds of broth. There are luxury hotpots too, that include Boston lobster and Wagyu beef. The large contemporary dining room comes with a lively and convivial atmosphere.

此火鍋店以鮮為名，意指店內供應的全是最新鮮的食材。除了價格實惠的火鍋自助餐外，喜歡波士頓龍蝦和日本和牛的朋友，可選擇價格較高的精選套餐，且共有七款湯底供食客選擇。午市時段，還會供應燒味和新派中式點心。

TEL. 8113 1200
L1, Sheraton Hotel, Cotai Central, The Cotai Strip, Taipa
氹仔路氹金光大道喜來登金城中心酒店 1 樓
www.sheraton.com/macao

■ PRICE 價錢
Lunch 午膳
à la carte 點菜 MOP 280-600
Dinner 晚膳
à la carte 點菜 MOP 280-600

■ OPENING HOURS 營業時間
Lunch 午膳   11:30-15:00 (L.O.)
Dinner 晚膳 18:00-23:00 (L.O.)

Ying
帝影樓

XXX   ⚷ ← 🍽 🅿 🍴30 🕐🍴 ፠

It's not just the breathtaking views looking north to Macau that set this restaurant apart – the beautifully styled interior has been designed with taste and verve; the beaded curtains, which feature gold cranes and crystal trees, are particularly striking. The Cantonese dishes are prepared with contemporary twists and much flair. Try the prawn with herb-scented pear in tangerine paste, and the beef short ribs with red date essence.

帝影樓北望海港及澳門繁華景色，環境宜人。餐廳設計品味獨特，風格絢麗；珠簾上飾有金鶴和水晶樹圖案，使裝潢更添神采。餐廳的粵菜融入了新口味，大廚的烹調技藝精湛。專業的服務態度令人賓至如歸。值得一試的有這裏的柑桔蝦球桂花梨及紅棗炆牛肋骨。

TEL. 2886 8868
11F, Altira Hotel, Avenida de Kwong Tung, Taipa
氹仔廣東大馬路新濠鋒酒店 11樓
www.altiramacau.com

■ PRICE 價錢
Lunch 午膳
à la carte 點菜 MOP 150-1,700
Dinner 晚膳
à la carte 點菜 MOP 200-1,700

■ OPENING HOURS 營業時間
Lunch 午膳 11:00-15:45 (L.O.)
Dinner 晚膳 18:00-22:30 (L.O.)

Zi Yat Heen
紫逸軒

With a large glass-enclosed wine cellar at its centre, Zi Yat Heen is an elegant yet intimate restaurant, located within the Four Seasons Hotel Macau. By using first rate ingredients and minimal amounts of seasoning, chef Ho prepares a traditional Cantonese menu but one that is lighter and fresher tasting. Interesting creations include the baked lamb chops with coffee sauce, while a more traditional dish would be pigeon with Yunnan ham.

地方寬敞，格調高雅的紫逸軒位於四季酒店一樓，正中位置設有巨型玻璃餐酒庫。大廚何先生烹調傳統菜式時採用最新鮮的食材與最少的調味料，炮製出更鮮味清新的粵菜。有趣創意菜式包括咖啡汁焗羊排，較傳統的選擇有酥香雲腿伴鴿脯。

TEL. 2881 8818
GF, Four Seasons Hotel, Estrada da Baia de N. Senhora da Esperanca, s/n, The Cotai Strip, Taipa
氹仔路氹金光大道 -望德聖母灣大馬路
四季酒店地下
www.fourseasons.com/macau

■ PRICE 價錢
Lunch 午膳
set 套餐 MOP 1,288-2,088
à la carte 點菜 MOP 250-1,500
Dinner 晚膳
set 套餐 MOP 1,288-2,088
à la carte 點菜 MOP 350-1,500

■ OPENING HOURS 營業時間
Lunch 午膳   11:30-15:00 (L.O.)
Dinner 晚膳   18:00-23:00 (L.O.)

Street Food 街頭小吃
Popular places for snack food
馳名小食店

Aboong 韓國鯛魚燒乳酪雪糕

Korean yoghurt ice cream.

華夫餅、韓國乳酪雪糕。

$ 28-32   12:00-21:00

MAP 地圖 36/A-3
129 Rua dos Mercadores, Macau
澳門新馬路營地大街 129號 A

Chong Shing 昌盛

Cantonese steamed buns.

粵式包點。

$ 10-20   07:00-20:00

MAP 地圖 36/B-2
GF, 11 rua de Tome Pires, Macau
澳門新橋道咩啤利士街 11號地下

Dai Gwan 台灣帝鈞碳烤胡椒餅

Taiwanese pepper meat bread.

台灣胡椒餅。

$ 20-30   11:00-22:00

MAP 地圖 36/B-3
1 Rua do Monte, Macau
澳門大炮台街 1號

Fong Kei 晃記餅家

Almond cake; egg rolls.
杏仁餅及蛋捲。
$ 30-50   10:00-20:00

MAP 地圖 42/B-2
14 Rua do Cunha, Taipa
氹仔官也街 14 號

Lei Ka Choi 李家菜

Cantonese snacks such as duck's blood soup, wontons and noodles.
鴨血、炸雲吞及魚球麵。
$ 30-90   11:00-03:00

MAP 地圖 40/B-3
Shop E-G028, Broadway Macau, Cotai
路氹城澳門百老匯 E-G028號舖

Lemon Cello 檸檬車露

Gelato.
意大利雪糕。

$ 30-50   12:00-23:00

MAP 地圖 36/B-3
Trav. Se 11r/c, Macau
澳門大堂巷 11 號

Lord Stow's Bakery 安德魯餅店

Portuguese egg tarts.
葡撻。
$ 20-30   07:00-22:00

MAP 地圖 43/A-1
1 Rua do Tassara, Coloane
路環撻沙街 1 號

Mok Yee Kei 莫義記

Durian ice cream; mango ice cream.

榴蓮雪糕及芒果雪糕。

$ 25-40　　　　　　　　11:00-21:00

MAP 地圖　42/B-2
9 Rua do Cunha, Taipa
氹仔官也街 9號

Neng Meng Wang 檸檬王

Preserved fruits.

甘草檸檬、川貝陳皮、檸汁薑。

$ 10-35　　　　　　　　12:00-01:00

MAP 地圖　36/B-3
GF, Lai Hou Garden, Rua Coelho do Amaral,
Macau
澳門白鴿巢前地麗豪花園平台

Sun Ying Kei 新英記

Pork chop buns.

豬扒包。

$ 20-40　　　　　　　　07:00-17:00

MAP 地圖　36/B-2
GF, 2B Rua da Alegria do Patane, Macau.
沙梨頭惠愛街 2B地下

Ving Kei 榮記荳腐

Tofu products and noodles.

豆腐、豆腐花及麵食。

$ 20-40　　　　　　　　08:00-18:30

MAP 地圖　36/B-2
GF, 47 Rua da Tercena, Macau
澳門果欄街 47號地下

Yi Shun 義順鮮奶

Fresh milk custard; milk custard with ginger juice.

雙皮燉奶、薑汁撞奶。

$ 30-40   09:30-23:30

MAP 地圖   36/B-3
60 Avenida de Almeida Ribeiro, Macau
澳門新馬路 60號

HOTELS
酒店

HOTELS IN ORDER OF COMFORT
酒店 — 以舒適程度分類

Altira
新濠鋒

High quality design, a serene atmosphere and wondrous peninsula views produce something quite spectacular here. Guests arrive at the stylish lobby on the 38th floor and the luxury feel is enhanced by a super lounge and terrace on the same level. Bedrooms face the sea and merge tranquil tones with a contemporary feel. There's also a great spa and a pool-with-a-view.

酒店設計獨特，舒適典雅，位置優越，澳門半島的環迴美景盡入眼簾。38樓的大堂時尚尊貴，同層的天宮備有室內酒廊及露天陽台，豪華瑰麗。客房位於較高的樓層，海景一望無際，寧靜的環境與現代設計相互交織，氣派超凡。顧客享用附設的豪華水療設施時可飽覽美景。

TEL. 2886 8888
FAX. 2886 8666
Avenida de Kwong Tung, Taipa
氹仔廣東大馬路
www.altiramacau.com

RECOMMENDED RESTAURANTS 餐廳推薦
Aurora 奧羅拉 ХхХ
Tenmasa 天政 ХХ
Ying 帝影樓 ХхХ

♦ = MOP 2,000-5,000
♦♦ = MOP 2,000-5,000
Suites 套房 = MOP 3,500-70,000

Rooms 客房　184
Suites 套房　32

Banyan Tree
悅榕莊

Forming part of Galaxy Macau, this luxurious resort comprises 246 suites, as well as 10 villas which come with their own private gardens and swimming pools. The very comfortable bedrooms all have large baths set by the window and the array of services includes a state-of-the-art spa – the biggest in the group. Guests enjoy full access to all of Galaxy's facilities.

作為路氹城澳門銀河綜合渡假城的一部分及毗鄰澳門國際機場，澳門悅榕莊共有246間套房和10間擁有私人花園和泳池的別墅。所有寬敞套房內均設有私人悅心池，酒店提供一系列貼心服務，當中包括集團最大及最頂級的水療中心。住客更可享用銀河綜合渡假城內所有設施。

TEL. 8883 8833
FAX. 8883 6108
Galaxy Macau, Avenida Marginal Flor de Lotus, Cotai
路氹城蓮花海濱大馬路澳門銀河渡假城
www.banyantree.com/en/macau/

Suites 套房 = MOP 2,899-14,888
Villas 別墅 = MOP 9,899-70,888
☕ = MOP 273

Suites 套房 246
Villas 別墅 10

Conrad
康萊德

The largest of all the Conrad hotels is on the Cotai Strip and its guests have access to an abundance of shopping, gaming, dining and entertainment opportunities. The Himalayan and Chinese inspired décor creates a relaxing environment; anyone requiring extra stress reduction should book a restorative session in one of the ten treatment rooms in the luxurious spa.

座落於路氹金光大道上的康萊德，是全球規模最大的酒店，這裡有為數不少的購物、賭博、餐飲及娛樂場所。陳設靈感取材自喜瑪拉雅和中國地區，感覺悠閒舒適。豪華水療中心內設有十間套房，客人可盡情享受水療服務，令壓力和疲勞一掃而空。客房空間寬敞，設計時尚。

TEL. 2882 9000
FAX. 2882 9001
Estrada da Baia de N. Senhora de
Esperanca, s/n, The Cotai Strip, Taipa
氹仔路氹金光大道望德聖母灣大馬路
www.conradmacao.com

RECOMMENDED RESTAURANTS 餐廳推薦
Dynasty 8 朝 ☓☓☓

👤 = MOP 2,640-9,320
👥 = MOP 2,640-9,320
Suites 套房 = MOP 3,900-12,650

Rooms 客房 430
Suites 套房 206

Encore
萬利

For VIPs wanting an even more exclusive resort experience than the Wynn, there is Encore – their luxury brand. The word 'standard' certainly does not apply here as the choice is between suites or villas, all of which are lavishly decorated. You also get an exceptional spa offering bespoke treatments and Bar Cristal: as small as a jewellery box and just as precious.

欲享受比永利更獨特尊貴的服務，可考慮同集團旗下更豪華的萬利。酒店提供豪華套房及渡假別墅，兩者均以紅色與金色裝潢，特顯富麗堂皇。貴賓級水療中心為你提供度身訂造的療程，酒店內的Bar Cristal一如其名，像珠寶盒般嬌小高貴。賭場內附設多間貴賓娛樂房。

TEL. 2888 9966
FAX. 2832 9966
Rua Cidade de Sintra, Nape
外港新填海區仙德麗街
www.wynnmacau.com

Suites 套房 = MOP 15,000-22,000
☕ = MOP 130

Suites 套房 414

RECOMMENDED RESTAURANTS 餐廳推薦
Café Encore 咖啡廷　XX
Golden Flower 京花軒 ✿✿　XxxX
99 Noodles 99 麵　X

Four Seasons
四季

The luxurious Four Seasons fuses East and West by blending Colonial Portuguese style with Chinese traditions. The lobby acts as a living room, with its fireplace, Portuguese lanterns and Chinese lacquer screens. The hotel also has a luxury shopping mall and connects to The Venetian and Plaza Casino. If you want peace, simply escape to the spa or one of the five pools and the charming garden.

2008年開幕的四季酒店融合了東西方元素，將殖民地時代的葡萄牙風格與中國傳統融為一體。大堂設有壁爐、葡國燈籠和中國雕漆屏風，猶如置身家中客廳。酒店設有豪華購物商場，直通威尼斯人酒店及百利沙娛樂場。想離開五光十色稍作喘息，可享用酒店的水療設備和五個泳池，還有迷人的花園。

TEL. 2881 8888
FAX. 2881 8899
Estrada da Baia de N. Senhora da Esperanca, s/n, The Cotai Strip, Taipa
氹仔路氹金光大道望德聖母灣大馬路
www.fourseasons.com/macau

RECOMMENDED RESTAURANTS 餐廳推薦
Belcanção 鳴詩 XX
Zi Yat Heen 紫逸軒 ⊛⊛ XxxX

�r = MOP 2,088-10,888
♠♠ = MOP 2,088-10,888
Suites 套房 = MOP 4,088-64,588
⌣ = MOP 228

Rooms 客房 276
Suites 套房 84

Galaxy
銀河

MACAU 澳門

The striking exterior of Galaxy is one of the most recognisable landmarks of Taipa. The guestrooms are very spacious and impressively well equipped. Another of the attractions of the hotel is its 2,000sqm artificial beach and the world's largest wave pool; there also are cinemas and assorted restaurants. It's just a few minutes' walk from the Old Town.

外觀金璧輝煌的銀河渡假城是氹仔的新地標。作為渡假城內三間酒店之一，銀河酒店予人國際化的印象。1500間客房，每間都裝潢時尚、空間寬趟、設備齊全兼現代化。最吸引的設施是佔地2000平方米的人造沙灘及大型衝浪泳池。戲院和餐飲設施一應俱全，與舊城區只有一條馬路之隔，便於觀光購物。

TEL. 2888 0888
FAX. 8883 3988
Estrada da Baia de N. Senhora da Esperanca, s/n, The Cotai Strip, Taipa
路氹望德聖母灣大馬路
www.galaxymacau.com

= MOP 4,988
= MOP 4,988
Suites 套房 = MOP 6,488-13,988
= MOP 148

Rooms 客房　1350
Suites 套房　150

RECOMMENDED RESTAURANTS 餐廳推薦
Gosto 葡軒
Myung Ga 名家
Terrazza 庭園

Grand Hyatt
君悅

With its striking 22m ceiling and fabulous artwork, the lobby sets the tone – the droplets appear to be falling from a cloud. The contemporary bedrooms are split between two towers. Along with contemporary and luxurious suites, the Grand Club on the top floor provides a dining service where customers can order any kind of cuisine they choose.

君悅酒店的大堂設計獨特，從22米天花上空墜下的吊飾，配合藝術設計營造出水珠從雲層落下再匯聚一起的壯觀景象。設計時尚的房間分佈在兩棟大樓內。位於頂層的嘉賓軒裝潢高雅，有多間貴賓廂房，按客人喜好提供不同餐飲服務，是舉辦私人商務聚會的理想場地。

TEL. 8868 1234
FAX. 8867 1234
City of Dreams, Estrada do Istmo, Cotai
路氹連貫公路新濠天地
www.macau.grand.hyatt.com

RECOMMENDED RESTAURANTS 餐廳推薦
Beijing Kitchen 滿堂彩 ХХ
Mezza9 ХХ

♦ = MOP 5,588-6,588
♦♦ = MOP 5,588-6,588
Suites 套房 = MOP 6,088-33,788
☕ = MOP 228

Rooms 客房　503
Suites 套房　288

Grand Lapa NEW
金麗華

MACAU 澳門

Plenty of Portuguese character and a relaxing, peaceful atmosphere set this hotel apart. There is also a lovely tropical garden behind the main building, along with a swimming pool and spa. Bedrooms come with large windows and face either the harbour or the city – ask for one with a balcony on floors 16-18. Prices are reasonable and the staff are eager to please.

於1984年建成，是澳門早期的豪華酒店之一。大堂面貌多年來改變不大，頗富葡國色彩且有一種寧靜優雅的感覺。房間裝潢並不時髦，然方正寬敞，16至18樓的客房更設有露台可觀賞海景。大樓後的熱帶園林邊設有水療中心及露天泳池，是澳門鬧市中少有的幽閒設施。

TEL. 2856 7888
FAX. 2855 4298
956-1110 Avenida da Amizade, Macau
澳門友誼大馬路 956-1110號
www.grandlapa.com

RECOMMENDED RESTAURANTS 餐廳推薦
Kam Lai Heen 金麗軒 ✕✕
Naam 灆 ✕✕

👤 = MOP 3,000-4,200
👤👤 = MOP 3,000-4,200
Suites 套房 = MOP 4,600-36,000
☕ = MOP 198

Rooms 客房　378
Suites 套房　38

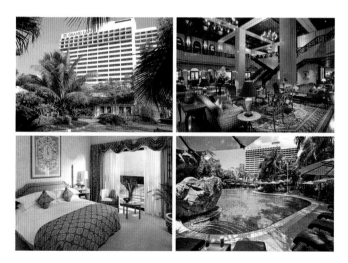

Grand Lisboa
新葡京

Impossible to miss, the Grand Lisboa can be seen from miles away with its eye-popping, brightly-lit lotus design atop a shining diamond. Opulent soundproofed bedrooms feature Asian paintings, and offer grand sea or city vistas. If you have a corner room or a suite, you'll get the added bonus of a sauna; if you have neither, you can make use of the sumptuous spa.

2008年12月開幕的新葡京外型像一片耀目的黃蓮葉，座落於一顆閃爍的鑽石之上，遠處可見。客房隔音設備完善，擁有典型的棕色牆壁、紅色扶手椅和亞洲油畫，並坐擁豪華海景或澳門的秀麗風光。角位客房及套房設有桑拿設施，其他客房亦可享用豪華的水療設施。

TEL. 2828 3838
FAX. 2888 2828
Avenida de Lisboa
葡京路
www.grandlisboahotel.com

RECOMMENDED RESTAURANTS 餐廳推薦
Don Alfonso 1890 當奧豐素 1890　XxxX
Robuchon au Dôme
天巢法國餐廳 ✱✱✱　XxXxX
The Eight 8 餐廳　✱✱✱　XxxX
The Kitchen 大廚　✱　XX

♦ = MOP 2,400-3,200
♦♦ = MOP 2,400-3,200
Suites 套房 = MOP 4,480-48,000
☕ = MOP 150

Rooms 客房　381
Suites 套房　50

JW Marriott <small>NEW</small>
JW萬豪

A soaring lobby forms the centrepiece of this impressive hotel within Galaxy Macau. The Grand Ballroom can host up to 1,600 and the hotel offers every service you'd expect in a resort. The well-equipped bedrooms may lack a little personality but they make up for it in square footage. Restaurants include the contemporary 'Urban Kitchen' with its international buffet.

宏偉的酒店大堂和完備的休閒設施如水療按摩及健身中心等服務，令你怦然心動！匱大的客房裝潢風格一致，設備齊全，雖稱不上別致，卻不失明亮整潔。酒店內的大宴會廳能容納千六人，不論是大型私人宴會或業務交流會議，都不愁找不到場地。設計時尚雅致的名廚都匯提供早、午、晚國際自助餐。

TEL. 8886 6888
FAX. 8886 6300
Galaxy, Estrada da Baia de Nossa
Senhora da Esperança, Cotai
路氹望德聖母灣大馬路澳門銀行渡假城
www.jwmarriottmacau.com

👤 = MOP 1,888-3,588
👥 = MOP 1,888-3,588
Suites 套房 = MOP 5,000-60,000
☕ = MOP 208

Rooms 客房　944
Suites 套房　71

MACAU 澳門

Lisboa
葡京

Thanks largely to its 1970s style façade, The Lisboa sports a relatively sober look for Macau, and so stands in stark contrast to the glitzier Grand Lisboa. There are ten types of guestroom available and the decoration is a mix of Chinese and Portuguese styles; it's worth asking for a Royal Tower room, as these are larger and more luxurious than those in the east wing.

仍然保留着七十年代外觀的葡京酒店，帶出澳門較為樸實的一面，與閃閃生輝的新葡京酒店可謂相映成趣。酒店共有十種客房，其陳設融合了中葡兩國的風格與特色；當中尊尚客房比東翼的客房更大更豪華。酒店設有多家餐廳，提供多國菜式。

TEL. 2888 3888
FAX. 2888 3838
2-4 Avenida de Lisboa
葡京路 2-4號
www.hotelisboa.com

RECOMMENDED RESTAURANTS 餐廳推薦
Guincho a Galera 葡國餐廳 XxxX
Tim's Kitchen 桃花源小廚 ⁂ XxX

♦ = MOP 1,180-1,980
♦♦ = MOP 1,180-1,980
Suites 套房 = MOP 3,780-23,880
☕ = MOP 140

Rooms 客房 876
Suites 套房 50

Mandarin Oriental
文華東方

The Mandarin Oriental is a non-gaming hotel but that's not the only reason it stands out – it is also a model of taste and discretion. Local artists' work adds a sense of locale to the bedrooms which come in muted, contemporary tones and offer great views – even from the tub! Those in search of further relaxation can choose between a very serene spa and a slick bar.

於2010年開業的澳門文華東方，除了不經營賭場外，更是品味的典範。本地藝術家的創作，為色調柔和時尚的客房添上韻味，即使在浴室裡也能欣賞醉人景觀。想進一步放鬆身心，可到幽靜的水療中心或雅致的酒吧。此外，服務質素保持極高水準。

TEL. 8805 8888
FAX. 8805 8899
Avenida Dr. Sun Yat Sen, Nape
外港新填海區孫逸仙大馬路
www.mandarinoriental.com/macau

RECOMMENDED RESTAURANTS 餐廳推薦
Vida Rica 御苑 ⅩⅩ

👤 = MOP 4,300-5,900
👥 = MOP 4,300-5,900
Suites 套房 = MOP 8,300-63,800
🛏 = MOP 299

Rooms 客房　186
Suites 套房　27

MGM
美高梅

Its iconic, wave-like exterior makes MGM one of Macau's more instantly recognisable hotels. The interior is pretty eye-catching too: topped by a vast glass ceiling, the Grande Praça covers over 1,000 square metres and is where you'll find an assortment of bars and restaurants. Spread over 35 floors, bedrooms are suitably luxurious and have glass-walled bathrooms.

標誌性的波浪形建築設計讓美高梅成為澳門最矚目酒店之一。店內設計同樣出色:巨型玻璃天幕下的天幕廣場佔地逾一千平方米,設有多間酒吧和餐廳。如果看膩了浮華的裝潢,不妨前往恬靜的水療中心。酒店有35層,客房華麗得恰到好處,景觀優美,浴室採用玻璃間隔,感覺寬敞。

TEL. 8802 8888
FAX. 8802 3333
Avenida Dr. Sun Yat Sen, Nape
外港新填海區孫逸仙大馬路
www.mgmgrandmacau.com

RECOMMENDED RESTAURANTS 餐廳推薦
Imperial Court 金殿堂 ⅩⅩⅩ
Square Eight 食・八方 Ⅹ

♂ = MOP 6,000-7,000
♂♂ = MOP 6,000-7,000
Suites 套房 = MOP 12,000-50,000
☕ = MOP 190

Rooms 客房　468
Suites 套房　114

Okura
大倉

Looking for sanctuary from the outside world? Try this tasteful, discreet and elegant hotel, which is part of Galaxy Macau resort. Charming staff provide excellent service; bedrooms are up-to-the-minute; and all suites have private saunas and steam showers. Dining options include Japanese and international fare.

裝修典雅與品味並重的大倉酒店讓賓客感覺如遠離了凡塵的一切。身穿日本和服的服務員服務親切貼心，時尚的酒店客房寬敞舒適，套房內設有私人桑拿及蒸氣浴。

TEL. 8883 8883
FAX. 8883 2345
Galaxy, Avenida Marginal Flor de Lotus, Cotai
路氹城蓮花海濱大馬路澳門銀河渡假城
www.hotelokuramacau.com

🚹 = MOP 1,388-3,888
🚹🚹 = MOP 1,388-3,888
Suites 套房 = MOP 2,888-30,000
☕ = MOP 140

Rooms 客房 429
Suites 套房 59

MACAU 澳門

Pousada de Mong-Há
望廈迎賓館

A very good value hotel with a distinct difference – it is run by the Institute for Tourism Studies, so you will be welcomed at the desk by students learning their trade. The hotel benefits from a very peaceful position, away from the casinos and surrounded by a lovely garden. Its bedrooms may not be big but they are quiet and come with some nice Asian touches.

這家與眾不同的超值賓館由旅遊學院營運，因此全部服務員由學院的學生擔任，為你悉心服務。它位處寧靜的望廈山半山腰，遠離娛樂場的煩囂，更給可愛的花園重重圍繞。客房地方不算大，不過環境寧靜，設計帶有亞洲風格。教學餐廳是品嘗澳門美食的好去處。

TEL. 2851 5222
FAX. 2855 6925
Colina de Mong-Há
望廈山
www.ift.edu.mo/pousada

RECOMMENDED RESTAURANTS 餐廳推薦
IFT Educational Restaurant
旅遊學院教學餐廳

♦ = MOP 700-1,300
♦♦ = MOP 700-1,300
Suites 套房 = MOP 1,300-1,800
☕ = MOP 140

Rooms 客房　16
Suites 套房　4

Pousada de São Tiago
聖地牙哥古堡

An exquisite boutique hotel, built into the hillside on the foundations of a 17th century fort alongside traditional Portuguese villas. Ancient steps lead up to reception; by contrast, the interior is modern and stylish, with subdued taste the key feature. Guestrooms boast cool marble floors and rich colours and fabrics – all look onto the Straits of Macau.

這家座落於山腰的精品酒店，由一座十七世紀的城堡改建而成，毗鄰傳統葡式住宅。古樸的石階別具風情，拾級而上可經入口到達接待處。內部設計十分現代時尚，獨樹一格而不浮誇。客房採用大理石地板、鮮明的顏色和布料；每間客房都坐擁澳門內港景色。陽台設有戶外泳池。

TEL. 2837 8111
FAX. 2855 2170
Avenida da República, Fortaleza de
São Tiago da Barra
西灣民國大馬路聖地牙哥大炮台
www.saotiago.com.mo

Suites 套房 = MOP 3,500-5,500
☕ = MOP 126

Suites 套房　12

RECOMMENDED RESTAURANTS 餐廳推薦
La Paloma 芭朗瑪　XX

Rocks
萊斯

This seaside hotel's ambience is inspired by the Victorian era and, as part of Fisherman's Wharf, is a good choice for those who prefer the quieter side of Macau. It has a lobby full of Victorian-style décor and furnishings including a fireplace and paintings, as well as a big marble staircase. A terrace overlooks the bay, while bedrooms have balconies and sea views.

酒店座落於澳門漁人碼頭，設計採用維多利亞時期風格。酒店大堂佈滿維多利亞時期的裝飾及傢俱：火爐、掛畫及大型白色雲石樓梯。舒適怡人的花園盡收海灣醉人景色，設有海景露台的臥室讓你身心放鬆。這裡不設賭場，專為嚮往澳門寧靜一面的遊客而設。

TEL. 2878 2782
FAX. 2870 8800
Macau Fisherman's Wharf
澳門漁人碼頭
www.rockshotel.com.mo

♦ = MOP 1,650-2,530
♦♦ = MOP 1,650-2,530
Suites 套房 = MOP 3,600-5,500
🛏 = MOP 130

Rooms 客房 66
Suites 套房 6

Sheraton
喜來登

Currently the biggest hotel in Macau, Sheraton Macau forms part of the resort complex of Sands Cotai Central and is connected to a huge shopping mall. Needless to say, the facilities are comprehensive and include a varied choice of restaurant, three outdoor pools with private cabanas and an impressive spa. There are Family suites and special amenities for children.

作為全澳門最大規模、位於金沙城中心的喜來登酒店，連接大型購物商場，便於閒逛購物。酒店內設備亦相當完善：設有數間餐館、三個戶外泳池及舒適的水療設施，吃喝玩樂與休憩，一網打盡。酒店還設有家庭套房和兒童遊樂設施，適合一家大小住宿。

TEL. 2880 2000
FAX. 2880 2111
Estrada da Baia de N. Senhora da
Esperanca, s/n, The Cotai Strip, Taipa
氹仔路氹金光大道望德聖母灣大馬路
www.sheraton.com/macao

👤 = MOP 1,388-5,088
👥 = MOP 1,388-5,088
Suites 套房 = MOP 5,988-20,838
☕ = MOP 188

Rooms 客房　3603
Suites 套房　260

RECOMMENDED RESTAURANTS 餐廳推薦
Xin 鮮　XX

StarWorld
星際

Opened in 2006, StarWorld Macau is a comfortable, well-managed hotel in a good location. Its bedrooms are bright and contemporary and the bathrooms are smart and well-equipped. Along with various restaurants and assorted gaming, the hotel also offers comprehensive entertainment and leisure facilities and these include a bar with live music every night.

在2006年開業的星際酒店地點便利之餘，亦是一間管理完善的酒店。光猛的房間設計風格前衛，時髦的浴室設施相當完備。除了各式餐館和娛樂場所外，酒店內還附設各種休閒設施，例如每天晚上都有現場音樂演奏的酒吧 。

TEL. 2838 3838
FAX. 2838 3888
Avenida da Amizade
友誼大馬路
www.starworldmacau.com

RECOMMENDED RESTAURANTS 餐廳推薦
Feng Wei Ju 風味居 ❀ ✕✕✕
Temptations 品味坊 ✕✕

♦ = MOP 1,980-3,080
♦♦ = MOP 1,980-3,080
Suites 套房 = MOP 3,960-5,760
☐ = MOP 158

Rooms 客房   501
Suites 套房   4

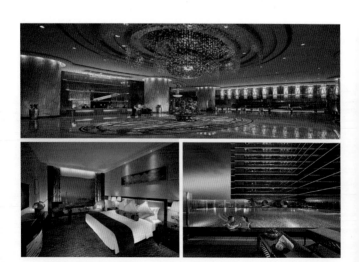

The Ritz-Carlton NEW
麗思卡爾頓

All bedrooms are suites at the exclusive Ritz-Carlton hotel, which is located on the upper floors at Galaxy Macau. They are impeccably dressed and come with particularly luxurious marble bathrooms. They also provide great views of Cotai, as does the outdoor pool. Along with a state-of-the-art spa is an elegant bar and stylish, very comfortable lounges.

講究的裝潢、精緻的藝術擺設、舒適的座椅,甫踏進設在51樓的接待處,心已給溶化!風格典雅的套房除了設有舒適奢華的大理石浴室外,還能俯瞰欣賞銀河渡假村景觀或遠眺市內風光。與接待處同層的麗思酒廊設計優雅,且能飽覽氹仔景致,是與摯愛親朋把酒談心的歇息處。

TEL. 8886 6868
FAX. 8886 6600
Galaxy, Estrada da Baia da Nossa
Senhora da Esperança, Cotai
路氹望德母灣大馬路澳門銀行渡假城
www.ritzcarlton.com/macau

Suites 套房 = MOP 6,000-90,000

Suites 套房 233

RECOMMENDED RESTAURANTS 餐廳推薦
Lai Heen 麗軒 ✕✕✕✕✕
The Ritz-Carlton Café 麗思咖啡廳 ✕✕

The Venetian
威尼斯人

One thing you'll need at Asia's largest integrated resort is a map to find your way around. Expect vast shopping malls and even canals with singing gondoliers; there are frescoes, colonnades and sculptures everywhere – it's easy to get caught up in the sheer scale and exuberance of it all. Identikit luxury is assured in a towering bedroom skyscraper with 3,000 rooms.

你需要一張地圖才能環遊這間全亞洲最大型綜合渡假酒店！在這裡你會找到大型購物商場，更有貢多拉船夫一邊掌船一邊唱歌。遍佈各處的壁畫、柱廊和雕塑裝飾，具規模且色彩繽紛，令人目不暇給。高聳的摩天大樓設有三千間套房，全部房間都很寬敞。

TEL. 2882 8888
FAX. 2882 8889
Estrada da Baía de N. Senhora da
Esperança, s/n, The Cotai Strip, Taipa
氹仔路氹金光大道望德聖母灣大馬路
www.venetianmacao.com

Suites 套房 = MOP 1,898-9,000
☕ = MOP 190

Suites 套房 3000

RECOMMENDED RESTAURANTS 餐廳推薦
Canton 喜粵 XXX
The Golden Peacock 皇雀 ❀ XX

Wynn
永利

      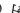

The Wynn's easy-on-the-eye curving glass façade is enhanced with a lake and dancing fountains, while the classically luxurious interior includes Murano glass chandeliers, plush carpets and much marble. An attractively landscaped oasis pool forms the centrepiece to corridors lined with famous retail names. Comfortable bedrooms display a considerable degree of taste.

弧形的玻璃外牆十分奪目，更設有表演湖及噴池。酒店內部散發着古典豪華氣息：穆拉諾穆玻璃吊燈、豪華的地毯，觸目所及皆是大理石。走廊中心設有一個造型迷人的綠洲池，而兩旁滿是名店。客房融合了傳統與現代兩種設計風格，盡顯卓越品味。其吉祥樹同樣令你印象深刻。

TEL. 2888 9966
FAX. 2832 9966
Rua Cidade de Sintra, Nape
外港新填海區仙德麗街
www.wynnmacau.com

RECOMMENDED RESTAURANTS 餐廳推薦
Il Teatro 帝雅廷　XxxX
Mizumi 泓　❀　XxX
Wing Lei 永利軒　❀　XxxX

♞ = MOP 3,700-7,600
♞♞ = MOP 3,700-7,600
Suites 套房 = MOP 16,500-41,000
▢ = MOP 210

Rooms 客房　460
Suites 套房　140

MAPS
地圖

麻雀嶺 Ma Tseuk Leng
沙頭角 SHA TAU KOK
古澳洲 CROOKED ISLAND
平洲 PING CHAU

荔枝窩 Lai Chi Wo
鹿頸 Luk Keng
三椏村 Sam A Tsuen
往灣洲 DOUBLE IS.
大鵬灣 TO PANG HAN
赤洲 PORT IS.

烏蛟騰 Wu Kau Tang

大美督 Tai Mei Tuk
船灣淡水湖 Plover Cove Reservoir
塔門洲 TO LO CHAU
塔門 GRASS ISLAND
石牛洲 SHEK NGAU CHAU

大埔 TAI PO
汀角路 TO LO

荔枝莊 Lai Chi Chong
海下 Hoi Ha

馬鞍山 MA ON SHAN
恒安 Heng On
榕樹澳 Yung Shue O
赤徑 Chek Keng
短咀 Bate Head
鹹田 Ham Tin
大浪咀 Fung Head

香港中文大學 Chinese Univ. of H.K.
九肚 KAU TO
火炭 Fo Tan
4
北潭涌 Pak Tam Chung
西灣 Sai Wan
清水灣 Clear Water Bay

沙田 SHA TIN
小瀝源 Siu Lek Yuen
西貢 SAI KUNG
大網仔 Tai Mong Tsai

大圍 Tai Wai
塔咀洲 KIU TSUI CHAU
滘西洲 KAU SAI CHAU
牛尾海 NGAU MEI HOI (Port Shelter)

九龍塘 KOWLOON TONG
香港科技大學 H.K.U. of Sci. & Tech.
牛尾洲 SHELTER IS.
吊鐘洲 TIU CHUNG CHAU
火燒洲 FU TAU FAN CHAU

九龍 KOWLOON
尖沙咀 TSIM SHA TSUI
觀塘 KWUN TONG
將軍澳 TSEUNG KWAN O
火石洲 BASALT ISLAND

紅磡 HUNG HOM
鯉魚門 Lei Yue Mun
大坳門 Tai Au Mun

銅鑼灣 Causeway Bay
太古城 Taikoo Shing
佛堂門 (Joss Bay)

香港島 HONG KONG ISLAND
柴灣 Chai Wan
小西灣 Siu Sai Wan
糧洲群島 Ninepin Group

黃竹坑 Wong Chuk Hang
東龍洲 Tung Lung Chau
大潭灣 Tai Tam Bay

海洋公園 Ocean Park
深水灣 Repulse Bay
石澳 Shek O
藍塘海峽 TATHONG CHANNEL

赤柱 Stanley

蚺洲
螺洲
橫瀾島

蒲台島 Po Toi Island

N

◀ 10,125m米(比例尺 Scale 1:337,518) ▶

A   B

美城苑
May Shing Court

城門隧道路 Shing Mun Tunnel Rd

利苑酒家 (沙田)
Lei Garden
(Sha Tin)

新城市廣場
New Town Plaza

嘉御山
The Great Hill

1

美林邨
MEI LAM ESTATE

大埔公路・沙田段 TAI PO RD · SHA TIN

沙田公園
Sha Tin Park

城門河 Shing Mun River

大埔公路・沙田段 TAI PO RD · SHA TIN

1

曾大屋

文禮閣
Man Lai Fat

CHE KUNG TEMPLE 車公廟

泰石邨
CHUN SHEK
ESTATE

大埔公路・大圍段 TAI PO RD

楓林小館
Fung Lum

TAI WAI 大圍大道

TAI WAI RD

紅梅谷路 HUNG MUI KUK RD

大圍
TAI WAI

新田村
Sun Tin Village

豐盛苑
Pung Shing
Court

獅子山隧道路 LION ROCK TUNNEL RD

2

名城
Festival
City

新翠邨
SUN CHUI ESTATE

車公廟路

新田圍邨
SUN TIN WAI
ESTATE

2

雲疊花園
Carado Garden

金獅花園二期
Golden Lion
Garden II

田心街

N

← 606米(比例尺 Scale1:20,202) →

陳亭邨
NG HANG
ESTATE

A   B

呈祥道 CHING CHEUNG RD

樂仁學校
Lok Yik School

A   B CHEUNG

荔枝角 LAI CHI KOK

龍

祥

善導小學
Good Counsel
Catholic
Primary School

深安邨
Chak On Est

南華中學
Nam Wah
Secondary School

蘇屋邨
So Uk Est

大埔道 TAI PO RD

大角中學
Tai Kok College

聖公會基愛
小學
SKH Kei Oi
Primary School

CASTLE PEAK

長沙灣道 CHEUNG SHA WAN RD

李鄭屋邨
Lei Cheng Uk Est.

石硤尾邨
Shek Kip Me

1

深水埗運動場
Sham Shui Po
Sports Ground

坤記竹昇麵 (長沙灣)
Kwan Kee Bamboo Noodle
(Cheung Sha Wan)

元洲邨
UN CHAU
ESTATE

李鄭屋
游泳池
Lei Cheng Uk
Swimming Pool

N

← 545m(比例尺 Scale1:18,155) →

幸福邨

幸俊苑
Fortune Est.

WEST

荔枝角 RD LAI CHI KOK RD

亞洲高球會
Asia Golf Club

怡閣苑
LAI KOK
ESTATE

長沙灣道 CHEUNG SHA WAN RD

劉森記麵家 (福榮街)
Lau Sum Kee
(Fuk Wing Street)

石硤尾邨
SHEK KIP
ME

2

循道中學
Tsung Tsin
Christian
Academy

九龍走廊 KOW LOON CORRIDOR

怡靖苑
Yee Ching
Court

泰潮
Thai Chiu

2

協和小學

深水埗公園
Sham Shui Po Park
Swimming Pool

英華女學校
Ying Wa
Girls School

深水埗公園
Sham Shui Po
Park

順寧道

安盛邨
LAI ON
ESTATE

深水埗道 SHAM SHUI PO RD

公和荳品廠
Kung Wo Tofu

坤記糖品
Kwan Kee Store

聖瑪加利
小學
St.Margaret's

合益泰小食
Hop Yik Tai

添好運 (深水埗)
Tim Ho Wan
(Sham Shui Po)

欽州街

A   B

10

好運印尼餐廳
Lucky Indonesia

利苑酒家 (觀塘)
Lei Garden (Kwun Tong)

灉家
Wonton Master

MIC Kitchen

龍皇 (觀塘)
Dragon King
(Kwun Tong)

觀塘避風塘
Kwun Tong Typhoon Shelter

觀塘
KWUN TONG

觀塘公眾碼頭
Public Pier

← 462m米 (比例尺 Scale 1:15,385) →

觀塘渡輪碼頭
Kwun Tong
Ferry Pier

甲邊朗
Kap Pin Long

天主教墳場

西貢崇真天主教
Sung Tsun

豐城
Tan Cheung

油麻莆
Yau Ma Po

灰窰下
Fui Yiu Ha

旺泰特食
May's Sawaddee Thailand

新安村
Sun On
Tsuen

西貢墩
Sai Kung Tuk

西貢戶外康樂中心
Sai Kung Outdoor
Recreation Centre

灰窰角街
Fui Yiu Lane

勝記
Sai Kung Sing Kee

Lakeside Garden

六福菜館
Loaf On

全記海鮮菜館
Chuen Kee Seafood

西貢
SAI KUNG

碼頭
Pier

對面海
Tui Min Hoi

官門漁村

塘頭村

漁民新邨

西貢對面海路

西貢公眾碼頭
Sai Kung
Public Pier

西貢警署

西貢體育館運動場
Sai Kung
Tang Shiu Kin
Sports Ground

西貢游泳池

滘西洲
南涌球場碼頭
Kau Sai Chau
PGC Pier

西貢中心
李少園

滘西洲高球場
停車場

西貢公眾碼頭往榕樹澳，
鹽田梓

← 400 m 米 (比例尺 Scale 1:13,323) →

11

491

桂寶雞窩高米線
Gainmore Cuisine

九龍城
KOWLOON
CITY

村
TSUEN

JNDARY STREET

E EDWARD ROAD WEST

窩

九龍醫院

打

公

JUNCTION RD

ARGYLE STREET

馬頭圍
MA TAU WAI

馬頭涌道

MA TAU CHUNG RD

九龍城道

土瓜灣
TO KWA WAN

8度海逸
Harbour Plaza 8 Degrees

MA TAU WAI RD

KOWLOON CITY RD

TO KWA WAN RD

7

NCESS

何文田
HO MAN TIN

FAT

KWONG ST

馬頭
圍道

添馬頭圍

1

5

2

5

MARGARET

ROAD

香港
理工大學
Hong Kong
Polytechnic
University

AD

添

HUNG HOH RD

紅磡

巧饍坊
Qiao Cuisine

竹家
Takeya

詠黎園
Wing Lai Yuen

紅磡
HUNG HOM

黃埔花園
Whampoa
Garden

九龍海逸君綽
Harbour Grand Kowloon

岡田和生
Kazuo Okada

玉蕾
Yù Lěi

炉端燒
Robatayaki

3

香港科學館
Hong Kong
Science Museum

香港體育館
Hong Kong Coliseum

SALISBURY RD

C

19

雄多利亞港
VICTORIA HARBOUR

D

← 278m米 (比例尺 Scale 1:9,260) →

C

D

1

右竹樹路
TAI HANG TUNG RD
丹珠路
OSMANTHRUS RD
大坑東
一村學校
一二村學校
TAT
鐵道廣場
CHEE AVE

街 蘭苑饍館
Lan Yuen Chee Koon
SAI YEUNG CHOI ST

BOUNDARY

界限街迴遊樂徑 FLOWER MARKET PATH

界限街迴樂場
Boundary Street
Recreation Ground

旺角大球場
Mong Kok Stadium

STREET

PLAYING FIELD

旺角警署
Mong Kok Police Station

PRINCE

FLOWER MARKET RD

PRINCE

西

帝京
Royal Plaza

純山東餃子
n Shandong Dumpling

太子
PRINCE EDWARD

KOK

NATHAN RD

NULLAH RD

叁薯
Three potatoes

新世紀廣場
Grand Century Place

旺角東 MONG KOK EAST

2

鳳城 (旺角)
Fung Shing (Mong Kok)

旺角中心
Pioneer Centre

TUNG

FA

SAI

YEUNG

CHOI

奇趣餅家
Kei Tsui

YUEN

ELLEN

WAY

旺角
MONG KOK

CANTON

NATHAN

KOK

旺角
MONG KOK

SOUTH

街
STREET

利苑酒家 (旺角)
Lei Garden (Mong Kok)

HONG LOK ST

HAK PO ST

FIFE

NELSON

ST

明閣
Ming Court

朗豪坊
Langham Place

PORTLAND

泉章居 (旺角)
Chuen Cheung Kui
(Mong Kok)

PEACE AVE

PAK PO ST

YIM PO FONG ST

3

康得思
Cordis

雅蘭
Grand Tw

RECLAMATION

Joyful Dessert House

SHANTUNG

SOY

STREET

STREET

好旺角麵家(花園街)
Good Hope Noodle (Fa Yuen Street)

YIN CHONG ST

KWONG WA ST

C

D

A   B

1

海麗邨   HOI LAI

WEST KOWLOON HIGHWAY

西九龍公路

HOI FAI RD

LIN CHEUNG RD

覽翔道 Express & Tung Chung Line

HOI TING ROAD

海庭道

HOI WANG ROAD

海旺道

LAI CHEUNG RD

麗翔道

FERRY STREET

渡船街

LI YUEN ST

利源街

DUNDAS ST

敦梳街

富榮花園
Charming Garden

油麻地
YAU MA TEI

HUI CHEUNG ST
匯�575街

2

西九龍 九龍公路
KOWLOON HIGHWAY

海�നෝ路

JO WAH ROAD

租華道

LIN CHEUNG ROAD

連翔道

YAN CHEUNG RD
欣翔道

MAN CHEUNG ST
文昌街

MAN WAI ST
文威街

MAN YUEN ST
文苑街

MAN YING ST
文英街

MAN WUI ST
文匯街

SHIP STREET
船街

有線小敍
Yau Yuen Siu Tsui

老趙 (佐敦)
Lo Chiu (Jordan)

摩天半島
Sorrento

JORDAN ROAD
佐敦道

3

天璽
The Cullinan

Union Square

漾日居
The Waterfront

君臨天下
The Harbour Side

凱旋門
The Arch

KOWLOON 九龍

LIN CHEUNG RD

田舍家
Inakaya

天空龍吟
Ryu Gin

天龍軒
Tin Lung Heen

Tosca

環球貿易廣場
International Commerce Ctr

麗思卡爾頓
The Ritz Carlton

廣深港高速鐵路
(香港段)
工程進行中

Guangzhou-Shenzhen-Hong Kong
Express Rail Link
Under Construction

Temporary Road D1A

HUI CHEUNG RD
匯翔道

WUI MAN RD
匯民道

AUSTIN
柯士甸道

AUSTIN ROAD WEST
柯士甸道西

士甸 AUSTIN 西

A   B

長沙街
CHANGSHA ST

ST

打
王
街

WATERLOO ROAD

廣華醫院
Kwong Wah Hosp

HAMILTON ST

富
豪
街

PITT

九龍華仁書院
Wah Yan College
(Kowloon)

← 278m米 (比例尺 Scale 1:9,260) →

PRINCESS MARGARET RD

主
道

何
文
田
山

ST

油麻地
YAU MA TEI

NATHAN ROAD

老

道

京士柏
KING'S PARK

WYLIE RD

RECLAMATION

文
ST

恩
寧
道

ARTHUR

柏
十
道

KING'S PARK RISE

KING'S PARK HILL RD

KING'S PARK RISE ROAD

ST

永
星
里
WING SING LA

北京道 CITY RD

PUBLIC SQUARE ST

南十二號路
NIGHTINGALE RD

伊利沙伯醫院
Queen Elizabeth Hospital

SHANGHAI

市
政
署

MARKET ST

KANSU ST

加

QUEEN ELIZABETH HOSPITAL RD

廠
興
街

北海街

PAK HOI ST

士

賓
臨
道

結
業
學校

HK Chinese
Civil Ser Assn
衛理道

SAIGON

茂
林
街

西貢街

拔萃女書院
Diocesan
Girls' School

RECLAMATION

NING

佳佳甜品
Kai Kai

道

教

GASCOIGNE ROAD

TEMPLE

寧
波
街

CHEONG
LOK ST

廣東道

和

ST

NANKING

吳
松
街

十八座狗仔粉
Block 18 Doggie's Noodle

JORDAN

佐

敦

ROAD

WOOSUNG

白
加
士
街

PARKES

德興街
TAK HING ST

裕成街
TAK SHING ST

ODES

PATH

JORDAN

九龍木球會
Kowloon
Cricket Club

槍會山軍營

JORDAN

Gun Club
Hill Barracks

BOWRING

庇
利
金
街

PICKEM ST

松
街

ROAD

AUSTIN

柯
士
甸

山林道
HILLWOOD RD

道

聖瑪利
嘉諾撒書院
St. Mary's
Canossian Coll

香港童軍
中心
HK Scout Ctr

尖沙咀警署
Tsim Sha Tsui
Police Station

聖安德烈堂
St. Andrew's

香港天文台
HK Observatory

AUSTIN AVE

香港歷史
博物館
HK Museum
of History

18

柯士甸 AUSTIN
CANTON ROAD

KWUN CHUNG ST
SHANGHAI ST
上海街
PARKES ST
白加士街
TEMPLE ST
廟街
WOOSUNG ST
吳松街

PILKEM ST

避風塘興記
Hing Kee

1 柯士甸道西 AUSTIN RD W

The Victoria
Towers

尖沙咀警署
Tsim Sha Tsui
Police Station

港景峯
P
HK Scout Ctr
香港童軍
中心

富豪 (尖沙咀
Fu Ho (Tsim Sha Tsui
新同樂 (尖沙咀
Sun Tung Lok (Tsim Sha Tsu
翠亨邨 (尖沙咀
Tsui Hang Village (TST

室內體育館
Sports Centre

Landmark
Centre
Piece

國金軒 (The Mira)
Cuisine Cuisine at The Mira
Whisk

中港城
China HK City

九龍公園
KOWLOON PARK

港景大廈
Gateway

China Ferry Terminal
中港客運碼頭

海港
HARBOUR

香港文物探知館
HK Heritage
Discovery Ctr.

清真寺
Jamia Masjid
Islamic Ctr.

(北座)
World
Commerce
Centre
(南座)

CANTON ROAD
廣東道

和宴
Wa-En
禪八
Zenpachi

HAIPHONG
海防 RD 道

九龍太平洋會
Kowloon Pacific

阿一海景飯店
Ah Yat Harbour View

2 鼎泰豐 (新港中心)
Din Tai Fung (Silvercord)

世界商業中心
World Comm Centre

新港中心
Silvercord

九龍中心
ASHLEY RD

宜蘭街

LOOK RD

新鴻基中心 力寶太陽廣場
New T & T Centre Lippo Sun Plaza

朗廷
The Langham

唐閣
T'ang Court

HARBOUR
CITY

GATEWAY BOULEVARD

海洋中心
Ocean Centre

PEKING RD

北京道一號
Peking Rd.

北京道
KOWLOON PARK DRIVE

美岸海鮮廳
The Bostonian

Épure

海運大廈
Ocean Terminal

夜上海 (尖沙咀)
Yè Shanghai
(Tsim Sha Tsui)

半島
The Peninsu

瑞樨閣
Chesa
Felix
吉地士
Gaddi's
嘉麟樓
Spring Moon

逸光行
Star House

香港太
香港
空館

3 往中環
To Central
天星碼頭
Star Ferry Pier

往灣仔
To Wan Chai

香港文化中心
HK Cultural Centre

鐘樓
Clock
Tower

九龍公眾碼頭
Kowloon Public Pier

尖沙咀
TSIM SHA TSU

N

← 250m米 (比例尺 Scale 1:8,333) →

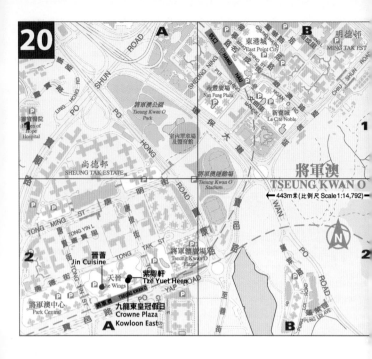

A

B

SHUN ROAD

LING HONG RD

LING PO RD

將軍澳公園
Tseung Kwan O
Park

靈實醫院
Haven of
Hope Hospital

室內單車場
及體育館

尚德邨
SHEUNG TAK ESTATE

CHUNG WANG

東港城
East Point City

SHEUNG NING

TSING NIU

MONG KU

南豐廣場
Nan Fung Plaza

NGAN

CHIU SHUN

明德邨
MING TAK EST

新寶城
La Cité Noble

1

將軍澳
TSEUNG KWAN O

HONG ROAD

PO TSUI

POPING

TONG MING ST

TONG YIN L

TONG TAK ST

CHI MING ST

晉薈
Jin Cuisine

天晉
Lic Wings

P

將軍澳中心
Park Central

TONG YIN ST

TSEUNG KWAN O

將軍澳運動場
Tseung Kwan O
Stadium

將軍澳廣場路
Tseung Kwan O
Plaza

紫玥軒
Tze Yuet Heen

九龍東皇冠假日
Crowne Plaza
Kowloon East

PO YAP

PO WAN

PO CHOK

至寶寧路

2

← 443m米 (比例尺 Scale 1:14,792)

N

PO

PUNG LIN AVE

盛寶隆

A

B

A
B

高樂花園 Connaught Garden

干諾道 西 CONNAUGHT ROAD WEST

WEST

德輔道 DES VOEUX ROAD WEST

西港城

P

奇靈里 CHING CHING ST
西源里 SAI YUEN L
石棧里 HING L

皇 西 營 盤

SAI YING PUN

1

西安里 SAI ON L
安泰街 ON TAI ST
興隆街 HING LUNG L

正街 CHIU KWONG ST
北街祥坊
西安里

第二街 SECOND ST
西邊街 WESTERN ST
中街 CENTRE ST

水街 WATER ST

曹湘門第(西環)
Café Huhan (Western District)

三多里 SAM TO L
蘇杭里 SAI SAU L

聖類斯
St. Louis

第一街 FIRST ST
西草里 SAI FUEL
薰里 TAM L

西園 Western Garden
北街 NORTH ST
德星里 HING ON ST

ROAD

POK FU RD
薄扶林道

餘樂里 YU LOK L

玫瑰里 ROSE LANE

THIRD ST 第三街

巴依 Ba Yi

西寧街

扶 林 道

聖士提反堂
St. Stephen's

般 咸 道

聖保羅書院
St. Paul's College

HING HON RD 興漢道

英皇書院 King's College

聖士提反里 ST STEPHEN'S LANE

2

本部大樓 Main Building

香港大學
THE UNIVERSITY OF HK

般咸道

美術博物館

BONHAM ROAD

光景台
聖嘉勒

巴丙頓道

BABINGTON PATH

列道

巴丙頓道

P

BABINGTON PATH

地質博物館

柏立基學院
Robert Black College

大學道
UNIVERSITY DRIVE

龍虎山
環境教育中心

旭龢道 HATTON RD

R
R
R

R

R
R

R

KOTEWALL ROAD 千德道

寶珊道1號
No.1 Po Shan Rd

寶珊道

3

A
HATTON

B

鴨巴甸街東

WILMER ST

修打蘭街

皇后街

P

德   輔   道   西

西源里

華里街TSZ MI ALLEY

威利麻街

SUTHERLAND ST

蓮香居
Lin Heung Kui

KO SHING ST

文咸東街

QUEEN'S RD W

帝后
華庭

1

荷李活道 MUI FONG ST

ST

P

大   街   SUTHERLAND ST

朝光街

和興街 WO HING ST

KOM U ST

PAN WAI ST

QUEEN'S RD W

摩羅上街 LOK KU

磅巷

大笪地 OAK LANE

上環

EASTERN ST

五福里 NG FUK LANE

菲廟
牙科醫院
Philip
Dental Hosp

贊育醫院
西營盤賽馬會分科
Tsan Yuk Hosp

西   醫   院   道

樂善堂
繁錦瑤

新街 NEW ST

SHEUNG WAN

S(建築中)
under construction

郭亞里

SOUTH LANE

香港佐治五世紀念公園
KING GEORGE V
MEMORIAL PARK

商業匯
College view

HOSPITAL   ROAD

聖公會
聖馬太

東華醫院
Tung Wah
Hospital

PO YAN ST

太平山街 TAI PING SHAN ST

FO YEE ST

新   街   NEW   ST

HOLLYWOOD RD

普慶坊

卜公花園
Blake
Garden

PO HING ST

西摩道 WEST PORT

STREET

高   街

西營盤社區
綜合大樓
Community
Complex

PO VIEW LANE

寶翠里

磅巷街

NG LANE

BONHAM   ROAD

磅巷 WING WO LANE

普仁街

鴨巴甸街

FRUITER ST

POUND ST

般咸道官立
官立

般   咸   道

PARK ROAD

東邊街

士丹頓街

BREEZY P

CAINE RD

St. Stephen's
Girls' College

聖士提反
女子中學

LYTTELTON   ROAD

RD

香港科技
專上書院

樂善堂

SEYMOUR RD

柏道

KLANDS AVE

ROBINSON   ROAD

羅便臣道

英華女學校
Ying Wah
Girls' Sch

近卑路乍街

ROBINSON ROAD

3

帝豪閣
Imperial Court

ROAD

聯邦花苑
Realty Gardens

干   德   道

CONDUIT

半山區
MID-LEVELS

N

SHAN   ROAD

← 168米 (比例尺Scale 1:5,587) →

C   D

SERVICES STREET

皇后街
QUEEN'S RD W

中港環
CHUNG KONG ROAD

香港消防總部、海事處及海務處總部
HK L, Is & Marine Fire Command HQ

海偵分區總部

CONNAUGHT RD W - 干諾道西

NEW MARKET ST 新街市街

永樂街 WING LOK ST

德輔道中

新威靈頓街

東里 TUNG LOI

干諾道中

海澳碼頭

香港國際機場
Hong Kong Heliport

港澳碼頭
HK-MACAU FERRY TERMINAL

信德中心
Shun Tak Ctr

招商局大廈
China Merchants Tower

林士街多層停車場

Queen's Terrace
帝后廣場

上環
SHEUNG WAN

文咸東街

ING

WING

LOK

文安中心
Wing On Centre

陳勤記鹵鵝飯店(上環)
Chan Kan Kee Chiu Chow (Sheung Wan)

荷李活道公園
Hollywood Road Park

SHEUNG WAN

新園興記
Sun Yuen Hing Kee

Wagyu Kaiseki Den
李

桃花源小廚
Tim's Kitchen

永

上環 - SHEUNG WAN

印尼餐廳19
Restoran Indones

新紀元廣場
Cocoa Town
Grand Plaza

Upper Modern Bistro

Blake Garden
卜公花園

普慶坊

Moon Thai

志魂
Sushi Shikon

尚品
The Mercer

麵店
Noodlemi

四川擔擔麵
Dandan

Bibo

麵鮮醬油房周月(中環)
Shugetsu Ramen (Central)

大班樓
The Chairman

Cocotte

九記
Kau Kee

名人坊
Celebrity Cuisine

文武廟
Man Mo Temple

聚賢居
Centre Stage

BRIDGES ST

永利街 WING LEE ST

LADDER ST

蘭桂坊
Lan Kwai Fong

香港醫學博物館
HK Museum of Medical Sciences

合一堂

CAINE LANE

堅道

SEYMOUR

Aberdeen Street Social

Isono

一宝
Ippoh

大平伙
Da Ping Huo

英華女學校
Ying Wah Girls' Sch

香港花園
HK Garden

美麗台
Merry Terr

CASTLE RD

衛城道

麻辣燙
Chilli Fagara

富景花園
Scenic Heights

美麗閣
Merry Court

猶太廟
Ohel Leah Synagogue

羅便臣道
Robinson Place

高樂台
Goldwin Heights

Le Souk

凱旋門
Blessing Garden

碧翠苑
Excelsior Ct

輕雲峰

ROAD

Tate

Buxey Lodge

承德山莊
Scenecliff

雙明苑
Elegant Terr

CONDUIT

清真禮拜堂
Jamia Mosque

ROBINSON

嘉諾撒聖心商學書院
Sacred Heart Canossian College of Commerce

康威園
Conway Mansion

康苑
Cliffview Mansions

ROAD

MOSQUE ST

MOSQUE JUNCTION

嘉兆臺
The Grand Panorama

羅便臣

全景大廈
Panorama

1號碼頭
Pier 1
中區海濱長廊
2號碼頭
Pier 2
往珀麗灣
To Park Island
Caprice
龍景軒
Lung King Heen
3號碼頭
Pier 3
往愉景灣
To Discovery Bay
4號碼頭
Pier 4
往榕樹灣
To Yung Shue Wan
往索罟灣
To So Kwu Wan
5號碼頭
Pier 5
往長洲
To Cheung Chau
6號碼頭
Pier 6
往坪洲
To Peng Chau
往梅窩
To Mui Wo
7號碼頭
Pier 7
往尖沙咀

1

民耀街 MAN YIU ST

民祥街 MAN CHIU ST

民寶街 MAN PO ST

民光街 MAN KWONG STREET

Central Pier
Waterfront

天星碼頭
Star Ferry Pier

四季
Four Seasons

金融街 MAN KAT ST

香港站停車場

國際金融中心商場
IFC Mall

民祥街 MAN CHEUNG ST

國際金融中心
Inter'l Finance
Ctr IFC

國際金融中心二期
Two International
Finance
Centre

利苑酒家 (國際金融中心)
Lei Garden (IFC)
正斗粥麵專家 (國際金融中心)
Tasty (IFC)

2

IFC Mall

HONG KONG 香港

HARBOUR VIEW ST

交易廣場
Exchange Square

翠玉軒
The Square

郵政總局
General Post Office

文華廳
Man Wah

怡和大廈
Jardine House

置地廣場

26

文華扒房+酒吧
Mandarin Grill + Bar
Pierre

遮打大廈
Chater House

CONNAUGHT PLACE

文華東方
Mandarin Oriental

CONNAUGHT RD C

CENTRAL

8½ Otto e Mezzo - Bombana

香港會所
HK Club

唐人館
China Tang

CIAK

歷山大廈
Alexandra House

北京樓 (中環)
Peking Garden (Central)

太子大廈
Prince's
Building

Dot Cod

Sushi
Ginza Iwa

Arcane
ON

QUEEN'S ROAD

L'Atelier de
Joël Robuchon

Mott 32

HSBC Main
Bank Building

中國銀行大廈
Bank of China
Bldg

立法會大樓
Legislative
Council Bldg

遮打花園
Chater Garden

都爹利會館
Duddell's

Amber

CENTRAL
BATTERY

港島廳
Island Tang

Le Dôme
de Cristal

3

長江集團中心
Cheung Kong
Center

置地文華東方
The Landmark
Mandarin Oriental

終審法院
Court of Final
Appeal

ALBANY RD

港中醫院
HKC hospital

HKSAR Govt HQ

Cathedral

C   **D**

26

GRAHAM ST

Man Yee Building

🅿

MAN YEE

POTTINGER ST

沾仔記 (威靈頓街)
Tsim Chai Kee (Wellington St) 🅿

旅
Ta Vie

COCHRANE

Pedestrian Escalator

中環 (中區)
CENTRAL (中區)

LI YUEN ST W

中環石板街
The Pottinger

GUTZLAFF

GAGE

蛇王芬
Ser Wong Fun

王府
Wang Fu

一樂燒鵝
Yat Lok

波士廳
The Boss

LI YUEN ST

QUEEN'S

CENTRAL DISTRICT

擺花街

LYNDHURST TERR

星記(中環)
Sing Kee (Central)

STANLEY

陸羽茶室
Luk Yu Tea House

新同樂(中環)
Sun Tung Lok (Central)

伊 沙 里

HOLLYWOOD RD

Bombay Dreams

WELLINGTON

世紀廣場

OLD BAILEY ST

中區警署
(已停用)
Central Police
Station (Closed)

WO ON L

玄鮨
Xuan Sushi

Café Siam

ST

Fofo by el Willy

2

域多利監獄
(已停用)
Victoria Prison
(Closed)

WYNDHAM

D'AGUILAR

蘭桂坊
LAN KWAI FONG

賢善里 CHANCERY L

中央
廣場
The
Centrium 🅿

蘭桂坊
LKF

Carbone

環貿 🅿
Universal
Trade

ARBUTHNOT

ST

下 亞 厘 畢 道

會督府

LOWER ALBERT

ICE H

聖公會

港中
醫院
HKC
Hospital

天主教
總堂
Rome
Catholic
Cathedral

CAINE RD

聖保羅堂

聖約翰堂

Church
Guest Hse

3

聖母無
原罪堂

GLENEALY

下 亞 厘 畢 道

里 畢 道 UPPER

ALBANY RD

ALBERT

明愛大廈
Caritas Hou

A

← 98m米(比例尺 Scale 1:3,250) →

B

N

EDINBURGH PLACE

C.A.W. Quarters PLA Berth

LUNG WO ROAD

Fenwick Pier
分域碼頭

龍和道

CITY HALL
大會堂

Central Barracks
中環軍營

行政長官辦公室

Legislative Council Complex
立法會綜合大樓

LEGISLATIVE COUNCIL RD

CHATER RD

Bank of China Tower
中國銀行大廈

紫玉蘭
Shanghai Garden

Hong Kong SAR Central Government Offices
香港特別行政區政府總部

Citic Tower
中信大樓

FENWICK PIER ST

LAMBETH WALK

HARCOURT ROAD

HK Red Cross Headquarters
紅十字會總部

金鐘

ADMIRALTY

Lippo Centre
力寶中心 力寶中心1期 力寶中心1期
Lippo Ctr Ⅰ Lippo No 1

海富中心
United Ctr 4

ROAD 夏慤道

MTR Construction Site
港鐵工地

Caine House
堅尼樓

Harcourt Garden (暫時封閉)
夏慤花園

Bank of China
中銀大廈

Bank Plaza
銀行廣場

COTTON TREE DRIVE

Lippo Plaza
金鐘廊
Queensway Plaza

DRAKE ST

RODNEY ST

QUEENSWAY

Police Headquarters
警察總部

Arsenal House
警察大樓

Arsenal House East Wing
警察大廈東翼

Museum of Tea Ware
羅桂祥茶藝館
KC Lo Gallery

High Court
高等法院

Queensway Gov't Offices
金鐘道政府合署

The Continental

HONG KONG PARK
香港公園

QUEEN'S ROAD EAST

港島香格里拉
Island Shangri-La

Café Gray Deluxe

KENNEDY ROAD

SUPREME COURT RD

PACIFIC PLACE
太古廣場

港麗
Conrad

龍蝦吧
Lobster Bar and Grill

珀翠
Petrus

金葉庭
Golden Leaf

PARK AVENUE

奕居
The Upper House

萬豪
JW Marriott

JUSTICE DRIVE

JUSTICE DRIVE

夏宮
Summer Palace

British Consulate
英國領事館

意寧谷
Nicholini's

Ammo

BORRETT ROAD

KENNEDY DRIVE

BOWEN ROAD

Island School
港島學校
Island Club

HK Electric Ctr
港燈中心

寶雲道網球場

MAGAZINE GAP ROAD

Magazine Heights
馬己仙峽

BOWEN ROAD

寶雲道花園

A ROAD **B** PEAK ROAD

N

← 236m米 (比例尺 Scale 1:7,851) →

LUNG WO ROAD 龍和道

分域碼頭
Fenwick Pier

LUNG KING ST 龍景街

香港演藝學院
HK Academy
for Performing Arts

香港藝術中心
HK Art Centre

電訊大廈
Telecom House

稅務大樓
Revenue
Tower

LUNG WUI RD 龍匯道

分域碼頭街

中信大廈
Citic Tower

紅十字會
總部
HK Red Cross
Headquarters

夏慤道 HARCOURT RD

夏慤道

告士打道

Grand Hyatt Steakhouse
Grissini
港灣壹號
One Harbour Road

君悦
Grand Hyatt

New

博覽海濱花園
Expo Promenade

博

香港會議展覽
HKCEC Ne

博覽道 EXPO DRIVE

博覽道 EXPO D

會議道

香港會議展覽
HK Convention
Exhibition Ce
(住會議展L

灣仔政府大樓
Wanchai
Tower

消防

港

入境事
務大樓
Immigration
Tower

MTR
Construction Site
港鐵工地

警察總部
Police Headquarters

堅偉樓
Caine House

美國萬通大廈 夏慤樓

Mass Mutual Tower

警察大樓
Arsenal House

Harcourt Garden
(臨時封閉)

警察大樓東翼
Arsenal House
East Wing

QUEENSWAY 金鐘道

告士打道

星記 (灣仔)
Sing Kee (Wan Chai)

莎巴 (灣仔
Sabah (war

車氏專菜軒
Che's

留園雅敍
Liu Yuan Pavilion

國福樓
Guo Fu Lou

永華雲吞麵家
Wing Wah

益新
Yixin

辣椒會
Chill Club

生記
Sang Kee

遨舍衛蘭軒 ●
Ozo Wesley

八日
Youka

福臨門 (灣仔)
Fook Lam Moon (Wan Chai)

灣仔 WA

Butchers
club

悦木
The Vietnam Woods

The Pawn

Beef & Liberty

Kelly's Cape Bop

杏
Qi

Akrame
Atelier Vivanda

Bo Innovation

KENNEDY

St Francis Canossian
聖方濟各嘉諾撒書院

ROAD 堅尼地道

BOWEN DRIVE 寶雲道

寶雲道網球場

KENNEDY ROAD

BOWEN ROAD 寶雲道

合和中心
Hopewell Ce

QUEEN'S

胡忠大廈
Wu Chung Hse

永興街 FUNG WONG TER

灣仔渡輪碼頭
Wan Chai Ferry Pier

HUNG HING ROAD

MARSH ST

WAN SHING ST

伊利莎伯大廈
Elizabeth House

環球中心
Great Eagle Centre

海港中心
Harbour Centre

HARBOUR ROAD

新鴻基中心
Sun Hung Kai Centre

灣仔運動場
WAN CHAI SPORTS GROUND

TONNOCHY ROAD

灣仔游泳池
Wan Chai Swimming Pool

灣仔體育館

告士打道

ROAD

香港會議展覽中心
HK Exhibition Centre

華潤大廈
China Resources Building

HARBOUR DRIVE

灣景中心大廈
Causeway Ctr

GLOUCESTER

蘇浙滙
Jardin de Jade

東來居
King's Garden

富聲 (灣仔)
Fu Sing (Wan Chai)

強記美食
Keung Kee

灣仔警署
Wanchai Police Station

ROAD

鷹君中心
AXA中心

史釗域道

家全七福
Seventh Son

浙江軒
Zhejiang Heen

利苑酒家 (灣仔)
Lei Garden (Wan Chai)

莊士敦道

北海中心

SPRING GARDEN

軒尼詩道

天樂里

活道

TALLOCK ROAD

MORRISON HILL ROAD

CANAL ROAD WEST

ROAD EAST

SHARP ST W.

Times Square

芬名
The Fleming

ROAD

再興
Joi Hing

臨時街市政大樓

HENNESSY ROAD

甘牌燒鵝
st Goose

杭州酒家
Hong Zhou

靠得住(灣仔)
Trusty Congee King (Wan Chai)

衛生署

灣仔道

Catalunya

BOWRINGTON ROAD

LEIGHTON

美味廚
Megan's Kitchen

CROSS LANE

BURROWS ST

養和醫院官立中學

摩理臣山游泳池
Morrison Hill Swimming Pool

摩理臣山
MORRISON HILL

QI

SPORTS RD

鄧肇堅醫院
香港專業教育學院

香港足球會會球場
HKFC Soccer/Rugby Field

鄧肇堅
SKH Tang Shiu Kin

KWAN

香港賽馬會
HKJC Headquarters

律敦治醫院
Ruttonjee Hospital

吟彩
Gin Sai

鮨魯山
Sushi Rozan
Wagyu Takumi

灣仔公園
Wan Chai Park

灣仔
WAN CHAI

e Phoque

港華仁書院小學部

皇后大道東

QUEEN'S

QUEEN'S

OI

伊利沙伯體育館
QE Stadium

HAU TAK LANE

黃泥涌道

賽馬博物館
Racing Museum

看台入口
Stands

香港足球會會球場
HKFC Soccer/Rugby Field

AST
Methodist Church

香港華仁書院
Wah Yan Coll,HK

KENNEDY RD

高主教書院小學部

回教墳場
MUSLIM CEMETERY

← 161m米(比例尺 Scale 1:5,376) →

A

B

海底隧道

奇力島
KELLETT ISLAND

臨時
直升機坪

香港遊艇會
Royal
HK Yacht Club

CROSS HARBOUR TUNNEL

R

醫官俱樂部
Police
Officers Club

HUNG HING RD
鴻興道

1

WAN SHING ST
灣盛街

MARSH RD
馬師道

告

太湖海鮮城(銅鑼灣)
Tai Woo (Causeway Bay)

信和
Sin Hua

鵬利中心

富臨
Forum

ROAD

蛇王二
She Wong Yee

ROAD

PERCIVAL STREET

GLOUCESTER

ROAD

伊利莎伯大廈
Elizabeth House

JAFFE

岩
Iwa

銅

LOCKHART

南翔饅頭店(銅鑼灣)
Nanxiang Steamed Bun
(Causeway Bay)

何洪
Ho Hur

2

TANG LUNG ST

WEST

Penthouse

利小館
Lei Bistro

RUSSELL ST

MORRISON HILL

TIN LOK LN

軒尼詩道

百樂潮州(時代廣場)
Pak Loh Chiu Chow (Time Square)

雲陽
Yun Yan

CANAL

EAST

SHARP ST

利舞臺廣場

Plaza

莆田
Pu
(Cause

新羅寶
Se
(Cause

伊斯蘭
中心

BOWRINGTON

CANAL

SHARP ST W

YIU WA ST

MATHESON ST

潮江(
Wu
(Cause

灣仔道

駱克道

堅拿道西

軒尼詩道

耀華街

禮頓道

LEIGHTON ROAD

皇冠假日
Crowne Plaza

LEIG

3

A

B

銅鑼灣避風塘
Causeway Bay
Typhoon Shelter

VICTORIA PARK ROAD

1

維多利亞公園
VICTORIA PARK

怡東軒
Yee Tung Heen

德林(銅鑼灣)
ng Tak Lam
useway Bay)

VICTORIA PARK

告士打道

加寧街

CLEVELAND ST

KINGSTON STREET

京士頓街

銅 鑼 灣
CAUSEWAY BAY

百德新街

EAST POINT RD 東角道

百德
大廈

珠城大廈
Pearl City
Mansion

GREAT GEORGE ST

記利佐治街

AY BAY

香港大廈

怡 和 街

怡隆
中心
Hung Lung

皇室大廈
Windsor House

GLOUCESTER

CAUSEWAY

2

威

道

霎東街

鼎泰豐 (銅鑼灣)
Din Tai Fung (Causeway Bay)

富聲 (銅鑼灣)
Fu Sing (Causeway Bay)

登
龍
街

樂聲
大廈

YEE WO ST

百德
Palibury

JARDINE'S BAZAAR

JARDINE CRESCENT

Seasons

權八
Gonpachi

安南
An Nam

AN FONG RD 渣甸坊

嘉蘭中心
Caroline Care

HYSAN AVE 希慎道

SUNNING RD 新寧道

PENNINGTON ST

敬誠街

YUN PING RD

伊榮街 IRVING ST

IRVING ROAD

Lanson Place 聖保祿學校
St. Paul's Convent
School

TUNG LO WAN RD

聖馬利
亞堂

何東
中學

3

KA NING PATH

州(希慎道)
Chiu Chow
Avenue)

HOI PING RD 開平道

LEIGHTON

禮頓道

希雲街 HAVEN ST

希雲街

Ramen Jo

郵政
體育會

聖保祿醫院
St Paul's Hospital

何東
分校

丁壽司
ni Ta-ke
Town

農圃
Farm House
雪園
Snow Garden

蓮 山 道

路政署
港島區

COTTON PATH

聖保祿修院

寶 花 道

記律人員體育
及康樂會

保良局
o Leung Kuk

C

D

保良局
歷史博物館

A

禮頓山
Leighton Hill

連

加路連山
CAROLINE HILL

B

掃桿埔運動
SO KON P
RECREATION G

南華
體育會

加

南華體育會運動場
SOUTH CHINA ATHLETIC
ASSN STADIUM

印度遊樂會

黃
泥
涌
道
WONG NAI CHUNG RD

LEIGHTON HILL LINK ROAD

連

山

東

CAROLINE HILL

路

道

連

山

道

1

聖馬加利教堂
St Margaret's

樂活道

BROADWOOD RD

HAPPY VIEW TERRACE

比華利山
Beverly Hill

孔聖堂
Confucius Hall

奧運大樓
Olympic House

院

道

EAST
HOSPIT

跑馬地馬場
Happy Race Track

雲地利道

**聖保祿
天主教**

**聖保祿
中學**

**香港三育
中學**

樂翠台
Villa Rocha

香港大球場
HONG KONG
STADIUM

*HAPPY VALLEY
RECREATION GROUND*

St.Paul's
Sec Sch

道

掃桿埔
SO KON PO

跑馬地
HAPPY VALLEY

VENTRIS ROAD

樂陶苑
Villa Lotto

← 234米(比例尺 Scale 1:7,4

2

N

BROADWOOD ROAD

源公廟

養和醫院
H.K.Sanatorium
& Hospital

彭慶記
Pang's Kitchen

奕蔭街 YIK YAM ST

景光街 KING KWONG ST

馬

師

道

合和里
HO WO LANE

駿景
台
Valley
View
Terr

藍
塘
道
BLUE POOL ROAD

古
松
山
村
道

昌明街

毓秀街 YUK SAU ST

山

村

道

蟠龍道

昇平街

菜市街 TSUI MAN ST

禮頓山

書局街

**英皇
駿景園**

WING TAK ST

SHAN RD

聯文街

大坑道

駿景軒
Golden Valley

VILLAGE TERR

山光苑

山光道 SHAN KWONG

東蓮覺苑
猶太墳場
JEWISH
CEMETERY

跑馬地
警署

和合坊
KWAI FONG ST

成和道

SING WOO ROAD

景星街

桂芳街

松柏新

TSUN YUEN ST

奕蔭街

新村街

STUBBS

古松山村 FU FUNG FAT TERR

玫瑰新邨
Villa Monte Rosa

ROAD

司

徒

拔

道

STUBBS ROAD

SHAN KWONG ROAD

賽馬會
體育綜合大樓

HAWTHORN RD

南

道

山光道

WOO

SING

ROAD

藍塘別墅

寶瓊坊
GREEN LANE

賽馬會會所
Jockey Club
Clubhouse

連青道 HOLLY RD

A

ROAD

B

← 200m米 (比例尺Scale 1:6,667) →

A

B

富澤花園
Fortress Garden

COMFORT TERR

泡台山
FORTRESS HILL

MERLIN ST
美輪街

WATSON RD
屈臣道

KING KING RD
英皇道

SHELL ST
蜆殼街

Sushi Mori
Tomoaki

JUPITER ST 木星街

廣福道
TEMPLE RD

銅鑼灣
避風塘
Causeway
Bay
Typhoon
Shelter

黎明邨
萬國寶通銀行
銀行中心(銅鑼
Citicorp Ctr (銅鑼

威菲路道
WHITFIELD RD

MERCURY ST 水星街

甘飯館
Kam's Kitchen

WING HING ST 永興街

Belilios
Pub.Sch.
庇理羅士女子

1

GORDON RD 歌頓道

ELECTRIC RD 電氣道

VICTORIA PARK RD 維園道

TSING FUNG ST 清風街

遠風街

電氣街

東院李澗田
Lee Ching Dea
Mem.Coll

蒙特梭利
Montessori

維多利亞公園
VICTORIA PARK

LAU LI ST 琉璃街

KING KING RD 英皇道

WAN OKS ST 雲華街

石記廚房
Shek Kee Kitchen

YACHT ST 帆船街

銅鑼道

天

新東方台

NEW EASTERN ST
新東方街

維園
Swimming
Pool

華姐清湯腩 (天后)
Sister wah (Tin Hau)

留仙街

LAU SIN ST

銅鑼灣
CAUSEWAY BAY

柏景臺
Park Towers

天后
TIN HAU

避

龍

道

DRAGON ROAD 金龍道

NEW EASTERN TERR

2

銅鑼灣維景
Metropark (Causeway Bay)

皇仁書院
Queen's College

I M Teppanyaki & Wine

KING RD 英皇道

YEE KING RD

士他花道 CAUSEWAY

FIRE DRAGON PATH 火龍徑

銅鑼灣運動場
Causeway Bay
Sports Ground

中華遊樂會
Chinese Recreation Club
Sports Ground

LAU TAK TSUEN 流德村

3

香港中央
圖書館
Central Library

MORETON TERR

TUNG LO WAN DR 銅鑼灣徑

TUNG LO WAN RD 銅鑼灣道

SCHOOL ST 書館街
FIRST LANE 第一巷
KING ST 京街
SECOND LANE 第二巷
SHEPHERD ST 牧羊街

安庶庇街

WUN SHA ST 浣紗街

大坑
TAI HANG

SHELTER

何東中學
Hotung

KA NING PATH
嘉寧徑

豪園
FONTANA GARDENS

大坑
TAI HANG

SUN CHUN ST 新村街

WATER LANE 水巷

五谷
Go Ya

No.5 Italian

ILLUMINATION THR 照明台

A

B

← 375m米(比例尺 Scale 1:12,500) →

N

1

2

VICTORIA HARBOUR 維多利亞港

ALDRICH BAY
愛秩序灣

QUARRY BAY 鰂魚涌

ISLAND EASTERN CORRIDOR

EASTERN CORRIDOR 東區走廊

TAIKOO SHING 太古城

東區
East

TAIKOO 太古

SAI WAN HO
西灣河

ISLAND EASTERN CORRIDOR
港島東區走廊

OI TUNG
ESTATE

YIU TUNG
ESTATE

KINGS RD
英皇道

WESTLANDS

MOUNT
PARK RD

HONG SHING ST
康城街

GREIG RD

YIU HING ROAD

QUARRY BAY 鰂魚涌

QUARRY BAY

粥麵館
Congee and
Noodle Shop

難勒醬油房周月(鰂魚涌)
Tulsi (Quarry Bay)

麵場醬油房周月(鰂魚涌)
Shugetsu-Ramen (Quarry Bay)

裹園上海小廚本古城
Grand Cuisine Shanghai Kitchen

大潭郊野公園
(鰂魚涌擴建部份)

A

B

C

515

MACAU
澳門

36 | **37**

青洲
Ilha Verde

花地瑪堂區
Na. Sra. Fatima

澳門半島
MACAU

內港
Inner
Harbour

聖安多
尼堂區
Sto.Antonio

望德堂區
S. Lazaro

大堂區
Se

外港
Porto Exterior

風順堂區
S. Lourenço

南灣

38

西灣
Sai Van Lake

友誼大橋
FRIENDSHIP BRIDGE

39

西灣大橋
SAI VAN BRIDGE

澳氹大橋
MACAU - TAIPA BRIDGE

←2,222m米(比例尺 Scale 1:74,074) →

40 | **41**

氹仔島
TAIPA

42

氹仔
Taipa

珠海市
ZHU HAI
CITY

蓮花大橋
LOTUS BRIDGE

路氹連貫公路
ESTRADA DO ISTMO

Cotai

澳門
國際機場
Macau International
Airport

路環島
COLOANE

黑沙
Hae Sa

黑沙灣
Hae Sa Bay

九澳
Ka Ho

43

路環
Coloane

竹灣
Baia de Cheoc Van

A B

珠海市
Zhuhai Shi

1

ESTRADA MARGINAL DA
英樂花園
青洲

青洲山
55.6
Ilha Verde
福榮新邨
Fok Tak Sun Chun

紀念孫中山市政公園
Sun Yat Sen Park

威苑花園

逸麗花園
Jardim Iat I

AVENIDA DO CONSE

AVENIDA DO COMENDADOR

canal da Pata

海鳥新邨
Grey Fle

AVENIDA DA CONCORDIA

老記 (筷子基)
Lou Kei (Fai Chi Kei)

RUA DO GENERAL IVENS FERRAZ

筷子基
北灣

2

筷子基南灣

AVENIDA MARGINAL DO LAM MAU

筷子基
Fai Chi Kei

AVENIDA DO ALMIRANTE LA

紅街市

昌盛
Chong Shing

龍華茶樓
Lung Wah Tea House

新橋
San Kiu

新英記咖啡麵食
Sun Ying Kei

RUA DA RIBEIRA DO PATANE

六記粥麵
Luk Kei Noodle

白鴿巢賈梅士公園
Camoes Park
Patane

牛記咖喱美食
Ngao Kei Ka Lei Chon

RUA DO VISCONDE PAÇO DE ARCOS

檸檬王
Neng Meng Wang

ESTRADA

鏡湖醫院
Kiang Wu Hospital

濠江�”記美食
Hou Kong Chi Kei

天主教藝術博物館
Museum of Sacred Art

REPOUSO

Cemite
Mic
Arce

3

內港
Inner Harbour

榮記荳腐麵食
Ving Kei

大三巴牌坊
Ruins of St Paul's

大炮台
Monte Fort

AVENIDA DE ALMEIDA RIBEIRO

AVENIDA DE S. PAULO

台灣帝鈞碳烤胡椒餅
Dai Gwan

果欄堂

祥記
Cheong Kei

陶陶居
Tou Tou Koi

韓國鯛魚燒乳酪雪糕
Aboong

A

義順鮮奶
Yi Shun

檸檬車露
Lemon Cello

大堂
皇冠甜
Wong Kung

B

← 469m米(比例尺 Scale 1:15,625) →

N

關閘邊檢大樓
Border Gate
Frontier Post
關閘
Border
Gate

澳門特警總部

馬場北大馬路 A. NORTE DO HIPODROMO 友誼

馬場
Hipodromo

CAMINHO DAS HORTAS

RUA CENTRAL DA AREIA PRETA

賽福安花園
Jardim
Kong Fok On

明珠
The
Pearl

環宇天下
La Cité

海名居
La Baie Du
Noble

黑沙環新
填海區

康福祥花園
Jardim
Kong Fok
Choeng

保利經

陳林達花園
Polytec
Garden

黑   沙   環

望廈迎賓館
ada de Mong-Há

建華大廈
Kin Wa

金海山花園
Kam Hoi San

濱華新邨
Kwong Wa

AVENIDA DA PONTE DA AMIZADE

E. MARGINAL DA AREIA PRETA

海濱花園
Hoi Pan
Garden

AVENIDA

南灣花園

東華新邨
Tong Wa
San Chun

Areia Preta

RUA DE MA KAU SEAK

DE

MAIO

-Há

望廈新村
Mong Ha Sun
Chuen

Jardins Sun
ck

八總新村
Pat Tat Sun
Chuen

NORDESTE

RUA NOVA DA AREIA PRETA

南華新邨
Nam Wa
San Chun

學院教學餐廳
tional Restaurant

福海花園

普濟禪院
(觀音堂)

望廈
新西洋墳場

羅理基公爵

馬交石炮台馬路

漁翁街 RUA DOS PESCADORES

葛羅石
天后廟

友誼大橋

FRIENDSHIP

BRIDGE

治安警察廳

ESTRADA DE D.MARIA

通訊博物館

父紀念館
Mem. of
Dr. Sun

螺絲山
花園

松山纜車
Cable
Car

東望洋山
Guia Hill

Reservoir
貯 水 塘

發車看台 GrandPrix Control
Tower

AVENIDA

DE

CACILHAS

RODRIGUES

東望洋燈塔
Guia
Lighthouse

聖母雪地殿教堂

東望洋炮台
Guia Fortress

ESTRADA

松山

海之聖母
瞭望台

阿露娜印度皇室咖喱
Aruna's Maharaja Indian Curry

DE

D. RODRIGO

外港客運
碼頭
Macau Ferry
Terminal

港澳直昇機坪
Helipont
Platform

澳門綜藝館
Macau Forum

大賽車及
葡萄酒博物館 蓮世紀花
Grand
Prix & Wine 蓮世紀花
Museum Lotus
Monument

唐城
Tang Dynasty

火山
東西滙聚
East Meets
West

C   口   岸

外   港

Outer   Harbour

D

38

A

北河 RUA DO FOLCENÇO PEREIRA MARQUES

RUA DA ALMIRANTE SÉRGIO

1

下環

Praia de Manduco

船屋
● A Lorcha

媽閣

Barra

B

PRAIA G

DR STANLEY HO

A PANORÂMICA DO

南灣湖
Nam Van Lake

AVENIDA DA REPÚBLICA

聖地牙哥古堡
Pousada de São Tiago
●

RUA DO LAGO NAM VAN

RUA DO LAGO SAI VAN

西灣湖
Sai Van Lake

芭朗瑪
La Paloma

2

A PANORÂMICA DO LAGO

西灣湖景大橋路

南灣湖

A

何東圖書館

路 A DA PRAIA GRANDE

時代商業中心

中央廣場

時代廣場

中央廣場

聖玫瑰堂 樂伯多祿
（三巴仔修院）
Theatre

AVENIDA DO DR. STANLEY LOBO

陳光記(羅保博士街)
Chan Kuong Kei
(Rua do Dr. Pedro José Lobo)

AVENIDA DA PRAIA GRANDE

AVENIDA DR. MÁRIO SOARES

友誼巷

中國銀行

帝皇樓
King

當奧豐素 1890
Don Alfonso 1890
天巢法國餐廳
Robuchon au Dôme
8餐廳
The Eight
大廚
The Kitchen

澳門陸軍俱樂
Clube Militar
●

新葡京
Grand Lisboa
●

葡京
Lisboa
●

3

音樂噴泉
Cybernetic Fountain

南灣湖
Nam Van Lake

AVENIDA DA PONTE

B

葡國餐廳
Guincho a Galera

桃花源小廚
Tim's Kitchen

MACAU BRIDGE

澳氹大橋

帝雅廷
Il Teatro

永利軒
Wing Lei

Mizum

C D

新口岸
Outer Harbour
Reclamation Area

外
Outer

嶺
南
綜
合
大
廈
Legend Wharf

週圍密館

文化中心
廣場

澳門藝術
博物館

1

萊斯
Rocks

港海新填區
NAPE

美高梅
MGM

參考下面
See below

澳門科學館

文華東方
rin Oriental

御苑
Vida Rica

金殿堂
Imperial Court

食·八方
Square Eight

N

2

←469m米 (比例尺 Scale 1:15,625) →

金麗軒
Kam Lai Heen

金麗華
Grand Lapa

人
範
頭
漁
Fisherman's
Wharf

新口岸
Outer Harbour
Reclamation Area

風味居
Feng Wai Ju

品味坊
Temptations

lld

藍
Naam

澳門回歸賀禮
陳列館 文化中心
Macau 廣場
Handover
Pavilion

澳門文化中心
Macao Cultural Centre

澳門藝術博物館
Museum of Art

利
re

ower
es
APE

宋玉生公園
SONG YOK SANG

加路
Carlos

觀音像
Statue of
Kun Iam

N

3

D

←356m米 (比例尺 Scale 1:11,856) →

521

A

B

← 627m米 (比例尺 Scale 1:20,909) →

N

西灣大橋
Sai Van Bridge

澳氹大橋
Macau-Taipa Bridge

海洋花園大馬路
Est dos Sete Tanques

氹仔雕塑
Taipa Monument

110.8
小潭山

奧羅拉
Aurora
天政
Tenmasa
帝影樓
Ying

觀音岩
Unive

將軍馬路

新澳
Alt

菩提禪院
Pou Tai Un
Monastery

海洋花園
海洋花園

玫瑰山莊

百姓
Banza

氹仔炮臺

柯維納馬路
Est Governador Albano Oliveira

西面佛
Four-Faces
Buddha

澳門賽馬會
Macau Jockey Club

澳門
運動場
Stadium &
Aquatic Centre

Taipa
Village

賽馬場
Macau Jockey Club

奧林匹克
游泳館
Stadium &
Aquatic Centre

東亞運大馬路

Avenida dos Jogos da Asia Oriental

大倉
Okura

悅榕莊
Banyan Tree

萬豪
JW M

8 1/2 Otto e Mezzo

咖東
Katong Corner

麗絲卡爾頓
The Ritz-Carlton

Lai H

李家菜
Lei Ka Choi

麗思咖
The Ritz-Carlton

珠海市
ZHU HAI CITY

皇冠小館(百老匯)
Wong Kung Sio Kung (Broadway)

Avenida de Cotai

路

人工濕地

通往珠海市，橫琴
To Zhu Hai City

蓮花大橋
Lotus Bridge

ESTRADA

A

B

友誼大橋
Friendship Bridge

澳門氹仔臨時客運碼頭
(北安碼頭)
Taipa Temporary Ferry Terminal

北安大馬路
永安街
Estrada de Pac On
Avenida Son On
信安馬路
Avenida Son On

Estrada da Ponte da Cabrita

氹仔
159.2
大潭山

天文台斜路

雞頸馬路

Tai pa

Avenida Wai Long

客運大樓
Terminal Building

澳門國際機場
Macau International Airport

鼎泰豐 (新濠天地)
Din Tai Fung (COD)

Avenida Dr Sun Yat Sen

大潭山壹號
澳門
科技大學
Macau University of
Science &
Technology

金坂
Shinji
The Tasting Room

君悅
Grand Hyatt

滿堂彩
Beijing Kitchen
Mezza 9

金 Golden Peacock
nton
苑酒家 Garden

譽瓏軒
Jade Dragon

路氹連貫公路

金光大道

康萊德
Conrad

朝
Dynasty 8

an 四季
Seasons

喜來登
Sheraton

鮮
Xin

城

ISTMO

DO

ESTRADA

十二生肖雕像

otai
路

澳門東亞運動會
體育館(澳門蛋)
Macau East
Asian
Games
Dome

蓮花路

42

A

B

RUA DE TAI LIN

ESTRADA GOVERNADOR NOBRE DE CA

RUA DE EVORA

RUA DE NAM KENG

AVENIDA DE GUIMARAES

賽馬拉斯大馬路

埃武市街

RUA OLIMPICA

奧林匹克

RUA DE BRAGANCA

大連街

埃武街

AVENIDA DE SENG TOU

RUA DE COIMBRA

1

澳門
賽馬場
Macau
Jockey Club

澳門
運動場
Eetadio
De Macau

PONTE NEGRA

晃記餅家
Fong kei

Castiço

葡國美食天地
A Petisqueira

奧林匹克
游泳館
Piscina
Olimpica
De Macau

RUA DO DESPORTO

體育路

RUA CORREIA DA SILVA

安東尼奧
Antonio

RUA DE CUNHA

告利雅施利華街

迷仔住宅式博物
Taipa Houses-Museu

莫義記
Mok Yee Kei

AVENIDA DO ESTADIO

AVENIDA MARGINAL FLE DE LOTUS

蓮花海濱大馬路

澳門
三育
Escola
Secundaria
Sam Yuk

RUA DO REGEDOR

新陶陶
San Tou Tou

2

望德聖母灣大馬路

銀河
Galaxy

葡軒
Gosto

利安
Café Leon

名家
Myung Ga

庭園
Terrazza

ESTRADA DA BAIA DE NOSSA SENHORA DA ESPERA

迷仔市區
TAIPA TOWN

←325m米 (比例尺 Scale 1:10,850)

43

A

B

里斯本地帶
Espaço Lisboa

石

ESTRADA DO CAMPO

田畔街

ESTRADA DE CHEOC VAN

竹灣馬路

安德書餅店
Lord Stow's Bakery

居
場
前
地

炮仔園

連沙街

里斯本總統前

RUA DA CORDOARIA

打纜路

1

十月
初五
馬路
A. DE CINCO DE OUTUBRO

鹹蝦巷

客
商
街

中

陳勝記
Chan Seng Kei

打纜街

打纜
前地

新利街

水
京
公
地

情
人
街

永
安
街

亞
美

街

RUA DA CORDOARIA

LARGO DA CORDOARIA

2

船鋪前地

民國街

天后廟
前地

菜園
園巷

路環市區
COLOANE TOWN

←157m米 (比例尺 Scale 1:5,220)

PICTURE COPYRIGHT
圖片版權

64 - Aberdeen Street Social, 65 - Above & Beyond, 66 - Michelin, 67 - Ah Yat Harbour View, 68 - Akrame, 69 - Amber, 70 - Ammo, 71 - An Nam, 72 - Michelin, 73 - Arcane, 74 - Arisu (Tsim Sha Tsui), 75 - Atelier Vivanda/ Michelin, 76 - Ba Yi, 77 - Michelin/Beef & Liberty, 78 - Bibo, 79 - Bo Innovation, 80 - Bombay Dreams, 81 - Café Gray Deluxe, 82 - Michelin, 83 - Café Siam/Michelin, 84 - Caprice, 85 - Carbone, 86 - Catalunya, 87 - Celebrity Cuisine, 88 - Celestial Court, 89 - 91 - Michelin, 92 - Chesa, 93 - Michelin, 95 - Chilli Fagara/Michelin, 96 - China Tang, 97 -99 - Michelin, 100 - CIAK - In The Kitchen, 101 - Cocotte, 102 - Michelin/Come-Into Chiu Chow, 103 - Congee and Noodle Shop/Michelin, 104 - Cuisine Cuisine at The Mira, 105 - Michelin, 106 - Dandan, 107 - Michelin/Din Tai Fung, 108 - Din Tai Fung/MICHELIN, 109 - Dong Lai Shun (Tsim Sha Tsui), 110 - Dot Cod, 111 - Michelin, 112 - Dragon King/Michelin, 113 - Duddell's/Michelin, 114 - Épure, 115 - Michelin, 116 - Felix, 117 - FoFo by el Willy/Michelin, 118 - Fook Lam Moon (Tsim Sha Tsui), 119 - Fook Lam Moon (Wan Chai), 120 - Michelin/Forum, 121 - Michelin, 122 - 123 Michelin, 125 - 126, Michelin, 127 - Gaddi's, 128 - Michelin, 129 - Gin Sai/MICEHLIN, 130 - Go Ya, 131 - Golden Leaf, 132 - Golden Valley, 133 - Gonpachi, 134 - 135, Michelin, 136 - Grand Hyatt Steakhouse, 137 - Grissini, 138 - Guo Fu Lou, 139 - Michelin, 140 - Ho Hung Kee, 141 - 142, Michelin, 143 - Hugo's, 144 - IM Teppanyaki & Wine, 145 - Inakaya, 146 - Michelin, 147 - Island Tang, 148 - 149, Michelin, 150 - Jardin de Jade, 151 - Jin Cuisine, 152 - 153 Michelin, 154 - Kam's Roast Goose/ Michelin, 155 - Michelin, 157 - Kazuo Okada, 158 - 159 Michelin, 160 - Kwan Kee Bamboo Noodle/Michelin, 161 - Michelin, 162 - L'Atelier de Joël Robuchon, 163 - Michelin, 164 - Le Dôme de Cristal, 165 - Le Soleil, 166 - Michelin, 167 - Lei Bistro, 168 - Lei Garden/Michelin, 169 - 172, Lei Garden, 173 - 174, Michelin/Lei Garden, 175 - 178 Michelin,, 179 - Lobster Bar and Grill, 180 - 181 Michelin, 182 - Lung King Heen/Michelin, 183 - Man Wah, 184 - Mandarin Grill + Bar, 185 - Mask of Sichuen & Beijing/Michelin, 186 - Michelin, 187 - Megan's Kitchen, 189 - MIC Kitchen, 190 - Ming Court/Michelin, 191 - Michelin/ Moon Thai, 192 - Morton's of Chicago, 193 - Mott 32, 194 - Namo, 195 - Nanxiang Steamed Bun, 196 - New Shanghai/Michelin, 197 - Nicholinis, 198 - Michelin, 199 - No.5 Italian (Tai Hang), 200 - Michelin/Nobu, 201 - Noodlemi/Michelin, 202 - Olé/Michelin, 203 - On/Michelin, 204 - One Harbour Road, 205 - 8 1/2 Otto e Mezzo - Bombana, 206 - 207 Pak Loh Chiu Chow, 208 - Michelin, 209 - Peking Garden, 210 - Penthouse, 211 - Petrus, 212 - Pierre, 213 - Michelin, 214 - Putien, 215 - MICHELIN, 216 - Qïao Cuisine, 217 - Ramen Jo/Michelin, 219 - Restoran Indonesia 1968, 220 - Robatayaki, 221 - Michelin/Ryu Gin, 222 - 224 Machelin, 225 - Seasons, 226 - Michelin, 227 - Serge et le phoque, 228 - Seventh Son, 229 - Sha Tin 18, 230 - Shang Palace, 231 - Shanghai Garden, 232 - 234 Michelin, 235 - 236 Shugetsu Ramen/Michelin, 237 - 240 Michelin, 241 - Snow Garden, 242 - Sorabol, 243 - Spoon by Alain Ducasse, 244 - Spring Moon, 245 - Summer Palace/Michelin, 246 - 247 Sun Tung Lok, 248 -

Michelin, 249 - Michelin/Sushi Ginza Iwa, 251 - Sushi Mori Tomoaki, 252 - Sushi Rozan, 253 - Michelin, 254 - Sushi Ta-ke/Michelin, 255 - Ta Vie, 256 - Michelin, 257 - Michelin/Tai Woo, 258 - Michelin, 259 - T'ang Court, 260 - Tasty, 261 - Tate, 262 - Michelin, 263 - The Boss, 264 - The Bostonian, 265 - Michelin, 266 - The Continental, 267 - The Pawn, 268 - The Square/Michelin, 269 - The Steak House Wine bar + grill, 270 - The Swiss Chalet/Michelin, 271 - 274 Michelin, 275 - Tim's Kitchen, 276 - Tin Lung Heen, 277 - Tosca, 278 - Town, 279 - Trusty Congee King, 281 - Michelin, 282 - Tsui Hang Village, 283 - 284 Michelin, 285 - Tze Yuet Heen, 286 - Upper Modern Bistro, 287 - Wa-En, 288 - Michelin, 289 - Wagyu Takumi, 290 - Michelin, 291 - Whisk, 292 - 293 Michelin, 294 - Wonton Master, 295 - Wu Kong, 296 - Xuan Sushi, 297 - Yan Toh Heen/Michelin, 298 - Michelin, 299 - Yau Yuen Siu Tsui, 300 - Yè Shanghai, 301 - Yee Tong Heen, 302 - Yin Yue, 303 - Michelin, 304 - Youka, 305 - Yù Lěi, 306 - Yuè (Gold Coast), 307 - Yue (North Point), 308 - 309 Michelin, 310 - Zenpachi, 311 - Michelin, 322 - City Garden, 323 - Conrad, 324 - Cordis, 325 - Crowne Plaza, 326 - Crowne Plaza Kowloon East, 327 - East, 328 - Four Seasons, 329 - Gold Coast, 330 - Grand Hyatt, 331 - Harbour Grand Kowloon, 332 - Harbour Plaza 8 Degrees, 333 - Harbour Plaza North Point, 334 - Hyatt Regency Sha Tin, 335 - Hyatt Regency Tsim Sha Tsui, 336 - Icon, 338 - Indigo, 339 - Intercontinental, 340 - Intercontinental Grand Stanford, 341 - Island Shangri-La, 342 - JW Marriott, 343 - Kowloon Shangri-La, 344 - Lan Kwai Fong, 345 - Lanson Place, 346 - LKF, 347 - Mandarin Oriental, 348 - Metropark (Causeway Bay), 349 - New World Millennium, 350 - Ozo Wesley, 351 - Panorama, 352 - Royal Plaza, 353 - Sheraton, 354 - The Fleming, 355 - The Landmark Mandarin Oriental, 356 - The Langham, 357 - The Mercer, 358 - The Mira, 359 - The Peninsula, 360 - The Pottinger, 361 - The Ritz Carlton, 362 - The Royal Garden, 363 - The Upper House, 380 - 383 Michelin, 384 - Aurora, 385 - Michelin, 386 - Beijing Kitchen, 387 - Michelin, 388 - Café Encore, 389 - Michelin, 390 - Canton, 391 - 395 Michelin, 396 - Clube Militar de Macau, 397 - Michelin, 398 - Don Alfonso 1890, 399 - Dynasty 8, 400 - Michelin, 401 - Feng Wei Ju, 403 - Golden Flower, 404 - Gosto, 405 - Guincho a Galera, 406 - Michelin, 407 - IFT Educational Restaurant, 408 - Il Teatro, 409 - Imperial Court, 410 - Jade Dragon, 411 - Kam Lai Heen/Michelin, 412 - Katong Corner, 413 - Michelin, 414 - La Paloma, 415 - Lai Heen, 416 - Lei Garden, 417 - 420 Michelin, 421 - Mezza 9, 422 - Mizumi, 423 - Myung Ga, 424 - Naam/Michelin, 425 - Michelin, 427 - 99 Noodles, 428 - 8 1/2 Otto e Mezzo, 429 - Robuchon au Dôme, 430 - Michelin, 431 - Shinji, 432 - Square Eight, 433 - Temptations, 434 - Tenmasa, 435 - Terrazza, 436 - The Eight, 437 - The Golden Peacock/Michelin, 438 - The Kitchen, 439 - The Ritz Carlton Café, 440 - The Tasting Room, 441 - Tim's Kitchen, 442 - Michelin, 443 - Vida Rica, 444 - Wing Lei, 445 - Michelin, 446 -, 447 - xin, 448 - Ying, 449 - Zi Yat Heen, 458 - Altira, 459 - Banyan Tree, 460 - Conrad, 461 - Encore, 462 - Four Seasons, 463 - Galaxy, 464 - Grand Hyatt, 465 - Grand Lapa, 466 - Grand Lisboa, 467 - JW Marriott, 468 - Lisboa, 469 - Mandarin Oriental, 470 - MGM, 471 - Okura, 472 - Pousada de Mong-Há, 473 - Pousada de São Tiago, 474 - Michelin, 475 - Sheraton, 476 - Star World, 477 - The Ritz-Carlton, 478 - The Venetian, 479 - Wynn

Michelin Travel Partner

Société par actions simplifiées au capital de 11 288 880 EUP
27 Cours de L'Ile Seguin - 92100 Boulogne Billancourt (France)
R.C.S. Nanterre 433 677 721

Although the information in this guide was believed by the authors
and publisher to be accurate and current at the time of publication,
they cannot accept responsibility for any inconvenience, loss or
injury sustained by any person relying on information or advice
contained in this guide. Things change over time and travellers
should take steps to verify and confirm information, especially
time sensitive information related to prices, hours of operation and
availability.

E-mail : michelinguide.hongkong-macau@cn.michelin.com

Maps : (C) 2012 Cartographic data Universal Publications,
Ltd / Michelin
Printing and Binding: Book Partners China Ltd.